Edna Manley

Edna Manley

THE DIARIES

EDITED BY

RACHEL MANLEY

HEINEMANN PUBLISHERS (CARIBBEAN) LIMITED
175-179 Mountain View Avenue, Kingston 6, Jamaica

HEINEMANN PUBLISHERS (CARIBBEAN) LIMITED
175–179 Mountain View Avenue, Kingston 6, Jamaica

ISBN 976 605 084 8

Printed in Great Britain by
Ebenezer Baylis and Son Limited, Worcester

Contents

List of Illustrations

Introduction

On February 10th 1987 the island of Jamaica awoke to the news that Edna Manley had died at dawn. It may seem strange that the death of an eighty-six-year-old woman should stun a nation, but with this news a book closed in Jamaica and both this country and the century lost a woman who seemed to belong to them so specially and inexorably.

What then was so remarkable about this woman? The length of her life, which almost spanned the century, and gave her the rare opportunity to see Halley's Comet twice? Her accomplishments and renown as a sculptress? Her unique position as wife of Jamaica's first Premier and the mother of a Jamaican Prime Minister? These are the biographical details of a life that touched so many people in Jamaica, but ultimately the answer lies in her spirit, which was possessed of a creative fire and an infinite capacity to love.

Edna Manley was born on Leap Year's Day 1900, the fifth of nine children of an English Methodist missionary and his Jamaican wife, in Cornwall, England. While studying art in London, Edna married her first cousin Norman Manley, a decorated World War I veteran and Rhodes Scholar studying at Oxford University. After his graduation they returned to his home in Jamaica. There she entered a society that reflected the dislocation of a people from its traditions and culture; a society that mirrored only the culture of its colonial masters, forced to relinquish not only the rights of its own history, but even its tribal memory . . . as though the Middle Passage had been a veritable passage of Lethe.

She began her struggle not only to establish herself as a serious artist in her new country, but to conceive an art form that reflected her new realities, and to sow the seeds of a nascent national culture. She emerged as a visionary mother of the arts in Jamaica, as teacher and friend to other artists, as editor of the first successful literary journal, *Focus*, and inspired one of the most vibrant cultural forces in the West Indies.

Edna Manley was a Piscean, a sign known for paradox, so with the closure of one book came the opening of another. She left not only a living legacy in the spiritual and cultural fibre of Jamaican life, but also four diaries which she kept privately for almost fifty years. These diaries she bequeathed to me, often reminding me of their existence and my eventual responsibility for them. I once asked her what I should do with them. She said when the time came I would know. As a Jamaican I knew the historic value of these documents. As her granddaughter I turned to them for comfort and reassurance after her death. What I found was a superb work of literature from which emerges the struggle of her long and 'endless-going' journey.

In these diaries Edna often mentions the idea of writing a book. In one of the entries she says: 'I have a profound feeling for the surrealists to whom art was a way of life. The telling of this story would be part of the story itself.'

So as we read these diaries a book is written and a life unfolds.

It is the story of her union with Norman Manley, which inspired heights of creative energy in both of them, and yet often faced her talent with a dilemma. A portrait of this famous man emerges nowhere with more insight than in this tender and painful reconstruction of their time together. Through it we witness the growth of Jamaica's national movement towards independence and Norman's role as its spiritual father.

It is the story of a family, and all the pride and anguish of a mother's heart are woven through the entries on her two remarkable children.

It is the story of a woman with talent, the creative process behind her art and her spiritual search for truth, from the depths of her first memories in Cornwall almost to the end of her life.

It is the story of a humanitarian and friend and her great love for Jamaica.

As the editor of these diaries I have tried to be true to the text, always aware that this work was her final testament. Apart from a few adjustments it remains as she wrote it. Legal and financial constraints made it necessary to reduce the whole to a publishable length. I looked for content that could be lifted without affecting her journey. Four sections account for most of the reduction. A short story included in Diary One, a travelogue of China in Diary Two, a list of odd, hallucinatory incidents listed separately at the end of Diary Three, and finally the poetry dispersed throughout the diaries which will be combined with other poems she wrote, and published separately. These omissions I regret, but assure the reader that her thoughts and opinions remain intact as does her journey.

Although Edna Manley was not to last this century, this was truly her century; not one that drew her along with it, but one she seemed, within the limits of her sphere, to pull along behind her, creating a tide and momentum in which we as Jamaicans continue to live. I invite the reader to share these diaries remembering the words she cherished, the last ones spoken by her beloved father before he died: 'Oh the power and the glory and the wonder of it all!'

I would like to thank:

Douglas and Michael Manley for their enthusiasm and cooperation. They considered her legacy paramount and left me free to exercise my judgement over content, even that which was private and sensitive.

The Edna Manley Foundation for its support.

Pamela O'Gorman, David Boxer and Michael Manley for help with factual references in the notes.

Corina Meeks, Easton Lee and Wallace Campbell for assistance and support throughout the project.

Ian Randle whose expert advice led the diaries to their publisher.

The publishers, André Deutsch and Tom Rosenthal for their faith in the venture; Sheila McIlwraith and Jill Thomas for their work on the manuscript.

Georgia Wood, Audre Brown, David Cover and Patrick Phillips for their help during a technical crisis.

Maria Layacona for providing us with photographs.

Mike Smith, Tony Bogues, Carole Edghill, Barbara Thompson, Beverley Burrowes, Rosie McDonald and Donald Chung for their help along the way.

My husband, Israel Cinman, who helped where he could, and coped with me throughout. His faith in me gave me courage.

Finally, Glynne Ewart, not only for her incalculable help time and time again in so many ways, but also for just caring so much.

Their generosity is a reflection of the deep love that Edna Manley inspired.

Rachel Manley
Berne, 1988

Diary One

February 1939

Tragedy is the individual's refusal to accept reality.

I feel sometimes that life is just a struggle to free oneself from oneself. At some period one achieves complete self-consciousness, and the realization comes that one's mind is like a cocoon, that such time as one has lived has only succeeded in enveloping one in layers and layers of ties and conventions – and then the rest of life stretches out as a saddeningly brief time in which to struggle out of the wrappings to some kind of intellectual and emotional freedom.

To carve the Negro isn't to travel a road. To find the secret of the African carvings, to penetrate the vision of the Mayans, to get out of oneself and into the ideologies of other peoples isn't easy, but that is travelling a road and a hard one. Then, having felt experiences other than one's immediate own, to discover a free world, where one can definitely choose a direction uninfluenced by caste and tradition-bound shibboleths, that is to travel a road; and even, then, to lose yourself in the direction of the group to which you belong and so to live as to create a channel for its life force to pass through in the medium of form, sculpture, talk, music, anything that comes easiest and nearest to one.

You ask me to explain the little Renoir (the 'Woman Reading'); it is so difficult because it is true painting in that its real quality cannot be translated into any other terms. It depends on the power of appeal of paint on canvas. Paint just as paint, sensitively, subtly, powerfully applied and that independently of colour. Paint can go on the canvas so many ways, smoothly, roughly, irritably, full of flicks and swirls; it can go on spontaneously and with speed and this is obvious in every mark left behind, or it can go on ponderously, broodingly, slowly. So much for paint, and then take colour, how it glows framed in its sombre black! And painted on with such a world of wisdom, such knowledge of the capacity to leave colour and paint to make their own suggestions, their own statements, with such loose, self assured guidance from the brush. And the simplicity of the design that carries the

2

colour and paint. The flying wings of eyebrow and eyes, echoed with the swift turn of the open book, and mark you, all of it in deep black against the tender, intimate glow of the flesh on face and neck. Has the face a neck? I don't even remember, for I write from memory! And crown it all with the glory of the hair, such hair full of vitality and softness and, more than everything else, full of the lamplight that lights the picture. How the French love with their senses and yet such a detached, such a connoisseur's love. So much sophistication, so much cynical indulgence. All that and so much more is there, so much that is intimate, and yet so much that is secret and rare. Not to be had by snatching or possessing. Only the disciplined appreciation that is backed by a knowledge that to completely have is to completely lose. This I think the French understand in an extraordinary way. This world of controlled senses is, I think, their greatest contribution to painting.

April 1939

The shadow moved away through the gloom of the woods, soundless and without direction. Where there had been a nucleus of consciousness, there was now only eternity. What had been and what might always be. A single note of a bird and a leaf falling reluctantly down.

Perhaps there is warmth somewhere and an end to roaming, perhaps the world one day will cease spinning and the day will no longer follow the night. Perhaps the fear of never ending will succumb to the fear of being at an end. Perhaps death will not follow life in an endless succession of shadows, perhaps only one shadow will cease to pass through the gloom of the woods, with the note of a single bird and a lone leaf falling reluctantly down.

The world is drenched in the whitest of white moonlight and the hill slips away down to the pond at the bottom that is black and full of mystery.

Pain and realities hang suspended and doubts retire till the dawn comes, only the white moonlight and the deep black pool.

Do they ever penetrate one another, or does the moonlight but strike alive the surface and leave the depths untouched, and does the blackness of the pool but hold a smiling mirror to the moon's wan face and lie indifferent and inert.

Shouts of boyish, childish laughter and the barking of the dogs, so much to fill one's heart with, so much of love and joy and need for sympathy and care, warm lights indoors and kindly servants, cigarette smoke curling from the depths of comfortable chairs, a friendly circle, a kindly domestic god.

Outside at the bottom of the hill lies the deep, still pool, without a ripple, without a movement, so secret, so inscrutable, holding its imperturbable mirror to the drifting wan white moon. The moon moves on, so many pools,

3

so many seas full of the blackness of the night and the children's laughter and dogs at play over the dew-drenched grass, but the time-ridden circle is eternal.

Only the pool knows peace, only the children know reality, but no kindly god stays the restless trailing of the moon.

The moon moves on, it wasn't human, it was but a light, perhaps creation, perhaps God's face.

How could it stay? Something so precious, something so dangerously vital, it came to visit life and then move on. We can't live with it, nobody can, and besides it has so many pools, so many seas full of the blackness of the night. But it leaves something, something to remember, something to care for, something to develop and make grow, something that not everyone understands to build on.

So often have I cried aloud for the moon to come back — back with its light and its magic, left alone in the darkness.

But now I know that inside you and me and all of us who have seen the light — and such a light! — is left the chance to create something — something that is made of sun and wind and rain, something without magic, but born of it.

Truly the moon moves on, but the pool carries the light deep in its breast and the hills hear the memory forever deep into the earth.

25 August 1939

It was a very still corner at the bottom of the common where the mango tree leant against the stone wall — the path that the village folk took always happened to turn the other way and no one troubled to cross the grass to the mango tree which was old and disreputable and useless. So it was still, so still that it seemed to be forgotten. The yellow days passed over this corner of the world in a timeless procession, and at nights the nearest approach to a visitor was the roll of the old toad's drum from a neighbouring pond.

Then one day two creatures found it, this quiet little corner, and with a littler heartbeat of excitement, they ran from the path to the mango tree and down to the old gate that complained, and they looked at each other and knew that here they would build a house and here they would find a little peace.

The house was built and the world rolled round and children were born and the years brought fruition and maturity.

Arthur's Seat[1], November 1939

You say that life doesn't resolve itself into the struggle between the individual and society, that that is something that is settled once and for all times, as a preparatory move, before growth can commence at all. That *after* that has taken place, the individual can call himself adult.

But are you sure, isn't the adjustment a changing and perpetual one? Is there a final self that can be finally adjusted to anything? Isn't it the new and growing self that comes into new conflicts. Oh, isn't the whole problem of growth a perpetual struggle between realization and responsibility? How much of you is your own to reserve to yourself, how much must you control and discipline and how much leave free, and finally how much must you yield to the demand of something whose demands must perforce be inexhaustible.

12 December 1939

The first time that I saw the phrase that life begins at forty, I thought it nonsense and I have thought it so for many years. I thought that life began every time I found a new experience, every time that I learnt to look at life from another angle, I thought it was always beginning and incidentally I often felt that I was at the end, a dry, bitter, disillusioned end. Perhaps that was the result of the attitude of mind that made all those new beginnings possible.

Next year I am going to be forty, and I now discover with a dawning surprise, that I am looking forward to it in truth and in fact as something I am regarding as a beginning.

1 January 1940

And so perhaps the time has come to look back and remember and even to make lists of the rememberings. Of the rememberings that make an end, for every beginning draws the final line in some conclusion and all the forty years of end are important in this first year of a beginning. For the wise old fools say life begins at forty and they are right, and viewing one's own originality how often one has to wilt at the *wisdom* of great folly.

And so at this beginning I try to dig back into the past, into the last beginning, into the time when the knowledge of a beginning, let alone an end, to be followed by a further beginning, had not been born yet, and this is what I see, confusedly it is true, and with no order or merit, and nothing that can be of interest save to myself. I see two paths, inextricably bound to each other, and yet in some curious way almost irrelevant one to the other. Irrelevant, inconsequent, but caught up by some inner magnetism into a parallel frame that had a beginning and so some day must end.

These two paths travel through country. One country is full of people, people seen objectively and people seen subjectively, people in relation to myself, where the image is vivid, where the music is loud, sometimes overwhelmingly loud, and where the vision is nearly always distorted like a face seen reflected in the back of a spoon. The nearer you get to it the larger appear the features that are closest to your centre of interest. That is, I think, a fair analogy of the way one sees the people who have got caught up in the emotional development of one's life. You look, and perhaps you only see a distorted image of something that is a reflection of your own mind working on a bit of objective material. Like the making of a picture, the paint is there and the canvas too, and the subject may be something as remotely detached from you as a cotton tree or a string of gleaming fish, selling from some fisherboy's hand. But by the time it is a picture it is so much you that either you are tree or fish, or tree or fish are you. Those are the people who have made you, carved you, produced you.

Then there are, of course, the swarms of people, who have come and gone 'like shadows on a sea that move on glassily' and because they have not formed part of your growth, you wonder if you ever knew them at all. Ever even met them, or were they like the creatures of sleep or anaesthetics, that come to make a little fun of you and with you, only to pass through the wall, a miasma, a proof of madness in an otherwise sane world.

But the other path passes through a country that is without sound or sight or contact. It is a world of twilight and in it something grows, something intangible, something that could move on the water like a great octopus at rest, drifting with the sea, nebulous, yet capable of the most instantaneous and tremendous tension. Something that knows pain and that most vivid and biggest of all experiences, the cessation of pain — that creature that is the inner you, that is there whatever people and things and sets of circumstances come and go, that something that is the perpetual justification of all the confusion of wrongs and rights, of all the inabilities to discover final spiritual values, in a country that knows only being and not being.

These two paths moving through these two countries make up the past out of which this beginning is being born. To describe one or the other would be easy — to grasp the connection between the two makes a job, or seems to make one, that is doomed to failure.

How did the silent creature in its detached fluid world react to Peter or Jane, did it even know that they were there, did it shift a tentacle, or tense a muscle as they came and stayed or passed? Or did it lie and absorb and absorb and grow, looking with reluctant eyes at the Peters and the Janes who had to stay out of range and objective? It is a question that the world will answer swiftly and peremptorily for the artist, determined to deprive him of his detachment or at least of his outside-the-worldliness. But it is not a question that in all sincerity and after the most ruthless probing I have ever been able to answer for myself. I do not know if the creature lives as a *result* of the world or *in spite* of the world, and therefore I do not know what is the direct source of his growth. Certain I am, however, that although the magnetic flow between the two sources of his being may be continuous and powerful, that a direct transition from one to the other is anything but possible or likely. One is a world of natural phenomena, of light and rain and people passing down the roads, of things happening of excitement and peace, and of music ending. The other, is nothing, yet everything. Nothing happens, nothing comes, only a growing in the dark and a state of being.

25 January 1940 – Moneague

Can you imagine a contact with life that is like the umbilical cord? The world can be full of meat and nourishment, but to the child in the womb, it would be death.Only the food that flows through the life-giving channel of the cord produces sustenance and the means of existence and growth. Take the child and cram it with the richest, the most delicate, the most powerful fodder and you will only kill it. It has only one source of life that it can respond to: it is a simple but a delicate mechanism, which can handle all the abundancy of food supply admirably. You can give the mother all the rich food you like and this particular mechanism will translate it into terms that the child can thrive on. But the simple fundamental law must first and always be observed. (Hence the complete extinction of the creative artist during wars etc.) To translate the metaphor: the creative artist has only one contact with reality and life and that is through his highly sensitive and delicately adjusted sensory system approach. He trains it to register every nuance of change and impression. Through it he can receive the most powerful stimulus. Stimulus that would render the average human being a total wreck. And whilst he receives his shocks and his excitements through this one channel, he can exhibit a toughness and a balance that can rival the toughest campaigner in any other field.

Now what happens to me in the political world is what happens when I step out of my sphere into any other world. I start getting emotional experiences crammed down my throat through entirely foreign and wrong channels and the result is that the creative artist in me starts stifling and struggling most frightfully for air and the means of life. Then the channel, from lack of proper use, begins to atrophy and so, even when I fling away the foreign influences, it has been so damaged by ill-use or no-use that it can't immediately resume its function.

The contact with life, however sordid, however brutal, is essential, but it is *through* the creative awareness, not through any other way. To the artist, the lack of perceptiveness of the average human being makes him think that he (the average man) only sees men as trees walking. To the average man it looks as if the artist is refusing to see men any other way. Both are right.

The average man looks at the artist, poor fish, and wonders how in God's name he breathes, living under water, and the artist looks up from his glassy depths and, in one effort to understand the average man's ability to live in an unlimited quantity of breathing matter, flops to the surface dead from shock!

7 March 1940

Lunching with Sir Harry Luke of the BC[1] & Paget[2] ... Whilst waiting for N.* to arrive, Dr Burgin passed and stopped for a chat ... Sir Harry says 'truly the West Indies are becoming the hub of the world – every ten steps I meet some ex-cabinet minister or worse drifting past,' and now today comes Eleanor Roosevelt.

8 March 1940

The reception for 'Eleanor' was unenjoyable – I felt the antagonism of many and hurried off to my art class after half an hour of it. Kirkwood[1] had 'too many' and went all over the crowd saying 'the PNP[2] is a pack of crooks, bastards and anti-British and Manley tolerates it.' He also said to many people, 'And this man Wills Isaacs[3] is one of them – the press have suppressed his attack on Lady Huggins,[4], but I'm going to carry it all over Jamaica.' He and Lady Huggins are apparently pretty matey. It's curious for they are very alike – generous impulses but Lord God, what egoists. She has a more generous mouth than he has though. It's funny, because when she came to see me she said she didn't like him, he was all 'I – I – I.' So is she, poor darling.

Noticed for the first time that Amy Bailey, who was at the reception, wasn't pleased to see me and clung to Edith Clarke. I guess she is being disloyal and is unhappy. I couldn't teach afterwards – I felt tired.

Tonight he has the Party Executive and I have my art class so we'll both be late again. The law work has slackened pressure a bit and I am glad. I don't

*N. – Norman Washington Manley, Edna's husband. Also referred to as 'N.W.'.

know how much longer he can carry the financial burden of the Party, but whilst it is still necessary he has to work full capacity at his legal work to face it.

Talking to Domingo[5] this morning, he described the recent investigations in the party as 'a good purgative – but not actually a purge!' He has had a long talk with that stubborn fellow Fairclough, who is feeling his strength as the editor of what should soon become a daily. His fear of left-wingedness has become an obsession, understandable but a bit . . .!!

There is a devil of a drought and I love it, and shouldn't – It fills me with a sense of a mighty past and the old rites to the rain-god. 'Send us rain, oh God' but the sun god is a flaming power and goes down each evening smouldering red, behind the fine little logwood and parknut trees. And the drought throws Indian red lights and mauve shadows.

April 1940

I am just beginning to understand that perfection of anything in life is quite, quite valueless. A perfect relationship, a perfect happiness, a perfect adjustment, is finality, conclusion.

What is valuable is something which makes sacrifice worthwhile, something which gives self-discipline a meaning. That is one of the values of marriage. Perfection in marriage would only lead to self-satisfaction and dead contentment, but marriage, with all the difficulties and dangers that it entails, can make these inevitable steps towards growth worth doing.

Arthur's Seat, Summer 1940

The old toad is rolling his drum down at the foot of the hill, and the crunch, crunch of the cows is near to my window over the barbecue.

The dark and the light have lain down in each other's arms to sleep in a bed of silver moonlight and a little shifting wind brings the scents from the nearby woodland on the other hill.

28 January 1941

Human relationships are entirely dependent on a gift for objectivity.

The biggest mind achieves the highest pinnacle of thought – but in its development it often appears crude and half formed to a lesser mind who has already achieved a lesser, but complete peak. I write this as a very minor artist.

Minor artists are essential and valuable because by crystallizing early they achieve complete 'realisis', where the bigger mind is in a state of *process* – and unrealization.

Poetry should not depend on the 'right word'. Poetry is the art of *building** realization out of a sequence of words – realisis that can be achieved by the use of one word is scientific.

This does not conflict with the fact that poetry must not descend to the *process* of thinking, but must be the last nucleus or kernel of it. Because poetry is not thought, but awareness.

Realisis is Smith's[1] coinage.

Awareness – me.

1941

And there was a green, keen light in the world as the dawn came, and in that light desire moved away across endless waters, back to the hot, dark land where the dark god abode, a land of countless millions of inhabitants, where animals march in pairs and insects know flux – where men and women crawl back to the warmth of an endless womb – a Noah's Ark procession – and the land of Ham and Shem and Japheth.

But where the green light grows keener, desire has departed and an endless freedom springs like a young wind amongst the trees.

Oh lovely morning with the mists new furled, listen to the circling music and follow the footsteps in the grass towards an endless light.

For my god is the light god, the dark god is my brother's.

11 July 1941

Oh but I want to carve my two gods – dark and light.[1] I'd like to carve them where the echoes of the mountains would take up the song, where the mists and the rain breathe round, where there's freedom and light and no desire. And the laughter of the faun falls like jewels on the past. Where there's a beginning and an end, detached bodiless creation. I want an icy silence and an icy stillness and an icy loneliness.

(*building or finding – creative or interpretive – inverted forms of the same act?)

23 September 1941

For there is nothing in failure, nothing in success, nothing in youth, nothing in age, nothing in crowds, nothing in loneliness, nothing in pain, nothing in peace, only the glory of the endless going.

10 October 1941

Comedy and tragedy are the subjective approach to the drama of life. Timon and Lear are false: the first produced, I imagine, as the result of the collapse of a positive love, the second by the rediscovery of faith through kindness.

Hamlet and Caesar are, I think, superb, having neither good nor evil – but only understanding.

Carving is *process*, there's no pause anywhere. The whole thing, from the first picking up of the tool must be lived. The idea of roughing out and finish is false. It is produced by a developing mind, and the lift or falter of the mind at work will be the sum total at the end, there's no way out of it. Get down to *process* and leave the means to the end.

Sometimes I think it is more unjust to understand a person too well than not to understand him well enough.

28 October 1941

I have a little pupil, twelve years old, an elementary schoolboy; he only wants to carve, he hates painting, his hammer goes like mine. I went to see him work at about two o'clock and to tell him to go home. He was so intent he didn't notice me, he went on banging away and the chips flying. I put my hand on his shoulder and I said: 'Look here, Ferdinand Escoffery, you have to go home.'

His eyes went so dark and his hands dropped quite still; the afternoon sunshine seemed to doze for a second and I felt such a feeling of kinship, it just swept over me from head to foot. I knew his urgency so well, I knew the fatality of stopping – so finally. He climbed down and we walked together to the gate.

'Goodbye, Ferdinand – till next Saturday.'

'Yes ma'am, next week I finish he.'

Oh Ferdinand, Ferdinand, you're so little and your feet are so big and bare and your eyes, why did they go so dark? And now the sunshine isn't the same, it looks shabby without you.

January 1943

In the green light of the dawn they rose from the void of the past — Kablan, the great feminine principle, with the snake of wisdom spreading away over the foothills to the valleys, and his head lying with easy power in her lap. Then Dilmoon, the two-headed mystic, moving away and up beyond the dawn — beyond all life — neither male nor female —

A small procession of goodly ones lying between them. Next comes Hooman — the perfect one with a still and steadfast profile and the single power of the prophet, facing to the last of the mighty ones — the August Pair, cloud-topped and mighty, all male, all female, all human, all divine, balanced, faulty, aloof and yet aware.

Here they dwelt and here they ruled, all-powerful, all-compassionate, blessing the days and nights as they passed, calling the winds for changes, driving the mists for possession and breaking the thunder for freedom.

When the great rains washed for passion and the white lightning tore for vision, only the movement on seemed endless. The birds, the beasts, the insects, even the fishes and the worms moved endlessly on to the beginning.

The Blue Mountain Peaks in procession from Nomdmi ... from St Catherine to Blue Mountain Peak.

In another world of light and dark where man had been born — all this was changed, terrible bonds of right and wrong had grown, terrible laws and terrible liberties. And fear walked side by side with birth and death. Here man had lost the power of the future, and spiritless and servile he trod the ways of subjection to an unknown, unjust and capricious omnipotence.

Driven by a deep, unconscious memory of his birthright, he left the certainties that dominated him and returned weary, saddened, and under much suffering across the seas to an unknown destination.

15 April 1943

The mountains help me to realize that I mustn't strain to work, not worry over what I produce. For me it must flow lawlessly. Of a choice of flawless and lawless it must be the latter. It wasn't always so, however.

9 October 1943

I have been through a lifetime of theoretic domination in the arts. I find that I writhe over theoretic domination in politics. Theory should be the guide – never, never the master. At any rate we have had an orgy of theory the world over – a necessary orgy, but now the fundamental creative energy of a people must be the source of their action. That, I feel strongly, in the arts and politics, moves with the big streams of forward thinking.

8 January 1944

I notice that the young people, particularly the writers, glance at my work (on rare occasions when it is about the place) and look away quickly as if it made them uncomfortable – and they are very obviously not interested at all. Whether this is due to the badness of the work or their own self-preoccupation I do not know. It isn't making contact anywhere at all at the moment, with the exception of an odd stray person and moment.

This is caused by the fact that, I think, that I cannot, no matter how hard I try, get that extra something into it that will make it inescapable. The stark crudities are so apparent that the little voice inside creates no impression at all. I feel quite cheerful and detached about it, and I know it will be always so – I don't any longer believe that a new kind of concentration can be born that can make it otherwise. I feel really happy about it and lots of other things.

Doug and Michael* – growing big and hefty and assured.

Norman I worry over always, though he gets sweeter than ever before – and calmer too. He misses Michael mightily and aches to see Doug – though he can't say so.

The horse is a bit of a flop – but it taught me many things, so no grousing.[1]

1. The way and other than the way.

2. Planning can ensure a safe proportion, but it is death to discovery.

Care must come after spontaneity or things will be still-born. I learnt a good deal too about concentration and handling oneself in the hours when one can't work.

5 March 1944

We left home at about 4.15, Vivian[1] driving and picking up Allan Isaacs[2] on the way. At Guava Ridge we picked up eight people including a policeman, three driving on the running-boards, and drove to Content. There we met the village band, which bugled cheerily and the drum beat up. After a pause of fifteen minutes, whilst people began arriving over the mountainsides, we

* Edna and Norman Manley's sons.

walked a mile to 'Pompey's Shop'. A completely isolated spot with one shop, and there Norman moved about and chatted to various people of the crowd for about an hour. I sat on a rock and enlivened things for myself by making special requests of the band ... it soon became a popular idea and more than one person asked me to 'ask for something'.

A crowd of about 150 gathered and speeches began. Two speakers from Tower Hill, (beginners), astonished me. Particularly the first, who was sincere and extremely fluent. Then Vivian followed with an impassioned declaration, showing remarkable flexibility of voice and manner and with a use of scripture and hymn singing that was charming. He's a bit violent for a country audience, but he has travelled a far way in mob oratory and he's a lovable soul even on a platform. Then came Isaacs, and it was interesting and also a little irritating. Isaacs is a realist, if a realist is a man who understands the material things of life. He is also a hard worker, intelligent, sincere and full of ingenuity. But, Dear Lord let no one not admit, he is an agitator. He held my attention mightily for the first half hour and then he began repeating himself a bit and ramming the points home to an enthusiastic crowd. But his sharp, harsh voice was like a wooden mallet on my head, and at the end I was surprised to find myself with my fingers rammed into my ears. When he finally stood down and Norman was called upon, he was standing on the rock just behind Isaacs, swaying on his hips in that way he has, with his face turned up to the night. Lit faintly by the moonlight and with the mighty peaks behind him, he looked a quiet, impressive figure.

When he stepped up, the storm lantern threw its uneven yellow light up under his face, making the hollows in his cheeks look carved and his eyes enormous. He took over a crowd already a shade tired and cold. *All* the speakers had been too long and too noisy. But I could feel a different interest all around me — something quieter and in a way more normally hopeful. He has learnt to speak to the poor in the language of the poor, in a way that is full of warmth and sympathy and strength. Tired and cold as they were, they listened and went with him.

There was a lightning patch when an 'enemy' intervened and agreed that to follow the party was right if the 'government approved'. Like the crack of a whip came the answer ... 'My God, that I should live to hear a man say that, and I tell you, sir, that it is for us to tell the government of this country when *we* approve, and not for us to wait for their permission to think and form our own opinions.' The crowd yelled and the troublemaker never opened his mouth again.

The walk back in the moonlight was very good — I was left with the impression that at that meeting, if at no other, the women were the most alert, the most wholehearted and the most unselfconscious. Isaacs told me they had been largely instrumental in beating up the crowd.

We got home a bit tired, but not too much so. Norman has had a trade union meeting to address in the afternoon and a large area council meeting all morning. He said when he got home, a trifle whimsically, 'actually I don't feel very like work after an evening like this.' But even so I went to bed and left him up.

Now, when I listen to him speaking, I know that he will never have to struggle to speak again; it comes with sureness and power.

10 March 1944

Norman is out at a house meeting tonight, and tomorrow has to go to Port Maria on a case. I went to *Public Opinion*[1] and helped judge the prize for the party emblem. It was pleasant coming home in the tram, and over the gully the full moon rose. I wonder if I'll see it full again before completing my carving 'The Moon'[2] – it went better today. Going to bed early. Just got Claude Thompson's[3] scene for the pageant – it is powerful – it quite upset me.

12 March 1944

Sunday and an empty house. Domingo has gone off to work and N. is away for the weekend ... You go into practical work and what happens to you? Everything is judged by standards other than itself. You can't say to a group of men, 'do this' because it is right. They just don't understand. Rightness, truth, honesty, integrity are the last measuring rods men ask of you. Everything is twisted, distorted and dragged down. I give myself five years more and then I'm coming *out*, and after that I'll live and act as my inner self bids me – solely. 'No honey – you go on carving – it's true and honest.'

He has a meeting today in Manchester, and yesterday he was off to St Ann. He was talking to teachers and the business of a subject was worrying him. He felt that the teachers particularly need practical guidance; that this is no time for ideologies or generalities. I wish a reporter had gone along.

Lady Huggins shows her self-willedness and is apparently determined to run her *own* new organization in spite of all advice to the contrary. There is also written evidence that she is mixing herself in politics, which is just as bad as it can be. The hopes of a WI University are bright this morning. It is thrilling. The party's 'no land' policy ought to be distributed in pamphlet form – it's a grand bit of work.

Nethersole[1] and Isaacs are resigning on this question of taxation[2], in deadlock with the governor. I hope it is well timed and proves valuable. Haven't heard N.'s opinion yet, but he seemed cheery.

14 March 1944

Nethersole resigned from the KSAC[1] and gave a magnificent statement to the press. Gerald Mair opposes his re-election. Mair as a member of the JDP[2] is funny. He is colour conscious and often bitter about the upper class. But he runs with them all the same. He does their auditing. I wonder what his son will think – Michael will blaze when he hears! Isaacs didn't resign, it was decided so. (N. was away for decision). So we're in for a bitter election campaign. Nethersole asked me to come to his meeting on Wednesday – you bet I'll be there. He's a grand lad. Heard from Sherlock, sounds as if University is a cinch. Praise God.

Victor Manton came in to see me and he was telling me how bitterly Ansell Hart's social professional set hate him. The Lindsay Downers, Samuels, Audley Morais. And yet I think Ansell is one of the finest people that even literature has created. He understands purity of motive, intellectual honesty and integrity of being and all these are the things that his enemies wilfully misunderstand. I think his attitude to his son Richard[3] one of the most remarkable things I have ever seen, and the courage that he showed during his internment was magnetic. No, they can sit at their old Liguanea Club and tear Ansell to shreds, not even God would hear, he would be listening for the sparrows.

N. has more evidence (written again) of Lady Huggins' political activities. On his tour in the weekend, N. lectured Jamaica Welfare on co-operatives[4] and his audience of over two hundred visibly sulked because they wanted politics. He didn't win them over till nearly the end.

18 March 1944

A terribly rushed four days. N. speaking all over the place, have hardly seen him except at meetings. The mass meeting at Edelweiss over Nethersole's resignation was a great success – he made a very powerful and sincere speech which was excellently received. It was a huge crowd, around eighteen hundred – a cross-section audience. The middle class are becoming very conscious.

Last night went to a house meeting and signed up seven members myself – great fun. The JDP are trying to make it a party issue, which it is not, and the unscrupulousness of their cashing in on an issue[1] between the Corporation and government is being made by our speakers. But public opinion is still so undeveloped that it takes a good deal of ramming in. Waiting for N. the other evening at Edelweiss, got chatting with Arnett[2] and Grubb[3] and ultimately N. Fairclough and King[4] joined us and it was so pleasant, like old times before the split. It was the *Gleaner* strike[4] which drew us all together. Middle class girls have been picketing, and it has aroused great enthusiasm; it certainly makes history! Anyway they are back at work with the bonus won. If only paper would arrive and let PO launch forth as a daily — how we need it!

My own work has gone slowly this week but I am fighting to learn patience over it. I would to God I could work twelve hours a day, but there is so much needing support.

20 March 1944

Yesterday was a full day for both of us. N. had an all-island party conference and at night we went to King's House to meet the parliamentary delegates.[1] In the morning I had some students in doing landscape, and the pageant in the afternoon.

We quite enjoyed the affair at night. The Governor left in the middle to meet the Colonial Secretary to discuss 'the strike'. They're obviously in a state of fret over it and Lady H. kept lashing out over it. I tried to say nothing.

It's amusing: we discovered from other sources that government is expecting a general strike, and all sorts of fantastic precautions are being taken. Even the Brigadier was summoned and water, lights etc., etc., are all to be guarded. All for *exactly* nothing. I'm sure Busta only called the strike in the hopes of wringing something out of the wharf people — so as to get even with Wills Isaacs, who has taken some of his people from him. Tonight there is a meeting at Edelweiss in memory of the internments. I have a cold, but wasn't going in any event. I can never regard the 'heroism' of that little group[2] as other than childish disloyalty, except of course for Domingo.

Was glancing at '*Native Son*'[3] this evening and had to put it down — too depressing. It's journalistic filmdom with a deadly lack of any artistry. But it had to be written and it ought to be read, if your nerves can stand it. What a Nemesis America is laying up for herself with her colour prejudice.

23 March 1944

Government has again 'played ball' with Bustamante.[1] Wilmot (British)[2] of the P delegation met the PNP and PO here two nights ago. He is a fairly honest and fairly conservative labour person. A trade unionist, not a socialist, knowing *nothing at all* about the colonies and insisting that the average person in England was as ignorant as he is and not very interested. He answered questions for about one and a half hours, sometimes heated ones, and was always good tempered and courteous, if sometimes a little embarrassed and worried. He had taken the trouble to go into the slums, however, and was like everyone else appalled at conditions and high rentals. He reproved us for permitting Bustamanteism, and someone said: 'Yes, and the tie-up with the wealthy JDP makes it even more difficult.' He admitted that, and Harold Dayes stated: 'Mr Wilmot, it's not the tie-up with the JDP we mind, it's the tie-up with government.' And Wilmot muttered, 'Yes, I've seen that for myself.'

Kirkwood launched his blitz yesterday, defending Molly and damning us all. Pity he couldn't be recalled. The *Gleaner* went back to work, and the negotiations appear to have broken down for today and they are 'out' again. I hope Glasspole[3] knows his onions and can handle the situation. Still PO awaits paper. The St Andrew ladies are in a flutter over the election for Mair. That at least too has been achieved!

26 March 1944

Writing up at Nomdmi. It has been an eventful weekend. The *Gleaner* is still 'out'; apparently the men 'precipitated'. Rumour has it that Issa[1] is trying to become *au fait* with the strikers by appearing to sympathize. It's a political stunt, I have no doubt, and may or may not succeed, but there are masses of people who dislike his appointment and feel it is evidence of partiality from now on from the *Gleaner*. Also the bus drivers and mechanics have struck and Lindsay[2] is prepared to smash them. I felt quite ill this evening when I saw the police manning the buses. God bless my soul! But it's ugly all the same. Nethersole is in hospital, quite ill, and N. has left all unionism in his hands. There's no doubt about it, Huggins is a desk man and 'scary' over strikes. His speech in Council still awaits publicity in the *Gleaner*. I believe the *Express* had something of it but I didn't see it. Meanwhile the Russians pour across Europe and we await the invasion. Public opinion is tense, even in Jamaica, and feeling is that it may come even this weekend. N. had a meeting at Tower Hill last night. We reached Guava Ridge at 6 p.m. I walked up here and he went on to Mavis Bank. He rode two miles from there – they had 250 extremely enthusiastic people with two bands! Allan Isaacs is moving with great speed. If only we didn't have the impulsive Kirkwood to cope with, but I think not. He didn't reach here till midnight, whilst I tried to keep dinner hot. He seemed all set for hay fever and nerves by 2 a.m. but it passed and he slept peacefully till seven-thirty. Today he is working on his brief for Port Maria tomorrow. He leaves Drumblair at 9 p.m. and expects to be away all week and plans a meeting for every night in St Mary.

27 March 1944

Work hasn't been going very well. The upset over Vivian shook me, and also Marjorie Stewart[1] came into the class to tell me of the savage attack on Jamaica Welfare in Council, led by Kirkwood on one side and Campbell and Anderson on the other. I hear Simbys have collapsed. Really it's heartbreaking; all these years of patient work being savaged to suit the personal venom of selfish and indifferent people — indifferent to the ultimate good of Jamaica. No *Gleaner* so no news. Bus strike settled satisfactorily, thank God.

Had lunch at Greta's.[2] Lady H. was there and when she asked me about the *Gleaner* strike I told her, 'It isn't only pay or only conditions — it is also too that they still have a manager who still says, "Get out of my office you d--d nigger," and the time for that has passed.' She agreed and looked puzzled — queer creature, full of mixtures — very sobered though.

4 April 1944

Norman returned very cheerful from his week in St Mary. He had had excellent meetings and a very good spirit in them.

Today *Public Opinion* was launched as a daily, and it has made me inexpressibly happy and proud. Long may they go, and from strength to strength.

The JDP are electioneering madly with a lavish expenditure of money on every detail. The second the *Gleaner* Board knew for certain PO was coming out, they *instantaneously* settled their strike,[1] and had the effrontery to tell the arbitration board that it was a political stunt to cripple Mair's campaign and give PO a boost. Silly asses — they needn't be in such a hurry to identify *themselves* with the JDP!

Nethersole is still ill.

11 April 1944

Well, tomorrow is election day and the result is very obscure. From front to back the *Gleaner* is JDP; it's the devil, but it will have a good effect on PO. We took the weekend off and went to Dunn's River. We really rested and swam and saw some friends — it was wonderfully beautiful. The full moon rising behind palm trees with the sound of many waters, river and sea. The whole thing was cheery and good — and as they had had floods of rain it was a relief from the drought, which was appalling.

Think I'm going to the meeting this afternoon and tonight — can't resist it!

It's difficult to carve just now, d--d difficult — if only I don't spoil it before the election. It's equally difficult to leave it alone!

16 April 1944

Well we won and we're happy. A very orderly election, all things considered. The roads were almost blocked with JDP cars and the PNP rode in the JDP cars and won. We had against us money, publicity, transport. It was hard on Mair, because he kicked off with a lead of 350 and had to sit down and see it slowly dwindle as the 'out stations' poured in for Crab. The hardest way to 'take it', and then all his party left him there alone except for Mac. Seivright[1] and I took them out of the station.

The crowd carried Norman and Crab out shoulder high and a little boy, all dressed up, galloped a thin horse up and down through Half Way Tree! The one bad exception to good conduct was the reception of that ass Major Nathan[2] at the polling station. It wasn't good, but it was understandable.

The feeling among the masses is definitely one of pleasure, and of course Busta keeping out of it made the issue less confused and difficult. The *Gleaner* stayed partial to the end and the *Express* since has been revoltingly vulgar at Crab's expense.

My work goes fairly smoothly in spite of everything.

Insert on Drumblair stationery at Nomdmi[1] — no date

The house is surrounded by fog — which lies white and still on the top of the hill. Outside, the voices of the children, shrieking as they chase their ball through the trees standing like ghosts in the heavy mist, sound like the disembodied spirits of all children of all epochs since the first children of man.

Racing, darting in and out of the pine wood — sometimes looming almost clearly and almost instantaneously vanishing — with the chime of their laughter as the only evidence of corporeal life. After the green and gold ball they go.

Last night, coming up from the city at dead of night, driving the car to where the road ends, five mules turned their heads and flicked all ears forward to the bright headlights.

The road ends where the inky black shoulders of the mountains rise on either hand and tower to meet the stars, which seem to get entangled in the minute foliage on the mountain edge.

Five mules and men with lanterns — mules are like humans in some ways, but older and more experienced, and whether for vice or virtue move all of a piece.

Five mules for two people.

That tall blonde she mule — that one they call the Queen of the Mountains — Morgan's mule from Guava Ridge, Cripp's mule from Queen's Hill, Lloyd's little fiery black three-year-old from Lime Tree, and Dixon's mule from Little Content — a great pack mule that's slow but steady and no kicker. Which mules to take — Morgan's mule the first pick — she just come down from Cinchona and she tired — if there is another mule to take. Then Cripp's with a fine Mexican saddle — a steady creature — one-pace mule.

13 June 1944

Talking to Sealy[1] yesterday evening, he said: 'Happiness is a bad thing.'

What has the world come to when people can say a thing like that ? Sometimes I think happiness is the one measuring rod of a set of moral values—

Altogether happiness—

Christ, who made that great, painful journey — if he had given happiness too, perhaps they wouldn't have crucified him — he asked too much pain of them. But perhaps I take it out of its context. Because the soldier who gives his life can't do more than do so forgivingly, that life should weave the pattern thus. It would be inhuman and perhaps not god-like that he should do it with a smile. So it can't be happiness that is needed, it must be some inner harmony born of a new time-sense; not to be confused with an after-life.

Bob[2] said at dinner the other night: 'I do think that pursuit of goodness is the most thrilling thing in the world.'

And I said No! No! like Sealy over the happiness.

What on earth is the cause of this repudiation of harmonious values, as if they were stuffy and dead!

19 June 1944

Today I finished the Moon carving — but the carving doesn't matter anymore — I cannot say anything — I have no answer to the sense of failure when I look at it. So I won't look at it anymore — I will only keep my eyes on every moment of every day — for there reality lies.

Today, too, I reached a crisis with the Institute Committee — I think I cannot sit under the chairmanship of so cynical and contemptuous a person anymore (Esther Chapman).[1] And one who has no conception of the rights and integrity of artists, not only in this country but everywhere.

1 September 1944

As we walked up from the car I could see from way down in the valley that the line of pines looked thin — and then, as we got nearer, I knew it was true: the windows of the house of God had been blown out.

As we passed in through the wicket gate, I couldn't look — I had to climb over some of the trees to get down the path and I knew my heart had cracked. Whatever of faith I had found, I had found under those trees, whatever of faith I had been able to hold on to, I had kept because my temple was there to return to. All the journeys ending in a hand on their fine, rough trunks, and the returns down to the plains with strength and sureness.

Perhaps I had placed too much importance on the outward symbolism. Perhaps the artist always does, perhaps a human being cannot help becoming attached to the outward appearance of the invisible source.

God knows how or why — my heart cracked a fine hard line that afternoon — and for hours after I felt I was recovering from a heart attack. Though I think it was all safely concealed.

Norman went to work next morning to clear it for me — and we grew happier over it by twilight. A new symbol took its place — the symbol of his vision of the unending capacity of man to move on.

He cleared it and he left the one mighty stump in the centre, shaped like a flame — a pillar of cloud by day and a pillar of fire by night. And last night we three, Doug and N. and I went out on nigh full moon and talked nonsense for half an hour lying on the pine needles.

I went with N. and Allan Isaacs for a fourteen-mile ride through the storm area, and after that distress I could accept the fate of my high altar in a different spirit.

21 November 1944

We spent a fantastic week in the hills, campaigning in remote villages like Halls Delight and Westphalia.

There was one particular evening I shall never remember without a queer feeling in my heart. We had ridden and then scrambled down a fantastic track to come upon one of those queer little flat ridges thousands of feet up, with a sheer drop on either side. Over one edge you could hear a river thundering below in the valley, over the other side the lights of Kingston twinkled immensely far away.

On the ridge was a table, two chairs and a storm lantern dully glowing. No shop, no hut, only a wild wind pretty damned cold − and a flake of a crescent moon drifting down and across, accompanied by one brilliantly faithful star.

And N. speaking with such clear gentleness to a vast audience of twenty-one adults and five children!

Back in Kingston a mass meeting at the racecourse; over twenty thousand cheering and singing themselves hoarse as he mounted the Judge's box to speak.

Which is more real, answer me that − and I can tell you many things.

28 December 1944

I can't write of the election −

Now I can smile −

But N. carried a lamp of truth wherever he went. Fine, unforced and beautiful. 'Him that hath ears to hear, let him hear.' He has lost nothing − only gained in wisdom and quiet and maturity.

Jamaica − well Jamaica has such a rough road to travel that my heart is often troubled over it. But she has her laughter to make it bearable.

So Fagan[1] 'represents' us −

A just fate for us all I suppose −

Trying to put truth against greed and ignorance. But these things can't be hurried. I shall never forget the rich people rolling in in their hundreds to vote 'Labour' so as 'to keep Manley out'.

But you can't keep the truth out − it always comes knocking at the door − and the 'House' is no symbol of being 'out' or 'in'.

I felt my mistakes and my lack of ability very intensely through the whole campaign − wish I knew about people and that they liked me more.

There is something that you find in the stillness that follows complete defeat, that will stay with you till your journey's end.

It isn't exactly a pain, nor is it a sadness, it is as if everything ceases, everything has ended − as if there is no movement in the world, no going on, only a clear cut silent realization.

Yes, but realization of what? Not that life is ugly or painful, not that it is stormy or difficult, nor even that it fails. It is merely a realization, perhaps for the first time and hence the only time, of what life really is — of all its component parts of good and evil and in-betweens.

It is the knowledge that comes, that failure ends nothing, that life goes on and goes on going on. That a human being doesn't cease because his values have ceased, he isn't even any different, except that now he knows everything. Everything that is worth knowing. Life can't fool him anymore and he can't fool life, and most of all never, never again can he fool himself. That always in future will he know that there is no chartered course for himself or his hopes or even for his despairs. Always inside him there is a cold, an icily cold calculation of what is possible — it could, I imagine, be like being born knowing exactly what life is like.

Never again will the dawn bring the same hope, never again will the night drop on the same despair — always he will be different, with that small nucleus of silence.

7 March 1948

Exhibition in progress.[1]
In the inscrutable face of the night all chords find their harmony and that is why one can be unafraid.

29 July 1948

I am working on my 'Sun'[1] carving and waiting and waiting, trying to catch the ebb and flow of an authentic direction. It's a strange discipline. Anytime I take the bit between my teeth and try to dominate it or to know more about it than is to be known, I end up in a crash and the doors close against me. So I wait and work at other things — for what seems wrong is often some unknown truth presenting itself.

20 November 1948

Last night we went to hear Robeson[1] sing at the racecourse — the largest crowd we had ever seen. The sound system was hopelessly bad, and one could hear the words but the tone was hopelessly distorted — thousands of people heard nothing at all. The crowd was around seventy thousand. We were wading through the crowd to a spot where we could hear better, and the crowd around us, quite a small part of it, began to snowball behind us — so

Norman stood still. It was terribly disappointing not to hear, and to feel the disappointment. We felt completely flat when we got home and phoned Bob, and Stanley who was in charge of the sound — they were distressed and depressed. We took the staff here with us in two cars — the other car-load heard nothing at all. It was difficult to go to sleep and I woke early and went to look at the cows.

Nine a.m. Went to the airbase to see Robeson go — he was in a terrible mood — savage over the failure of the 'sound system' and deeply hurt over the death of the child and injuries to the others.[2] So typical of the *Gleaner* to headline the accident and give the type of presentation that almost made Robeson responsible for the tragedy. He swears passionately that he will come back. Jamaica may hurt and disappoint him if he does, and I wouldn't want that to happen. I tried to warn him off, but he was as stubborn as a mule. Actually I have a sort of presentiment that he won't. But the desire to come back to help us is very deeply felt — and he's very sincere about it.

Norman went up to Papine at six. He's trying to get some people settled on some land there. The ones that have been disinherited by the University. He's gone off tonight to the Executive and then afterwards to a street meeting at Providence Pen.

24 November 1948

Went up to Mona quite early this a.m. and did a cheering morning's work — in time it will take shape, but it is extraordinary how nearly I never saw the damned thing was still quite embryonic. It's quite wonderful to go to the length of a hundred foot room and lie down and look from that distance at so large a carving — it helps one to be very detached.

26 November 1948

Robeson phoned down from New York to ask Norman to contact the parents of hurt and killed children — to pay the hospital bill and funeral expenses — a generous act.

I didn't get a chance to write anything yesterday — too busy. Decided to take today quietly. Norman has just been invited by Munoz and the American Government to go to the ceremony that makes Munoz Governor — they are paying transport too — which makes it possible for him to go — otherwise with the elections ahead we couldn't afford it. It will make a heavenly (break) for N. and I'm so glad — we all are.

Hazel Scott and her Congressman came to dinner — she is a direct, honest sort of person, and very lovable. He is a strange creature — Robeson says he could and would be a Bustamante if he weren't too intelligent! Still it was a jolly evening.

Tonight N. is up in the mountains — he is driving hard at his constituency and covering every inch of it and leaving nothing to chance.

I wish we could find some way of appealing to and agitating for domestic employees — they have a ghastly time and there seems no way of getting through to them.

4 December 1948

The hill people are incredible — obeah, malnutrition and lack of steady work — I wonder how reliable they are. Sometimes I think they are almost a lost people. It is sad beyond belief.

N. has gone to the Agricultural Society meeting at Gordon Town tonight. We are on the last lap with *Focus* II.[1] It should be out at the end of the week — I hope it'll sell out and give us no trouble. It was heavenly working up at Gibraltar today.

7 December 1948

Focus II is almost finished. I scribbled a foreword to it today, and it should be out on the stalls next week. I'd like to do Smith's poems[1] next. Edith James is back and we hope better. She is in good spirits — we love her so much.

Norman was in good spirits tonight and telling tales from court, which is always such fun. There's a moon and I'm watering the garden and then going to bed early. The end of the week is always the hardest for me, with clubs nearly every day.

8 December 1948

Busta has let loose a sheet of an attack on Kirkwood!

9 December 1948

This morning spent two hours discussing with Louise Bennett[1] the possibility of getting her to work in the youth clubs and in this constituency she feels that she could earn back her salary in a year. I like her very much and I feel that to get really down to developing the cultural side of the clubs and providing some sort of entertainment in the hills is absolutely essential.

14 December 1948

Norman's new assistant Forrest has started work. I hope it will go well. Focus the second is out today. Had a busy morning fixing up with booksellers and reviewers. Norman has his inaugural meeting at Papine tomorrow night and we are fixing for a cinema show on Monday. On Sunday I took a message up to the end of the bridle track to Cambridge and was flabbergasted at the wildness and primitiveness — it's as bad as Queen's Hill. They are a tragic people, these mountain people, and it's quite incredible how they live. For actually those areas ought to be in trees.

A lovely photo of Rachel[1] came this evening — we both long to see her. Salvador Ley[2] is coming to stay for two weeks at Xmas, it ought to be a wonderful change — I'm glad for Norman's sake.

17 December 1948

On Wednesday night N. had his inaugural group meeting at Papine — or rather at Hope Flats. Just coconut boughs against the hillside. About two hundred people came and they got nicely started, when rocks started rolling down the hillside on top of them. Pandemonium! — finally Norman got hit by one, and about fifty men dashed up the hillside — one of the guilty ones got caught and beaten and went to hospital in an ambulance, and then peace was restored. He got in late — the tone of the meeting changed considerably. His wrist was quite swollen, but he and Vivian and Forrest looked bright in the eye from the scrap and the mass of the crowd were with him. It's funny, no one really approves of this stone throwing, and on the other hand everyone hates the culprits to get caught.

Actually N. doesn't think it was a political difference, but much more a bitter personal antagonism, that caused a political difference. Anyway I trotted off next day to see the wounded fellow — a wild creature with a beard. I don't think the party organizer had handled the whole thing at all well — too much hate and fanatic partisanship, and not enough attempt to view it all as a human problem. I'm wondering if our cinema show will be a success now, or if people will be afraid to come. There's no doubt the whole atmosphere of Papine is now very upset, but we can work on and in it, I feel quite sure.

19 February 1949

I wish I had a dictionary so that I could look up the word 'obsession'. All that is beauty, all that is truth, is destroyed when the flow of events starts to circle about one particular state of mind.

I have been in the grip of an obsession for the last few weeks – not a very harmful one, but nevertheless – and this evening I stepped out onto the verandah, whilst a Brahms Intermezzo played by Bachaus was being played on the gramophone. It was late dusk and the little Japanese tree was leafless against a last fading glow – the studio and the guinep were black shadows in the distance – there was a dark little toad hopping along the grass – and slowly all of my life kaleidoscoped, with the most extraordinary sweetness, a sweetness that recognized and praised its fullness – its mistakes – its richness in loves and hates – in steadfastness, as well as in its brief and glancing casualness –

Maybe tomorrow will be another day, but tonight, as the obsession lifted from me – and it spread out fan-wise – I knew great peace.

Maybe, too, obsessions are creative, perhaps they are the complete essence of something that, if it isn't isolated from its context, cannot bring the awareness that has in it the germ of an arrived at truth.

14 April 1949

Across time and space certain truths interweave – certain struggles go forward – certain faiths are kept, and the smile on God's face is very tender.

29 May 1949

Today the first chips came out of the carving of Papine[1] – it was quite early up there, cool and sweet. The golden light on the grass and trees. All the world was young and fair. A grand old, tough old, piece of wood that I love – to make the mother of all men, and the child of all women.

There was a big, strong, steep hill – and above it a cloud – a cloud that was full of light and everywhere was quiet.

Oh lovely morning with the mists new furled, follow the footsteps through the grass – into an endless light.

The American Negro Anthology of Poetry – I am horrified at its quality. The few good things are drowned in a sea of bathos. Dear God, here in Jamaica we know better. Poetry isn't description, it isn't argument, it isn't meaning well, it isn't respectable platitudes. Poetry is fire and air and water and earth, it is the realisis of the moment – in mood – it is experience, and above all it is simplicity, economy, and after all that, it is style.

Poor old America — what do they know about it? They are too, too material, too, too, bloody damned *earnest!*

24 September 1949

We are running close to the general elections again and everyone is getting 'het up'. I feel that it is on the pages of history and nothing we can do can alter its course. That isn't fatalism altogether — it's a sort of quietude of spirit, born of eleven years of insecurity and strain and the discovery that people can't and don't change overnight. You can't tell a person and expect them to believe it. Believing things is part of one's own growth and development and it can't be hurried or changed.

8 October 1949

From today, 12.30 p.m. Saturday, I am taking a vow of silence — not to say anything that is unnecessary for one week, until Saturday midday of next week.

This decision follows an attempt — fairly unsuccessful for the last few months — to stop using oaths or unnecessary expletive expressions, in order to be able to check the bad language used in all the youth clubs.

Now I would like to control the tendency to talk when it is more helpful to be silent and to listen. And to add to that the ability to be more careful and more sincere in expression.

Finally to face the tendency to talk as a result of, and as a cloak for, fear or even nervousness.

3 January 1950

Dear young people — I have been waiting for an opportunity to write to you about the great events of the last eight weeks and to give you a close-up picture of Dad's campaign, which was quite one of the most thrilling experiences of my life.[1]

Unfortunately, two days after election day, I went down with a touch of pneumonia and was in hospital consuming vast quantities of penicillin and sulphur and so I had to wait to write. But in a way I believe I can give you a truer picture now.

It was a wonderful campaign — a wonderful fight — full of colour and drama and above all, poetry. We had the toughest fight of all on our hands, as you can imagine — everything was used against us and technically it was a tough and a fascinating problem.

The first decision was to have no speaker, except he was actually from Eastern St Andrew — in other words, no mob-excitement and no demagogues. This was important for the obvious reason that without vast middle-class sections — bang up against our depressed areas — what you would win one way, you would lose the other way.

Secondly, and this is private, Dad decided that for the sake of party discipline and his own safety in the party, he wasn't going to allow any man to be able to say that 'he put the party leader in', and finally he had decided on a line of speaking that was emotional and spiritual all at once, and which needed a carefully built up atmosphere for it to be considered as sincere and genuine. It couldn't be effective after the chicanery of some of our best mob orators.

Dad used as his time signal a girl with a lovely street-singing contralto voice, and whenever he spoke, she sang in a slow, dragging way, 'There were ninety and nine ... that safely lay.' The effect of it was amazing — for miles away, when it could be heard, you would pass someone on the street and they would say, 'Manley going to speak now,' and then he ended every speech with James Lowell's famous poem,

> 'Once to every man and nation,
> Comes the moment, to decide.
> In the fight twixt truth and falsehood,
> On the good or evil side.'

He would recite the whole poem and by the end of the campaign you would hear the whole crowd muttering it after him.

And how he used to roll it out — it used to make the hair on my head stand on end. In the last week of the campaign he would also use —

> 'Ring out the old
> Ring in the new
> Ring happy bells across the sky
> The year is dying
> Let it die,'

etc. etc. and the crowd used to almost leap in the air with the thrill of it.

One of the extraordinary and obvious things was that from the drop of the flag we had youth with us — both working-class and middle-class youth. All the new young voters seem to be PNP. Dad built up an extraordinary speech using all the archetypal images, translated into modern terms. He used to say, 'All the young people, eating their hearts out, scuffling around day after day looking for work, they too want to feel that their country needs them, they too want to feel, all the young men, that when Sunday comes they have earned enough to put on their long coats and go out and cast an eye at a pretty girl.

And the young girls, they have their dreams too, they want to put a ribbon in their hair and put on the ballerina and the be-bop. They want one day to have a little place of their own, nothing very grand, just somewhere where they can open a gate and lock it behind them and walk through the little flower beds with the roses they have planted themselves, and lift the latch of their own home, and when they go inside and close the door after them, they can talk to their man as they like.'

Mercy! Night after night he fairly pulled the place down with it. And the strange thing, that except in the hills, anywhere he spoke, whether at Coronation Market or anywhere else, he was always the biggest drawing card. Speaking slowly and with humour and deep feeling all mixed up, he created the most extraordinary quality of a sort of *young* patriarch. From the start they called him the Father of the Nation, and as weeks went by he more and more grew into the part.

Fortunately he has learnt to make people laugh, and that, in Jamaica, is almost everything.

But the hills — ugh! Every time we turned the car up the hills, the same feeling of gloom descended on me. Poor souls — they are faithful to Fagan. But they are dark and desperate and really very stupid — it's sad, but it's true. I hate to even write the word, because there are such wonderful, shining exceptions.

But the brutal way Fagan and even Allan talk to them is terrible — it's got to be cuss words and personalities all the time, and it leaves me feeling sore and depressed. The truth is that the older generation can't change, but the young things must be given a great new chance, somehow, somewhen, somewhere.

I find I can't work with or for older people — they lack freedom, they are so set in a pattern — but the young people of either sex are so longing to be released, to be set free — to laugh and be glad.

But the last night was the most unique experience of all. He planned nine meetings, all on the plains of Eastern St Andrew, all for the one night. We had a loud-speaker fitted to the car and we went from meeting to meeting with Dad announcing them all himself as we drove: 'Come and hear Norman Manley for the last time, speaking at Papine — speaking at Papine — we're going to MOVE them — move them — it's "time for a change",' and then after speaking: 'Goodnight, goodnight, God bless you all!'

Up and down the roads we went and everywhere cars, bikes, people actually running from meeting to meeting, tearing after the Vanguard and Vivian's truck full of the Four Roads' young men singing our songs. From meeting to meeting, in the end getting caught in the traffic jam from our own meetings.

It was the biggest bit of showmanship ever devised and I am rather proud to say that I did the driving!

And then the last meeting — such a vast crowd, you couldn't see the end of it; twelve midnight and Dad saying, '*Today* you will vote — and comrades don't make me suffer in 1949 what I suffered in 1944,' and that was the end.

I actually saw people crying — over and over again.

How we worked — every detail — nothing was omitted — we had a team of voluntary workers that touched supreme heights.

The middle class voted as if they had gone mad, and all the lies and the propaganda never touched them. They had made up their minds and nothing could shake them, and our working-class vote just broke Fagan's heart. All the areas where we had swept in like Four Roads and Barbican, Papine and August Town.

It wasn't a wild turning away from him. Slowly they began to understand the party and to believe that Dad must be the better man — because when they howled their awful lies and slanders against him and then afterwards they heard Dad speak, the two things didn't make sense, and gradually we drew them to us.

And then so many people came forward to help — working like tigers. Three young barristers did amazing organizing and street speaking. Everywhere you turned, people trying to help, and deep down one sensed that what people really felt was that they loved him and felt he'd had a hell of a time and anyway when all was said and done, there lay the deep faith that he, of anyone, could solve some of the problems that beset us.

We didn't win a majority all island, but we only just missed, and on the figures, anyway, we polled more votes.

So we're happy, my young ones — we're happy and full of confidence and hope — we aren't fighting a losing cause — one day we're going to win and in the meantime we're growing up and learning what it will be like to take responsibility one day —

God bless — Mother.

7 March 1951

Around comes the drought again and the creative moment. Deep underground things are stirring —

The children¹ have been here for nearly a year — and I have given as much as I possibly could to attach them to Jamaica and Drumblair and a sense of home here. Not altogether successfully, I am afraid — but the best I could do. And now it's time to work again — for the years are fast slipping by, and I am conscious that the spate of work that I did in the years that followed 1940 has spent itself. The inspiration that was Nomdmi has rolled away. Somewhere, and secretly, I always knew it would. I couldn't have admitted it consciously, for it seemed something so permanent – but always, even the sequence which ended with the phrase 'and man was born,' I felt that – as I drew and drew – for the crucifix – for 'All Saints'² – I wonder if they'll accept the drawing and I wonder if I'll get the chance to do the carving.

When I did the radiant drawing, that was the philosophy of Nomdmi. But the parson said it was heresy, because I had done the resurrection (that would be permissible) – but in grave clothes. So I went home and thought over that one and I went on – savagely trying to get past the radiance, and lo and behold I drew a corpse. When I looked back to the first drawing it seemed as if the radiant figure was standing on guard before the cross, and when that was torn away, inside there was a stark and tragic little corpse.

Then came Norman's detention³ – and all alone, since no one else knew, I struggled to see it in perspective – not to succumb to terror. I couldn't fail to see it imaginatively, loving him as I do, I knowing his strange loneliness, and out of the struggle came the big drawing of the head.

And finally, after weeks, the drawing that is a flight – an upward movement and the arms long and like wings – Eloi Eloi – and the spirit mounting to God, and the body with its large and dusty feet, still rooted in the earth, or should I say *on* the earth.

2 April 1951

Yesterday I was able to break down the wall of inability to understand what is the truth (for me) that lies behind the crucifix story. I prayed, and now I see enough to release the creative spring in me.

Christ was a man – a very great man. He had all the qualities of intellect and simplicity and imagination – he was a mystic. Then he had his vision – his vision of one-ness with God – the true mystic vision of one-ness and light and love. And he tried to carry it to men. There were two planes of consciousness: the one where he was holding on to his vision and the other where he was striving to translate it for all men. When he said that he was the Son of God, he meant that we are all sons of God – and when he decided to put his vision to the last and final test of physical suffering and death, the agony was that much greater because it need not have been. The element of free choice in it made it so much the harder to hold to the sense of purpose.

If a man has to face death – well we all have to face that and the more philosophical we are about it, the better, but when a man tests his vision by accepting what is on one plane an unreal death, then the act of control is colossal. The vision of a moment can change one's whole life because it makes all other moments both brave and fearful; relatively real or unreal. The mystic's experience is a cruel doom unless it finds itself in a society that accepts.

Actually it is, more or less, a death in life and a life in death. And Jesus took it to its logical conclusion and that is why it makes such a strange contrast to the mountain isolation of some Indian mystics.

To sum it up crudely — the whole story of Jesus comes clear to me when I see him as a vivid person who saw God-ness and held to that experience through the ultimate catastrophe. He could have lived within himself and he could have had a great deal of personal influence, but he felt that his experience had to be given to all men, and the only way he could do it was by paying the price of death.

But right to the last moment, his eyes were holding fast to that one eternal moment of his transfiguration. All through the walk to the Cross. At an earlier stage he had refused, or been unable to see his mother, but when death was close he made a gesture to her — I don't know why that seems significant, but it does. And his head could only have dropped when it was indeed all over.

8 April 1951

Dear ... It's the most extraordinary thing. For weeks now I have been struggling with the basic idea of this crucifix I am doing. I have seen it as agony and torture and pain. I have seen it as the man of authority and vision — as the mystic in union with God. As the Son of God and the son of man. As the intellectual with the vision — even as God himself.

And now this morning I wake and I see it, I think, finally, as a quiet floating spirit — eternally rising — eternally hanging quietly over this world of men and women. A spirit that has hung for nearly two thousand years. So light, so quiet — so wise and so above it all.

Do you think, dear friend — that I can carve it like that? And will they understand? A figure floating before a cross and yet nailed to it?

You believe in it all — you are inside the fold — I am only watching through the doorway — so perhaps I am not worthy to do it. You say —

God Bless

9 April 1951

A Day to Day Diary of Carving the Christ.

I started work at around 9 a.m. I knelt and prayed — not only for guidance and inspiration in the carving, but that a new era of peace and honesty should invade my life whilst I worked, and that the work would never prove a strain or cause an irritation. As I put the first cuts in, Jim Gore[1] knocked on the door to speak about tiling the house. It took a few minutes and then I got to work. The wood is old and brittle and it will require great care working from front to back — the back will always tend to splinter off. One big bit did fly off and I must make it a warning.

I had to get Wright[2] to hold it for about ten minutes whilst I worked off the back, and this means that I have to think out just how I can fasten it for carving.

I also am seeing the possibilities of a halo — conceived rather like the rays of a sun.

I became more peaceful as I worked — and wondered if I could volunteer to be Norman's press contact.

11 April 1951

Yesterday went smoothly. I had Anita in the studio and she was very good, doing her little drawings. I started roughing out the figure's left arm — the wood on that side seems more brittle.

This morning people poured in. Women with children 'starving', men wanting to go to America, then to say thanks that they had had a 'call'. Someone with blisters, some with this, that and the other, all hoping to 'pass' the test. Constie had lost his apprentice job at the University.

Dear old Gallimore came[1] in and smiled at his 'join' in the wood and said: 'It's looking fine.' So I'll start now. Nita is peacefully on the couch.

The morning work was so short that I came back for three quarters of an hour in the afternoon, with Rachel cutting soap on the couch. I've got the top of both arms roughed out and the bottom of one and half of the other done. I think I'll do the same to the body leaving the head and feet in the block for later. I haven't cut the front surface yet — or the flat pattern. The work going on in the house is fierce and nothing ever seems to be finished. Hope it'll be over *one* day!

12 April 1951

Worked for one hour peacefully and completed roughing out of both arms — that's the end of work for the week, till Monday. Taking the kids out for lunch to get away from floors being torn up in the house.

There's a more harmonious feeling within and without today. Last night saw the W.Indian table tennis and Norman 'met' the team. Took Aimee[1] with us and she stayed on and worked on the book with N. afterwards and I went to bed.

It's a great drought and the air is full of spring. The guangos are in young leaf, it's such a resurrection –

If I put feet on the same side as head, there would be a great feeling of soaring flight. Shall I alter my design or carve another one that way some day?

14 April 1951

Came down from spending a day with Muriel[1] at Stony Hill with Nurse[2] and the kids – with a deep conviction to swing the legs across to the same side as the head, in order to create the feeling of soaring.

Had a bath and changed into evening clothes and then went into the studio and with paint changed the legs. I haven't moved them more than two inches and the effect is startlingly different. Will have to wait and see how it looks tomorrow a.m.

N. in Sav-la-Mar so can't ask his opinion.

The guineps are in blossom and the bees are working still, although it is dusk.

15 April 1951

Awoke feeling fresh and confident this morning. At last, with the hot weather, I can keep my window open to my beloved hills, without disturbing Rachel with the night wind. I got through unemployed, servants, children and carpenters by nine-thirty and have worked for two hours. Washed out the legs again and waiting for a more inspired moment for settling finally the sideward slant. But went ahead merrily on the figure's left arm.

N.B. There is no part of this wood *or* this figure where you can chance hitting too hard or taking off too large a chip.

It's BRITTLE and tricky.

It will require great patience.

16 May 1951

After that things went awry and I took the kids to Pine Grove for a week, and then got back to send Anita to school and had Vera M.[1] for a couple of days, before sailing for England. She looked lonely going off, but was very brave. After that I worked for four days, two hours every morning – and forgot all about my promise to keep a diary. Then Norman had his accident – Grey[2] turned the car over, coming home late from Montego Bay, right on the hood, and they had quite a job getting out and the engine was running – and oh – well –

After that I went *completely* to pieces, crying at nothing at all, and with a splitting headache. Just as if I had had the accident. Meanwhile Norman was cheerful and assured and only fed up and puzzled by my taking it so badly. I was so all in yesterday that I thought I was going to collapse. The class at night was a failure, and I came home with a blinding headache. Norman had gone back to Montego Bay with the same chauffeur. So it was difficult. Anyway at midnight he phoned that he had got over safely. I lay awake for hours with a headache and nervously just spinning in circles.

This morning I am driven back to face the fact that physically and spiritually I lack something. I feel in a dim and confused way that there is an unreality about my approach to religion and to the future and death, that is leaving me utterly unreconciled to the shocks and changes of life, and that until I get it straight, I will still go on enduring this sense of catastrophe.

Faith – whether it be truth or fiction – is a state of being, whereby one achieves a more harmonious sense of reality. This, as the first step on a road, is as far as I can go. I also can see and feel that God was too all-powerful, too distant and remote – until man brought him near through the birth of Jesus.

6 June 1951

A week ago, I moved the Christ up to the University – to have peace and to find sureness. Also to have that 140ft room – with its gloomy space – near enough to the lighting of 'All Saints' and the distance. So it has moved forward again and I am deeply conscious of my inadequacies – of all the years that I have passed when I have not given objectively to carving or to drawing – or to anything, in fact, except this feverish search to free myself of myself. Such a strange thing happened when I was working today. My thoughts, after the first hour's work, began to stray in that weird, worried half light that exists when you think you are completely concentrated. I stepped back to look at my work with my mind slightly wandering on to some election speech that N. had made, and bang, crash – I hit one of the pillars with my head so hard that I actually reeled, and then struck my bare foot against the stand and smashed a toe nail and the blood spurted.

And in a flash I knew that it was like the anger of God – there I was carving the most important job of my life and, even then, I was doing it with only part of me — not good enough.

So for now I am being, or trying to be, ruthless, and cutting things out in order to be fair to this great opportunity. All these days I haven't even kept a diary, that I seriously swore to keep. But now, this must all change, and more than ever I know I haven't the technique or the clarity of vision for the job — I can only do it if in peace and sureness God leads me through it step by step.

The legs seem short and heavy — I may add a piece of wood at the bottom in order to lengthen the carving from the ankles down. The wood is cutting very true, now that I have got to grips with it.

The idea of the Biblical drawings is coming clearer in my head — I must start drawing a great deal again.

16 June 1951

Everything has crashed again. Norman's statement in the House and all the savage, ruthless diversion that the *Gleaner* made of it, has made an ugly, exhausting nightmare of our lives. So I won't bother to carve anymore. (The Palisadoes murder[1]).

There are things in my life that I must get straight. It is quite impossible to go on like this. There are things that I must make my peace with — my whole relation to the political work, both as an artist and as a person. It's funny that it has never been put properly straight, but I must set it right now and find a pool of peace — something to measure all this by.

13 March 1952

Of course the carving was finished in December and the dedication service was held the same week that the great split took place in the party.

After June I went to the hills with the kids for the summer, and the day Norman came up for his holiday, the hurricane smashed up the east end of the island. It was an immense experience, five of us packed into the little upstairs room, whilst the cottage rocked and creaked like a ship and the rain lashed under the shingles and poured in on to us.

Rachel touched us off with great humour the next morning by saying: 'Mardi — you and Pardi was a bit *fidgety* last night, wasn't you!' That became a classic — that reached into far corners! All our pine wood was smashed and lay like fallen giants on a titanic battlefield.

Next day some Eastern St Andrew men cut their way through to us, and

Norman went down to town to offer his services to help with relief. Water, light, power, and communications quite gone, and a mammoth problem of feeding and sheltering thousands of people. He, and all who served on that epic occasion, worked day and night and did a wonderful job. Up in the hills I couldn't do much — but I went on some prodigious hikes seeing people and conditions and making a few reports. Not much else I could do, with two children on my hands. And all this, of course, was still part of that strange carving awaiting completion down in the city. The roof was blown completely off the hut and it stood, so N. tells me, face up to the open sky, quite unmarked and unmoved.

After eight weeks we came down again. By now N. was more than ordinarily tired, and we resumed work and life as if his holiday had been spent in the conventional way.

I moved the carving down to the Church, and started work again. And then I knew that the subject was a great strain, and that I could only stand carving it if it achieved a strong peace and beyond pain quality. I couldn't do it in agony, or full of self pity. It must rise — and even the head must have gone beyond pain. So for better or worse the die was cast. I wish I had written an account of the hurricane whilst the experience was fresh in my mind — but it was so mixed up with my concern over Norman, and coping with the children and trying to keep adjusted, that unique as the experience was, everything slid.

Carving in that dark old church helped me greatly. The simple working-class people who came and looked, or expressed opinions, made it a precious experience.

In the first week, late one evening, plain clothes police arrested a case of larceny hiding behind the organ. That made me a bit jittery for a few days, and I developed a tendency to look over my shoulder at every slight noise — but I soon overcame it, and even the height of the scaffold in a sense gave me a feeling of being in another world, and so secure.

As it got near to completion, and all the plans got under way for the Dedication, I realized that I had made something that at least was functional, and that comforted me for what I felt was the inadequacy of the carving.

And then came the thunderbolt of the Party split.[1]

We asked both left wing and right wing to the service. The left wing came, the right wing stayed totally away, even Seivwright.

It was a lovely service — all the ritual of the church was used, the Bishop leading every rector in Kingston. Bearing the brass cross held high, they filed in and then the service started.

At the end, when the two standing tall candles, and the two candles that were being carried, and the borne cross were reared high in front of the carving, whilst the whole congregation stood, Governor and all, I looked up at the lonely figure above it all, and did I imagine it, or did it seem incredibly lonely, incredibly not a part of it, *incredibly* as if he had never meant it to go that way — with all the robes and the ceremony and the ritual — with all the Godhead.

What a strange story and what a strange sequel, oh, son of man.

Finished and dedicated 10th December 1951.

21 April 1952

I have told Michael that it is his job to write the story of the 'probe' and the 4 H's. He was in and out of it all with that passionate, youthful vigour — so let him record it.

2 June 1952

Have just got back the studio from hurricane relief after nine months of clothes distribution.

I did a little terracotta[1] down at the Art School, which Lady Foot bought.[2] So I have started a little bit of satin wood — direct carving without an idea in my head — let's see what happens. And there's the 'unknown political prisoner'[3] turning and stirring in my head. I'm not sure yet. I hope to take it to the country for the summer to carve.

I am trying to create a little pool of peace at home — the political world seethes and boils and it's too, too much. It looks as if Fagan[4] is coming over to us — it's all so odd, after the passion and the bitterness. There are no permanent values in politics — but the mallet and the gouge are always there, and the sound of the chips coming away. We'll see, tomorrow!

Michael is a darling and *so* helpful.

6 July 1952

After a tough 'post-probe' period things are at last smoothing out again. N.'s birthday marked a remarkable re-birth of spirit in the Party and in the whole self-government movement, which had deplorably slipped back to almost 1938. Also Campbell of the FF[1] has created a stir, by speaking favourably of our Plan for Progress.[2] Norman's old dynamism seems to have returned, and in the house and on the streets he has launched a great campaign to seize the dynamic in the country again. His broadcast, too, was lovely and well received, with the lovely Blake poem: 'Give me my bow of burning gold.'

Eight weeks ago I took a bit of satin wood and, with nothing in my head, decided to do a preparatory carving to get my hand in for the competition. Tonight I finished it — 'The Secret'[3]. I think my technique is quite good now — and my ability to keep relaxed. I hope I sell it quickly, as I am broke. Anyway it's good to have a temporary break and be happy for a little while and do a happy little carving.

14 July 1952

Mayoral election — sitting in studio and awaiting result — fairly calm.

Would like to transform the University carving into the competition carving for the 'Unknown Political Prisoner'.

Won election. Fagan our candidate as Mayor and Barnswell Deputy.

Norman really did a master-job over the situation with Fagan and may it be the forerunner of many others. He will be very relieved and I guess I go back to my original idea for the carving! It must have been nerves!!

Actually, I create best in the hurly-burly of politics — it gives one less chance to become over-concentrated.

20 July 1952 — Sunday, Nomdmi

We came up this morning, four children, Miss B., Nurse and myself. It took the day to get settled in. Rachel fell down the stairs, such a pity as it got her all ruffled, although she wasn't hurt much. Anyway they've gone to bed now, quite cheerily, if a little tired.

I am sleeping in Minni[1] with my clay sketch and the block of wood. I know that only God in my heart and mind, and peace emanating from me, can make it a success — for the others — and make me able to do the Political Prisoner.

Harmony — which is contact with all things — will come, I feel sure, and detachment and relaxation. I felt more than a little sad to leave Norman — he would have so loved to come. However, I feel that his trip to Barbados is going to be good. He has been very brave this year. I can't help remembering last year and the hurricane. There was such magic the few days before — everyone felt it — an all-pervading sense of peace. But this year is different — there is no magic — so perhaps there will be no catastrophe. Please God, help me at the least to receive and pass on harmony, and out of that may the inspiration grow.

21 July 1952

Had a rather miserable night — couldn't sleep, and the remains of my cold made me feel achey. The little cot was very hard.

But I went out and drew, and a strange different head came, which couldn't 'go' with the figure I have prepared. So feeling stiff and out of practice I did a large, finished pencil drawing with the new head — and a rising, almost flying figure. The two ideas are totally different, so tomorrow I hope to be able to do a large, complete drawing of the old idea and then on Thursday I'll take them both down and show N., who I will be seeing off to Barbados on Friday. So I'll go to bed and hope for a better night. It was a heavenly day and the kids and Miss B. and Nursie were very sweet. Hope N. and Michael are OK.

23 July 1952

Well that makes four days of concentration for work and four large drawings and a lot of small ones. I've gone back to the original idea for the Prisoner — but the other drawing is very symbolic of a lift over difficulties and being cluttered up. I think the idea is clarifying now, though it's still difficult to 'see' anything in the wood.

No bad news from Kingston, and this evening the papers were full of Norman's call for unity in the House over Self Government (a successful appeal). So I hope he will leave for Barbados in good spirits.

I have loved the four days of drawing. It's such ages since I drew continuously — about twelve years.

27 July 1952

Started carving this morning — made everyone give the wood a pat for me.[1] It's old and very tough, but true.

I saw N. off to Barbados on Friday. He had a wonderful week in the House on the Self Government issue and actually achieved unity over it. But it had taken a lot out of him and although he was bright, he was tired and thought he was getting a cold. I hope not — but I hated to see him going off alone. Michael and Graham[2] and I got him down in good time. Glasspole and Wills were down to see him off and we made it a jolly affair. I got back with Michael to hear Rhoden and McKenley win at Helsinki[3], and sent off a cable to Wint. Oh they're a great set of boys!

7 August 1952

Well that makes nearly two weeks work on the Prisoner, and it's finally committed in embryo. The roughing out rather suggests that it should keep a completely simple and basic silhouette and be quiet beyond belief. I love it — tonight I found myself putting my arms around it and the wood had that acrid sweet and blessed smell of cut mahogany.

Last weekend N. came up for a day — a blessed day. He looked well and cheerful and I think that the Barbadian trip had been enjoyable and successful. The issue of the ICFTU[1] had been dealt with by Adams[2] quite independently and, I rather think, finally. Busta had cut no ice in Barbados. They're too critical and sober for him; but now he holds up so much that he doesn't understand, intent only on retaining his present position.

I heard that our paintings and my sculpture had been well received in Puerto Rico, and that the 'Horse of the Morning' had created a sensation!

Outside the wind is tearing and I can't help remembering last year's hurricane. Minni shakes under the wind and the full moon has come and gone again without rain. Still it's heavenly weather for a holiday, even if it is a quite severe drought.

I wrote Adolphe Roberts to congratulate him on *Six Great Jamaicans* — it's a fine job. He has such a clean, incisive style. Well, this is the end of the first stage of the Prisoner and the die is cast. If God would only guide me to a simple and profound result, I would learn so much.

I have done a drawing of Anansi[3] for a carving. I just went and sat in the old woodland and it came to me. I must do it — it's important, really it is. He just came out of a tree trunk, in the gold afternoon light, coming flickering through the trees down near the fork. Great little, wise little, cunning little man. You saved the slaves, you saved our people, you alone brought us to emancipation from the white dominance, and the shackles of the past.

17 August 1952

This is the anniversary of the hurricane. And it's a warm, sunny, golden day. N. has been up for a week and it has been wonderful. He found it hard to sleep for the first night or two, but he did mighty deeds of carpentry, making another clothes shelf, '*à la* Nomdmi', for the new bedroom. He also, with the help of Robinson, sealed the downstairs room, and the children carried shavings to pack under the floor. They had a glorious time. Rachel carried her little box on her head in the appropriate style. Then the great event came of going upstairs and pouring water into the 'chimmie' on the floor in an effort to make it sound like a little girl peeing at 6 a.m., and it was decided that those occupying the lower room would wake when those upstairs used the potty — but as it was no longer *very* loud, they would be able to go back to sleep. N. thought that was satisfactory.

The carving is going slowly, as I brought up a bit of wood that was a good deal bigger than required. Anyway, all surplus is off now and next week I will have to find a guidance of how it must go.

30 August 1952

So this is the end of one of the loveliest and most important holidays we ever had. Norman has had three weeks with very few interruptions and he integrated into the busy, quiet life of planting and clearing, and long games of cards in the evenings. We slept in Minni and left the house to the children and visitors. We have been nearer to each other and more in harmony than ever before. I stopped working a week after he came, and just gave up myself to holidays and peace.

The rain has come at last so we will leave everything green and even some water in the drums. I don't know what sort of life we will move into — hectic as ever, I expect. But we will take down some of the peace and harmony, I feel sure. Rachel too is vastly improved and it will be nice to see Michael again, and in two months Carmen and the baby will be here.[1]

Thank you Nomdmi — for a return to balance and strength.

1 December 1952

Just finished the Prisoner — it took four months after all — four uneven, uninspired months, packed full of other engagements and activities. Carmen and little Norman are here. Mike[1] and Mary came. All sorts of things, good and bad, and through it all, intermittently, I carved. It's a dull little figure, but at no time did I ever feel that I was working on something that would blaze out any aspect of the truth, and it's compromised too, in spite of my desire to be free. But it is sincere, and a sober statement of philosophy, I suppose. It moves no one, I wish I could feel that it did, and it will pass unnoticed in England. But I feel that I kept faith with myself in working to completion. One thing is important — I have finally broken out of the Nomdmi cycle.

Eleven years is a long time. Michael says that I escaped the difficulties of my life into a flying mysticism and I think he is right, but it seemed so radiant, so sure, and then slowly I have discovered that I was being held by the past —

the fallen chain in the Prisoner may be of some significance to me too.

So the carving is finished and with it a new road is opening up. I don't know where it is taking me, but I feel it is to somewhere mature and good.

1 April 1953

The Little Prisoner did end up in the Tate — it wasn't in the catalogue at the end, but at least it didn't altogether fail. I am sending off the 'Horse', 'The Generations', 'Old World New World' and 'Tomorrow' to the London Group.[1] They're old works, but perhaps I should see if they can make any impact in the big outside world, amongst all the abstractions. I hope I won't get too hurt over it!

We were to have gone to the Federation Conference in London, but it had to be cancelled. Bustamante decided not to go on grounds of health (I wonder) and N. couldn't go and leave the by-election wide open.[2] Allan's death comes at a critical time and we must at least make a bid for it.

His funeral was a macabre affair. The public appeared to take it as a sort of public spectacle and a vast crowd turned up. The JLP had run quite a few trains and truck loads of Portlanders over to it. Busta was parading up and down and making much political capital, but as Allan of St Elizabeth said, 'Never have I seen such a big funeral and so few mourners.' It was really quite horrible. We all felt that it was ballyhoo.

So perish all our decency and values.

The studio has been jacked up and run down to a quieter spot in the grasspiece, and I am making a great effort to keep things peaceful in spite of the election and the pace all around.

Michael has just flopped into bed to get a long night. He's a simply wonderful kid and of enormous value to Norman and the movement. He's a great boy in the Trade Union field. There is peace and knowledge and understanding.

Zonarich and Millard were here last night. They are great fun and great boys and I think they're going to help the NWU in the bauxite fight.[3] We need it.

14 November 1953

Well — three terrific weeks of excitement — Simmonds dismissed and the HHO scandals.[1] Norman carried the fight in the House with restraint and drama, and then the arrests of Truman and Simmonds.[2]

We all know that HE would not have 'moved' to do a thing if N. hadn't gone all out, and if the knowledge had not spread that he had evidence.

Of course Trotman[3] is involved in the worst way too, but it's impossible to prove it.

Sealey's three *Gleaner* editorials have almost stolen the show. Meanwhile Issa and DaCosta[4] will pay the earth to preserve silence.

The Foots are working hard on the Royal visit. How odd and unreal the Royal procedure is. You curtsey here, you curtsey there — in fact you curtsey everywhere. Give me the new democracies, where a friendly handshake is all that is necessary, with or without gloves.

I have just read *The Man on a Donkey* and, in truth, the crimes of the Royal line need a great and a humble expiation.

It's so wonderful to have Douglas back — mature and solid and a little distinguished.

Foot is a charming, likable, infinitely clever person, and he is surrounded by people who admire and flatter him. Personally, I like him, but I feel he has that ancient fault of demanding higher standards of his own people and his own country, than so-called semi-Barbarians like us — and that gives him an irrational tolerance, which is easy of self-justification. Sylvia is warm hearted and kind, completely devoted to his career and his interests — in another world and circumstances, she would be a charming friend of artists and a happy member of a cultured group.

Graft — the country is rotten from top to bottom with it, and the amoral cynicism of the *Gleaner* staff, which dates from the old regime of DeCordova,[6] is a root of the dilemma.

Anyway, this time quite a large section of the public is alert.

15 December 1953

And then Norman became ill — a slight coronary thrombosis — it's so difficult to write about it.

Moody, Aub and Levy have looked after him and I have nursed him. He's been wonderfully good and cheerful, except for a chronic tendency to do too much. He's still confined to his room but he's stronger. It's so difficult to know how much he ought to be allowed to do, because he can confuse us all with how he feels, in his determination to get back to work. In spite of many upheavals he has to rest until the end of January, and after that the important thing is to help him to moderate the pace and keep to certain set rules which will safeguard him from too much excitement or fatigue. I see some difficult days for him ahead, but somehow I feel that he will set a slower pattern and keep it.

His illness coincided with the Queen's visit, and there were the wildest rumours that he wasn't really ill, but being a 'communist' he wouldn't shake the Queen's hand. I did all the functions for him, and it was the sort of day one doesn't remember with any pleasure except that from 7 a.m. to 1 p.m. I was wanting to be at home, and faces and voices and movement were an odd blur in front of my face.

Once at dinner, for about half an hour, Charteris, the Queen's assistant secretary, kept me fascinated with his lively, quick mind. The Queen herself is puzzling — one wonders how much she could achieve if she were Mrs Smith and had to fight for recognition every step of the way. Obviously she has the character and stability to carry the role that she has been born into, and that is saying a great deal. But there is no sparkle, as indeed there could never be.

The Duke is a nice young man. He landed into a bed of well-watered begonias trying to get to his chair, and exclaimed: 'Oh dear, I am playing Sally in the Alley round my chair.' And when the Queen's ermines arrived, he said: 'Good God — it's not as cold as all that, is it?' How he stands it all, I don't know.

Next week we are off to Nomdmi for a week and then to the sea for three weeks and one more week at home.

I am so conscious that something has happened to us, with Norman's illness, but nevertheless I feel we mustn't think of it as a milestone, but as something that with patience and cheerfulness we can adjust ourselves to. There has been great sympathy and he felt that very deeply — his fan mail has been vast and so comforting!

Jamaica needs a spiritual revival —

Michael has been a tower of strength in it all and is doing great things in the NWU.

3 March 1955

Sometimes at moments of hurt and confusion, the only way out is to look back over the years and try to remember the pattern.

The sea is roaring on the Palisadoes, the trade wind is only moderately strong, and the good keen sun is cooking us firmly as the fine spray from the sea puts a light coating of salt on lips and hands.

If I try to remember — I see a hilly field in Cornwall in the early dawn — and a wave of emotion goes over me, two roads out of a great loneliness.

There's something in the *process* of finding something or someone even lonelier that oneself — a lonely man, woman or child, and out of the effort of help, comes a shield, a bulwark.

The lame pony, the deserted dog, out of this process of healing, there is fulfillment and release.

That is one road and it doesn't last longer than the period of recovery.

The other road is the creative path – out of hurt and confusion you make something new, something 'other than', something different. You make order out of confusion – you make peace out of hurt.

The sea comes thundering in, curling and dazzling and antiseptic, the sun is too hot now – and the two roads in that hilly field of emotion away back in that youthful Cornwall have welded into one.

And remotely I have detached myself from the process, and now I see it all.

2 April 1955

So much has happened as I look back over the election campaign. Chiefly I remember Norman and I setting out in the Humber Snipe with Graham at the wheel and Davidson[1] beside him. Such a vivid campaign with always, deep-rooted in me, a calm conviction that we would win. 'Not by much – but by a little' was the simple phrase that kept running through my mind: when spirits soared – Norman so full of humour and so full of fight, and the two men so selfless and so untiring – and election night, when there was a moment of horror when the score didn't look so good in the Eastern end and Henry Gray and Fagan fell[2] – 'Not by much – but by a little.' I always remember Harry Dayes[3], a good sportsman, with his big chin steady: 'I think we're coming through,' and Norman trying to comfort Seivwright. Ah well, it was a great fight and, in the retrospect, a phenomenal victory. It has taken me from January to collect my emotions and my wits, to even mention it. Sorry I didn't keep a record, but that was impossible – too much was at stake, and if we hadn't won it would have made grim reading. That, of course, is why men don't keep more diaries during a war – one mightn't live to read it.

Then we had two flying visits to the States and one to Trinidad, and the two hours of Magloire[4] and the Princess.[5]

May I go on record once and for all – I hate to bend the knee, except to God, and even then not too often. Whatever the magic that attaches to a throne it belongs to the past. The modern press can't replace the awesome mystery of the ancient rulers with the gaping, gossiping curiosity of a modern throne; and the odd and humble service of the modern king more befits an ardent social worker, than anything else that I can think of. But let it all rest in peace.

Here we are with a job on our hands – demanding, amongst other things, humble service – but with it all a need to remain intact and oneself.

After two months of suppressed but acute worry, I begin to breathe again – the job is to achieve a routine, a routine that can render possible a chance to live and to create.

The whole studio was filled up with junk and last week I went in and cleaned it out.

Friday, all day, I will spend at the office, keeping in touch with constituents.

Monday and Tuesday nights I will spend at the groups — sometimes alternating to Wednesdays.

Saturdays and Sundays are there in case Rachel needs me — and the other nights are between Norman and the world. It's all a question of keeping relaxed.

Michael and Thelma,[6] who were so wonderful during the election — Michael made a massive contribution — need a little help to spread themselves a little more socially — and Carmen needs much consideration with this difficult pregnancy of hers. Doug seems settled for the moment and little Norman, who is in a bumpy patch, can come as often as he likes.

Big Norman is happy and settled, and so far keeping good health. Provided he can be got to sleep enough, and get the odd weekend, he is so unfrustrated that he should keep well.

Gradually he will get a chance to get things started and we all pray that oil may turn up!

Last night the oil expert came to dinner, a nice Canadian, progressive, humorous and keen. It was a good evening.

And this big carving in the Studio — little by little, bit by bit, I can touch it, if only I can keep relaxed — a flame.

7 December 1955

I feel that we will lose this silly old by-election in N.E. Clarendon, and perhaps it is for the best, as it will teach us to be humble and to keep near the earth.

Re-reading some of this old record, I realize how personal and passionate it all is and how harshly I have judged our opponents.

8 December 1955

To get a pattern of behaviour and an ethical pattern — and above all a creed of faith.

I can't accept the tenets of the church — whenever I hear the apostle's creed, it seems to have no inner life — but as the years go by one longs to believe in something that never waxes nor wanes; something that can keep one silent at the right moment and will make one always interpret through love and not through criticism. I believe in a state of being when, through humility and quietness, one can accept life and people as they are.

It's so strange, but I do think that the desire to change things and to change people can often be a refusal to change oneself. No, that isn't it — because why should one change oneself, if all things as they are, slowly grow. The finding of peace between one another doesn't imply change, it only means the recognition each of the other's being as a whole.

The Godhead, the stillness at the core — out of which flows understanding and sympathy and love.

13 March 1956

Could I start now and write a book on the theme, 'I saw my land'. Seeing Jamaica through the years, a shifting, changing pattern, leading inevitably towards its new constitution.

People, places, moments of awareness and moments of crisis.

The atmosphere, the physical splendour — the grim reality of its problems.

January 1957

This is an important three weeks — with the Federation talks on. No one knows the outcome of the knotted question of the site and everything is in a state of suspense.[1]

It's a problem to keep calm — and to wonder how much longer we can stand the strain of life.

11 January 1959

On Thursday the 8th I took Rachel to school at Knox — it's nearly nine years since she came to us. It was a sudden decision on her part, arising out of a little bed-time talk about education, and next morning she made up her mind and in five days I had taken her. She was very brave until the end, when she broke down — and coming home with Michael driving, I remembered how I had cried when he and Douglas went to boarding school and here we were, hurtling through the night, and the tears flowing again, and then I looked and saw that the same little boy I had cried for was driving me, so I needn't have cried and it comforted me.

Of course it's the end of a period again, for the house has been teeming with children and there has been no time to write or to dream or even to carve. Now the quiet will come back — it's been a great experience trying to integrate her and I haven't altogether failed or she couldn't have gone with such courage.

And today Norman has gone with Wills Isaacs to Trinidad on the Regional Planning Conference.

I refused all invitations and have spent the day quietly here, tidying up and reading and thinking and playing Prokofiev No. 5. Lonely and basic thing it is, with some fabulously lovely, melodic lines. I would have gone to Trinidad myself, but I didn't want Ra to feel I had walked right out on her.

So this is the last year. One more great effort until election, and after that — freedom. The whole issue of Federation is clouded with suspicion and doubt and an awful lot of dishonest politics. Perhaps it will survive — who knows.

I don't feel very intense about it all. We seem to have given half our lives.

If it is quiet, I will often write in this old book again. I have begun to read again — a remarkable life of Picasso, and Errol John's play, 'Moon on a Rainbow Shawl' — very sensitive.

Douglas is down in the South Caribbean, and Carmen is doing brilliantly in the Pantomime.

I am working on a little carving for the Cadburys[1], and some small terracottas — one for Dawbarn. I tried this summer to experiment and break out, but it wouldn't come. Only 'feeling' was there. Clay is lovely, though, and if I can get the time, I believe I could do good work.

Norman had a lovely two weeks at Nomdmi — Xmas turkey and a Xmas tree and *such* moonlight, and the kids were excited and very good — only little Norman gets too excited. But he can imitate the whistle of a bullet and when you hear it in the mist, it's very realistic. Michael came up for the day.

I'll go to bed now — it isn't late, but it's the first day I have had alone for years. My mind wanders to my little girl with a hope and to Norman with a prayer.

24 January 1959

Ra has been through such a storm, poor little kid — she really touched bottom — but now her spirit is soaring. She has sent one or two remarkable poems and letters, 'and when you come to die and life throws back her golden hair.' I think the worst of the homesickness is over and we all feel more at peace.

I have got a fascinating commission from Jock Campbell for the West India Committee's office. He wrote a very interesting letter and a copy of a remarkable speech he had made about the West Indies — and in it the phrase: 'they were striving forward in hope.' There, I think, is the carving.[1]

So when I finish Cadbury's I'll go away to the mountains and think.

Tomorrow night the new art teachers are coming to drinks and I am asking all the artists and one or two writers. We must try to get the art movement together again — it has drifted so badly recently.

Norman is in St Catherine tonight with these party conferences. I wish now that I had gone — I would have done, but Monday is my carving day and I want to be fresh just to finish the little girl with the goat.

Monday 16* 1959

The Cadburys' carving is finished — my first commission. It made me so happy and I hope they will like it, for they are dear, intelligent, lovely people. It's a child with a little goat. I tried to keep the tree effect of emergence — only the top of it is worked out. The rest disappears into the wood. It's a dark little piece of Guatemalan wood.

My aim was to learn to carve with the tremendous pressure of political and social engagements, and not to falter nor to get confused. I think I came pretty well — the carving has tremendous feeling, though it is slight in intention.

And now comes the big effort right through till the election. How to keep serene and sure — and how to keep Norman well and on his feet. To keep near to the Almighty and to keep humble and yet unafraid.

I will write often this year — it is like communing with the still small voice.

23 March 1959

So Crab died — 17.3.59.[1]

And that great funeral — from East Street to Half Way Tree — a solid mass of people, and when they broke through the police into the cemetery, thousands of them, and then stood so silently for the masonic rites — nothing like it had ever been seen before, and Norman reading the lesson, 'and God shall wipe away all tears.'

25 March 1959

Dear Harold — Tell your friend Ben for me that there is only one point in time when a man can say that sculpture is finished.

A man can depart from an art, or an art can depart from a man.

Sculpture is endless — when it is finished, man is finished. Man is finished.

*Month omitted.

I'm glad I didn't meet him — I would have so hated him.
Edna

5 April 1959

1940 — it's a long time ago and so much has happened — I realize now that in spite of my age, I was still young then — and outside stimulus lifted my spirit soaring, and new things broke through.

Now one must find a way to look inward and brood — or to take the passing scene and hold it, for always.

As the molten rock in the beginning of time had, at some given moment, to petrify and stay forever in the form of the moment.

31 August 1959

It all started with that brilliantly impudent declaration of an early election.[1]

I wanted to write an account of it, but it has all been spoilt now in one way.

24 February 1960

Today for the first time there was a review of art in the paper, and they referred to my carving as 'dated' and in a cold, clear way, I heard a clock strike and I remembered something that had happened at the end of last year. I was driving along, I don't remember where or what time of day, and suddenly the thought swept over me that I am sixty and that it is all nearly over.

This thing called life — that is so much oneself — the thing that one felt to be eternal — the onward movingness that could never end — this — was nearly over. It's quite incredible, really. It's well nigh impossible and somewhere inside one there is a hard lump, a hard and final lump — what does one do with the last little bit of the arc that is sloping so swiftly down?

It's a hard decision, but I think it's important to make up one's mind and to spend it to the full, in the way one wants to.

It's impossible to go on putting off — and it's equally impossible to squander in a sort of impulsive reiteration of patterns that have become mechanical — but to release oneself to a deeper reality requires considerable courage and more self-knowledge than most of us have.

But I don't think I can put it off any longer. This is the beginning of a new and a last phase and how does one spend it? Is there a story to be written about it all — is there a chronicle of events that should be recorded, and have I the gift to do it? It has been an eventful sixty years — too eventful, perhaps, to have allowed time for keeping a record unless I were a methodical person, which I am not. And yet if one could remember with accuracy and with a particular point of view, for the latter is important. I have a profound feeling for the surrealists to whom art was a way of life. The telling of this story would be part of the story itself. I think it should start at the end and work back to the beginning. Only by the unfolding from the outside, which is nearest to one, could one achieve the perspective to give form to the early days.

At this moment I picked up the phone and spoke to Mike Smith. This was my first gesture — a step outside the patterns. Mike is often so cross when you phone him, not wanting to put down his beloved work to speak to anyone — to me at any rate — but he was calm and cheerful and we talked of George Campbell,[1] carrying his job and his responsibilities in New York with part of his mind and his consciousness just aching to get back home and to get a chance to write again. I told him, too, that I wanted to write a book of all of this and I waited a little nervously, knowing he would speak his mind. He said yes — but it would have to be the truth and I would spend a good deal of time steering off libel — so it had better be the sort of book that was published after my death. I said OK, and that I felt in such a hurry I would do it and die in five years. He laughed and said, 'That's a bit short!' We talked of this and that. It made me feel good! that perhaps it could be done. He said will it be politics or people — it should be both. Then he suggested, in his oddly practical way, the use of a small dictaphone, which would be less laborious. I could try that. But when I said I could start from now and work back, he said, 'Well, Anthony Eden has done that already — he started from Suez and worked back,' and I said, 'Damn'.

We talked of Derek Walcott[2] and the *Gleaner* review published whilst I was in Trinidad, which tore him to shreds, and called his work 'pastiche'. I didn't argue with Mike — it's never any good, you can't convince him and you daren't allow him to influence you, not too much anyway. He has one of those positive minds, which combine an amazing range with a fantastic self-opinionatedness. I believe in him, though, and deep down I like both him and Mary. I like to know that they are getting somewhere, and I like to think that Mary is keeping her bright mind and ways in spite of much that is difficult in their relationship and in her life. But I don't like to see them often, it's just that they are real and very uninfluenced by superficial and casual things.

I don't really think they meant to tear up Walcott — I think it was a solid attempt to appraise him, but paying the compliment of showing that it was worth doing.

How can I start this story? I think that day on the truck when we waited for Bustamante to come out of gaol.[3]

St William Grant[4] was there and Fairclough and all the battery of speakers who were mixed up in that early turmoil of explosion. People whom I grew to fear in the days that followed: W.A. Williams, Scarlett[5] and a group of Garveyites, Aggie Bernard[6] whom they called Joan of Arc.

And Bustamante arrived in a sea of acclaim — and the famous story of the extra half pence that N.W. had got the workers whilst Bustamante was locked up — and hearing his voice announce it as his own achievement with utter and complete ruthless falseness. That was when the pattern was set, and out of it grew this strange, deadly struggle. But the bitterness has passed now and one looks back a little wonderingly at it all.

Now, in spite of Anthony Eden and Mike, I think that is the way I don't want to write it. You see the way I go back emotionally — to 1938, and this I don't *want* to do. I want to see 1938 through the peace of mind of 1960. Can one do that, though? Can one ever really recall the past as an act of memory without becoming immediately the person who lived through the events. It is easier to go in a car with Ruth Williams up to Spanish Acres and to watch Grantley Adams going through the motions of a charming host — but not asking one to sit down — not until one was almost in the car, admitting that there was only a little sherry and perhaps a little brandy in the house, and he foresaw that neither would be welcome. And the ghost of one Grantley watched the ghost of the other Grantley speaking with a little self-love and a little self-pity, or both.

Do we all come to this? Sooner or later, this lack of total contact at the same moment and in the same place — is this old age? Are Jung and Bertrand Russell like this — a little, perhaps, and what is the difference? Is it perhaps only a memory that can still throw so large a shadow, that even the end has shape and meaning, but the trend is the same.

Driving home from Spanish Acres the two ghosts of Grantley receded and I remembered Grantley at Drumblair for the first time — and I, being twenty years younger, saying, 'Grantley, here's a cushion, sit on the floor, all West Indian politicians have sat on this floor at one time or another.'

And he gave his little secret smile and sat. His knees cracked a little because he was big and heavy in those days and he told jokes about Barbados and we sang West Indian songs and raised a rumpus generally — he danced, too, in a courtly and Victorian manner. He seemed so forthright in those days. He spoke at the St George's Hall to a conference and was humorous and tough, and very socialist. I'm not sure how old he really is — I wonder! He always seemed older than Norman. He was a good friend and devastating about Bustamante and dictators, and of how the Barbadians wouldn't have accepted him for a second, which was true enough.

And another memory — when we were in Barbados at the time of the rumpus with Walcott,[7] and Walcott's passionate protest that Grantley wouldn't accept help, wouldn't accept the organization of the party on PNP lines, based on group structure, how he ignored everyone and just issued statements — but Grantley beat him, though, and changed him.

He was a huge man, with a head like an unborn child — the same protuberant forehead, with the nose sort of folded under.

Then, of course, there was the time when he came to see us after he was so desperately ill at the University, and I remember putting my arm through his to steady him down the steps, and as he drove off we thought, is it a stroke or maybe Parkinson's disease?

Did I say we didn't sit down that afternoon at Spanish Acres? Indeed we did — Ruth made him take us in to 'the chamber of horrors' — his study. It was like a 'collage' picture — the first thing we saw was the waste paper sitting in the middle of the desk, which was just a shambles, and all over the room were strewn letters and files and newspapers. We did sit there, almost from shock; the windows were closed, the blinds were down, but we sat. Actually we were sitting now with the real Grantley. This room was a symbol of Grantley's life. But for all his failing life and energy, he wasn't a small person. He had pioneered and fought for freedom — he had been restless and dogged and a flat-footedly dangerous debater — merciless, ruthless — crushing all opposition, and at the same time, crushing all new life and new ideas.

And somewhere in all of this was Grace, his wife.

Generous, charming, well-read, affable, and quite, quite independent — in that, a Barbadian to her core. We spent a week in Barbados once, and every single afternoon Grace would come with her car alone and drive us all over her beloved Barbados, talking and telling us about it. Norman used to sit beside her and tease her about her driving and about the width of Barbadian roads, and sometimes they would talk of books.

But it wasn't until we met Bathsheba that I really understood Grace. The one little spot in Barbados that is wild, jagged rocks and a tearing trade wind and huge Atlantic breakers, and this was Grace's love spot. This was the place where she came alone to recover from a term at school — to sleep and read and walk and rest.

'Grace is at Bathsheba,' Grantley would say. They never invited us to their house in all the years — we never knew their home, for good or ill.

When Grace wouldn't go with Grantley to Trinidad, there was every kind of explanation. She had sacrificed too much already — she wouldn't leave her home, her work.

But once, when she was in Jamaica after a Canadian tour, I took her in the car from King's House to the Institute and she was in a great state of excitement over her students' Cambridge exam results. Thinking, this is the

First Lady of the West Indies, I said, 'Grace, why don't you go to Grantley in Trinidad?'

Her voice was sharp for the only time I can remember: 'Edna, Grantley knew I wouldn't go – I told him frankly that I wouldn't.' What could one say? Nothing at all. Only Grace could know her own secret. It was a great chance lost for the West Indies, for she was a wonderfully nice and charming woman.

26 February 1960

When we got back down the hill, Ruth and I, we heard at the hotel of the invitation to go to the calypso tent with the C.L.R. Jameses. We went, and Eric Williams[1] turned up too, and he came round to the hotel afterwards. I think he was making an effort to be relaxed and as he used to be in the old days – all the suspiciousness dropped away and his face smoothed out. If only he had a family, and some relaxation with home life, and a break from the endless tension and work. It's quite awful, really – on and on endlessly – nothing but work, and then the paranoic tendency comes in. It is Trinidad – because Grantley is now suffering from the same thing, though not as a result of too much work. But Eric has great honesty of purpose and he wants all the right things. I hope that the people around him won't spread such a carpet of arrogance, that he will succumb and lose his original simplicity.

28 February 1960

My birthday today and the family gave me the Cleveland Morgan of the 'Little Girl'. I am so thrilled over it.

How can I tell the story of Eric Williams? I remember him first in Washington at the time of his divorce.

What a strange thing divorces and separations are. How people become involved in a tight spinning whirlwind of emotion, how they clinch and separate and clinch again and all the world becomes blurred and unreal and only an intense, violent passion of hate and love takes charge, to which everything else is secondary – dear God, what a madness it is.

This was Eric in Washington when we first knew him, or at least when I first knew him. His wife is a nice woman and quite a real person, but she just didn't know what she had married when she took on Eric. Eric's egotism and drive, and almost his egomania, were things that she didn't understand and couldn't cope with. His eternal wars with everyone, his perpetual suspicions and passions, his ceaseless tendency to be over-intense about even the smallest details in life, and his total lack of comprehension about a woman's world. He could go on forever – all night it raged – and whenever we weren't otherwise

occupied, all day too. One felt it all so intensely, one was so deeply sorry –
but there it was – a great bird had taken charge of the nest, and a wife and her
children were just pushed over the edge to hold perilously on in a great void.

So they parted – and our paths often crossed after that – and an odd,
lopsided friendship grew. He had a fine mind, critical, clear, but in his soul he
was always looking over his shoulder. He had a great trust and confidence in
N.W. because N.W. let him expand and held his own personality back and
often his own views.

Then, years and years afterwards, he travelled across the world to bring his
second wife to meet us. She was a wonderful woman and she loved and
understood Eric and was proud of him. He was so deeply happy – I was very
touched – and a year afterwards she was dead and he was left alone again, with
a baby daughter. It was quite awful, and whenever nowadays the worst of him
shows, I remember that bit of tragedy and forgive everything.

Nomdmi, 5 March 1960

The next time I remember seeing Eric, though I think there were many
forgotten times in between, we were passing through Piarco airport –
spending the night there to change planes. It was a few weeks or even days
before his fatal decision to go into politics, and he had come to the airport to
'put it' to N.W. Should he, shouldn't he – and Norman threw the full weight
into the decision on the side of urging him to do it. As usual when they got
together, they talked till almost dawn.

I remember circling above Port of Spain in the early morning light, and the
fine little mountains etched like wave caps in the dawn – and N. saying, 'My
God, I told him to go ahead, but can he do it? Someone has to lift Trinidad out
of all this.'

And then, just a year later, spending a night before the election, Eric's first
election, and all the PNM[1] people pouring out to Piarco to meet us. I
remember particularly his women's auxiliary, and the white-hot enthusiasm
and confidence – I've never seen anything like it.

Well, they won – I don't think it would have happened without Norman's
pioneer work in Trinidad as well. Just a year before, he had spoken at
Woodford Square and prophesied that they would enter party politics like the
rest of the Caribbean. Trinidad, which has since become so arrogant, was all
those years after everywhere else.

Writing of Eric's character – one night he was dining at Drumblair, and he
was full of fun and affable, and then quite suddenly the power failed and the
lights went out. There was the inevitable scramble for candles, and there in the
half light of the flickering candles, Eric's whole character changed before our

very eyes. In the flash of a second he was literally, as well as figuratively, looking over his shoulder. His voice dropped to a sibilant whisper, and he began to talk of what the English had done to him when he was at Oxford, of how his letters were opened and messages intercepted and Washington!! – it simply curdled one's blood.

It's odd how circumstances like this can repeat themselves, for the same thing happened to Paul Robeson. But he didn't look fearful, he merely told us more, but in a different way, about why he took the stand he does over communism – how, by refusing to deny, he increased the tension, and in that way put greater pressure on to the legislators to speed up the reforms on the race question. Sheer fear that he would develop a following of left-wing support in Harlem and the other big cities.

It did have that effect, but I am quite convinced that Paul misread the coloured American, who is even more anti-communist than the white, and for entirely different reasons.

7 May 1960

It's funny the sort of things that bring back the past – the other day the use of the word 'dated', and last night in Seaward Pen. We had come down from the mountains and I felt so sad. I didn't want to come down, it had been a cold, wet weekend – quite lovely – and we sent home Graham, no engagements for the night. And of course as I walked in, there was the telegram reminding me of the banner unveiling in this little St Andrew group.

I changed like mad and went, rather glad of something to lift me out of my depression. It was the usual rip-roaring affair, and a wonderful young man sang and sang, and we all had a jump-up, merrily sweating, and then he sang:

> 'So Comrades greet the dawn
> Salute the rising sun
> My country turns towards the light
> New day begun!'

and in a flash I was back in Gordon Town, fifteen years before. We used to go in for special 'days' in those years; Nethersole's Day, Lloyd's Day, etc.

This was Manley's Day – and the valley in Gordon Town was crammed with tens of thousands of people. The day was over, really – the moon was coming up over the steep, black hills and the Shortwood Boys' Choir was singing, 'The Voice of the City is Silent'. Because of the shape of the gorge, their voices echoed from side to side on the hills – that vast crowd hushed, except for little knots of tipsy people around the rum shops who were past knowing what was happening. Dear God, the passion, the power, the thrill of those hard fought days – 'Manley's Day' in Gordon Town. They still vote against us, but all Jamaica came that day, more than all the people of Gordon Town.

24 June 1960

And this all started[1] when Fairclough, along with H.P. Jacobs, was offered the management of the Jamaica Standard by Kirkwood. That was a great opportunity for Fair C. but of course he was Secretary of the newly formed People's National Party; it was he who had worked like a tiger beating up the first Ward Theatre Conference on an all-island basis. Now he was at a cross-road. A cross-road, incidentally, which altered the whole course of his life, and ultimately caused him much embitterment.

He had to find a secretary to take his place, and he ultimately went down to Trelawny and found the man Vernon Arnett, who for twenty-two years held the job – and in an honorary capacity after he became Minister of Finance.

It also altered to a great extent the whole character of the PNP. Fair C. was a nationalist, and in a rather high sense of the term, a racialist. Arnett – well look at Arnett's face: over close-set, dark, brooding eyes, a narrow face, a narrow head, and a slightly bitter mouth. Fair C. was an extrovert and Arnett is an introvert, and very pronouncedly so at that.

Fair C. was a middle of the road liberal – Arnett was, and possibly still is, a left-wing socialist. He is also a passionate nationalist. Whichever one N.W. had to work with would have had its difficulties. He was far left of Fair C. and a nationalist, but not a racialist. But Fair C. being an extrovert, it would have been a happy combination as N. is, and always has been, an introvert, and in those days an extremely nervous and highly strung person.

With Arnett he was much more in sympathy politically, but in character they had too much that was alike for them to be of great help to each other, personally or socially.

I think I should correct any impression that Fair C. was a racialist. Actually he has eternally been attacked for being a snob and a lover of the company of white people – particularly women. He defends himself on this charge on the grounds that as he is not an avid reader, he depends very much on the company he keeps to keep his mind alive and up to date. So that any good company means much to him.

12 June 1961

Busta has declared in favour of secession, and N. has come out with his statement about a referendum.[1] So the fight is on. Jamaica I think on the whole, solidly supports the idea, though I see by the press that Ulric thinks not. My bones tell me otherwise. But the South Caribbean has totally misunderstood, and think that he is blowing hot and cold, etcetera, etcetera.

C.L.R. James[2], who is a darling as a person, hasn't a clue as a politician and he advises Eric in the African pattern. Eric himself is inexperienced. Anyway, I believe we will win through and we go on Thursday.

We are tearing ahead with a new Focus; it's happy work, and Micky Hendricks is a new voice in poetry — he's half French and Jamaican coloured of Dutch lineage. Interesting combination. Tonight George Campbell's poems, set to music by Salvador Ley, are being performed for the first time and I am excited and happy.[3] Pam O'Gorman piano and Vela Vincent. It's something new, piano and voice, two separate entities meeting on a point of harmony; in 'Listen Moon' the voice carries the voice of the lover and the voice of the moon, but the piano is like finely splintering glass falling, falling 'and residue of nothingness'.

It's a wonderful effort, and I love it. But in one song, 'Birds Sing with Me', I feel that here there is not enough of a *call* to the birds, and later to the wind, to come and join in the great rejoicing that his 'inspiration is in love' with him. I must tell Salvador this — also — in 'Listen Moon' the line, 'I looked for you and you had fled' is too agitato. The whole song is a *lament,* someone going through the blackest night — looking, looking for the moon — like a lost soul.

24 July 1961

'Last week a comrade die — you know, mother, him come from just round the corner in Upper King Street. Him die of a haemorrhage and the only shirt and pant him have wash up in blood. I go to a friend and I borrow a five pound and me go to the comrade who sell second hand clothes and we search and search till we find a dark coat and pant and we take it to the tailor man next door to me in Beeston Street and him cut it down the back and fit it on the comrade and we get shirt and tie and sock and put it on him.

The undertaker charge twenty-two pounds and my girl friend she collect and some give eight pence and some give six pence and some give one pound, and we get it and take to the man and him agree to bury him and I pay back the five pound I borrow, we don't owe any man.

And mother, him gone to meet Scarface and Adinah Spencer and Marquis[1] looking decent.

And last thing we pin the Federal button on him coat so that when he get there they will know where him stand.'

'Yes, Linwood,[2] God will bless you.'

'I hope so, Mother, I hope so. I need it — we all in Beeston Street need it.'

Undated

I was on the platform in May Pen, July 1961. The microphones were booming. Davidson was singing 'Clap your hands for joy', there were speeches – and then we were tearing through the night and N. was drinking hot coffee and not spilling it, with the car doing seventy, and we were in Spanish Town – with the old square mysterious in the lights from the truck and the people were singing 'Manley wear a crown someday'. Dr Leslie[2] climbed on to the truck in an African cap and handed N. the Rastafarian report[3], just as he got up to speak, and we danced all the way from the truck to the car, hundreds of us, and the old, beloved smell of the swamp passing Ferry on the Spanish Town road coming home. It was very late – the fourth meeting for the night – and then it was Port Antonio, such a vast crowd listening and listening, not restless as in the old days or ebullient. 'Goodnight, Comrades, I must leave you – the people of Buff Bay are waiting and it is late.'

'That's Mr Wills, sir, I'll stop.'

'Damn, why did you stop, he's coming from Buff Bay and we will be late.'

'Just courtesy, sir.'

'Hullo Wills, how was it?'

'Fine.'

'Night.'

And Buff Bay was waiting at five past ten p.m. 'There were ninety and nine that safely lay –'

The cold fog on the junction at eleven-thirty.

'Gosh, can't we stop and have a drink?'

'Get out the basket.'

'Stop, Witter.'

'Anything wrong, sir?'

'No, only stopping for a drink.'

Anything wrong, anything wrong, no only a drink. Anything to eat? No thanks. Go on Witter, let's get home.

After midnight at Drumblair, and a great wheel reversing in my head – speeches, cheering, silence, microphones, singing, dancing, a swinging car with hot coffee. A thousand years of elections, some won, some lost.

A thousand songs, 'Let the fire fall on them my Lord' – 'Manley you win the referendum'. Into bed listening to a long relaxed groan of relief from the next bed. Norman, which election is this? I can't remember what year it is – are we going to win? It isn't an election, dear – just feeling out for the Referendum – go to sleep. Yes. Night.

18 November 1961

I haven't written a word about the loss of the Referendum. Of what use? I could write reams about our journeys, 203 meetings, and about 7,000 miles in six weeks. Hardly anyone else worked, only Blake, Michael, and the younger set. Let it all die — and now we face our last election, our last fight. Drumblair[1] is sold, that's the end of a very long book. I'm building a little house on a toehold of land. As one gets older it's fatal to recount anything. The days slip by and somewhere at the back of one's mind one knows it is nearly over — strange, because life seems so short, now.

But there is still kindness and a growing love of people and the desire to know what makes them go the way they go.

Carmen and I have done a little book — a little, very, very short story — and it comes out this week.[2] It has been a happy experience — so many miles I have travelled finding animals to draw!

'The Bush Was Not Consumed'[3] is finished and we, N. and Batiste[4] and I, polished it today. Technically it was very interesting — it wouldn't have been my choice of subject, but there it is. I am drawing Rastafarians[5] and I am half-way through a carving of one. Trying a totally new and more integrated method of roughing out — all the emphasis is on technique.

N. has been pretty wonderful since the Referendum — such courage and resourcefulness. We're hoping to get two weeks in December at Nomdmi — we can both do with it.

3 September 1962

So much has happened again since last writing. We have been in Regardless[1] now for four months.

Drumblair has been taken down and sold for old lumber.

We have lost the election[2] —

But it is a rainy afternoon, the thunder is rolling around, and for the first time I have put Debussy's 'La Mer' on the gramophone and picked up a pen to write. Suddenly this little house, which I have always loved since we moved in two days after the election, has an atmosphere of peace, and I feel like writing.

I feel older and calmer and oddly freer. Norman has picked up his law again. He has never complained and has been so fantastically sane and steady. We are very near to each other.

There is so much that one could write about the election and Russian ships and foolishness and fear, but why bother? For me the book is closed and can never be opened again. It is better to pick one's own way, testing one's values as one goes and not looking to other worlds for reality. I half believe Norman has closed the book too — he worked for independence and it's here.

Looking back at the long years — the campaigns, the sharing everything with people, the songs, the speeches and the sheer hard work trying to help. It has all ended — and if the book ever opened again, one's youth could never be part of it — that would be a different job and a different world.

Meanwhile I am working hard at Sheraton,[3] carving every morning. The scaffold is high and a trifle precarious, and oh dear, it is BIG — but it's coming slowly, and it's a wonderful discipline for me.

Nothing more to say.

7 May 1963

At last I am free of the burden of responsibility that started in 1938. And now I will go into a great quiet and experiment and find a new free road and a new free philosophy. I'm not going to sell anything or show anything. I'm going to find a way through alone — to a synthesis of flesh and spirit and form and the disturbance of the moment of truth.

The owl is my great symbol — it always comes to me in moments of crisis, and I am doing an owl[1] now, and two nights ago one flew onto the logwood tree and called to me — a great white owl. Do you realize if I weren't free it would have to be a great *black* owl. How foolish! And yet no one can order back the tides, nor save the waning of the moon.

17 June 1963

After the Sheraton carving was finished I did the carving for Jock Campbell — ghastly difficult thing with a violent grain.

Alright now, we begin at the beginning again — right down at the bottom, a fresh look and a last start.

A new medium and one that is quicker and allows of free movement — and anyway a lovely one.

Clay — fired — earth and water and fire. The kiln when it is white hot — ha! so like life, and what comes through has stood the test.

So I do a little goat's head and then a whole goat.

Then an owl —

And a Tyger, Tyger — and each time it must be unforced — with no striving for effect — only an attempt to understand what clay can do, and to get the owliness of the owl. Nothing really matters except to find a core of simple truth.

Sometimes, like today, I am too weary to try — so I sit and I wait — I write a little —

America was FULL of race tension. James Baldwin has swept USA and people are being killed.

28 July 1963

So Tyger[1] is finished — not fired yet though …

And now a nude[2] — to try a further technique. The kiln is small so I will do the figure too large, and fire it in two pieces and re-assemble. What is the nude — a young girl — black, three-quarters length, standing in a pool of water. I do this — to find my own handwriting in a nude. My own emphasis and simplification, a very young girl — utterly wild and untamed — not fully mature — caught standing in a river — kinky hair, uncombed — slim arms — very negro.

And Cecil will have to make the pool for me or perhaps we will build it with grey cut stones. Life hasn't begun yet for this girl — the men, the childbearing, the weary loads — no — I have chosen 'a bright morning'.

26 November 1963

We are just back from the States and the whole colossal tragedy of Kennedy's death.

We were in a jammed packed theatre in Philadelphia, listening to the orchestra, and after the third movement of the Mendelssohn, Ormandy limped off the stage with everyone staring and wondering where he had gone, and then they sent a little man who announced the news. It was quite awful — it made me feel I was living through Lincoln's death in a packed theatre long ago.

When we came out, the gorgeous Christmas decorations were up and I found that my teeth were chattering and I was shivering, and Norman looked like a man in a nightmare.

For weeks now I have been suffering from terrible nightmares, every night. It has perhaps something to do with future uncertainties. What Norman intends to do in the future. When we got back from the States, Michael said to me, 'You realize, don't you, that Dad is totally committed to politics — don't you?'

And then some things came up to the surface in my mind — whither from here?

What kind of road, for both of us; of course, living ahead is death in any walk of life — there is only the moment that is now. All the same — one has to *know* what will one be, what will one do. I know that for right now, the best thing for me to do is to withdraw, and if the gods would give me one last sense of inspiration and creativity before it all happens, this would be — above all — happiness. And then if the odd dimension of public life descended again, one could perhaps go through, like a fish in a glass bowl.

Long ago I had the idea of landscape and cosmic consciousness and then people, people kept coming in between. Now, God – for a flash that could combine the two.

12 April 1964

Two years ago from today we left Drumblair. Two days after losing the election on April 10th I said to Norman, 'Let's move,' and he said, 'No. I haven't the energy,' and I went to work to clean up his PM's office at the Ministry.

I said to myself, 'Regardless is ready, it's finished, and I can't sleep in Drumblair for the last time *knowing* it is the last time.' So I summoned the family and we held a Council at nine-thirty. Everyone said MOVE. So I summoned Charlie[1] and Dacres and TRUCKS. I went to Regardless and left Miss B.[2] and John Burrow[3] at Drumblair. In other words, I remember Drumblair as it was, and I settled Regardless.

We worked fluently, efficiently and almost silently. At 3 p.m. I phoned N. and said: 'Stop in at Regardless on the way home as I want to plant a tree.'

When he arrived the beds were made up and dinner was on the stove. He looked a little stunned, and he went back out to a Party meeting and when he returned at midnight, the lights were on and the pictures were up and he stood in the doorway with his nice smile and said: 'I think I rather like this house, it's a friendly house and nothing bad has happened here.' And we went to bed and slept like logs.

You see – the building of Regardless was opposed on every side – everyone thought it was madness, but I had that funny, mad intuition, that *something* would come one day and that it would be needed. I didn't know how soon, nor how utterly.

I remember walking across the parched common from Drumblair and climbing up over the cliff and saying to Scottie,[4] 'put it *here*.' Silver white seymour grass, three little cashew trees and nothing else. And then, when the little house began to go up, I would go and sit and dream – I will plant this here and this there and when they grow, the shade will be here and there. And the world will think it a hard and pokey little house, but I will soften it and hide its small hard straight lines, and by the time they see it, they will only see the garden and the dear old, lovely old furniture.

I took up whole shrubs and young trees and brought them over on the roof of the Jaguar, and not a leaf faded. I even took up the old lignum vitae trunk with the gorgeous orchids blooming on it, and not a flower faded, and sometimes in the moon light I would go and sit and dream – how it would all look one day. And it's two years after now and the dreams have come true and even better — trees, flowers, grass — everything little, but lovely and gracious. And across the gully I can see the little houses going up on Drumblair where it was all giant trees and lawns and paddocks, and where one's whole life has grown and lived and passed. Drumblair with the moon coming up behind the guango tree. Drumblair with a horse saddled, in the dawn, and the cows strolling in for milking. Drumblair on a gala night with the trees floodlit and the vast crowds and the smoke from the barbecued midnight suppers. Drumblair in triumph and disaster. The studio hidden down in the grass piece — and Norman's study with all its memories.

And the children, Doug and Michael, and Xmas trees, and Race Days and Roysterer.[5] Doug's room at the back and Michael's in the front, and romps and skirmishes — and I remember the dance when they came home and the lights and fun.

That was Drumblair, and this darling new two-year-old house, with the chairs hidden in the corner and watching the full moon rise. In spite of everything, we have found something new in Regardless. We are very near to each other, and although there has been great sadness — with Michael and Doug divorced — still we have been very near to each other and they are still young enough to find a future, Regardless —!

19 November 1964

Now listen Ra. I took a little trip down to Spring Garden, Stony Gut in St Thomas. I went and sat on the old stone foundations of Bogle's[1] little church. We had to cut our way through the bush. An old lady went with us — her father had been Bogle's great friend — and her son, another old man and an ex-school teacher. It was fairly early and the sun wasn't hot yet and we were very quiet and relaxed — not raising our voices at all.

I said to her, 'When they stole the guns from the courthouse what did they do with them, dear? Did they fire on the soldiers?' And she said, 'Pappy say them didn't use the guns, them didn't know how to load and fire gun.'

'But what did they take them for?'

'I don't know, but I know the men of Stony Gut couldn't use gun — maybe they took them to keep the soldiers from using them.'

'But Bogle carried a cutlass, he killed the Custos with a cutlass, all the books say that.'

'Yes Bogle him carry cutlass.'

'And the men of Stony Gut carried cutlass too?'

And a look came over her face as if it had all happened two weeks ago and she was still defending the men of Stony Gut: 'I don't know nothing about that — I know them don't carry cutlass — is stick them cut and is stick them carry.'

'Only Bogle carried a cutlass?'

'Yes Bogle carry cutlass — But Bogle a BOLD man.'

'Which way did they march — from here?'

'Yes in the morning the church bell ring and everyone gather and them pray and then them march — but — Bogle him never come back.'

The earth was damp and warm under our feet and it was all so quiet and we were sharing it and deeply moved.

'I think them was going to make a little garden and plant flowers and have a man tend to it — here where the church was — but them don't do anything about it and I would like to see it happen in my time, for my Pappy really love Bogle.'

'When I go back to Kingston I will try to talk to them.'

'Yes, but the Kingston people want to do it in Morant Bay where Bogle die, and I think it should be here where him live and was happy — but you will try?'

And then we rose and climbed through the bush up the steep hillside and as I drove home I remembered, 'but Bogle was a BOLD man.'

You see, darling, I am not sure that as you say he was over-rated . . . even Lord Olivier in his book says that Bogle was the turning point. They could argue with Gordon but no one could deflect Bogle. Perhaps he was a terrible man because he chopped the Custos more than once, but he did it himself, and I suppose there are times when it takes a terrible man — history cries out for even a crime of magnitude. He wasn't a Jesus, who turned the other cheek, a gesture that has had a far greater impact on humanity. Bogle was no God — he was human and terrible but he flung off the cloak of a slave past in a gesture that, though brutal, has also had its impact in a small corner of the world, and watching the faces of the St Thomas people, it still lives on. I asked the old lady which she thought was the greater man, Bogle or Garvey — and she paused for a long time — for though she was poor and very old, she was highly intelligent, and then her face lit up and she said: 'They were both great men, but Garvey was a spokesman — but Bogle was a BOLD man.'

This I thought showed real insight and great loyalty to the past though one couldn't exactly pinpoint just what the word BOLD signified to her, for she used it several times.

Think about this, my pet, you with your great imagination, and tell me what does a BOLD man look like?'

Love,

Mardi

5 February 1965

It was in 1924 that we started seriously looking for a house of our own, after Atholl, Newington (Plummers) – corner of Lady Musgrave and Trafalgar – and Newaralyia,[1] opposite.

We wanted a house, and in those days I could occasionally coax N. on to a horse. We had two, House of Cards and Firefly.

So we rode off on a Sunday morning to have breakfast with Volney Rennie at a place called Drumblair. As we rode through the gate there were cows all over the grass in front the house – and many, many heaps of cow dung and a sound to the left, at a distance, of lowing and buckets and men moving about. We rode up to the old wooden house – no verandahs, steps straight into the huge front room. I noticed even then the pretty use of the wood on the side wall – like this (diagram). We sat and talked and ate and drank lots of very good coffee – and Volney said: 'There are thirty acres of land, only of course the gully does go through it – it runs over to the Kings House fence. Will you walk or ride?'

We walked – to the right of the house there was a big grass piece with huge old guango trees, and where the cow pen was, even bigger, more gorgeous guango trees – 'Good feed for cattle,' said Volney.

We crossed a small gully to another grass piece and then the big Sandy Gully, wandering very nearly straight down and over on the far side more land, and two fabulous ponds, one large and one small. The good but slow salesman walking with us said: 'Very useful in a drought.' At which I piped up: 'Oh but we love horses, not cows – and we have a jet black nanny goat.'

'You won't make much money out of those.'

Norman intervened: 'No we don't, but you know we more want the land for space and hobbies – my wife loves horses – but honey, we could keep a cow or two, and with all this wood about we should never have to buy for the stove. I used to cut logwood for my pocket money as a boy you know, Volney, on my mother's property – chipping logwood is quite an art, but the pay wasn't very high. On the other hand it kept me as fit and hard as nails. Helped me to keep good wind – I think it gave me the constitution I have.'

'There's some logwood here,' muttered the salesman.

'Well time for us to go – we'll let you know.'

July 1965

Tom Concannon,[1] the man from the planning department, went down to see the Morant Bay courthouse site for the Bogle, and I went along. When we got there a murder trial had just come to an end and the defence had been unsuccessful — some men outside were talking and the place was packed. Three men were saying that the lawyer had 'sold out' the case, that all lawyers were PNP and that's why they always sold out the small men's cases! I quietly joined the little group and one man stepped towards me very aggressively and said, 'Why you don't give Bogle back to us alive — he was a good man and we need him.'

'I don't quite understand.'

'Give him back to us alive.'

I climbed onto the bonnet of the car and thought a minute. 'You know, from the world began I only know one man who was ever raised from the dead.'

'Yes, I know that — it was Lazarus.'

'Yes, and it took Jesus Christ to do that — I am not Jesus.'

'Well we want him back alive.'

'Well I can't do that, and I don't think it would be a good thing either. You see I think the things he fought for are alive — and I think that his spirit is alive — what he died for, freedom and independence, these things have been won; the effect of them hasn't spread everywhere yet and you may not have felt it yet in St Thomas, but it is only a matter of time now and it will come.'

'But look what the white people do to him.'

'Yes, I know that is true, but every country has to have its martyrs — people who will die for a great cause — every country has to have its history, if it is to be great, and Bogle gave his life for his people and his country and his spirit will always live on and you shouldn't want him walking around the place like a zombie — and instead of attacking me, you should go home and pray for me that I might make a good statue of him. Pray for me to have the strength and the courage, because I'm putting everything I have into it and it's taking the life out of me.'

'But the white people are too wicked though.'

'Now you listen to me — doing this job I've had to read and listen to everything I can about this man and the history of the time, and let me tell you, not one of you would know one word about Bogle or care about him, if it wasn't for a white man, an Englishman. You know where it was written, "a prophet is not without honour"?'

'Yes, I know it come from the Bible.'

'Well, this prophet was without honour, not one of you and no Jamaican would have known the truth about him nor cared to know, if it wasn't for the white Englishman, Lord Olivier who wrote the book about him — a wonderful book. You shouldn't be so bitter, you should know the facts first.'

'Well I don't come from St Thomas, I come from St Ann.'

'Oh I know St Ann well — it's a fine parish and a fine people — I come from

Hanover[2] and we're a bit backward in Hanover, but still I'm doing the statue and I know about Bogle.'

He stuck out his hand and I shook it and he said: 'Well I guess we're one people.'

'And you'll pray for me?'

'I'll pray for you Sunday.'

There was a murmur from the crowd and I waved goodbye and left.

August 1968

N. had been ill and we were sitting for a quiet moment at Regardless on the patio about 9 p.m. before he went back to bed, when suddenly car lights flashed and Frank Hill called out: 'What about the dog? I'm terrified of dogs.'

I went out and got him out of the car and as I put my arm round him, I felt him skeleton thin.

'How's Norman? I want to see Norman.'

We went in, and he put his arms around Norman and said: 'I've come to apologize for what I said at Pine Grove — that you were wrong to retire. Since you've been ill, I've been regretting it ever since.'

We all had a drink and they talked. He'd been down at Muriel's for two hours piecing together family history with Tom Concannon, preparatory to the restoring of Roxborough[1] and also a book he was writing on Bustamante.

'When I'm finished I'm going to do one on you.'

He was instantly emotional. He referred to the removal of one lung from cancer, and said: 'I know I'm too thin and I'm losing weight — anyway, my voice is alright.'

And then, to my horror, I noticed he was smoking — I said: 'Frank, darling, how many drinks did you have down at Muriel's?'

'Only two, and this makes three.'

I said: 'Not much, but don't work too hard — or sit up too late.'

And he said: 'Yes it is late, isn't it. I must go, they'll wonder where I am.'

Then he put his arms around Norman and kissed him three times and said: 'Rest well and get well — we need you.'

I saw him to his car — he was driving himself — he stopped at the car door and said: 'You know what I should have done — long ago, I should have done it — I should have shot Richard[2]. Yes, I should have shot Richard, and nothing would have gone wrong.'

I said, 'Frank, don't think of those things, my dear — just keep well and do your broadcasting.'

He drove off, and N. said: 'Frank was in a very emotional mood, wasn't he?' And I said: 'Yes — come to bed you look all-in tired.'

N. said: 'He's very thin — I wonder if he's going to die. I believe he knows it, poor soul, and he's putting such a good face on it — he's putting up a good show.'

6 October 1968

This year has been an eventful year — this year and last year — but the culminations are this year.

Barbara[1] died — and two days after, Michael went away. And for the second time we cleaned up Michael's home. The first time was when he broke finally with Thelma.[2] We moved him into the flat we had used temporarily on Mountain View Avenue — I sat in the house alone, when all his most personal things had gone, and I remembered how I had sat there and tried to evoke some happiness in it after we had cleaned up after Thelma's leaving. It's a strange house — not a happy one — it has a sort of desperation about it. It's lovely, it's well planned, but it never seems to have an anchor. I remember Rachel's desperate unhappiness and her involvement with a young set who cared mightily for her free drinks and mighty little for her safety and well being. And Michael following a chimera of his own creation. And then he carried Barbara over the doorstep and life started again, and then Barbara got ill and Rachel won for herself the rebuke, well-earned it's true, of dismissal, and then Sarah[3] came and Barbara died. And I sat in that house waiting for the tenants to arrive, remembering the tenants who came in after Thelma, and how they had ended in a break-up, and I wondered: do places have a destiny or do people follow a pattern — I don't know.

Michael wanted Norman to declare his resignation beforehand, in order that the dice would not be loaded in his or anyone's favour. In a gesture Norman agreed, and the great banquet ended on a note of great sadness — seventy-five years old[4] —

But in the meantime Vera had died — away in England — the land she had always loved. And Michael returned — in a mood of partial collapse — hating the thought of leadership, torn and tortured over the personal failure of his life. Spiritually and emotionally in revolt.

And something in Norman, who had been visibly flagging, snapped. He was seriously ill and for one week we were afraid — but slowly he recovered. Recovered when we discovered that he had not wanted to live — that he wasn't trying — that what he felt at that time to be the failure of his life was more than he could live with — lacking the sheer physical strength to make a new start in a new field, and hating and loathing the thought of idleness.

But the background of much that happened had its roots in something he had done with tremendous determination.

It was October 1966 that he suddenly made up his mind, beset by financial problems and a sense of impending retirement, that he made up his mind to spend the rest of his life at Nomdmi.

No argument, no persuasion could change him. So we moved up. I think it was really the very end of September. It was an appalling shock to me and I took it very badly, and to cap it all, he continued his life as it was − leaving at 8.30 a.m., returning any time between 6 p.m. or if the House were sitting or party executive, as late as 1.30 to 2 a.m. It had a fantastic effect on me − I bought a horse and I took to gardening, but I lived there in a deafening silence, going quietly to pieces. I will never know how I survived − we rented Regardless and because N. simply couldn't function without the occasional night in town, we took a room at Michael's house and ate at Muriel's. Well, let's forget it − living, eating (when not at M's), sleeping, entertaining in the one room. Finally, when it became obvious that our relationship was cracking under the total chaos and strain, we took a flat at Mountain View. Norman loved it. I hardly ever came down, and when I did I couldn't sleep and I couldn't eat. The whole basis of our life, our sense of home, seemed to have crumbled. I became really neurotic, but the financial bogey still hovered over us and then came the election and our tenant left and after ten months of turmoil we were now back down to Regardless. There had even been occasions when the road had been impassable and N. had been in town and I had been on the hilltop alone.

I realize that I have got the sheer dates and facts of my double stay at Nomdmi muddled and I will re-write this after a little research!

6. October 1968

Norman's illness has been coming on for some time. The terrific strain of commuting from Nomdmi daily − often insisting on driving himself − I think had something to do with it, for he had been dragging and looking more and more tired. But the birthday banquet was quite fantastic as he waited for hours to make his resignation speech − the last on a long programme − and just before we left, poor Michael had a near collapse, which left him totally confused and in an agony of doubt about the wisdom of his decision. It all added up − the deep sense of failure over the Nomdmi experiment − financial-wise, and because I simply couldn't feel well or happy there as a permanency.

Anyway we came down to be nearer everything for the last few months. His blood pressure was giving him a lot of trouble. We went, the night before his illness, to dinner with the McNeils[1] and he came home feeling very ill, with Rachel having a weeping attack over her own problems. He woke at night with his first attack of cardiac asthma, and next morning Moody[2] came. By morning the blood pressure had steadied and Moody gave Norman permission to go up to Nomdmi with a party of people for a picnic. Rachel and I were not at all happy over this and we went round and asked Moody to reconsider his decision. He said, no − it's OK. So we went and had a happy day − the Gilmours,[3] the Binns,[4] Doug etc., but by 4 p.m. he was feeling pretty bad again. At around 5 p.m. I drove him quietly down and dashed round to Michael's flat to ask his advice − he said he would let McNeil know. I got home and Ra and I got him to bed, and got hold of Levy.[5] McNeil arrived with Stuart[6] − his pressure was up to 224/138 and the cardiac asthma was back again.

It was a tough two weeks and then he had a week up and about and we went down to Negril for two happy weeks and then back to town for a week and then, I think mistakenly, for two weeks to Nomdmi, which is after all the seat of our problem. It was a disappointing two weeks because all the time the shadow lay across us, of this future and difficult decision. Where do we live and what do we do with our lives?

When we got back down I realized that Norman's road back to health couldn't be hurried and that the best thing to do was to banish all thoughts of the future and just concentrate on learning how to live with this unknown future ahead of us. Learning to live with a pattern of a quieter effort and a more integrated sense of day-to-day peaceful living.

We've been back for nearly three weeks and slowly he is healing his wounds and I am very at peace. Let it stay this way for a while as the last November conference draws near and the final break comes − and then we will know.

7 October 1968

It's nice getting awake in the dawn and creeping out and making a cup of coffee whilst the house is quiet. I love Regardless − the sound of the traffic and Four Roads raising its usual racket of dogs and quite stupendous sound systems.

But in the early mornings you realize that the little house is like a tent − open to the air − and the big bogies seem to fade back.

10 October 1968

Looking back through this old book I realize that I have written very little about my children and yet they have played such an important part in our lives.

Tonight Doug came in with Roy[1] in an uproariously happy mood. He and Dorit[2] have had some tremendous problems − but this new job he has got with the UN based in Addis Ababa, will help him to solve a great many of his financial and personal problems. First it will give him a chance to have Roy get expert handling and training, which he just isn't getting in Jamaica and which is expensive. Roy, now that he has taken him over altogether, is becoming an altogether different person. He has a mind and strange depths, and could really make something of his life. Dorit will get a far better chance to handle her children and her affairs if Doug is abroad, and might even work out some sort of solution and be able to join him. I do hope so, for they seem to make each other very happy. Douglas has had half a lifetime of unhappiness, and in it all he has grown. I'm very proud of him really, and we share the same sense of humour — he is so good with young people and very full of understanding. He and Rachel were carrying on like a couple of wild youngsters tonight, both of them expounding techniques on how to land a man. The house was fairly ringing with it, whilst Roy listened — pop-eyed.

Early August 1969

It's funny, really, if one sets out to put down just the most vivid things one remembers from long ago — such strange things stick out and shine and glow and assume an importance that is unaccountable.

I remember, for instance, a rambling old house in Callington, Cornwall, where there were asparagus beds — a new and strange wonder to me — with an aura of social superiority which went no further, and a front staircase and a back staircase, which was also in a vague way an achievement, up which and down which we tore in the dark, racing and playing a game called 'moppee-up' ... How I remember that, and my mother looking more relaxed as if in far away Jamaica that was the sort of house she was accustomed to, roomy and with shady corners.

Then Halley's comet appeared night after night and brighter, and when it was at its zenith they called us all — we were summoned — my father was dying and we must come and say goodbye. As we filed in — a large family — he looked like white, white sculpture, he was already gone.

As we turned to leave I leapt forward before anyone could stop me — I kissed him on the forehead and then I shuddered and cried and cried — he was icy cold. This was death — he was gone, but all through the years the story that has haunted me, and I can hear my mother telling it as if it were yesterday: 'Just before he died he suddenly sat up and, with a look of radiance on his face, he said: "Oh the power and the glory and the wonder of it all."'

All men meet fate in the language and on the terms that they have lived — he saw the promise of the resurrection as Halley's comet blazed outside. What terms of defiance had Beethoven lived with when he faced death and he too had sat up and shaken his fist at the dying sunset.

So we moved to Penzance, this made our fourth Cornish town, St Ives, Penryn, Callington and now Penzance for a short while, and ultimately and finally to Heamore — where all the wildly inner excitement of adolescence awaited me. Where the spring came and set us stampeding over the moors — you could feel it in your blood, in your skin, in your bones and your heart. Spring with the surging underground of rebirth and growth. That I remember, and it's funny really what August and an August moon can do to the heart of a youngster — a sort of bursting gladness with the hay in stacks, and the rabbit chasing, and no one wanting to go to bed — just running and shouting for the sheer joy of life.

And always as a background to all things, the ever-changing sea — tameless and primeval, elemental. Hardly ever calm in Cornwall — dangerous and yet challenging — the swimming we learnt mocked at the later pool swimming — currents and winds and even quicksands.

My mother every summer engaged two army bell tents and took her tribe of nine children plus various attachments to the sea, to Sennen Cove, and just off the sea we pitched.

Bitter rancour between boys and girls. The boys being fewer, slept in the food tent — and at night, we knew, they raided the food supplies. Our mother, eternally and femininely being on the side of the boys, refused to believe this and rather despised us for making the charge — God help her!

But August 1914, as anyone alive then can bear witness, was a month of such magic in Cornwall that one could almost have predicted after this — the deluge.

Into this glory walked Norman Manley — fresh from Jamaica — scholar, sportsman, and a strange, strange personality. He had won the Rhodes, nearly died of typhoid, had a hundred yards record which was a world record for a schoolboy.

I came in to supper — full of sunshine and running. I was fourteen and he stood there in front of the empty fireplace — his hands in his pockets — swaying — handsome, faun-like — smiling mischievously.

We had been summoned peremptorily, not too pleased, from some wild game outside. I studied him and met a mocking smile — and something somewhere deep down touched — something stirred and died.

Where was supper, why all the fuss — the gang outside were calling to come and jump hayricks. My mother said — Edna shake hands with Norman. OK. So what, and yet — it had stirred me for a brief moment.

It was all over and we were gone with the dogs and the wild, wild moonlight, running from the farmers who were extra agile that night in protection of their ricks.

The moon and the magic were gone, and instead were glaring posters, war,

war, war. My brother went under age and was killed — my sister's fiancé went and was killed, and worst of all my eldest sister's husband went after six brief months of marriage and was killed.

It seemed only yesterday that she had stepped through the church door — so lovely, so trusting, and the organ had pealed out what for me has come to be a sort of swan song — 'Oh perfect love', the end to all happiness. I would have died rather than have it at my own wedding — it still always moves me to tears as I see her floating up the aisle — and then his death. My wealthy uncle from the north giving her away — instead of my father, my childhood's love.

So, we faced the war — and a school friend and I left Cornwall and went to London to do war work in 1916, just sixteen years old. We left our childhood behind and my beloved dog and the sea — the moors and the freedom and the utter beauty.

October 1969

It's the time of from 2 till 5 p.m. which I dread even more than a sleepless night and Norman has gone — gone for always — there's nothing to write really — except the last few days — we were very close and once I broke down and cried — and he looked at me so strangely as from another world — I wish I hadn't cried — I'll carry that memory with me for the rest of my life — but I will also carry the nearness.

And the glory and the pain of our life together — what an empty, empty world — why didn't he let me come with him?

4 October 1969

There are two last stories of Norman that I want to record — they both happened on the Sunday — he died on Tuesday.

Michael came in the morning and he asked Michael how the voting was going, and Michael explained that it was Sunday and the election was Tuesday, and they argued a little, gently, and Michael left. Norman called me to him and said: 'So it's Tuesday — the election is Tuesday — that's funny, I thought it was today — well,' and he gave a long pause and lifted his hands, 'that day the book will be closed.'

During the same morning he had started talking about a train that he had to catch, and he asked me would I look up a train schedule. I said: 'Norman, why do you want to go by train — why not go in the Benz and let Chambers[1] drive you?'

Later Michael came in and he asked Michael to look up the train schedule and Michael too said: 'But Dad, why go by train — wait till tomorrow — it's late now and it's raining — tomorrow we'll take you in your own car.'

'No Michael, I have a train to catch.'

We went outside and agreed to just handle it gently, and the doctors and Michael left.

I went back into the room and again he spoke of the train and I said: 'Norman, where do you want to go in that train, where is the train going?'

And he said: 'I don't think I know — I'm not quite sure — but I have to catch it. My suitcase is there and I know just the clothes I want to wear — they are there in the cupboard. I must catch the train.'

I said: 'Why don't you stay with us — we all want you — don't bother with the train — stay with us.'

He was silent for a long time and then he looked at me gently, but very penetratingly, and smiled very sadly, and said: 'No — life here costs too much.'

And those were the last words he ever uttered.

Later. I have a journey to take. Where did I get that from? I don't think he actually said it — I think that's the impression I was left with.

1969

The clouds are hanging low around the house in the mountains and the air is still and it is very silent — no sounds at all. A man has walked slowly — summoning the end of his strength — from the house to the glass doored library that stands a little distance away.

Gravely, he moves to the big desk and takes a seat in the swivel chair; his long sensitive hands move to the drawer and quietly he opens it — bending to look inside. He closes it — and gently he touches the objects on the desk — slightly re-arranging them with care.

With great effort he pulls himself to his feet — and moves to the book shelves, drawing his fingers across the backs of the books on his way to the great plate glass doors.

For a long pause he leans against them, his eyes going far across the crumpled mountains that are his country. He stands quite still — his face and particularly his eyes brooding and withdrawn.

The woman beside him can bear it no longer and draws him away down the path through the pine trees to the waiting car. He alone knew it was good-bye.

And then in reverse a series of flashing confused images — like a long film turned in reverse — and it is August 1914. Racing home to supper, dodging in and out of the hay stacks a tumult of young voices and an air of expectancy.

Someone will be there for supper — hurry up — be on time. Cold water over face and hands a comb through hair — into the living room — and up short, a man standing in front of an empty fire place — swaying on his hips and smiling – sardonically. Nine children shake hands impetuously and nine were greeted with a special look and a special smile.

Supper is over and one of the nine slips away with a small shaggy dog – full moon outside and hayricks to jump. August in Cornwall and that 1914 August in particular, pure magic – and no breath of warning of the holocaust ahead.

And then it came – war – war – war. The farmers had to go and so one milked the cows in the early morning on the way to school.

Out of the family of nine an older brother was killed at seventeen, a sister's fiancé was killed and the husband of six months of another sister also never came back. Everyone had been so gay – so carefree – so happy. And then the man who had been the visitor on that August evening, along with his brother, also joined to fight for what the world believed was the war to end all wars. Fighting for peace they called it. Norman and Roy Manley, field artillery British army –

I will find the letter that he wrote me from the Front in France – I still have it – I was breathlessly proud and bewildered when it arrived. They had said to him, 'Which of the nine did you like best?' and he had said, 'I rather think that little plain one – with the spirit.'

But that did not warrant a whole letter when you're in your mid-teens. Anyway, I slept with it under my pillow – I wasn't sure why – it was just a straightforward letter from a lonely man with no involvements.

A friend and I went up to London to do war work – very young and very frightened, perpetually losing our way home at night and walking warily with London packed with soldiers. War work – clerical work, remount depot work with half broken Canadian horses, flax pulling for aeroplane wings, a restless youthful inability to accept routine or discipline.

Then it was all over – wild excitement in London – bands playing, train loads of returning troops – but the wide empty gaps of a toothless smile for those who never returned.

Roy never came back and Norman did. A gaunt, haggard, unsmiling man. Strange tales he used to tell us, sitting with his magnificent hands stretched out to warm in front of a flickering coal fire. Not much coal in the house these days.

No self pity – just the problem of have to live *en masse* – close up – no elbow room – no place or time to think or expand. The limitations of danger, of responsibility – someone always had to be able to say – I will – be the last man out. And Roy going down to become only a memory of something that was a stake in sanity and contact with the past, the future, with life itself. No more Roy – only the endless noise and fury of war – alone.

The hands made ghostly shadows on the wall – spread out to the flickering fire in the safety of the room they seemed a bit of a mockery – but we were there — we understood — my mother and I — we tried to move in — to fill the gap. He loved my mother — who wouldn't.

The strange nightmares of war passed across his unconscious face and at night we would dash into his room as the memories of war made the night hideous for him.

Back to Oxford, war weary — where the body that had known triumphs in nearly every field of sport no longer responded — and where concentration and study seemed an imposition on a mind that had lived for four years with death as the great challenge. But time is a river without banks and all things pass as the world turns into spring and rebirth comes. So the mind that had carried Browning and the Bible through the shell fire was born again and began to read — everything — everyone.

At this time he was almost reliving his lost youth, encouraging me to face life with a sense of reality — to open my mind to new knowledge, new experiences and a new dedication. He was a tremendous talker and I listened — often it was far over my head, but the thing I absorbed was the world of ideas and mental freedom that he lived.

Einstein was hitting the world with his theory of relativity just then — and with great care he explained the little pamphlet that had been put out for public consumption. H.G. Wells and his world coverage of history and science, Shaw with his superman and his preoccupation with the life force. I didn't like Shaw — I hated his egocentric bolstering of himself. I got flashes of what he was driving at — but I dropped with a bang whenever his mind drove all emotion away before him. Like every young person I was afraid of dying — so the idea of the 300-year-old new life-span that he created in 'Back to Methuselah' gave me secret comfort.

But Norman went with his keen, merciless, intellectualism and I really disappointed him. I often did. I often did as I was emotional and fuzzy minded. We shared D.H. Lawrence and oddly enough we shared George Moore — that stylist from a lost past.

I remember going to Picasso's first abstract exhibition in London, and Epstein, with him. The press were giving them both hell — and we loved the storm and felt vastly superior riding on it.

Sometimes now, looking back over the years with all the honesty I can summon — I wonder what I would have been without him. As a boy he had been a tremendous reader — he had always been totally impatient of discipline — and mentally arrogant and isolated by a strange originality of mind and behaviour. He had never been one of the crowd — and such friends as he had were always the sort of people who relaxed rather than stimulated him. He loved the company of extremely simple people — the men who cut logwood — the cattlemen — the women in the kitchen. Stories are told of him that, coming off the athletic track, he would streak through the crowds applauding him and begging for autographs — apparently really and truly unconscious of anything but the problem of getting to the changing room and a dry towel, with his burning, intense eyes looking straight ahead.

Later he learnt to mask those eyes; awareness of his difference of race and colour in England of 1920 caused him to develop a cold arrogant mask which became the basis of something that stood him in good stead as a lawyer — no one ever knew what was going on behind it.

I had been a very different sort of child, a daydreamer, prone to going off for a whole day at a time over the moors or by the sea with just a dog for company. I had a fierce legendary temper which flared whenever reality struck across the dream world I had built up. I wasn't popular at home — I was too difficult and too unpredictable and too hypersensitive, flaring at any imagined insult. I loved all animals — especially horses and dogs — I loved the life of the countryside, trees and the turn of the seasons — particularly the sea spoke to me more than any human being I knew.

He was beginning to work again at Oxford and I was at art school. I had a hard time — I had no money and at half term he would come to London and feed me an enormous meal.

I remember a little room above a fish shop and every morning kippers for breakfast. I would eat half and put away the other for night, when I often walked all the long distance home — sometimes having had no lunch.

But they were great days and going to the station to meet him, striding through the fog of steam and smoke and that leap in one's throat at the sight of his lean, tense figure.

So it slowly ripened from friendship to something more — something that lasted a lifetime to that last journey down the mountainside in Jamaica. I know that other people sometimes flashed into our lives — but nothing ever shook that beginning — what I have always called the apple trees — the singing and the gold.

We married there in London in a little registry office and went off on bicycles to build our own tent in the New Forest.

Mercy how it all comes back to me, and the forest ponies muzzling around the tent in the dawn. A month in the woods and a month in Paris.

We were young and so in love.

27 November 1969

I woke this morning again, as I seem to have waked every morning since Norman died, with this aching, nagging feeling of much that I could have done in which I failed, and some things I had done which I wish that I had left undone. An aching longing for the dialogue — an awareness of how much he suffered in public life and of how blithely we all had pressured him in 1938. The old hurtful pain at the way the *Gleaner* had pursued him all his public days. Never ever giving him credit for anything and using him as a scapegoat for everything that happened. It has been going on and on in my head. And the last two years, could I have handled it differently and saved him?

So here I am on the morning of the 27th realizing over and over again how much I depended on him and leant on him and loved him.

But if I allow this condition to continue for always it will spoil all my memories of him — from now I am going to record every day until I have found a balance — I have to live with all the lovely things. Anything else will be weakness and will turn into self pity.

We had a wonderful life, a valid life, and in the big things I rarely failed him. He was such an independent fellow — he gave one only the rare chance to help in the little things.

So from today, I am going to try very hard to get out from under the pain and to remember that life gave me a very unusual man to live with and to share, and a chance that very few women ever have.

28 November 1969

Yesterday passed fairly peacefully, and I walked by the Mona dam with Uhuru.[1] It was misty with a slight tendency to drizzle, the air was very cool — flocks and flocks of white egrets went overhead — Uhuru chased at them when he could.

But at night I got awake at 2 a.m. There was a strange tapping which made sleep take off like a wild animal — I think it must have been someone in the gully. Anyway, I got wide awake and stayed like that for two hours. I refused the idea of a sleeping tablet and tried to face up to my search for peace? for understanding? for God?

I took out Rilke's Elegies, and there the whole thing was, the relationship of life to death, 'death as the unilluminated side of life, but also to show the true place of love within this extended whole.' He obviously thinks that life and death are aspects of the same thing — life the personal, and death a part of the whole.

But later on he seems to develop past this and sees death as somewhere where there is pure being without parting, without time, *without* death as the opposite of life. In other words you move from life into death, which is an open world. To be inspired by love — in life — not a possessive love, but love as a contact with people in the true sense, based on understanding and an appreciation of the free 'otherness' of people as distinguished from the harsh pattern of I and thou. I fell asleep at 4 a.m. and slept till 7 a.m. — honesty is very important.

29 November 1969

I took Muriel out for lunch — to Devon House — and we talked. I asked her what, if any, was her philosophy of life and death. She hesitated and then said: 'What I would *like* to believe in, because it seems to make sense, is some sort of reincarnation — you know, where whatever you failed to grow in, you come back and meet it again.'

Then she told me the story of Roma, who for two years after her husband died was sunk in bitterness, and one night she had a dream and he talked to her and explained to her that he couldn't get into touch with her because of the bitterness. If they were to be near each other, she would have to make the effort and throw off the bitterness, which she did, and ever since he seemed to be able to help her. She said, 'This is what she told me — mind you, she said frankly — it was a dream.'

So I told Muriel how I had had a really terrible night, and woke in the morning feeling totally wretched and pursued.

And how later I had gone back into my room and sat on the bed, realizing that it simply couldn't go on like this, that I would go to pieces, and suddenly it had come to me that Norman was trying to contact me, and I sat very still, feeling intensely: it is *you* who are enclosing yourself and he can't get through to you, so I kept quiet and gradually, like a benediction, I sensed that he was near me. And that he was reassuring me, and I became calm and the torture passed. And I realized that he could help me through the years if I would listen.

I also saw the pattern of one's relationships with people as being very important — as a big and unavoidable responsibility, and how it fitted in with Rilke's concept of love in the unpossessive but understanding way — and of death not as final, but something that was inextricably part of a whole, an experience — I think for a moment we were very close, and then we moved on.

So last night I got awake to hear Uhuru growling, but I wasn't afraid, and just lay quietly for about an hour with my mind running over the discovery of the day, and then I went back to sleep. I felt the leaden feeling when I woke again, so I started to write this, describing the day backwards, as it were, and coming upon the experience of the morning all over again.

30 November 1969

There was a dance at Four Roads last night, with a really challenging sound system. I had put out the light at 11 and 1 p.m. — I still couldn't sleep — so feeling that I had taken the challenge of a lot of fences during the day, I decided to take a sleeping tablet. Unfortunately, Uhuru woke me at six-fifteen, and I was pretty deep asleep, so I woke reluctantly with a headache, and the feeling of doubt back again. But I have a weapon to fight it with now, so I took coffee and Phensic and I'm feeling much better again.

Yesterday Rachel made up her mind, at least I think she did, to hold on to her teaching and not to go to Pan Am.[1] I think it is a good decision.

The morning of Norman's state funeral, which was a fantastic affair, she got up and left the house to get her driving licence. The day after the funeral she was quite whacked out, but the next morning she dressed and left the house early and took up a job at Kingston College. She has been quite different since she started teaching — there is something real in the challenge of those boys, that has helped her forward — and she also takes extension classes, where she has one student who has been in gaol twice.

She talks of it all in a semi-humorous, serious way, but I think she is learning from it to recognize people as something external to, and different from, her own moods and compulsions. It's a hard lesson to learn — it takes intelligence as well as courage. Norman loved her very much and I wish she had found herself whilst he was still alive — he was very worried over her — but it is just one of the things that his death has challenged. It seems as if he had to die to make us all take a step of growth without him. As Michael said today, up to a certain period he could move and take so much of Jamaica with him, and then creativity seemed to lose contact. Either he was too far ahead, or some confusion in the air around made the directions less effective; but from the moment he died, his life work and the size of the man re-established itself in the minds of people, particularly the young, and he became a symbol, not so much for his political directions as for what he was himself. His love of excellence, his integrity, even his sense of history. The very qualities which some people felt had earned him the right to direct a government. Confusing perhaps the true values — elevating the right to govern to a higher place in the hierarchy than it is entitled to. I sometimes think that if life had been different, Norman was a philosopher, or should have been, if life had given him the time. He read so widely and his critical sense was so strong.

The day yesterday was full of small things — the evening was difficult. Between bedtime and say 8 p.m., if no one comes it can be incredibly hard and lonely, and it is then one misses the comforting figure in the chair under the light, listening to music together, and doing battle with extremely advanced music, which fascinated him and baffled me. I haven't got past Shostakovich.

The week before he died, he wanted to hear over and over again the Shostakovich Fourth and the little quartet, till one evening it caused me to cry and he saw it and his eyes went dark and full of pain and we played something else. The quartet is one of the loneliest things in the whole world — man alone with his destiny, and the future a journey into another world.

Looking back from today I realize that when he came to help me the whole room seemed full of him — it's one of the most real experiences I have ever had. Perhaps, from the point of view of challenging one's consciousness, the most real except for his death and the birth of two sons.

It makes one unafraid to die.

1 December 1969

I had a strange day — Blake[1] came to take me to see his horses, and before going we sat and talked. I asked him about Gillian's death, and how long it had taken for the wound to heal. I told him, because I thought he would understand, how Norman had come to help me. He sat very quiet and I found myself saying *no one* can tell me now that death is just extinction. I have always believed that after death was nothingness, now I don't *know* what it is, but there is something that we don't understand.

He said: 'I'm afraid it took me five years for the wound to heal, but I know what you mean about death. I felt like you until this happened. Gillian had been getting attacks of fever and then quite better again and we were hopeful. But one night the fever was up and I had a dream, that my grandmother, who had been dead for years, came to me and handed me a scroll and told me to read it. She was very tall with white hair, and the dream got confused and she came back again and said: "Have you read the scroll? You should read it because Gillian is going to die and it is better so." I woke and I was on the floor struggling. I felt absolutely ghastly, but I said nothing to Phyllis or to anyone.

'Gillian got worse and we took her to hospital where she died. On the way home Phyllis said to me, "Do you know Gillian kept pointing to the doorway and saying, who is that tall lady there with the white hair?" So now *I* know — that no one can tell me that there is nothing.'

I told him about Rilke and his concept of life in time, controlled compartments, and how death is an 'open world'. I think he was very interested.

Aileen Cliggot showed us the horses, it was a lovely morning — and his yearling, Second Helping, is a powerful brute and might be very, very good. I hope so — I would love to see it win. Mrs Cliggot looked sad, I thought. She has a sweet face, and very gentle manners, but the eyes looked tired and a little haunted.

I gave the youngsters lunch when I got home, and they slept for the afternoon. A restful Sunday, and then in the evening I went with Greta and Henry to see Pat and Nell's photos on slides of their Argentine holiday. He had taken some magnificent shots, and there was a strange love of beauty and the isolation of a focal point of interest in his approach. A scarlet sweater against gleaming white snow. Peace and affluence, and a love of children and a quite remarkably beautiful house.

On coming home I realize that one returns to an atmosphere of pain and I wondered about it and about a poem Rachel had written – a poem directly concerned with his non-presence in our bedroom – clothes on hangers and empty shoes – I wonder – but I think one has to stay on here, where the memories are, painful though they are.

Jennifer, Greta's daughter whose husband left her, was very lovely – she is an extraordinary girl. I went in – in a black suit, black blouse and slacks. I hadn't anything else to wear, really, and Nell referred to it as looking like Hamlet, which rocked me for a moment. But I drifted away from her, until I lost my self-consciousness. I wear mourning, partly because of the people of Jamaica who loved him, and partly because I'm not ready for anything else.

3 December 1969

Longman's have written and made an offer for Norman's brief biography, to be published with a compiled collection of his speeches, writings and broadcasts. I think it would be a wonderful idea.

It was exactly three months yesterday that Norman died.

4 December 1969

I have been reading some notes Norman left in a diary over the last two years – it's pathetic, the struggle over health.

I may not keep this diary as it's not of value just recording day-to-day things. I think my next step is to try to keep from looking back, and this may encourage just that.

Sometimes I feel very strongly that I am moving forward and then some simple little memory hits me for a loop again. That's why it is perhaps better to get away next year, for a bit. A little thing like making coffee in the morning, and there is one cup instead of two, and this happens every morning – there's an awful lot to miss.

10 December 1969

My mind has become very preoccupied with the problem of a book about Norman. Longman's have written suggesting a compilation of speeches, writing, broadcasts edited around the two fragmentary autobiographies, and including articles written about him.

It's an idea that appeals to me enormously, far more so than either Vic Reid[1], who will take too long, but will probably turn out a lovely belated book, or Philip Sherlock[2] who was in the welfare world, but never in the epoch of street fighting and dangerous living, and who in any event will be preoccupied, to a certain extent, with not treading on people's toes. It isn't just a question of a collection, it seems to me that it should have a powerful picture, a strong picture of the period, the currents and cross currents, and, with due respect to research, by someone who lived through at least some of the experiences and can trace the growth and change taking place.

Longman's Carrington[3] was here this morning and I think we both agreed, although I was a bit staggered at his suggesting Ken or Frank Hill who were too involved in so much that happened, and could hardly be impartial, and as an alternative John Maxwell[4], who is very young and might even be out of sympathy. We ultimately agreed that Vernon Arnett would be nearer the mark. So I will contact him. I think ultimately, a small editorial board could do for a start, and I do passionately wish Douglas was here. We have found another diary of Norman's around 1938.

I am continuing to go through his letters — it's tough and disturbing work, but somehow I feel that it is so infinitely worthwhile.

Norman seems so near to me as I read, and the feeling of terror is subsiding to something more like our own relationship — the last two weeks of strain and fear are being swamped by the fullness of the memories, when he was well and full of work and life and love.

12 December 1969

After intense thought, I have come to the conclusion that the offer from Longman's should be handled in this way — a small editorial group, Hoyt to be paid to do the research in all speeches, writings, etc., and then a series of articles on the period, the background and the man.

Arnett, perhaps Dayes or Ashenheim, Blake, Michael, myself???

Let's phone Arnett first.

20 December 1969

The other night Michael was here, very much in the raconteur mood. Leighton Holness, Tito Jemmott, Pat Anderson[1], Rachel, and myself. And the talk drifted on to Norman and why he didn't go Federal, and someone said: 'I know why he didn't go, he wouldn't leave Jamaica to Wills Isaacs.' This

Norman had said himself. Foot had thought that Jamaica would have been safe with Glasspole, but Wills would have split the Party in two sooner than have let that happen.

And someone else recounted how Wills had said with absolute glee: 'He's going, he's going, I know he is.'

And if all this had happened, as it would have done, Busta would have walked in, as he did, and taken over Jamaica and taken Jamaica out of Federation — and that would have been that.

1 January 1970

It's a golden afternoon, as only Portland can be golden and green. Jess[1] and I fled here to escape the festivities and not know when the New Year came in. Michael and Bev[2] have been in and out too. There's a sound system playing down under the hill as it's a holiday — it always makes me think of the Four Roads sound systems which played so endlessly at night when Norman was ill — all night long, and I used to slip out and walk in the garden so as to keep steady.

Anyway I have employed someone to collect all N.'s speeches, tapes, writings etc., with a view to being ready when some definite plan is evolved. I won't have wasted or caused any time to be wasted. There are several suggestions afoot, but I need advice badly.

So the golden light pours all around, and somehow he's stretched in a chair nearby, lost in a book. And so starts the year 1970 —

What will it bring forth?

January 1970

To Mike Smith

I think there is going to be a wild burst of creativeness one day — not in the mountains, but near the sea, if I could find the place that could evoke it. Perhaps somewhere on the St Thomas road near White Horses, with the arid foothills on the left — or on the outside of the Palisadoes where the great sea horses come roaring in and the smell of salt and the tearing wind in one's face, and bits of cactus and driftwood.

Still, still the solitaire utters its lone cry and the mist covers the memory of my Norman in a shifting yet revealing movement and I go on — learning to carry him with me and without a backward glance.

Love to you all.

It's strange all alone at Miami Airport, not sure of the concourse — not sure of the forms and the tickets and then, all of a sudden, not really sure of oneself. Everyone else seems sure, except me. Will they be there to meet me? Will Michael be on the tarmac?

Will Norman come and stay with me — stay with me — stay with me — like the beat of a ship's engine or a long distance train.

I think I feel better now — the fight with the tears is kind of easier. Will Rachel be there and young Norman and Uhuru? Uhuru — nice boy — I'll take you for a walk to Mona, if only you will be 'down' in the car?

6 March 1970

I was getting quite a high temperature with some sort of aching virus, and I knew that I had to cross a river, step by step, over slippery stones that were placed like stepping stones with the water almost covering them. It was a very dark night and I was afraid that I wouldn't get across, although I desperately wanted to because I knew that it was the only way I could get to Norman. And he came and helped me step by step, holding my hand and steadying me, and he kept saying: 'Edna — don't look back, don't look back, just come on.'

And I steadied myself although I was frightened and almost in despair, and so tired. But we made it across and we sat on the ground in the dark with our arms around each other — but I knew in my heart that it was just for a moment that we would be together in that human way — that we would have to move on — separate, but part of one great whole — but very conscious of each other — and then I fell asleep.

Next day when I woke I felt it was just a matter of time that I would be ill and die and that he would help me across the journey of death.

This feeling persisted for two days, whilst I had the fever.

Today I went down to Westmoreland looking at cattle with Paul Bovell and handed out certificates, feeling pretty ill, and there sitting on the platform I wondered was it a message, and that I wasn't going to him at all — but was it once more that he was trying to tell me something that I couldn't accept. I don't know. I don't know. I can't give up the idea of crossing that river — to him — I can't.

19 June 1970

There is nothing very special about today, and certainly nothing very special about the date, which I don't like. I like things that divide by three or else it must be seven.

I keep saying to myself — shall I ask so and so if I could write a book, and so thinking that someone could give me confidence and the insight and the sheer sense of continuity. I so understand why Norman repudiated the whole idea. By the time all the research had been done — instead of something that flowed from his pen as words flowed from his mouth, all that sweat and all these modern youngsters with their talk of trends and factors and motives and what did and didn't happen *as a result* of unknown-to-consciousness backgrounds — it's no wonder he said: 'Hell, let someone else do it — it's all too much like a ruddy chore.' He seemed very happy with his little research team, but now that I know them better, I realize how claustrophobic it might have been making him feel. I used always to feel one could say of the dead, 'Anyway they are at peace now.' Now I am not so sure — not sure that it isn't they who we should be worrying over, with the unknown situations they may be finding themselves in.

But to return to the book. I think perhaps, when one has the long and lonely moments, one could spend some of it writing, not for publication, but just to console oneself and to help one to externalize things a bit. Writing as a profession is a different thing, but we all use words — the writers have no prerogative — and using the words one knows, in the way one has always used them, might build into the story of the past — the people we have loved and lived with — the things we have lived through — the problems we have sought to solve, and been defeated over and over again. Because it does seem that life never gives up in the battle, and you either grow, or you come up against it again and again, and when one dies — is that the end of growth? And the strange thing is that, to use a legal phrase, it is as if one were 'estopped' from solving the problem of growing by some prison in which one lives, and only utter catastrophe, and sometimes not even that, lets loose the ability to stride forward.

What is it — and why are we made like this? Prisoners within a pattern — a gramophone needle that has stuck?

So to take a pen and write when the loneliness, the emptiness comes on — might in itself help one to grow and to understand. For of this I am sure — it isn't wise to meet death without an effort of cognition — it isn't wise to go on with the assumption that courage is the only valid virtue. One has to have thought, one has to have wrestled with the angel.

So back to the book again. What is the fundamental construction — what are the important events — should it go with the flight of a mood — or should it go with hard facts — can one combine the two? Can I do it at all?

20 June 1970

I want to go back up to Moore Town one day. It has always left an indelible impression on my mind, because I associate it with the legend of the Russian ships.[1]

I think I have written an account of this before somewhere – but let me live it once more in case I have not left the record.

As I remember it, you climb a long, steep, winding road up the Portland mountainside, damp and lush, to Moore Town – the home of the Portland Maroons.

You come out on to a plateau with a river running across it and houses here and houses over there on the other side, scattered. We were having our meeting, which was always a complete waste of time with the Maroons, who arranged and pledged their votes through the leaders. But this time it was different. The young men of the village, tired of the reiterated boasts of 'freedom', and seeing it only in terms of what they got out of it, were showing signs of revolt. The leaders had always, more or less, voted JLP, and now when we arrived we were conscious of a split. The older people were gathered for the meeting, but the younger set were across the river bunched together in a restless group.

We held the meeting and we were coming back down when we were met with a telegram asking N. to return to Kingston at once. The story of the Russian ships had broken.

As we heard it, we looked at each other with strange icy hands on our hearts.

Russian ships had been allowed to refuel and even played a football match, and the JLP started and it took on like wild fire. Manley has Russian ships in Kingston harbour with their guns pointing to the city, and if you put the PNP in, he will bring them ashore and take you all prisoners, and turn Jamaica communist. The same tactics as the Tories used with the Zinovieff letter[2] and Russian troops landing in England.

All reason vanished – and it became a shambles. I even had a long distance call from someone in Lucea asking if it were true, and against a background of a microphone announcing the news and the threat that it involved.

It's funny how you *know* when you've had it, and always there are politicians who will use the weapon nearest to hand – so that was that – I don't say it affected the result, I just remind myself that the world is like that.

27 June 1970

Horses during the war
It came quite like a bombshell, the knowledge that 'gas' was going to be limited during the war and we were going back to horses for transport!

Norman, with his remarkable foresight, a sort of mixture of shrewdness and sixth sense, was the first 'public figure' out on the road with the smartest little two wheeler. It was built like a little English dog cart with motor car wheels – high and extremely nifty. I think he got it from a resourceful young man called Hourani, at the bottom of East Street, who *also* had foreseen what was coming.

I can't remember the order in which we acquired our horses. I know I had riding horses, and we must have broken them to harness, but I know we ended up with a good trio, Tom, Dick and Harriet.

Tom was a horse we had got from a woman who kept a riding school and who also used to organize trips to the Peak. I think he had the record for speed on a mountain road and also for the number of times he had made the trip during a given period of days. If I can find a certain letter, I could recall the time he used to take at night with Norman riding from Drumblair to Nomdmi, through Dublin Castle. But to return to driving, we did have a young ex-race horse who had been called Ole Massa, (not very successful!), but we called him Dick — he was slight with a high head carriage, a fiery chestnut, with all the characteristics that are supposed to go with that colouring, and with a turn of trotting speed, particularly when Norman was driving, that couldn't be matched. He wouldn't trot like that for anyone else, and to see him come up from Duke Street through Cross Roads was something to see. Norman still had his Chrysler, but that only came out when it was urgent and we could spare the gas.

In those days PNP meetings were held at Edelweiss Park, hours and hours of it, with microphones blaring, crowds cheering, much drinking and loud voiced argument on the periphery — and tied up and guarded was Mr Dick, often feeding was Mr Dick, getting more and more restless and nervous. He bit and kicked often, so no one went too close, but the noise and the excitement drove him nearly crazy. And then when midnight came, to see Norman turn Dick's head home and come out of Edelweiss Park's gateway and up Slipe Road!! — with one idea in his head, to get *home*.

Norman was a terrific and totally fearless driver — he had been brought up in what were called 'buggy days', of no cars, and he knew horse driving. People just loved to stand and marvel. The odd thing was that I was the one who rode every day, was passionately fond of horses and really could ride. But I just couldn't drive — I was terrified of it, terrified of slipping on the tarred road, was always convinced that the long, slender reins would snap, and hated the 'running on the bit' which good driving involved. Mind you, odd things did happen — we also had a four wheeler buggy, for taking the family, usually driven by the man who looked after my horses and Norman's cows. Tom and Harriet pulled this vehicle. But just occasionally Norman used Dick in it, as usual going at top speed and with great style. But the four wheeler couldn't take it and there was a big gully on the road before reaching Drumblair, now beautifully bridged, but in those days you went down and you went up, and he took Dick into it at top speed and quite unconsciously left the back wheels and the back half of the buggy in the gully, and arrived home, spinning round the gate and up the path home, with tremendous dash as usual, but with the front seat and the front two wheels only. 'Norman what has happened?'

He looked back and said 'Jesus Christ.'

But we were very lucky over one thing. For years before the war, we had always spent our holidays in St Ann, at Arthur's Seat, Epworth. But in 1939 I had bought a little bit of land in the Port Royal mountains at three pounds an acre, which was a normal price for those days, and on it we had built a little two-room cottage. We used to drive our cars to the forestry cottage at Guava Ridge and walk or ride the mile and a half up the hill. This took comparatively little gas and we were able to keep it up for some time, until things were really bad and gas was too short to allow for even this. So when we wanted to go, we rode from door to door, sometimes up the Mavis Bank bridle track from Gordon Town, and sometimes with a pack mule through Dublin Castle. I think we loved it – there was something young and different about it. Different from the sophistication of the city, different from the pent-up feeling our friends suffered from, and something above all that we shared and could do together. I often used to try to get Norman to ride with me for fun after a day's work before the war, but he always said he'd had such a ghastly time with horses during the fourteen to eighteen war, that he was out to launch a society for the abolition of the horse – so he laughed at me and wouldn't come.

But necessity changed all that and his old gift with horses came right back. To see Norman saddle a perverse and difficult mule, had an ingenuity about it that only a countryman could appreciate. He moved on a method of matching wits and I've never seen a mule he couldn't outwit. Even one famous mountain mule, Doris, who had 'a time' for trouble. She could spin like a top, tail and ears spinning too, and Norman would wait for just that pause that would inevitably come before she set off again, and he would almost shy the saddle and saddle cloth onto her back. Now Doris had a peculiarity – she could accept defeat, and always, if you could get the saddle on to her back, that was the moment when she would give in, not with relief, but in a sort of mood of predestination, and the girthing wasn't difficult. She treated me, in these moods, with total contempt; for one, she had discovered I couldn't shy straight, also I think she knew I loathed mules – women usually do!

The most romantic horse manoeuvre of all, though, was riding at night from Drumblair to Nomdmi through Dublin Castle, two of us and a pack horse called Tim. Tim had the record to the Peak, he was an ambler, and we'd send him ahead, loaded with hampers, to set the pace, and our horses would scramble after him. Sometimes on black nights Norman tied a white handker-chief to his horse's tail for me to see to follow. But sometimes after rain, oh magic of all magic, the fireflies — millions of them — peeny wallies — and in a wave all their lights would go on together and light up the track and the surrounding area, and then in another wave all would go out and it would be jet black darkness again. No one who hasn't seen this phenomenon could conceivably imagine — it would start from somewhere and follow like a wind across the hillside — a golden glory — with the tree frogs piping and the deep roll of the bull frogs — the mountains at night after rain.

We would get in so tired! A bite, a drink and roll into bed with a groan, aching happily in every limb. War, or no war, we had some incredibly happy times. Times that stretched us to the limit of our endurance, but brought new and challenging experiences. Not that we ever forgot that half the world was murdering the other half. The only way to forget was to plunge into activity that left one too tired to think — but that in the last analysis we knew was of immense value to our small world.

There was one last horse episode. We were going in full evening dress to an important show at the Carib, long dresses and all, and the narrow wheel of the four wheel buggy caught in the tram line and deposited Muriel and I out onto the road! Anyway, we got the buggy back up again and proceeded!

3 July 1970

We have just come back from the airport, where we met Burnham[1] and his wife. He has come to make the main address at the first Norman Manley Award for Excellence[2], tomorrow.

It went well — his wife is very nice, but I can't make contact with him at all — Michael and I talked of it in the car coming home.

I hope tomorrow will be helped by the love people have for Norman — everywhere one turns, the response is tremendous, you can feel it in the air. The desire to express *how* people feel about him.

We will go down to the grave in a family group in the morning, and the great banquet at night. I guess I'll survive — without a break — I'm not sure, not sure at all.

I have made a stunning discovery. If you have lived a long and complicated life, with someone you love, death doesn't alter the pattern at all — it's the same relationship going on, on a different plane, all the time — you react to everything exactly as if that person is with you — even the same explanations!

So you aren't quite as lonely — it's just that it takes a lot of faith.

20 August 1970

I finished the carving this morning.[1] Like all great efforts it is a great failure.

But it was a tremendous journey to take and these strange little lines keep running through my head:

> I will not see the shadows
> I will not feel the rain
> I will not hear the nightingale
> Sing on as if in pain.

I couldn't carve the drawing of the head again — not with the figure below it. *I couldn't.*

I know I am a minor artist, but no one, but no one, is a better wood carver. No one can bully, cajole, coax, batter, trick or beguile wood like I can!

11 July 1971

This morning I got up early to go and carve, but it didn't last very long. I think I am at last finished with carving. Perhaps I will draw or do terracotta, or perhaps — perhaps I will write.

Sorrow steals over one very slowly — it comes like a mist through the trees — slowly enveloping you. Nothing lasts forever — only memories are eternal, perhaps really eternal.

July 1971

Mike's poems have gone off to the publishers at last — it was a tremendous job — so many copies and variations — the typing was tremendous. I scribbled a simple little introduction, the way I think he wanted.

Now I am working with Clyde Hoyte on N.'s last interviews with Basil[1] — a back-breaking job as the tapes are shocking, some too fast, and background noises, and of course Norman thumping the table making each point as he always did. But it's all so alive and warm and there'll be no editing of his punches!

30 July 1971

Driving at eighty miles per hour, I suddenly remembered Norman — I was in St Ann, between Tower Isle and Ocho Rios, and I remembered how he and Princess Margaret fell for each other in a big way, and then we were in the Cathedral in Spanish Town, and she passed up the aisle, back view towards us, and he said in quizzical distress: 'But she hasn't got a bottom!!'

Diary Two

31 August 1971

Wayne has got my other diary, the old one, typing some excerpts from it for his book.[1] Risky thing to do, to give someone your personal diary. But saying yes and no is always such a complicated business.

I'm up in the hills nearly all the time, racing on with my carving now for this December show.[2] It was to be six, now I think it will be only five, because of the birthday of Rachel's baby. She still isn't sure if she will have it here or in England. I think George[3] is afraid of letting her go — she must be his one life line. In his own strange way I think he loves her very much, and her loyalty and pluck must appeal to a man of his reckless nature enormously. Her feelings for him must be complicated, because she has an uncanny insight into character sometimes, but there's something about him and his way of life that seems to hold her, and the fact that he is in trouble makes it more, not less.

St Ives[4] — I must have been four or five, but I remember it in a shadowy way. A long, steep pathway of steps between high stone walls with little peephole windows in the walls. The steps are very worn and uneven. I was small and had to go down holding someone's hand. I don't think we could walk abreast, it was too narrow, which made the descent awkward, and then at last out into sunlight on an open quay, with the light glinting on the water and a great sense of freedom and satisfaction of having arrived — great joy, and a relinquishing of the guiding hand.

This little incident seems to have happened many times. I would like to go back to St Ives to see if this is an imaginary or dream spot, because it has stayed with me as a sort of symbol — vaguely connected with periods of rather frightening loss of light and freedom, which, if endured, come out into achievement and daylight.

Rather like the periods in a carving when you lose sight of your objective, and ultimately have to relinquish it — to find a new and surprising sense of accomplishment. Perhaps this is pretentious nonsense — who knows?

3 September 1971

Came up back to Nomdmi — very tired — after terribly strenuous three days. Roy and Morgan staying with me — need quite a bit of looking after.

Amazing meeting on the night of the second at Bolivar[1] — vast crowd — Michael very relaxed 'talking' to the people, and then the candle-lighting and the march to Norman's grave — thousands of flickering candles across the park, planted on and around the grave. I thought how he would have twinkled and loved it, but we had to leave him alone with his candles and go home.

So tired today — double shopping, two houses running — but it's the only way to work, up here, alone with it. 'Mountain Women' difficult technically — they have to be remote and yet each a person — Grandmother, Mother, Daughter — I so love it.

Wrote M.G. a calm letter about his book of poems — he got so uptight, I'm dropping my hands. God, I get pushed around, but not anymore — this inner vein of weakness a sort of softness. Now I want to know myself a little better, and know and understand better what I am doing.

Deep down worried over Rachel. Doug dashed up to check on us — he looked happy but a little tired.

A quite *adorable* controversy raging over Bogle statue — terribly funny really, as I don't believe St Thomas people really hate it — not according to the TV quiz anyway. But you know it's kind of nice to be able to be violent and condemnatory, especially for councillors who have such a hard time themselves.

Reading a lot, listening to music too — have suddenly turned violently against poetry. I think it has a bad effect on my carving, makes it too romantic!!

So you see, step by step, I will find my way towards something perhaps newer and truer.

11 September 1971 — Nomdmi, 4 a.m., Saturday

Norman's book is out — just a few advance copies. Basil gave it a bad review, and the *Gleaner* only a moderately good one. The truth is the public wanted N.'s own story, told by himself — or that's what they will want.

Rex[1] has done a scholar's job, and the public will want journalism. I think we are right. The important thing at this moment of time is to keep the record straight, and by so doing, preserve in Norman's own words what he really believed in and stood for. I am going to read it through myself calmly up here. He's still ahead of his times. But criticism and reviewing doesn't upset me in the way it does other people. Vivian Carrington was foaming over Basil's review, which in a sense had a good point. He's a passionate person, Rex is a scholar, and that is the root of the difference — actually that says everything as to why they couldn't agree about how to handle that book.

I am happy over it and I am writing Rex before I go down, after I've had a bit of time with the book. It has integrity, I know.

Then the storm has been raging over Bogle. The Mayor and councillors, oh dear — it's so funny really — it should be torn down and cast into the sea.

I get a vivid picture of us all swimming out like mad and bringing it back, and this going on ad infinitum. Then the Mayor of Kingston says: 'Give it to us,' and the press have jumped in. Here again I'm not at all upset. I guess I had such a battering in the early days, when it really did hurt!

On September 2nd we had the meeting at Bolivar Place, and the candlelight march to Norman's grave. It was very moving — he would have loved all those candles so much and the singing and the size of the crowd. It had a mystique.

I had a hectic day on Thursday presenting the book to various people, and a fund-raising group of businessmen. In the evening my tummy was beginning to feel funny, when Michael and Bev sent me some flowers and I *pulled* myself together.

Then yesterday morning I shopped for both houses, in case Rachel arrived back from England all of a sudden, and got back up here by eleven. I was too tired to work, but I found all the old photos and papers we had lost and had been searching for.

I have to find someone to finally list and sort all of Norman's papers and photos, and hand them over to the right organization. I can't even find photos of all my work, let alone track down where they are for Wayne Brown. We have done a marvellous job of collecting all Norman's stuff, but it's chaotic still; not altogether, but not the way it ought to be.

I feel so well working up here and between today and tomorrow hope to finish the 'Mountain Women'. The Bergers[2] turned up as I was about going for a walk. They came straight off the plane, I was so touched. I think they wanted to talk about Rachel, but I headed it off. I can't talk about Rachel — it's still all too obscure and I don't want to make up my mind about her problems. I just want to be there to help if she needs me. But I still don't know whether I'll have to face England or not, and I still have at least one more carving to do.

Slowly my own mind is clearing and steadying, and I know that since Norman died almost everything that has happened to me has been rooted in a reaction away from reality — rooted in a refusal to face the future in terms that involved the finding of a path that leads somewhere.

Emotion — a sort of excitable dashing down roads that lead nowhere, and an almost frightening need to find someone to look after — such an unreal state of affairs, that.

I could have gone to pieces again over Rachel's experience, but she has managed so far to handle herself so well, that it has helped me to step across the sense of disaster.

So I am up here most of the time, carving for this small December show, and giving myself the quiet and the challenge of being alone to face the amount of running away which was building itself into my life. I'm not running now, but there is need for a lot of thinking, before reality and kindness take charge over fantasy and compulsiveness.

12 September 1971 – Nomdmi

In Rex's introduction he discusses the early decision to attack Bustamante. My clear recollection of this is that it was *not* taken as a decision. Totally against Norman's wishes, Ken Hill launched an attack at a Papine meeting and the news came to Norman and he shook his head and said: 'Damn.' I think the phrase 'Bustamanteism' might have come later, but it was from then that B.'s followers, who had been attacking Norman ceaselessly, and the PNP used this attack by Hill on Busta to justify much that they did.

I must remember to ask Michael to consider a function to pay tribute to Arnett for a life of service. He nearly died this year. Lucille was quite magnificient – I acted as her chauffeur, so I know the gallant fight that they both put up. He's back at work, but has to be careful. I admire him so *much*.

Another note on Rex's introduction. The chief opponent *within* the party of adult suffrage was Fairclough, whose political inspiration was largely based on his Haitian experience. The sheer aristocracy of the Haitian 'black man' appealed to him in a quite inspired way. To become a government was to him all important, far more important than ideas – win, and the rest that is good will follow. He saw adult suffrage as inevitably condemning the PNP 'to the wilderness', his own words. A wider suffrage would put power into the hands of people who could not, and would not understand. I well remember, we were on holiday, I think in St Ann, Epworth, and he came up late to put his point of view. He lost, and it was the first big difference between them.

I have found Norman's essays on George Campbell and 'Modern' art, the latter very brief. Lend Vic Reid?

There are some things about life I don't understand. Here is Wayne asking me questions about my life and today I go to an old woodshed, and under debris galore, everything from fertilizers to Coke, I find, worm-eaten, damp, mildewed, with the cover completely destroyed, a volume of an annual of modern poetry – 1917 or something – and in it the poem that influenced my whole life – 'Makeshifts', by Gibson, given to me by Jock Deansley, who committed suicide in 1918 – leaving a mute little heap of clothes on the sands and walking into the sea — forever. They gave me, or she gave me, her copy of Euripides, in memory.

Simon Watson Taylor came tearing up for ten minutes — why so short? I wanted to talk to Simon, but they were going to Wayne's lunch — to hell with lunches and parties — I'm so weary of them.

Finished 'Mountain Women' — Ha!

That is life without Norman, without a man to care or be cared by — oh God what a world.

24 September 1971

Rex, I read through the introduction a third time, and now I realize that it has opened up a hidden world of sadness that has been suppressed since Norman died. This is a good thing — I think your assessment of him and of his period has made me able to see the inevitability of much of his life.

I think I was bordering on bitterness (oh, very well hidden — the mask doesn't often slip) on what could be expressed as the deadly gimcrack tactics that were used against him, when to him the attempt at truth was all important. His very gift of compromise was born of his knowledge that truth has many aspects, many sides, and that therefore it must die in the hands of a wilful person. I hope that I do not do him an injustice with my inability to use words validly.

So your book opened to me an aspect of the truth about him which has set me free from my own complex pain.

I think he was far more philosophic about history than I was able to be. Women are so personal.

I have moments of agony since he isn't here anymore — moments when I wanted to ask questions. I don't mean personally — I mean the 'why' of life and history.

So I read your introduction again and it helped me.

God Bless.

19 November 1971

I am sitting in the labour ward feeling very shivery and funny, trying to keep steady. Ra has gone down to be X-rayed as, although the pains are pretty regular and severe, they're not sure about the position of the head — if it is 'down' enough.

For these four weeks this is the 'moment', and as one has lived so one will meet it. Birth is such an inexorable thing — I am not afraid — but I feel an umbilical cord pulling from her to me. I keep shivering — am I getting a cold?

Later

When they gave her an injection towards the end to relax and quiet the pain, I heard her murmuring to herself Keats' Ode — 'To cease upon the midnight without pain' — the whole of it she said — and then very softly she said: 'I love Daddy, I love George, I love Mardi — my baby is coming upon the midnight without pain —'

Little did she know!

21 November 1971

Letter to Mike Smith

Mike, you mustn't talk about Jung like that. Jung was the wisest man in modern times, and the most humane. Jung saved even people like Eliot from total disaster. He tried to walk into the unknown and to survive long enough to bring back knowledge.

I give to Freud everything that is his, but Jung has showed me the way to live. Do you remember when you and I discovered that to 'smile' was an approach to more than life, but to truth? I have watched death and birth — visibly, and at close range — in the last two years. The night of the 19th to 20th November 1971 has brought me near to my last doorway of growth; it isn't a smile this time, and yet the smile was part of it.

I am profoundly interested in the concept implied within the image of the alter ego. Somewhere, somehow there is an image moving in the back of my consciousness, of the peace of Norman's death, and the agony of Rachel's birth.

If Jung were alive, at whatever cost, I would go to him — for me HE is the image of the 'wise old man', and I would say to him; 'What was the image in that deep dark pool? Or in the deep dark blue?' And from him something would flow and I would understand.

Mike darling — life never stops, does it?

You and your beautiful Mary — a little like my Norman.

28 November 1971

A creepy little wind blows through the window. Outside the street lamps illuminate the trees in the square.

All the sense of loneliness and disaster is falling away — I've got a theme! a theme! a theme! and my revenge.

I'm going to carve

The laughter of a faun (disgruntled? perhaps, who knows)

Oh God — I'm happy

I'll carve it — I'll carve it — I'll carve it —
Don't tell *anyone*
I will summon that old symbolist Mr Freud from the shades to help me.
The Faun, Medusa and the Sea God.
  Death Silence Fear
The shades — look for drawings of Fear.
  And a baby, a baby within a form —
within a form — within a form, a baby.

To know and to understand decadence, is it an orgy of technique, a corruption of the spirit, or just an unqualified ebullience?

19 January 1972

I have been back for quite a long time now, and everything that happened in London seems a long way away. I can only vaguely remember the intensity — the sense of growing vision, the sureness. Back at home has been a long lesson in patience — real convinced patience. There have been abnormal January rains and this has deepened the sense of time passing.

Why do we try to hide our freedom from ourselves — we are free to come and go, free to love or hate. So what ties us to some situation, some involvement, and makes us behave like puppets on a string? And what hand pulls the string?

Is there a need to find and establish an equilibrium between an outside force and a 'will' within? Are we given a choice that makes us free? And is there such a thing as a wrong choice? Isn't choice an inevitable movement in the face of circumstances, so that we come back to the problem of the puppet and the string. We are all puppets on strings; some of us stay within the orbit of what is known and plumb the depths, others move on, never getting beyond a certain depth but covering a wide field, always ending with the same pattern.

Sartre says man perpetually chooses 'to be as he is'. I am not sure that he has a choice, and to perpetually make the same choice smells of automatism and that is the puppet again — except that now man pulls his own string.

I believe that sexual love is incapable of change, except within the confines of a greater control. Underlying its potential tenderness, there is always the problem of human will. The basis of sexual love is always possession, temporary or permanent — "Now you dominate me before I dominate you.' How can civilized man accept this as a way of life? It goes to the root of his unease, and the only way he can use it as a source of growth, if he chooses to stay within the orbit, is to learn that he can only walk the tightrope if he learns the meaning of forgiveness.

Sexual love is all geared to that supreme moment – possession of another – with its inevitable reversion to repossession of self – a perilous state of imbalance for civilized man to be subjected to.

An outside force and a 'will' within – here it is again – the puppet on a string. I so wish I could find the answer to the pulling of that string – I've watched two people just pulling each other apart. Can't help.

27 January 1972

It is remarkable to live in a world where quite suddenly, and for the first time in your life, you find yourself under perpetual scrutiny. If you happen to be the first person to pick up a phone ringing, this is regarded as a sign of some hidden enthusiasm.

Your letters are under surveillance, friends are watched, and there is a sense of a record being kept.

And slowly, step by step, your life is reduced to a matter of guilt or shame. Privacy, as a concept of the least of the freedoms, is an affront.

So how do I get *outside* of society – how achieve an atmosphere of unqualified "intouchness'.

Over that bridge we all have to go one day and for me soon – but before that bridge comes a few years of preparation – a few years of intouchness.

7 February 1972

This weekend the party opened its inaugural meeting[1] in Montego Bay – a tremendous flash-back in time – where was Norman?

One of the truly bewildering things about consciousness is the wide gap that separates the sound of the words consciously expressing a thought, an emotion – and another layer of consciousness which repudiates the whole thing. I *love* an election campaign – I truly do – the microphones, the crowds, the excitement, the love and the passion, the slow dawning of the archetypal pattern that the few great speakers evolve, the harsh calling out of the unconscious the things people want to hear you say, as different from those ideas which you want to implant. This you say and mean: 'I love an election campaign'.

But deep down in the dark pool of your own unconscious there is a shadowy movement. Is it fear – is it horror – or is it merely that what is taking place on top is so powerful that it shakes and reverberates down where consciousness ends, and some other existence begins?

8 February 1972

There was a vast crowd at the racecourse — thousands of candles, and a man handed me a six foot high torch and led me through the mass of people, who opened up a lane. Michael was following with an even bigger torch and we came to Norman's tomb, half completed, and they lifted me up on to a high wall, not even two feet wide, with a deep pit on one side abut ten to fifteen feet, and on the other a depth of about five feet, and it was quite dark — only the shadows of the lights from the platform. It seemed pitch dark on either side and I had to walk holding a man's hand behind, and another in front. I don't know how I kept my balance, it seemed a long way, and then they lifted me down on the shallow side and hoisted me on to their shoulders, higher and higher, as I strove to reach up and light the flames around the grave. I lit two, and then a young man siezed my torch and climbed up the parapet and lit the others,and then we started to come back along the wall, foot by foot, and there was Michael just back from lighting the everlasting flame, smiling amongst the crowd.

But I felt strangely cut off. I felt like a woman returning from some strange rite, unable to make contact with the people around, as if I had some other-dimensional experience. I couldn't smile, I couldn't cry — inside I was strangely still.

To wake from a strange enigmatic dream with a steel-like backward glance. Piercing the memory of centuries in a wild, improbable return.

I met you, to make amends, case hardened.

For one moment it had been deep sleep and a deeper dream.

Cruelty and life clasped hands.

10 February 1972

I think of youth in Jamaica. I think of a horse, my first horse, and that remarkable relationship that can build up particularly between a woman and her horse — the one horse — not horses. Horses have another significance. I knew that at the Remount Depot[1] when I had seven horses, caring for them through a bitter winter, rolling bales of peat for bedding, 'mucking out' with a straining back — being the first 'hand' put up on the unknown, half-broken mounts, sticking your knees in like a wild cat's claws (I weighed ninety-eight pounds) whilst all hell was popping under you. Going in with the feed on the side of a horse with a wall eye and lucky to get back out as he lunged across to pin you in. Overfed, underworked horses in freezing weather.

The first air raid over Harrow, maybe the only one, riding one and leading two, because so many of the girls were sick and absent. I never seemed to get ill – I never do when I am fulfilled and happy.

Bombs and aeroplanes and all the horses bolting – a woman and child and a perambulator ahead in a panic – let go the two leads and jump the bloody pram. All the horses galloped back to the stable, safely. The 'Forewoman', who had legitimate cause to despise me, said acidly: 'Why come back without the leads?' and turned away before I could answer.

Why did she despise me – because she cried in front of everyone when her boyfriend was killed, and turned to us for sympathy, and something in her manner stirred me, and I said, before I could stop it: 'Well there are other men in the world.' And then I knew what I had said, and for one painful moment I wanted to take it back. It was like kicking a dog – I was like that. I functioned on two levels and never knew which one was on top.

I think, in fact I know, I was hyper-sensitive and got hurt so often that it all turned into a sort of toughness that demanded the ability to hide what you felt from the world.

I still have it, only I can differentiate now. But after that I got all the worst mounts, all the tough jobs. I know she prayed for me to be thrown, to break my damned neck, to be humiliated.

And I learnt to stick on – I've never met any woman in my life who could just 'stay there' the way I could. I learnt a sort of premonition of what a horse could and was likely to do. I learnt to be aware just that fraction ahead, and to be ready. I have never in my life been 'thrown', only once a horse came down with me, and off I pitched. That was the same Jamaican horse I could write reams about – I loved him. But I never had a good-looking seat. I could never ride in a show. I was never taught the fine points of show-ring riding. I always looked on a horse, an outsider, glued to the horse, ugly, but with the saving grace of good, sensitive hands. This Forewoman was very conscious of this, and she gave me spiteful hell and I had no comeback because I knew it was true – but I rode more recklessly than ever – safe as a sandboy with my long legs, and this sort of clairvoyance about horses.

But my first very own horse filled a dream. He was my personal lean pony, carefully picked, but skin and bone, and as the months went by, filling out and filling my dreams. 'House of Cards' – you the first horse love of my youth, and as I remember you the air is full of the scent of logwood, the sound of bees and the faint chill in the air of early morning. How I loved you.

Creeping out in the moonlight to lean over the stable door, and the smell of the fresh Guinea grass – the stamp of your hoof and the crunch and rustle as you tossed the grass to get the best shoots.

God – the glory of a morning ride with life and the world ahead – a oneness. My throat goes tight as it sweeps back over me – the line of horses that followed. Norman always said I was never faithful to a horse, I was faithful to a dog. After a few years, I got to know a horse too well, and the feeling of fantasy would fade into reality.

Fantasy is the real world for me — it still is. I like people around whom I can hang my dreams and a horse's too. But they have to be, like Norman, inexhaustible. Dogs — well dogs are like an alter ego — inseparable and yet separated.

15 February 1972

Normalcy is only laziness!

I tell myself the truth comes from the surgeon's knife, work comes from love and vision — concentrate, concentrate, concentrate.

Good Friday 1972

The elections are over and won,[1] and the brief, wonderful honeymoon — and now one is conscious of the spotlight, oh what a spotlight, of people watching, hoping, believing. Small mistakes will begin to appear — little jealousies and slights stir the surface. What memories it brings back. What a treacherous, shifting road to go back on again.

It's difficult to run away — perhaps wiser — I'm just watching it. Why is it that the church can sound so meaningless when there is this desperate need for help.

It is 3 p.m. and I am totally upset. I have been for two days. I find I have even torn the back of my new curtain from bottom to top. I went and looked it up. Of course Christ has just died and the world is innerly dark.

This morning I lay in bed as the sun came up and I said, it is Easter. It was like jewels outside, the 'Woman Tongue' pods gleaming silver gold against the pale sky. The little fine-leafed tree outside the window was green gold with apricot blossoms. Somewhere a pea dove, the scarlet Hibiscus like small, irregular bursts of blood. The air had a musky smell like a long-closed vault when the door is opened. I said to myself, it can't be Resurrection morning yet, he hasn't died ... but that is the way it seemed. No clear definitions. Suddenly the joy in the air around me, the sense of birth, a kind of trembling beauty and life.

Like a Ravel orchestra shaking colours and sounds out on to a receiving world.

Now it is 3 p.m. and the curtain is torn and there is no sound from the hanging figure, but somewhere a long journey has started — an absence of sound and sight and touch. He is not in the tomb where they laid him. He never went there, just hanging above it, unable to detach himself entirely; the tiredness, the lack of will, of volition, a journey to take — all day and night long — a journey.

By morning with the first light, the spent force will have moved away, moved on.

Blue flowers follow the trail, springing up along the trail, blue flowers with deep green leaves.

Easter Sunday is a day with an open empty tomb — Easter Sunday is a day of fresh clothes and Easter bonnets with faces that smile through their tears and hopeful growing bodies.

There in the empty tomb a cluster of yellow flowers, upturned to the light.

But my curtain is torn and there is so much that I do not understand.

Easter Sunday

All day I have felt so strange, as if I were hanging, floating above life, unable to move away on a journey, unable to detach myself, and out of it a drawing is coming — an Easter drawing. It is the way I felt when Norman died — at that one spot in the garden which he couldn't bear to leave, and the music, is it Verdi's Requiem — Dies Irae — and this strangely almost conventional drawing of a hovering figure unable to depart, leaving so much sorrow behind. END.

Easter is first of all a time of death, in spite of all the Easter eggs. So let me go through the door of extinction and come out stripped of all the fantasies. Let me be what I am, a woman wrestling to find a final image.

I know that you honour me in spite of the fallacies, because I believe you see through the ability to love, to someone with a purpose and a passionate need for spiritual values.

18 April 1972

Can't you understand that as the light fails and the great depression descends, some men reach for a drink, and others reach for a telephone for a moment's brief communication with a friend.

The great baboons beat their breasts and trumpet to the darkening sky. But the depression is greater than personal loneliness, it is part of a cosmic turning from the light, the herald of the final journey into the dark, which all men fear.

4 June 1972

I am not working, partly because I have no energy, but even more because I am concerned with the difference between Being and Doing. I think it is the basis of all conflict, stating it badly.

Then there is memory. Somewhere I think that ... what do I think about memory? It's a very powerful ... powerful what? What is memory?

There's a scratch on a gramophone record and the words or notes repeat a little and then move on — is that memory?

At some moment in time you have been left with a great emptiness, a quite terrible emptiness, and you dare not walk back down that path again, so you go to sleep, and when the danger is passed, you resume life again — is that memory?

You'd be at night on a beach, under a vast sky, with a turbulent sea exploding near your feet, and you listen to anxious talk about the dangers of lost values or wasted energies — misplaced love.

But the moment is the sky and the sea and the moon making an incomprehensible riot of that one moment in time.

I cannot understand memory — it plays tricks. Some other life, some other time, I will walk back down that path and I will be on that beach, with sky and sea, without the escape of worry about how one lived, or to whom or to what one belonged.

7 June 1972 — 3.30 a.m.

An extraordinary night — fell asleep quickly, I was tired, and got awake round 1 a.m. to a dream that Carole[1] was calling: 'Mardi, Mardi'. I didn't get back to sleep and could have succumbed to fear, but slowly the value I have been gaining from the book by Krishnamurti I have been reading, helped me. Particularly what he has to say about the relationship between fear and thought.

So I turned on the lights and took comfort from the familiar sight of the bedroom — and my thoughts moved over the week Mike had spent here, and how much in understanding and calmness it seems to have brought me — and then Norman —

Now I can see that if I were to go on living at all, other than as a faint shadow of the past, I would have to lose Norman for a while. Now I am back on my feet again and I find that I am searching for him on a different level, a different plane, and it's tremendously comforting — reassuring. It's going to take quite a while to recapture his presence, but I think the garden is where there's still the best chance of contacting him.

July 1972

Now it has quietly started to move a little at a time, but surely and certainly the Faun[1] is coming — following the form has given the feeling.

12 August 1972

Uhuru died.

25 August 1972

I have a little theory — when someone has little or no family ties to look back at, no ties with an older generation, there very often are no deep ties with country or peoples.

For instance in a contemporary situation, I know that my tie with Jamaica comes very strongly through my mother, as well as through Norman. Also, in a deep acceptance of being coloured.

Undated

If you cannot touch to the quick of a friend with the reality of your own being, written words on a piece of paper are no substitute.

Sunday

I am totally unable to describe or evoke the sense of imminent danger and isolation of the dream. A little group of us, I think children, were on a narrow tongue of land, surrounded by an infinite space of sea, waves breaking, a light sharp wind — and the knowledge that at any moment a tremendous storm could spring up, and that there was nowhere to go or to hide — we were totally isolated.

M.G. seemed to come from nowhere, and appeared to be taking charge. The children seemed to be reassured. I went off on my own, and somewhere found some old brown maps — there were maps of the northern hemisphere with islands off mainland.

Then I found one that was obviously the area we were in and if we followed it carefully we could trace our way back to civilization. I took them to Mike, who looked at them carefully, and then looked up at me, and with a strange look on his face, said: 'No boats, no radio, no nothing.' And a cold shiver of fear went over me — a desperate and terrible fear of imminent danger and catastrophe from this vast sea all around us, and this tiny strip of completely bare and flat sand.

Wednesday

Very late — I dozed off to sleep and got awake after an hour or two to see a great, dark figure standing in the room. It was august, almost like a statue, and yet human. It was immensely tall, away up in the ceiling and the arms outstretched ended in a cloud of blurring. It was almost in the form of a cross, and the head seemed symbolic. I found myself gazing into great, dark eyes that looked back at me in a sort of implacable challenge. My heart was beating wildly, but I kept calm. We stared at each other, and slowly a cloud passed between us, and the room was empty as I stared at the opposite wall.

I lay for a long time, thinking and wondering about the experience, and in a mood of extreme rationality I tried to overcome my fear and understand what had happened to me.

I looked at the wall opposite the bed and there was a shadow similar to the one I had seen in the form of the great towering figure. I wondered if it was just a continuation of this, but slowly the realization dawned on me that the figure I had seen was projected from the wall because I knew that I had seen, not only the light on the figure, but a clear, luminous light *behind* the figure — in short, a light between the figure and the wall — a reflected light. What did it mean, of what significance had it for me? I simply don't yet know.

I had gone to sleep in a mood of deep distress, and had fallen asleep around 2 a.m.

16 September 1972

Today they dedicated Norman's memorial.[1] It was a terrible strain. We were on a high platform under the blazing 4 p.m. sky. I felt defenceless. I discovered that I haven't got a face, just something that registers or hides emotion.

> I could see him, I could hear him
> as we walked under the stars.
> I put out my hand but I couldn't
> touch him — that is the new way
> to learn.
> I asked him what way I should go —
> Why didn't he help me
> He said — You have never asked me
> before.
> I am asking you now.
> The way seemed to open up —
> I stood in the path — under the stars.
> It was three o'clock — the sky was
> blazing with stars.
> Suddenly the tears were pouring down
> my face — the darkest hour of the night
> and he had come.
> There was no one in the path now —
> except me — but he had come.

8 December 1972

Rilke's Ten Elegies, preface, page fourteen, marked passage, a portrait of Norman.

It was as if Norman accepted his fate that he had to be a symbol, an image, and that therefore it was important that he should be absolutely true to *himself,* and out of that whatever contribution he could make arose. Norman didn't drown himself in work — he worked like ten men, but that residual bit of himself was conscious of his family, his friends, the personal problems of his colleagues, his own spiritual and emotional growth. He was never a *desperate* man. He once talked to me about the discovery of detachment. I will never forget it. 'You will never grow up until you learn a degree of detachment in the face of your problems, a sort of inner acceptance and peace.'

He was a man passing through a stage, a stage only of a journey far longer than the span of his life. He hung over this garden for months after he died, and I am now doing a drawing of a Resurrection figure inspired by that experience.

17 December 1972

Herbert Read writes — "Far from being a playful activity — an expenditure of surplus energy, as earlier theorists have supposed, art at the dawn of human culture was a key to survival — a sharpening of faculties essential to the struggle for existence. Art, in my opinion, has remained a key to survival.'

This is in striking contrast to Freud who maintained that: "Imaginative activity is an escape.'

In either terms, the poetry of Wayne Brown[1] is a serious contribution to the writing of the West Indies. It is one more step in the brief and hazardous history of our literature, related as it is to the profound landscape painting of a wider world, where in the work of painters like Constable and Turner is evoked something of the terror of elemental nature. Wayne Brown in a single verse can do the same thing on a West Indian shore, facing out to sea:

> Even as the murmuring
> Sea unwraps and wraps its arms
> In turn around each dead, loved thing
> And the gesture may be fruitless but is made.

'Unwraps and wraps its arms.' I do not believe that a phrase like that is impulsively dashed off. I believe that the essence of W.B.'s poetry is that however inspired it may be in its beginnings, that it is also the outcome of tremendous hard work — nothing will be good enough until it has been stripped down to that last, final 'firmer grasp of reality', not scientific reality, but the reality of the original or ultimate symbol. And the introduction of 'each dead thing' in juxtaposition to the movement of the sea, introduces that element of fear which robs the wave of an appearance of protectiveness or deliberate kindness.

His poetry seems to me to be the journey, taken from intense observation and knowledge, to an expression in symbolic terms which relates to sort of cosmic consciousness.

In order to achieve this, he obviously discards, or is incapable of a sort of musical lyricism. He seems not to be concerned with the music of words so much as with their power to evoke the image. This, of course, puts him in line with what might inevitably end up in his case as great prose writing.

But 'On The Coast' is an entry which no lover of poetry can fail to pause and greet in the terms of Herbert Read's 'a firmer grasp on reality', a reality of which so vast a part of our public is so frighteningly unaware.

In the West Indian context, if we are to grow as a people, for survival surely depends on growth, then 'On The Coast' is also part of the terms of our survival, and we can't afford to ignore it.

Undated

At half past two I crept next door and looked at the first of the drawings for the Resurrection.

How much of life since September 1969 has been a fantasy?

Almost all of it.

And I am afraid now – of fantasies.

But I am afraid to be without them.

I will take something to make me sleep – another fantasy.

I looked at the scarlet velvet gown lying across the chair where I discarded it tonight.

Ownerless – possessionless – I wait for sleep.

The dogs bark – endlessly to phantom visitors.

Only the phantom visitor hangs above the garden, at a height, in a form I cannot touch. Each man, each woman, claim their own – only I embrace an empty night.

Only you – know all – you the phantom above the garden – out of reach.

January 1973

The heavyweight championship of the world[1], in the stadium that Norman built, organized in the Ministry that Doug heads, and sanctioned by Michael, Prime Minister.

I write this without pride — boxing has meant so much to our family — but I never dreamt this could happen. I felt like a small child on the great night, with the roar of the great crowd, and this magnetic youth striding through the lines of soldiers and police, so relaxed, so drawn within himself, suspended until the moment of release into action. A new young man, somehow different. Frazier, the old world — Clay, the man with vision and a purpose — and now Foreman — I wonder.

Joe Louis once said to me: 'How much did you come out at the races?'

I said, 'I won.'

He said: 'Good.'

I said: 'It was only fifty cents, though.'

He said: 'Mind how you publish that — these income tax fellows are pretty sharp you know!'

20 February 1973

Believe is a brother full of love

Believe is a friend

Friendlier than my only friend

Good air.

I asked Basil — which way shall I go — humanism or mysticism? He said — we are all human, we all have human experiences, very few have the other experience — surely it's in the nature of a command.

I wish I could be a little ill and be in bed and have time to think.

27 February 1973

'Only when man has been weaned from all that is purposeful, and does not know anything but his impulses, will the divine essence of an enchanted folly and great love be revealed to him.' — From Artur Schnabel's *My Life and Music*.

I sat for a long time with the big drawing, and it slowly came to me that there is an element of great bitterness in it. So — I repudiate it. Instead I will do a new Angel — perhaps a series of Angels. To me they are like the music of Mozart — the physical aspect of a wind blowing straight from God.

I will also do the dancers, men and women deeply and inextricably bound together by the incompletion of their own natures.

I have made peace with myself, and a new happiness is somewhere deep inside me.

24 March 1973

Reading Charles Norman's biography of Ezra Pound – can't think why it took me so long to catch up with Pound, but the book brings out what I have felt since I was a young woman, that Gaudier[1] was the one man in the world who should have lived to be old – he was bigger, more original, even more fundamental than all of them. His was an authentic surge forward – he had more to say than either Moore or Epstein – not more to say, but he was legitimate history of sculpture. Moore went off in one direction, Epstein, with the assistance of Donatello, in another – but Gaudier seemed to be carrying with him the whole new wind of formal thought.

27 March 1973

Quite extraordinary, came on this in book on Pound; page 151 said of Gaudier that he was 'the whole history of sculpture', almost exactly what I wrote on March 24th and have always felt about Gaudier.

27 April 1973

It is 6 a.m. and the studio is almost finished. I am having my coffee and trying to go back to work – just a small terracotta, it seems such a long, long time. I have become blown off my course and I'm irritable and explosive and a bit uncharitable. Funny how a woman fits herself into the routine of a man's life, and without it this anchorlessness is a constant nightmare. Norman's routine was really the shape of my life. I miss him, I miss him.

Undated (Between 27 April and 5 June 1973)

Coming back from St Ann through cattle country (though there aren't many cotton trees left) we slowed for a corner, a deep bend at the bottom of Diablo, and there was the old toad rolling his drum in the long grass in the pasture beside the road.

As I heard it, peace like a mist moved round me and I knew that we are all safe if we trust life and believe.

Believe not in what we want, but in what is expected of us. I have heard it in the dawn, in the moonlight, and I heard it again today. Why does it move me so strangely?

It is part of the Jamaica that I love, the sweet breath of cows, the boys whistling the cattle home, and dusk falling over the land.

16 June 1973

Today we met at the Little Theatre, Greta, Henry[1], Easton[2], Baugh[3] and me. We chose the wall and worked out the size and proportions to scale, seven feet by five feet ten inches.[4]

At first I have been terribly apprehensive, but now I feel the blood rise in me to accept the challenge. Not only for Greta's sake, but because I might make something very beautiful. I want to cast it in aluminium and possibly patina the background a different colour. I won't record anymore just now, as the drawings are still coming.

9 July 1973

Mandeville Hotel — Muriel and John and I drove over here yesterday. I am staying on for a couple of days to get away from the heat, and in order not to work. The temptation is always there, to work, if I am at home. Before leaving, I went down with some garden flowers to Norman's grave. The people are so kind to me when I go, and two young men spoke so warmly of Michael.

Today I feel slightly depressed — perhaps it is coming to a relaxing place and having to take sleeping tablets ... strange room, I guess. I don't like taking anything to make me sleep. I have worked out such a good routine of getting up early, making coffee and going into the studio and working, instead of worrying about how early it is!

The winning of the two elections in St Ann and East Kingston[1] has been a tremendous relief to me. I am conscious of a strange mood, chiefly in Kingston, the inevitable sobering down after the elation of the PNP win. They have had to do difficult things and the inevitable worry that it sets up in people's minds. But Michael was confident. He assured me that rural areas are firm, and of course East Kingston seems unshaken. I felt very wonderful at the swearing in, and I know Norman is somewhere, thrilled at Blake's[2] appointment. We have always been fond of Blake, in spite of the boat rocking. Actually, I think he has a strange kind of integrity; if you follow the course of his life it's there all the time.

Quite by accident I found a photo of Norman that I know is the one I want to keep with me always. I think it was taken when he was about seventy — it is strong and kind. It has helped me to make a firmer contact with him — it's strange how something to look at and hold on to can keep that contact firm. I make so many mistakes and I am so impulsive, but there is the sheet anchor as it has always been.

I have seen a bit of David Boxer recently[3] — he has an extraordinary kindness, plus I suppose a good deal of youthful arrogance — not a nasty variety, however.

He is working his way through this alignment with what I call the artists who are the prophets of doom — artists who genuinely are the expression of this period, the insecurity, the wars, the weapons of destruction, the loss of faith, the repudiation of spiritual props. And of course Freud ploughed up a sureness in surface values and left us all with emotional skeletons in our cupboards. And by that I mean the uneasy awareness that we all ought to have doubts about our apparent motives and springs of action.

This is where I cling, I literally cling to Jung. There must be a deeper, a more spiritual explanation. Jung's late books which refer to death, and something in Rilke, all seem to add up to me to a plus that this generation of artists have to discover, but they have to tear down in order to 'come upon the wonder' in their own way. I cannot go that road. I am a different generation, partly, and I don't feel it that way, and I think if I were even thirty now, I still would not see it like that.

I see it in terms of my Resurrection figure, a walking through something materialistic through a kind of telepathy, and through an understanding of sleep and dreams. I want to read everything that Kafka has written, just as I read Rilke for thirty years.

I want, too, to try to evaluate Bartok as against Shostakovich — there's something there that baffles me.

But Rilke's concept of the Angel, that is the most — and the most subtle concept I have come across in all my long life. Whenever he went to write, that would be something that is where these younger artists may be heading for, with their lacerated, tortured forms. I wonder how old Marini is; about sixty I think, so that it has been going on for a long time — but the English artists of the New Image, how old are they?

17 September 1973

Slept a little better — didn't get awake until 4 a.m. Still it isn't good enough, it's only five hours.

Anyway, I am calmer. I think I will try still to discipline myself and not take sleeping pills. I'll give it a few nights more and see if I can't get normal, longer sleep.

The carving is giving me a lot of concern[1]. I haven't got the feel of exactly how I want to handle it, and the tussle between the obligation to use the full depth of the wood and an effect that can be achieved in a bas-relief.

It's hard to get the planes, and repudiate the chip technique.

20 September 1973

I have to keep quiet and gradually make up my mind what to do with Nomdmi – it will take money to restore it, and a great effort of imagination, because in a sense it should perhaps be left intact in memory of Norman. That is where he loved, even more than Drumblair in the end, and the whole place breathes his spirit.

21 September 1973

We went over this morning, Michael and I, at 5 a.m. and made the final decision to revive Nomdmi in Norman's name, and I have decided, at whatever cost, to bring my carving up here and to work in solitude. Mike is right about that, and as I walked back into Nyumbani[1], Bev was playing that remarkable thing by Rachmaninov, 'The Bells', and on the back there was a quotation from a letter of his, 'creativity demands solitude.'

And this I daren't fail in – it shouldn't be human, and if I stay with people it will remain human and never take that step into the unknown that the drawing has so strongly made.

I am terribly afraid of this decision, but I know that the die is cast now.

In the back of my mind I am very concerned about Douglas and his case.[2] I firmly believe that there is going to be a new election and that is very hard on him – hard on all of us, really. But Doug hides what he feels, and it had upset him very badly, I know. It makes it extra hard for him to carry on his Ministerial work.

A little later Doug and Tonti[3] walked in, both very unhappy; they can't raise the lawyers' fees for the case, which will drag out the full three weeks. Doug's hands had vibrato – you see Michael's Algiers speech[4] is rebounding, his statement about Israel re trading from their military gains has started the rumour that he is anti-semitic. Very unfair, but it was unwise. In fact once again you face world fame at the price of the confidence of your own country – it's really hell. But it has been a happy two days here, and the decision to re-do Nomdmi has helped me. I've actually started and will return on Tuesday.

25 September 1973

I have been very busy and did such a good job with sleeping that I had no chance to write. When I got home to Regardless, Storm was so glad to see me and in some odd way he has changed; he was full of fun and galloped about, but he seems steadier – more independent and less clinging – he's a grand dog.

Now I have promised myself to put Nomdmi back into good order again, to get the garden going. We're having lovely rains, so a friend of Rachel's has been collecting plants from her mother who has a hill top place in St Mary, and I bought a few, and Batiste and I are going to leave at 5.30 a.m. and journey up. I think it will be great fun. And I also phoned Miss B and she is all excited about doing the curtains. It will do us all good.

I will miss carving today, but never mind, it will be there when I come back, and as I want to take it up to Nomdmi to finish later on, it's just as well to get the place warmed up. Michael and I agreed that Norman's presence is overwhelmingly strong there. It's quite extraordinary, and can be very upsetting — for years after he died I faced it at Regardless and slowly, out of it all, this Translation figure was born — in a simple way it's an attempt to come to terms with his presence. The carving gives me a great sense of peace — there is so much that is worrying just now, both on the personal front and politically. I'm trying to be positive about it all, and just to see it as a challenge — but the carving and my faith in it is a sort of rock to which I cling.

What an important thing in life — to need to be needed.

Doug and Norman and Rachel came to lunch on Sunday. Norman is growing into such a fine person — it's a great joy to watch — he's off to Barbados back to his law study.

Doug moved into a flat at Olympia and is finding it more cheerful and inexpensive than that mausoleum of a house. At night the Dwight Whylies[1] came in to dinner, and Albert, and later Doug and Tonti, on their way back from the airport, and it turned into a really happy evening.

Last night the Drumblair Dance Committee met[2] — they're a fine bunch and I think will work well this year. I find that after several years when I dreaded it, somehow the old spirit has revived in me, and as it may be a difficult year, we'll all have to work hard to pull it off.

Odel Fleming[3] rang me up — in a great mood of happiness in the work he is doing. He switched from the Children's Organization, the thing Carole[4] is in, to Operation Friendship, and this has put him into direct contact with people in every field, and he was his old self — just bubbling — but still as keen as ever on helping with the Dance. We're trying to make the Committee more businesslike, and cutting out as much as possible the 'talk'; for one I get desperately tired when they drag on after 11 p.m. as I'm working early in order to escape the sleeplessness.

27 September 1973

Today Roy Marshall[1] came in to see me, about accepting a doctorate from UWI. It's the second time he's spoken to me about it. I explained all the reasons why I thought it would be all wrong.

First, it just isn't my image. I've always functioned outside of the establishment and enjoyed it better that way.

Then it would dig up so much talk and jealousy, and maybe I couldn't quite even take the teasing!

He's a fine person, I like him very much. He stayed for over an hour. He has such a ghastly time at the University. I think he must have taken it with high hopes — it's not the students, it's the staff that have given him such a rough time as everyone knows. Racism is at a sort of peak at the moment. It was bound to come, and it has come in a lawless form — bad behaviour at cinemas, at sport — a sort of raucousness, and where the University should lead the way in at least stemming the tide with a certain impartiality, there you have a hotbed of it. The expatriate staff have a rough time and are often openly insulted. I stand by Norman's motto, 'Out of Many One People'.

Mind you, it makes it difficult to show up the selfish entrenchment of the monied and landed classes. The press has it all its own way, and oddly enough doesn't altogether reflect, in fact doesn't at all reflect, the opinions of the mass of the people. After all the abuse and the attack, Marshall doesn't say one bitter thing. You can see his mind move out from under the local scene and say over and over again: after all it is everywhere the same. But he did say two things that impressed me: 'Nowhere in the world is there a *greater* respect for individual freedom than in Jamaica. You can say what you like here and no one locks you up. I love this quality.' And later he said: 'Munro and Beckford have been the bane of my life, but God forbid that the day should ever come when government intervened.'

Doug dashed in this evening. His case looks a bit better today. Arthur Williams, I imagine, is stubborn and intellectually stupid, but is a very near to the people sort of man. Doug, who has a great feel for this sort of thing, was interesting about it, and humorous, and under far less strain.

It's a subject that has always fascinated me — what does and what doesn't tick in an election. Everyone is worked up to fever pitch and the old subconscious and the older collective unconscious are very busy! You can beat your guts out, selling a slogan, and just a whisper of something else and the whole place is seething with excitement.

'Russian ships', hostile ships on the horizon, and the panic runs like a bush fire.

Here, in the excitement, Williams seems to have got off with some sort of phrase: 'Don't use guns or knives but plus out Manley with the voting sheet and vote for the bell.'

Which is what everyone did, marked out Doug's name and X for the bell, and then it spread further and they marked out Williams' name from the other camp and voted for Doug, and so you got enough spoilt votes to confuse the whole pattern. I don't believe that Williams is that stupid. I think somehow that phrase came from him in a moment of heat and just spread like mad. That you could defeat a man by digging your pencil in anger across his name, instead of voting in the normal way!

Harry[2] came in later on – he is so much calmer for his trip to California and his arm seems to be coming on. He and Flo have fallen in love with California. And then Dossie[3] and Dorothea Carberry came in and Dossie talked about Doug's case. I like those two – Dorothea is a really charming person and Dossie is like family – he spent the holidays with us sometimes as a boy. Both Doug and Michael like him.

7 October 1973

Last night I handed out the Manley Award for sport at the Stadium. There was a vast crowd, thirty thousand, and a wonderful programme of sporting events, people even from Russia and Kenya. George Headley[1] won it – it was a tremendously popular choice.

I said to him: 'George, aren't you scared, I'm terrified to speak to such a vast crowd.'

And he said: 'When you're playing cricket you never see the crowd.'

10 October 1973

5 a.m. Yesterday was full – we left at 5.30 a.m. to continue gardening and cleaning up at Nomdmi: Miss B., Batiste and I.

When the October rain, which hasn't yet been as heavy as it should be, is over, I may take the Translation figure[1] up. I'm not sure, as I don't want to get too intense over it.

Have just written the Commonwealth Institute[2] – not sure I really want to give a show, and would only do it if it were a very comprehensive one – I need advice.

26 October 1973

The thing I remember most about my first year in Jamaica, other than the intense excitement I felt over Norman's start of a career – how we loved that and the rising confidence as it became apparent that he was making an impression – all the new people and sights and sounds.

But the dawn, I found the dawn again. Six years in London – with all its life and experience – but I never saw the dawn, and as a child in Cornwall, it was the oft-recurring miracle of my life.

So I got up at dawn and went riding, or on shooting parties, or to watch racehorses train. Then I remember the smell of logwood blossom, and in the dry weather the aromatic smell of dry earth and seymour grass. A Jamaican dawn is something special, because all the tropical flowers give off an aura of differing scents. All these things were new and were quickly absorbed and loved.

I don't remember very many people – there was a horse and buggy which by the second year had given place to a car. There were two older people, a doctor and his wife, that we played bridge with – and then slowly my health began to give way. Young Douglas by now was a much tougher baby, with all the sunshine and a nice old nurse who helped with lots of things.

I picked up malaria and completely lost my appetite. I remember I used to live on Nestlés milk and my weight went down to ninety-seven pounds, and I'm five feet eight. Meanwhile Norman was getting fitter, stronger and more confident every day and money was beginning to come in. My kidneys started to play up, and although I loved Jamaica and wept to go, he advised me to take Doug and go back to England for a month or two, to try to get rid of the malaria and to find an appetite again.

It was awful to go – leave Norman, leave home, and go back with a sense of failure – but we went – and on the way we ran into a storm.

November 1973

Oh what a day it has been – Michael came hurtling over with a bottle of wine to see the carving and to show me the synopsis of his new book.[1] It doesn't tire him to write, it's just the stimulus that his passion for life needs – I love good talk, like racehorses going – I miss it so much – with the tall carving standing over us and the bottle of wine.

And Opus III a miracle at night.

Talking with Michael is like going down a water chute and finding yourself in the same swimming pool, very much at the deep end.

I'm going around looking haggard and shaken.

30 November 1973

On the 27th Michael had the press conference for his book's release here, *Politics of Change*. It was a large turnout: including photographers, thirty. Bev came looking calm and lovely, and Easton and Corina[1] set the scene.

I unfortunately was placed beside him on the other side of Bev, under the bright TV light. I would have liked to have been at the back and been able to watch unobserved.

What I was impressed with — Michael refused to turn it into a cricket match. If ever he used the word involvement in action, it was at that conference. When the questions came, he very quietly — the whole thing was very quiet — went into them, drawing the questioner with him. It was very remarkable, so that after an hour it became almost a mutual conferring. I liked it very much. Two JLP reporters he handled very well — I think for the 'Voice'. Joe McPherson[2] tended to lead him off the subject of the book on to government policy — particularly land. M. could have legitimately refused, but he didn't, he simply used the opportunity to expound the policy.

Afterwards Aimee Webster said to me: 'What a way you always find yourself in the heart of things — all your adult life, at least. *You* should write a book.' And I looked back over the years and thought in very truth — and how I should have kept a practical day-to-day diary instead of just doing as I have done — recorded my own vague search for truth. There is so little time left — I realized that last month when I got flu etc., etc., and that night when once again I got those terrible pains around my heart. If there is just time enough to be kind to people!

Sylvia Foot wrote me that she had walked on Kit Hill — and there was the word staring at me out of the page, and a lifetime rolled away — Kit Hill and Brown Willy — Cornwall.

2 January 1974

6 a.m. Last night Mike and Basil were here; it was an interesting evening and the talk flowed. After I had gone to bed I lay for a little while and thought. How life gets itself into pockets, into ravines — and how difficult it can be to see the broad pattern.

I had quite a little while — in my own head — sloughing off the portcullis and the moat.

So the oil crisis is here. In some odd way, it's something like this perhaps we need, something that throws us into the melting pot where we suffer with the rest of the world — daylight saving — a demand that we yield from our entrenched habits of thought and ways of life. The farmers are happy — this I believe to be true — and I hope I am not wrong. But in spite of all the storms I sense a feeling that they don't want anyone else but Michael to lead them at this time.

2 March 1974

Came through the local government elections very well — the violence mostly confined to Kingston — not good, but not too bad. Very disappointed over result of Doug's case — can't understand why it was based on count, because it had been counted, is it three or four times, and D. had won every other time. But to have held it up for two years was a pretty inefficient business. Anyway, they say the Chief Justice is honest and a good lawyer — so that's that.

It was a shock but he took it very well. Doug worries beforehand, but in a crisis of this nature he is a real man. I feel very proud of him and he and Michael got on so well. Michael has grown and he has had such a series of problems, the fuel crisis topping everything — and in it all he has kept in touch with us all as a family in a wonderful way. Bev and her baby have delighted everyone. It's a gorgeous baby, there's no doubt there, and she is a great girl — strong and growing in confidence.

Michael has remarkable intuitiveness — it's a quality that can cause one to make mistakes, but in the long run it is essential in leadership.

Ra is a great comfort to me too — she is surely growing — she went through so much in her marriage, such an unbelievably difficult experience — we all watched with real grief. But she is strong in an insecure, nervy sort of way, and that child is the root of her life. Lovely kid too. But when things go wrong she never forgets me.

Heavens, I am lucky to have a wonderful family, because I know I am a difficult person. I must stop now and write to young Norman.

25 March 1974

Tonight, this night of March 25, with the Andante of Schubert's A Major Sonata stealing out into the night, I swear all I have of passion, all I have of love, I will pour into a message of faith as I carve.

Nothing else really matters now — I have lived too long.

But there is reason to hope and reason to love.

As the sparks fly upwards it is there.

22 April 1974

There, I have put almost the last tool on the figure of 'Journey' — there is the enveloping flame to do now — probably another two weeks. What a journey it has been. I think I have been the whole gamut of experience over it. Somehow I knew at the start that this was an effort that was truly beyond me. There were so many battles.

One, the struggle between the concept of a Resurrection figure, with all the glory and the triumph that that involved — the sense of arrival, radiance.

And my — to me — strange concept that I met that night in the garden, under the blazing stars — the sense of movement, going on-ness — the sense in very truth of a journey. It has entirely revolutionized my concept of death. I mightn't like the actual process, but I'm not afraid of death anymore. I couldn't understand so many things about the drawing, but it has proved valid the whole way — at least a root like inspiration.

And then it is not easy to carve a movement out of life. The feet still in this world and slowly moving up to a more cloudy and abstract top. I carved and recarved the whole thing all over — dozens of times — slowly inching the way towards this conviction that kept coming and going in my mind. I was ill once or twice, luckily, as it gave me time to think.

Now, all I can say is — I tried, I put everything I had into it — one night it was so bad I prayed and called on Norman to guide my hands — to take charge. As I look back I can't believe that I lived through all that.

Michael was so good — he would drop anything and come and help — and Phillip[1] too gave me confidence, faith in myself.

Mike Smith helped to keep me steady and spotted the fact that I had lost sight of that strange angle of the head and neck, that it was part of the movement away, that an upright head evoked the idea of arrival, and that this had not and would never arrive. The Journey goes on. I used the full depth of the wood willy nilly. I feel a little humble tonight that I was given the strength to stay my Journey to the end. It wouldn't hurt to die now.

And Schubert — I found Schubert — what music — I have a stack of records and I read about him and every night, last thing, I would play over and over the little Andante in the A Major Sonata. But the great Quintet 'C' and the Octet, but mostly the first.

Scottie came in and he said: 'But Edna it is the saddest carving in the whole world.' So tonight I will play my Schubert and know that tomorrow at 5.30 a.m., pitch dark, I will get up and make my coffee and start on the flame, but I have exhausted completely anything I can do about the figure.

Thank you God — thank you Norman and Michael, you believed. Even little Rachel hoped for me, and Phillip.

On another note — today it would seem that they have cracked open the gun-swop ganja racket.[2] Oh God I hope they have — we're all so weary of this sinister cloud that hangs over all our lives, rich and poor alike.

Tomorrow, too, Rachel's divorce comes up — poor little soul, she's scared of the court appearance, but more than all, the fear of the custody of Drum — he means her whole life to her. Tonight I say a little prayer.

Undated (after 22 April)

It's been wonderful getting the garden perked up again, with a nice little grandson of Blanche's. John B. drove me up, he has taken this shocking trumped-up crisis over the headmastership so well.[1]

Church people can let themselves down pretty badly — Bishop and all. You see — the act of faith that makes a man believe is one thing, but the moral fibre that decent, forthright, honest behaviour demands, is quite a different business, and so few of them have it. That chap Huddleston who Phillip brought to see me, that was, or rather *is*, a man — a real man — and out of his face pours a sort of radiance.

All my life I've loathed spiritualism, table rappings, contacts with the dead — the whole works — so I almost hesitate to record the fact that once again I have had the conviction that I was in direct contact with Norman. I was reading on the verandah and the sun was going down the way it does like a great fire opal. I was quite calm, and then it was as if I heard a little crying — and when I looked up I knew that it was my little studio, 'Minni', that was crying — so I went down to look, and there it was full of old junk, wheel barrows, shovels, fertilizer, any old rubbish too. The bed was dirty and dishevelled — I sat on the table — it was fairly dark in there and I wept. All the past came pouring over me — the days we had our little bunks in there and pump lamps, and washed in water from the drums outside. Days when we solemnly locked up Nomdmi and went down there to sleep to be near the sound of the pines.

And then it came to me this terrible presentiment I had — that there is a bad year ahead of me — especially August. Just full of fear and pain and insecurity. I hadn't been thinking of it — it just poured back over me. Perhaps partly an expression of the months of fatigue and worry, public and personal.

I let it wash over me — and then suddenly there was Norman — the room was full of him — just like the night on the path at Regardless. *That* time he was remote and warning me. This time it was a gesture of pure comfort — it was the happiest experience I have ever had.

I think perhaps he felt I had earned it because I had toiled so hard over the 'Journey' — no one will ever know how hard. I remember the night when I was working *late* at night and in despair I said aloud: 'I can't do it Norman — I can't — guide my hands — guide my hands,' when I was working on that difficult transition area — over the cage of the ribs. But this time he came and comforted me — it's no good anyone saying I imagined it — so what — suppose I did — what made that flash of imagination come with such total surprise — and what gave me that slow dawning sense of happiness and security, and the sense of his being there. Whatever it was, it was just as real as the rest of the day today — and I woke so happy this morning. I feel stronger — I feel saner.

Anyway I went in today and I completely cleaned out Minni, and from now on it will be locked — as it has always been. But I haven't inconvenienced anyone. I've cleared out the top tool room and everything will be stored there from now on — just as Norman would have done.

I think when I was weeping, he said: 'You have me, you know.' That is what he did say.

Goodnight — time to go back to Mr Blake.[2]
'The subconscious mind which sometimes presents us with mental pictures more vivid than the retina itself can present, is a world of reality where our primal emotions of love and fear and hope work like a sea.' Wickstead — in 1940.

26 April 1974

There! What a week fighting every step of the way with the carving. A ghastly night, full of disappointment. It's not a work of art at all, and I had hoped to get somewhere and find something, something radiant, serene, something that would give courage and peace.

But no — there is that face. The Journey goes on — the same challenges — the same failures or abilities to face up. What has all that to do with art? Vermeer and the peace of his interiors — so utterly at peace. Why do I have to travel this road?

Douglas said it frightened him: 'It is like the Exorcist.' And there I stood trembling — I ran out of the studio — I repudiated the whole experience, but saw him peacefully to his car.

I talked to Muriel in the morning.

But what did Norman say to me on the path that night — wasn't it just this — no reprieve — no escape — only 'the endless glory of the endless going' — that's a quote from me thirty years ago — but this face has no glory, only the endless going.

14 May 1974 — Nomdmi

'With all his vision Blake never deserts the earth. We miss all the virtue of his mighty sanity if we miss this fact. Vision did not transport him to another world. It enlightened him to see this one in its glory.' Wickstead — in a letter to Max Plowman.

'It is the very same thing that Wordworth has to say, indeed, as Shakespeare had to say and perhaps as all supreme genius has to say: ...' (Wickstead, continuing).

It's marvellous to get back to old Blake again, what a man, what a man. Each time I come back, I get deeper into him. I haven't read all the vast number of experts, but Wickstead stands the test of time. He's so direct, so tolerant, and not at all an idolater! And God knows Blake takes a bit of advocacy sometimes!!

Gun courts, ganja and all the vast problems of this year 1974 seem far away for a little while. Oh, I was tired – tired beyond belief – so although I have a new work lightly sketched out, I'm not allowing it to grip me, but trying to dream and work hard in the garden and walk when it is all over, feel tired and ready for bed. I had dinner with Bev and Michael at Nyumbani – they are people of *such* courage. I was still tired and shaky – could hardly make the hill, but we soon all cheered up and Michael played Berlioz, who I don't know at all.

8 June 1974

The relief for the LTM[1]. Put the wood horizontally – it will gain an added sense of size – the walls of the theatre are too high to compete with if the wood goes up vertical – it is only 6 ft 7 ins. It is the width that is within normal visual range.

Have finally decided on the theme – with the Angel between two human heads. An African mask between two – a man and a woman. Jamaican. In a sense a variation on the expulsion theme. To be driven from Eden – isn't it just another life, birth, death, birth cycle again? Eden, the mother's womb – and man and woman ejected into another life from which one day they will depart.

There are no angels in African mythology, clearly – but it is *all* supernatural, to put it crudely. But this dispenses with the need for wings. This new book by Franco Monti uses colour and creates or recreates the arrival of the elemental fear, mystery, secrecy which is the impelling force of African art. The mask is fear – that it also inspires is another matter.

But the serpent?

The snake, the symbol of the Roman God of medicine and a symbol of the medical profession.

2 July 1974

It's a difficult thing to put into words and I admit that *Journey to Ixtlan* has given my mind a shove into a direction that I might have fumbled around for the rest of my life, and never taken the step forward.

Twice now – at a moment of spiritual crisis – I have been so near to Norman that it was almost tangible.

The first time on the path that night two years ago – the second up at Nomdmi, in Minni, when he filled the room, and I felt that he put his arms around me and the words were there − not spoken, felt − 'You have me' − so full of comfort − but a comfort that one had to earn by taking a certain road. A road where one could see the truth and could wait for the truth to happen, without attempting to give it a direction. An entirely empty and useless thing to do.

So one has to stay near these two memories and allow them to dictate a certain validity of experience and behaviour.

And then − I was playing Bartok − it was somewhere around midday and slowly I became aware that light and shadow seemed to be flowing from the music − sweeping across the garden and out over the valley. At first I thought it was a cloud effect − it could have been sweeping across the sun − but when I stopped and thought about it, it seemed to stop too and then when I went back to the music, there it was again.

Perhaps an illusion − but the experiences with Norman were not illusions and this seemed to belong to the same world. I know that whatever it was, I will always remember it. I have a new record of the same work coming − Michael is bringing it − and it will be interesting to play it in town on the big gramophone and see what effect it has on me. This experience was at Nomdmi on my little portable machine.

3 July 1974

This evening, just after the sun went down, I was standing on the patio and a pale grey dove flew on to the garden bench about two yards away from me and stood looking up at me. It had a ring of darker feathers around its neck.

It was so quiet and gentle and quite unafraid − we stood looking at each other for a few minutes and Storm came out of the house and he too stood, but very tense, and looked at her and then he made a sudden spring and she flew away.

Later that night Paul[1] and Ra came in − he had taken her out to dinner − they were very happy and talked of having a baby.

There is that place on the garden path where Norman seems to be − standing like the evening star − no, not standing − hovering.

2 October 1974

Been to Germany and England and a very creative visit.

23 November 1974

11.30 p.m. Have taken the decision to stop drinking any alcohol until Xmas Day.

Today I started the big relief for the LTM.

I am certain that there is a kind of approach to people and life that should be sustained. A drink sometimes can cause a strange break in the continuity of one's consciousness — it is confusing — so let me try this.

January 1975

So I tore off the head of Adam[1] in a wild mood and then I waited — and working very late at night, I was very scared with the studio door open behind me. I put him back — with all the strength I had and all the love, and now it doesn't matter anymore what anyone says — that is my Adam, and for the first time I understand the story of Pygmalion — there in the cold, wet clay is someone I love. Perhaps it will be destroyed in the casting — clay is so perishable. But I have known a moment of great love that no one can take from me, and a moment of creation that passes all understanding.

Some deep nerve of birth saved him from the shallow platitude, some moment when that black night was on me — weeks ago — when defeat and failure left me defenceless and alone, and something from the heart of my forefathers refused to die —

Oh, Adam, my Adam.

8 February 1975

So — the Rainbow Serpent is finished and today the caster, Colin Jones, comes from London. I think we will end up in fibreglass, and that's an interesting material to be using — and at last I will be trying a method that does not involve shipping abroad and paying a fortune for a final cast. A lot depends on this young man. He is not a professional caster — I believe he's a ceramist — but a person who has worked in all sorts of media and methods. I ask my friends to say a lot of Hail Marys!

But I've lived through a big effort with, for me, an astonishing new confidence and calm. I've written the story of how this came about and I've tried to be faithful to that experience, so perhaps that will continue to the end.

Today we go to the plane to meet him.

So much is happening on the political front — a bit shattering sometimes. The violence, particularly, as Seaga stepped into the leadership of the JLP; all the guns are barking again, and the knives too.

For the first two years, it seemed almost like a one-party country — so many of the reforms were put through, more or less unopposed. Now everything is on the surface — all the opposition of class and privilege.

The problem is to get the civil service involved, without antagonizing them.

There is no doubt that there are men and women devoted to the welfare of the country, but there is no doubt that as a body they are shot through with a sort of inertia, that the service is just a method of livelihood. And yet there is an urgency attached to the word efficiency, that stems from the desperate needs those at the bottom of the economic and social ladder bring to any leader in this year 1975.

If one can keep calm, keep faith, spread confidence in however small a way, amongst the little group with whom one comes in contact. That's the only contribution one can make.

Even in one's opinion, the stage, the scene changes so swiftly that to offer advice would be a sort of madness. Perhaps the most one could do would be to let people talk, blow up, and say very, very little.

Right in my circle at the moment, marriage seems to be going through a terribly difficult patch.

Women's Year — rings a happy warm note — like a birthday, a well-earned celebration, recognition.

Women's Lib — seems cold and makes men a little revengeful — as if it dries up all the quality of protectiveness and gallantry; makes them try less hard to make the man/woman relationship work. And if you talk to the women who are involved, somewhere, all the time, there seems to be some unfortunate love grouse which is, after all, an entirely different thing. Anyway, there is no turning back now, of that I am sure. And the blonde Mrs Thatcher bounces on to the scene!

So, China[1] — I feel very calm and happy — surely even in the new China there must still be something of the old East, and to see the reaction to the new experiments must be a great experience.

Germany[2] gave me back my health and confidence — I was tremendously stimulated and inspired. To have built that country back in so greatly brief a time is astounding. They are a cultured and efficient people, and the S. Germans are wonderful — *Munich!*

Berlin is an august and mysterious city.

22 April 1975

Yesterday the 'Rainbow Serpent' was unveiled. I felt steady and sure of it. People were warm and kind — I think on the whole it was well received. Looking back it was a great and a happy adventure. The casting had some formidable problems — the usual beastly plaster — and Colin became impatient. The students were very good and it was a remarkable experience.

I cracked up in the end health-wise: not I think from overwork or strain from work, but because of a sudden loss of faith in an important friend. I think it's better to put it on paper in order to be objective about it. One builds these odd creatures in one's mind – endows them with all the dream qualities, and then, presto, they disentangle themselves from the unreality – and one is left in a state bordering on shock.

All this left me feeling ill – breathless, terrible problem with breathing – even at night waking out of sleep, and desperately tired and lacking in energy.

So now – here we go to get to the bottom of it – sort it out and find faith and vitality again, because I believe that those two are inextricably bound up together.

So back I go to a day-to-day entry, keeping a record of a climb back to an inner harmony – and from that will come a return of health because I *must* do my "Creation"[1], I simply must.

It's a strange thing, but rest doesn't do me the slightest good – it is the search that keeps me alive and well.

23 April 1975

Just going to Jamaica House where Barry[1] is presenting his portrait of Bev. I don't know what he has turned out – but I think that the one Susan Alexander[2] has done is utterly lovely. The circle of the chair, the greenery, and Bev sitting serenely in the centre of it – an excellent likeness too.

The breathing is coming on, I slept late this morning. The fear of it is going, which helps, and it is, I am sure, the result of a mistake I made years ago when I was afraid to walk alone without Norman, and so I found a series of people, two really, to cling to – and they proved human and left me in a greater panic.

I believe if through control and calmness I find harmony and wholeness inside, I will be able to unleash incredible energy to do 'Creation'. But it need not have that note of desperation in it. Somehow the speed of work and the energy of the top figure should be able to unite, with no fatigued exhaustion.

How wonderful to be free, to know that it is no longer even truthful to hanker and long for help – to no longer waste one's energies in a fantasy that only brings pain. Slowly I will think my way into this, and bend all my strength, my energy, to fulfill a great effort. Perhaps my first great – truly great – effort.

When I was young I was so bold in my use of distortion and then I became afraid – the public, Jamaica. Looking back I know I did not fulfill my promise – the odds were too great, and faults of my own temperament. Now there is a chance – now if I can look life and myself squarely in the face.

I went up to Nomdmi – and I went into Minni where Mike had fixed the cupboard and the shelves. It was dusty, but shadowy and cool. I took a bit of chalk which had been discarded and without stopping to think, I drew the

Creator on the cupboard door, trying to free it from naturalism. It has to be powerful but not clumsy – abstracted.

And Adam – back at Adam, the man in my present life – they must swing in an oral movement – but Adam has to be distorted to still look part of the earth – *please God!*

Later – moving through the day – still breathless but more cheerful and able to look back at the recent past and near escape of an illness with actually a shade of detachment. Went to Jamaica House to see the portrait unveiled – not as good as Susan's, but had a certain quality.

Went to the dressmaker – getting ready for the Queen's visit.

Did a bit of work on the second Serpent[3], bit of a chore working on it for the second time – another week, I fancy.

Going to Devon House to set up selection committee for purchases.[4]

Wonderful no longer afraid of an evening alone – listening to music and reading – nursing back, nursing back to health for the sake of 'Creation'. God I had become rocky, too many shocks.

Still anxious to know what to do about Muriel whilst I'm in China, she's so frail – it breaks my heart. Something may turn up.

23 April 1975

Had a shocking night coughing and unable to sleep – wrote to Wayne – am convinced that this is psychosomatic, so I am tracing deep down inside myself to eradicate resentment and unforgiveness, to feel whole and at peace with life. I will try today to be serene, also it's much too early to be thinking of future work – relax and let the world go by –

24 April 1975

Woke this morning after a long and normal sleep, feeling utterly happy that the second Serpent is at last finished. But not only that – free, free of the myth that has haunted me for over a year – realizing that I had projected that story into my own life, and was confusing and destroying many relationships in an effort to capture something. In the end I fell in love with my own Adam, and sublimated it in the work – like Pygmalion.

Now I know I will get well. I feel truly happy having broken the bonds that tied me to the work. Greta and Henry[1] have been utterly wonderful throughout the entire thing. There must be a great love between them, whatever the ups and downs – it's all there in the Adam and Eve. They have been thoughtful, efficient, comprehending and utterly darling to work for – it's been a joy – and they've volunteered an advance of three thousand dollars on the second Serpent, which I will dash around to my dear Mr Fung[2] who is beginning to look at me in a disapproving way.

I'm living madly beyond my means – and what to do, to do!

Sunday, 18 May 1975 – Shensi[1]

As a tribute to my obvious love of Art, the Chinese let me see these giant terracottas unpacked. We were having tea, and looking pleased and mysterious, they told me they had a surprise for me. We followed them to a door, which I was told to open after a little speech in which they declared: 'You are the first Westerner to see what you will behold, and certainly the first woman Westerner.' We went in and there they were unpacking from mountains of sawdust these great sculptures – masterpieces! There was a long, narrow box and they said, 'Open it,' and in ancient velvet lay a silver handled sword. I felt that it was the great moment of my life. The horses! life size, and soldiers, six thousand of them in all – the Emperor must have slept the sleep of death feeling very safe! What a great people!

12 July 1975

I have just read the account today of Barbara Hepworth's death. 'The greatest woman artist in the world.' It's true in a way – perhaps the most devoted, dedicated – but something a little cold – but all glory to her, and to her name and fame.

I'm alone. Albert[1] was to have come in to supper but he hasn't turned up – very unlike him – and my family don't often think of me as human and needing comfort, except for Rachel. Anyway, let me think of China. I have never recorded anything, and yet it was such a tremendous challenge. Let me put on the gramophone and quietly try to recall something of it. I should have gone alone, I know that now, but they wouldn't hear of it. And no one is very interested. It's odd too, the honorary award hasn't drawn a comment, except from Swaby[2], who had won the Manley Award and wrote a warm letter about both events.

Just out of hospital – missing the quiet efficiency, not even Adinah or Batiste are here.

So China – I learnt such strange personal things there – it nearly finished off my friendship with Mike. I got near to Doug in a way, perhaps nearer than I have ever been, but the last two nights when I was so ill, actually coughing blood, he left me to battle through alone. Mike stayed and helped me with blankets to combat the fever and ague. I was half conscious only.

So I came back with 'Creation' to do, and the "Horsemen"[3], and then, 'Nunc Dimittis'.

I like loneliness — it's a great preparation.

So, China — all the purpose, that faith, that drive, that endless toil. That *discipline* — all those thousands of bicycles without lights and the great square in Peking where Mao talked to his people.

Coming home late at night in the dusk and lines of workers still up to their knees in water, planting the rice, as the wheat nearby is being harvested. The faces of the people on the Communes, how long will it last? It's the crest of the wave. Going over the Children's Palace and the little boy who led me, stopping every now and then to blow on his little hand because it was hot and sweating, and he said: 'You see this once belonged to a British capitalist and only five people lived here, and now it's so big there are two thousand people here.'

The music somehow stirred me. Not the Western stuff that is being done for films and export, but the concert at the Minorities Institute. An orchestra of about forty pieces, a mixture of old Chinese instruments and some Western violas and basses etc.

Do I want to write about China anymore? I know deep down what I think. As of this moment, they undoubtedly are the greatest potential force in the world, but will they go the way of mud-slinging nationalism — the virulence of the attack on Russia goes too far in sheer unparliamentary language. Who is trying to please the US and who is trying to hold the Third World — that's the great open sesame, Third World.

Michael is in Cuba right now, receiving a tumultuous welcome — but China hates Cuba, and of Russia and China, I think I pick China. Perhaps this won't alway be so, but as of now, Mao leaves his touch on things, and there's a Chinese calmness and down-to-earth humanity even in the brain-washing. The Russians are different. Oh, let me stop and listen to music — if I can just feel well enough to get back to work.

And I can do it on my own two feet with no help from anyone — just my own hands. No I am not depressed, I am just facing the future — such as it is — in the terms that present themselves.

I have been led away by what seemed such endlessly comforting support — it was a mistake — I wonder why. A lifetime of close love and companionship, and somehow one is searching, searching, and the world is full of people who will make use of one, steal one's creativity and leave one that much weaker — that much drier.

The lesson of walking alone — that's what Scottie said. As the end comes near one learns to walk alone, because through that door one will surely pass alone. And yet I don't think I'm afraid. I'm glad I've kept this diary so free of politics — the changing scene should only be recorded by very experienced minds — the pattern changes so swiftly, and one is left holding on to the wrong end of the stick or the bone or whatever you want to call it.

Just then I realized I should go and take Muriel's dog for a walk at nine-thirty. It was damp and cold and I called to the police to come with me – as usual they had vanished, gone off on their own, so I put on a wrap to go alone. And then I thought I'd call Tangie, my beloved little next-door neighbour. She's a highly trained nurse, so we talked of my illness and many things, and all of a sudden I felt better. She's so warm and practical, and yet infinitely wise and understanding.

So I finished the talk, and put on a warm wrap and took Muriel's little dog for a walk, coming back feeling much better! It was 10 p.m. so I shared some chicken etc., with Storm and as it's going on for 11 p.m., I'm going to bed full of dope for sleep and dope for recovery and my own particular brand of utter optimism.

On Monday I'll head off for Nomdmi. We had at least an inch of rain, oh glory be, and everywhere smells so sweet.

Twelve midnight. I feel wonderful again, full of confidence. Only I think that Albert behaved badly, he could have let me know he wasn't coming and I could have organized something else. However, I expect there is a plausible explanation – *cherchez la femme*.

14 July 1975

Today has been lovely – John came in from jogging and we had breakfast and then off he went, and then it started to rain and Norman Jnr.[1] dashed in and looked hopefully for lunch, so we carved up a cold chicken and he had a gin and we had a marvellous talk. He said: 'Don't be hurt, but you know for the first time in my life I miss Pardi. I do an opinion. I've done eighteen now, and all of a sudden I think of Pardi, and I spend another two days on it, and even then I don't feel satisfied. They tell me it's a weakness, I shouldn't think of Pardi, but somehow it drives me on, and I think how marvellous it would be if I could sit and talk and argue with him. Because he was a great lawyer. Mardi, I've never told anyone this –' So we talked about the great ancestors, of how I believed in heritage and that in the great old totem poles there were images, and the ancestor of law must have been a powerful image, a powerful force. It was a magic two hours with the seeded rain pouring outside.

His mother is dying and he tries so hard to help – in his hidden, tough way. He finally left after I heard about how he collapsed when he got home from law school and met her. He is behaving so well, poor kid.

And Rachel had pulled Norman together by saying: 'Norman, I wrote you that she was dying and you didn't listen – now you see for yourself – well, we all have to meet our Waterloo, and now you've met yours.' She knows a lot about Waterloo, poor kid, with all she went through with her first marriage.

Then Norman and Roy[2] turned up for supper and we carved up some corned beef. It was such a lovely day, for I wasn't feeling too well with all the Cortisone and Ventolin inside me, and still coughing – and Greta came in too, full of flowers and gorgeous brown bread. Greta and Henry have been very close since 'The Serpent'. I hope I sell the second one soon as the bank is a bit overdrawn.

What would I do without people – the doctor wanted me to go to the hills after I came out of hospital – but it's been raining and people drop in and it makes the day so full and happy.

Hearne[3] comes in sometimes, and Ian[4], and they're so stimulating, and Marcella[5]. I'm reading a lot, still on China; they would let me go back if I wanted to, but perhaps India instead. Poor Indira! but I think she's right – if she stepped down who, but who, would take up the reins in that storm-tossed confusion. She was here for the Commonwealth Conference and really stole the show. Quite a woman. I think Bev got to get a glimpse behind the screen. Bev is good with people and she's such an honest person – she is growing.

Rachel was deeply moved and committed by Cuba – so is Michael. It's dynamite, but who knows.

There's a brilliant article by Toynbee on China in *Horizon* – I showed it to Hearne. China's stumbling block may be her nationalism, and of course she wants the safety over those little strategic American-dominated islands, but friendship with America now can lose her the faith of the whole Third World. Oddly enough, the Chinese Ambassador is coming to see me tomorrow at 10 a.m., and I'm just wondering?

It's strange I suffered so terribly over that fibreglass allergy. It was a *ghastly* experience, and yet my mind is burrowing behind it to know what psychosomatic condition set it off – and lying in the long chair watching the garden, it flashed into my mind that I had been suffering for at least two years from a deep-seated resentment, and now I know – to write it, or not write it – I'm not *sure*.

Let's get some coffee, it's 4 a.m.

5 a.m. Had the coffee – if I keep near Norman he will help me through the dead resentment. (...)[6] – they didn't understand – maybe I didn't understand – but one can't be swamped in other people's drownings when you are water-logged and going down yourself.

Perhaps I am selfish, but God how I needed help and friendship – John understood and even little Carole – 6–11, 6–11 and no car comes home.

Rachel had a long and stimulating talk with Castro on the plane – God, how that girl grows!

Castro said: 'Your father is trying to do it the *hard* way – I hope he succeeds.'

17 July 1975

Copy of letter to **Gleaner** — not public.
Dear Sir,
I know I owe a big bill which I am going to pay you as soon as I get myself straightened out — because I am basically fairly honest.

But I think it's HORRID of you to stop sending my *Gleaner* for over two months. I wouldn't even know if my own death notice had been suitably placed.

With NO kind regards,
Yours,
Edna Manley

9 August 1975

3 a.m. So the decision has been taken and I won't go to England with the show[1]. Osmond Watson[2] might be a good person to send in my place — I trust him and he's a fine carver.

When I was ill with that chest business, I came to terms with what little time I have left. The need to be honest every step of the way.

Read an article on Sartre this evening. Sartre at seventy, almost completely blind.

Very worried over Muriel, who is desperately depressed over her loss of memory and lack of ability to walk strongly. Flashes of anger and then an obvious attempt to be cheerful. The relationship with May[3] aggravates everything, and they won't be parted. Michael advises — try to keep conversation on an intellectually stimulating plane, and don't show that you notice the slips of memory. Aub[4] is the one person, and Cynthia, to a lesser degree, who seems to be able to produce a more serene mood and also a certain confidence about trying to be well.

29 November 1975

Well, back at work at last and feeling remarkably well. Not quite as tough as I'd like to be, but maybe it is coming back slowly.

I learnt such wisdom over handling one's health, and the philosophy I picked up from Dr Khouri[1] — he's a remarkable person. And this business of breathing with rhythm and control, you learn a lot about your reactions from it, of how under stress or work breathing can become superficial, shallow, almost non-existent, and so trouble builds up. I enjoy the exercises enormously — they seem to put me in tune with life; and in a crisis — and God knows there have been plenty of those — if one but remembers, and takes over one's breathing again, a sort of calmness, a detachment takes charge, and the problems don't seem quite as threatening.

The political scene has changed with lightning speed. The oligarchy are on the march, the merchants, and of course there's the brain drain, the trek away of the professional people.[2] It all runs true to type. It's difficult to know what even to think when one's friends go. There's freedom and there's also cowardice, selfishness, greed, and yet they are still the people you have loved and trusted. They haven't changed, it's just that you never really knew them. Odd this business of knowing and yet not knowing people. You each of you turn a section of yourself to your friends, rather like the tip of an iceberg, but the real bulk of the person is hidden, and then the pressures mount, and everyone sees everyone else, for the first time measured by the circumstances that prevail, and the friendship fades – like a ship moving over the horizon – leaving a trail of bewildered memories, and a series of question marks like sheep passing through a narrow gate, halting to be numbered.

In 1938 socialism was a bomb, in 1975 it *is* a bomb.

Let's make no comment and call no names, but the scene changed so little, only now the USA interferes, then England cracked the whip – damn funny really.

On the art front – I'm wrestling with materials, and here, strangely enough, the picture is that of 1924 with casting and bronzing problems[3]. 'Journey' is my final wood carving. Clay, which was my first love, I'm obsessed with again. Sometimes working, I think I'm back at St Martins, the happiness is so intense. The plastic moving quality, the chance for infinite change – my first real love, and leaving a lifetime of wood and stone carving feels very like a decently arranged and satisfying divorce, that has been achieved with no regrets and no recriminations.

10 December 1975

Michael's birthday today – I got him B. Russell's little book of letters, the sort of thing that one can get lost in for an hour when one is tired. He's not particularly my man, but he has a mind, original, clear and upsettingly debunking.

Doug and I are going up to Nomdmi for the night and over to Michael's for dinner.

Rachel seems to have found that lost self of hers in Barbados[1]. Her letters are quite unique, and two new poems. She sleeps well there, and the children will be healthier, and Paul – Paul will find himself now on his own for the first time.

December 1975

Spending Xmas in Barbados with Rachel and Paul and the children.

Barbados – cheerful, calm, with a style of its own. There is almost a cult of cheerfulness. The colours of and in the houses — admit it's tourist influenced — but even without that.

I got awake early as the others were coming in from Xmas Eve night club — lay and read Sithole's *The Polygamist* for a while — it's quite interesting. This is not a great novel, but it's honest and simple and, I imagine, accurate — it's interesting how in a hundred pages it can give you an insight that thousands of scientific pages don't achieve. But then I think that the novel is a very great art form. People, places, tensions, conflicts, mysticism, psychology, and above all, in great hands, the wholeness of man and the earth and the cosmic forces.

So Barbados — then I exercised and dressed and went for a walk. The air clear, with a sun-up clarity and stillness. The rolling little hills, and every now and then a peadove alighting in the road and fluttering off with a whir of wings, startled. I walked up to the house, empty now, that they hope to move into. A circular house with character, eccentric. An old, old cannon outside and a gorgeous old ship's anchor. Came back — got my own breakfast, coffee, coffee, and then lay and dreamt, waiting for everyone to wake and storm the Xmas tree — expectantly still in the corner.

The tourists in St James — let me be kind — if one suffers from inhibitions, and we all do of one sort or another, but you know — one is old, fat or skinny, aged, double-chinned. In the half light and the music and magic of one's own home, with the moon coming up over the mountains, all the sear and battle of life has marked one leaving one something that once happened — but so alive, so gloriously happy. Must one come and expose what life has made of one's body, one's face, to the glare of the minimum bikini, the see-through lace coat, the bi-focals half way down the nose, whilst outside of the trunks the belly-welly hangs, because some emotionally starved female secretary has inveigled one into a Caribbean holiday? Oh civilization, thy name is mirth!

The sea meets the shore — the sky meets the sea — since time immemorial, whether man knows or cares. God lasts so long and man is so finite.

Jamaica and Barbados: here in an exclusive hotel, Xmas Day, the staff are in the main dining room, the waiters being served by the executive staff — that wouldn't happen in Jamaica. Michael would like it to happen, but the people, the people of Jamaica don't want that to happen.

I'm so glad I came — life is short for me — but I've spent an Xmas with Rachel and Paul and I will go back having added to my life.

6 February 1976

Since March last year I have been very ill — fighting at the same time this damned diverticulitis and an almost impossible cough, and nights when I believed I would not see the morning, fighting for breath — I haven't told anyone — and a dragging lack of energy, that over and over has made me weep. But somehow I have got into touch with a higher power, so that step by step, life is becoming bearable, though I still fear the nights.

And then I conked out completely — couldn't breathe — couldn't call out, landed up in hospital — they even had problems with an intravenous injection — it just didn't 'pull'.

'The Sea God'[1] — fibreglass — the casting failed — and I built it up with my bare hands — I wasn't going to allow my 'Sea God' to vanish — to fail — damn — why should I?

I fought for days and nights — to just breathe — and on the fourth, at about 4 a.m., suddenly, I had such a vision. A great wave and a man and a woman crouching on a rock — the water, the shine of the rock, barely a foothold, the man with his arm around the woman, and the sea — wave after wave — so instead of dying, why not live and do that one carving — if only I could breathe, and then I saw even further, why had I gone back to fibreglass? Why did I laugh at the past — laugh at the doctors — what did I know that they didn't know? Fibreglass[2] — of course — I hadn't won my first fight — I had come out battered, but un-wise, un-free, so willfully, stubbornly, but *unconsciously*. I had deliberately taken up the challenge again, to die if necessary, but to break through the fantasies, the day-dreams that were holding me like ropes, to a limited understanding of myself and of life.

Dr Suite came in early and he said: 'Your breathing is very bad, but do you know you look different, absolutely different.' I made him sit right there, and I told him what I had seen, what I understood. It was a great moment for me — I had learnt so much.

Now, after a month, I can walk the Mona dam easily and fast — and have even done a half mile on a steep gradient at Nomdmi, plus altitude, and come home fine.

30 April 1976

I finished the 'Manchild' in a sort of record time, about five weeks. Then we cast it, and the table crashed with it — it was on the way to a ton in weight with the plaster mould still on top of the clay. So here I sit like an empty bag.

Fibreglass wrecks me — I come back with concrete and *it* wrecks me by total annihilation!

The house is empty, Adinah has gone home, so the two dogs, Storm and Anansi, and the gramophone pouring out Schumann's 4th Symphony.

Last night was tough and I had no tablets to help me sleep, so I got up at 2 a.m. and got a brandy and soda and sat on the porch breathing in the fresh night air.

Young Dan Berger[1] had brought me a new book, *The Denial of Death*, very rambunctious but wonderful. The section on Kierkegaard, he really is my man.

The strange thing is that trying to combat a deep worry over Michael and Jamaica, and even over Rhodesia and all it might lead to — all of Africa on a righteous boil — simmering.

The Israeli Ambassador and his wife had been to dinner and unfortunately the talk went on to South Africa and Israel, and the atmosphere was really tense! Oh, why oh why did that situation have to come about, however desperate Israel is — *not* South Africa. They were all embarrassed, we all were.

Angola and Nyerere growling, it's a horribly dangerous world at the moment.

So I was thinking of the power of faith and then Kierkegaard — the whole essay claimed that he was so profound that he was really *post* Freud and that he had been largely misunderstood. The pure, or so-called pure, science of Freud broke through, because that was the right moment and the contribution was immense, but Kierkegaard coming before Freud, explains Freud to us — and let me face the truth, scientific pessimism leads us straight to a world where there is only faith. Where does the concept of conscience come from, isn't that a miracle if man is all that Freud defines him?

I think perhaps conscience is a large part of the spirit that lifted man, with all his hideous faults, into something different from the animals — mind you, I think professional philosophers underrate the consciousness of some animals. A dog will be submerged with remorse. I think the developing theme of this book is that it is almost impossible for man to achieve his full possibilities as a mature human being — all the odds are stacked against him from birth and from conscious awareness — he shrinks and hides from himself his fear of decay and death. He even destroys himself in order to flee from the inevitable — and this fear of death causes him to so hide from himself that the result is a non-person who has neither the desire nor the strength to know himself.

Man himself does not accept the scientific truth about himself as the final word — somehow, somewhere he knows that he has deliberately blotted out, side-stepped another truth — perhaps even an aspect of the truth. Primitive man does not accept the evidence of his eyes — look at his art and you realize that this is so — somehow he is trying to relate himself to something outside of, bigger than, himself — and here comes religion and the act of faith. But *why* is this so? What brooding, troubled shadow moves behind him that makes him reach into the darkness to put himself into the safety of the hand of God?

So the 'Manchild' crashed and for two days I was empty and so tired, so weary, and then I thought back to how I realized what I was like — got a first glimpse of how utterly limited I am – when I thought I was dying, unable to breathe. Fibreglass made me know for the first time that life does end, as we know it – that in fact I wasn't unique – that I alone couldn't live forever – that death was near facing me and that if even I recovered it was still there, quite soon to be faced.

So I follow the pattern of a lifetime and plunge back into a new breakthrough in work – fit, well, strong. A grand bit of work. And now it's gone, vanished – and here I am, with that great experience, that doom still waiting for me. It was so shattering that I prayed for strength to withstand the shock. I identify prayer with calling to Norman to intercede for me. So you see, I did what primitive man did, and then comes Kierkegaard, psychology versus religion.

Freud and Kierkegaard – 'holding two totally opposed opinions of the reality of faith'.

Faith is real, say I – but it has to be so God awful strong to bear one up.

So I'll do the 'Manchild' again.

14 July 1976

We have been through the whole appalling storm of the organized violence of the JLP and with no doubt CIA support. I don't know if there is final evidence of the latter.

It's been a terrible experience, leaving the whole country quite shattered.

People are leaving in swarms ostensibly for that reason, which is far from the truth. Greed, love of their money, their special privileges, a refusal to face and accept colour and racial equalities – one's own friends shock one. Anyway, it is a free world, only they remove their money – money that has been made here – out of this country. It leaves one kind of peaceful!!

Michael has come through so far intact, and now the economic scene has to be rebuilt, because it is now clear that the violence was deliberately aimed at wrecking this.

If Shearer[1] were back leading the JLP Jamaica would be Jamaica again.

Someone said, 'Marx is a rogue and an idiot.' I am no Marxist – not at all – and certainly not a communist, and mostly not a totalitarianist, but it released a very demon of anger in me. I am not absolutely sure why, and I must get hold of a life of the man. I *can't* wade through *Das Kapital,* and it wouldn't help if I could.

Must talk to Michael – something happened at the end with Engels when the fundamental ideas had already been set in motion, and he did not (or could not?) gratify his thinking in a form that would not cause confusion.

All this and more — but why was I so angry — was it the abrasiveness of the form the words took?

Was it the short cut method of expression?

Was it the arrogance, or was it the negativeness?

Somewhere I am reading the danger of basing thought on the collection of statistics. What is it that statistics validates? I've got to get to the bottom of that one.

23 July 1976

So today I heard that Scottie, who had bought "Manchild', had thought that it looked dirty, and he has painted it with bronze paint — so that it should fit in with the sophistication of his gallery.

'Manchild' is all about people who our plural society would think were dirty — who sit on the ground and smell of the earth. That was what I meant, and I've been months studying *ciment fondu,* and what it can actually do.

So, bronze painted, it faces Carifesta — and I will never see it as it was again with its slate grey shadows and stonewhite high spots.

6 September 1976

I want to keep a day-to-day diary until the election[1] is over — there are several strands of strain just now. There is the tremendous problem of Muriel's future. She is in a very last stage, hating living intensely, hostile to any sort of nursing or care, quite unpredictable in her moods. She can't walk, and her lifelong independence makes her utterly miserable at being dependent on others. I feel desperately sorry for her and do my best to help, but it faces me with a strange fear of the future. Then I have a great financial worry as her money is nearly done, and the rest of us are under financial pressure ourselves.

Then there is looming over us all the election, with all that it involves of violence, danger, endlessly exhausting effort and control and patience.

This morning I woke with the memory in my mind of the story of Moses, and how, as the battle raged, he became weary of holding up his hands and began to flag, and how Aaron and another held up his hands as evening came, and the battle was won. I don't remember the story exactly. I must look it up. But I phoned Michael and told him that this was a moment for great faith, and asked him to read the story of Moses — which I felt was one of the great stories of a relationship of faith. He promised that he would, and I said you will often come upon the phrase, 'and the people murmured', but his faith carried him through.

Later I went to see Scottie and we talked of Jamaica and the future — it was a remarkable talk − he has an undying courage and optimism. I like and admire him very much, and he understands Jamaicans − he says, 'They are a frivolous people − they can't help it − you have to love and take them as they are.' I came away feeling better.

Then I went down to see Khouri, who leaves with his wife and children tomorrow. He is so sad − she simply can't take Jamaica − she's young and a German. I tried to comfort him, and she came in − so happy that she was going − and the nurse looked at her − utterly sad, even resentful − and Khouri torn in two.

It's been an awful summer, violent winds, and unbearable heat and no rain. I did an unusual drawing with a figure of the rain unable to fall because of a violent figure tearing across the foreground. I don't really understand it.

I am so troubled − one moment I am all in one piece, and the next moment I am in a storm, almost hysterical − so − I have done this before − I'll keep a day-to-day account of simple, practical things, and calm will return. I'll go and see Muriel now, and then Noel, and it will be dinner time.

This morning early I did one hour on the big figures, 'Tell No One'[2]. Tomorrow morning I will try to work again − it's six weeks since I touched it, and I do love it.

Perhaps tonight I will work on 'The Creation' drawing for Michael.

The visit to Noel[3] was a great success. She is, in spite of being nearly blind, full of music and pupils of promise − the place was full of creativity − I loved it.

Tonight I am going to start a first shot at Michael's drawing.

7 September 1976

Had an unaccountably stormy evening last night − irritable and a bit spiteful. So I went into the studio at about 9 p.m. and uncovered the big clay model of 'Tell No One'. One of the arms had dropped, and it was messy and over-wet − you see, I've left it since July − just couldn't work, what with the heat and worry over Muriel, and the men had to over-damp it so as to keep it in some sort of condition. I worked on it for a bit and then just covered it with the plastic and decided to leave it and face the problems tomorrow. So I made one more furious attempt at the 'Creation' drawing − just drawing wildly with a brush − with the ink running all over the place. Actually, I think it's almost arrived. I've actually been working on it for over a year in dozens of different variations, but this I think is nearest. 'Creation' is a struggle, not a miracle. I'll give it a day or two and have a go at it again. It depends what size it ought to be − on paper or canvas etc.

Anyway, I couldn't sleep before dawn. I crept out, driving with the car lights on, and went down to Hagley Park and took Mr Richards out of bed, and together we worked out some heavy wiring to hold the arms and heads of the clay.

Then I had breakfast and crawled into bed and slept till lunch and back to bed until 2 p.m.

The straw poll in the *Gleaner* tentatively prophesied a win for PNP of seven seats, which lifted this heavy load of worry, deep-seated, deep-hidden. Michael tells me he can't stand Jamaica House another month – he and Bev hate it -- all the PMs have hated it, and all that security every step you turn. He's moving into a government-owned house on Hopefield and he says they can put a whole army of police outside the fence – but just not one will come inside.

This evening I'm picking up Boxer and going to dinner with Pam.[1] I'm looking forward to it very much and hope that I will keep calm. Maybe we'll have some music, I would love that, but she has interesting friends so it should be good.

8 September 1976

Had an enchanting evening with Pam and her friends. They played a record of this young Korean violinist, in a Sibelius violin concerto. She was only twenty-two when recording, and had remarkable power and a clear, strong understanding. I'll always love that work! Then Richter playing Prokofiev's Sonata 7 Opus 83, all demonic, almost savage, elemental energy in the last movement – it would have been chaos, but for Richter's ability to sing through the whole thing with that marvellous rhythm of his. It's a magnificent work.

This morning went down to Marcus Garvey Drive on business, to find it quiet, orderly, with the streets swept, then on to Muriel's bank, only to find she has $286.00 left – oh *God*!

Kay[1] came in and we talked of drawing, which is a problem to her – she's honest and *very* talented – I like her so much. Sheila comes in at 5 p.m. I wonder if she has a problem. I hope not. And then tonight I'll replay the Prokofiev as I've borrowed it. I wonder what the neighbourhood thought – I made them turn the gramophone up and it certainly raged out into the midnight air!

I told Kay, if she wanted to learn to draw as distinct from sculpting, to go away by herself and draw and draw anything, no matter, and if necessary tear it all up and draw again – and slowly something would evolve. If one is not drawing from a given object or subject, but from within, a good drawing is ultimately an act of grace.

147

I did over fifty drawings at Nomdmi on this brief sixteen days, and lots of other things too.[2]

Sheila[3] wasn't depressed; she may get the job to organize the Caribbean area for the Nigerian Festival in January.

But Doug came in and he was depressed — the old devastation that fairly young left-wingers can create with their ...(sic) you know, I know, we all know — endless ideologies making endless ambitions, and women can be so silly over these things.

9 September 1976

So I woke at 3.30 a.m. very conscious that I had to face not only my bank, but Muriel's bank too. She had $284.86 left and I had an overdraft of $2,000.00. What a thought for 3.30 a.m!

Anyway I read until 5 a.m., made coffee, and went and worked on the 'Tell No One' clay. Terrific problem of supports and crumbling, over-wet clay, because of my absence. I was pretty weary by 7.15 a.m. — the bank, the bank. Went out and got Muriel's medicine and phoned Aub that I couldn't hold on any longer financially.

And then I went down and gave her hair a trim, sitting under her little almond tree.

I came back pretty low, and the phone went and David saying he had collected and they now could make an offer for 'Journey' for the National Gallery. Oh God — oh God — saved again, and 'Journey', my beloved 'Journey' will save Muriel and hold the fort for me.

Thank you God — oh, I'm tired — lunch, two aspirin and a little *bed*.

I walked round the dam this evening, wasn't at all tired. Came home and talked of Muriel's future with Rudolph — we had to make the final decision — the finances simply aren't there — so I have to search for a nursing home. After that I think I'll take a sleeping tablet and try to have a real night's sleep.

12 September 1976

Today is MONDAY. On Saturday night Michael came to see me about Muriel. We have been forced solely on financial grounds to take a room in a nursing home. It's going to be a terrible wrench, but it has to be done.

I went with John and Sue up to Nomdmi for a few hours to steady myself, and then went down to see her. She was in a bitter, bitter mood and blamed me for the whole thing. I came away shaken to my core. I shouldn't be the person to take her today, so John and M.G. are going and taking the nurse. Somehow I have to find my way back into her confidence. I told her — I am

1   *Edna's parents, Harvey and Elliie Swithenbank, taken in 1892.*

2   *Edna in London in 1937 to attend her exhibition at the French Gallery.*

3   *Nomdmi, Edna and Norman's rustic wooden cottage in the Blue Mountains.*

4   *Edna with granddaughter Rachel.*

5   *Edna's head of Norman*
     (plaster) *1924.*

6   *Norman flanked by sons, Douglas* (left)
Michael (right), *at Drumblair*
in the 1950s.

7   *Edna with 'Goatee the Goat'.*

8   *Edna at work.*

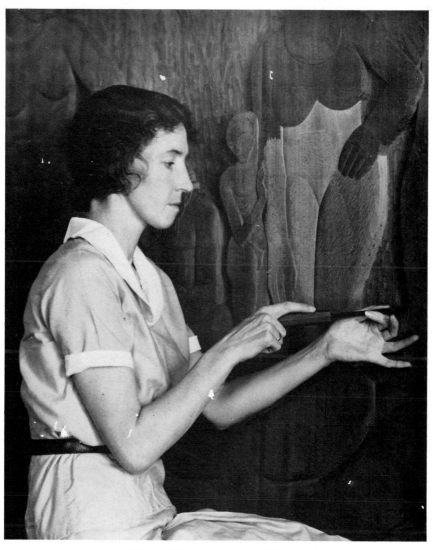

9   *Edna modelling the recreation of 'Tomorrow'.*

10   *'Negro Aroused', 1935 carving.*
(Her favourite photograph of
this work, taken by Dennis Gick.)

11   *'The Gossips', 1983.*

12 *'Ghetto Mother'* (ciment fondu) *1982.*

13   *'Bogle'* (ciment fondu), *1962.*

14   *Edna with 'Rainbow Serpent'.*

not a nurse, but I have tried never to let her down in all the practical and
financial facts and details of her life. And then there is the little dog — Michael
was terribly kind.

16 September 1976

I think this diary closes right here — the book is done, and in any event a new
chapter begins for me.

Many times I have been into homes for the aged, carrying a blithe spirit
across from another world. This week I went in to book a room for Muriel.

I was introduced to one old lady who had a face that suddenly lit up, like a
flame, to greet me and shake hands. Another passed with averted eyes. She was
supporting herself with that kind of contraption that anyone uses to learn to
walk again who has had polio — someone else was lolling on a couch.

We went into Muriel's room — it was small, but it wasn't bad because it had
two large windows with a cherry tree outside. We talked a little, the Matron
and I, and I left.

As I backed the Benz out, suddenly something happened to me — for the
first time in all my brashness and high spirits, a door opened in my mind, and
I saw the numbered days ahead — each day, each hour, each minute. How
could I find a role, an image, a reality to carry me through those lengthening
shadows.

Oh lovely evening with the mists new furled — how to move into it — how
to shed the past.

Savouring the moment — the coming of day — learning new tastes, jasmine
tea instead of gin and tonic — more reading, less talk, and music, music all the
way.

That's one plane — but how to find a new approach to people. H.G .Wells
writes: 'And now only does life pass plainly into a phase of complete finality,
so that one can apprehend and anticipate its end.' That's it — that's the driving
away from Fairway Avenue in the morning sunshine, traffic all around me —
the strength, the exuberance of the day calling to me, and I so suddenly seeing
it all through the doorway of finality.

28 January 1977

Last week I was ill — I had diverticulitis and at the same time a violent attack
of asthma (?) — that's not the real name — I really was ill — but not, as I
thought, too seriously — and yet now that I am better, I realize that something
happened. It was as if, for the first time in my life, I could look back and *know*
that a shadow had appeared and hovered behind me as it were obliquely — and

moved away as I recovered — and knew that it was death — and that being ill is not anything to do with dying, it's a loss of will to go on.

Very interesting — I felt as if I began to improve — that two more arrivals and I would go.

I don't think the fact of illness — even in the most extreme cases — is actually what causes the cessation of life. The will to live is like the mercury in a thermometer.

Loose pages from Diary Two

Norman was an unusual person in that he had so few friends, and yet he knew so many people.

For the span of his life there were two people who were very, very close. One was his sister Muriel. She was for thirty years the doctor at the Children's Creche in Kingston. As young people leaving home and going to England for education, she was his anchor. She was a fiercely loyal friend to him, and isolated as they often were by colour and race in the England of the 1920s, a bond grew there that lasted the rest of his life.

She was a very intelligent woman in her own way, realistic and practical. A woman with a sharp wit and frankness that could often be disconcerting.

But there was an honesty and a penetrating ability to debunk any over-romantic approach to people or things that I think her brother really valued. She demanded high standards, her mind was essentially scientific and sometimes unimaginative, but they laughed at the same jokes and could be wise in the same way. One difference between them lay in the fact that she lived so long abroad that it was almost impossible for her to integrate back into her homeland. Whereas he couldn't get back quickly enough, and never at any time would have been able to live in any other country. Jamaica was deep in his heart and in his blood.

The other friend who came from childhood days was Leslie Clerk. He was friendly with Leslie I think from when he was in his teens — and the friendship deepened when his two sisters, Vera and Muriel, had left for studies in England, and he was on his own and then became friendly with the whole family, whose home became his holiday base.

They were an interesting family, and shared a unique gift, an absorption with ESP. Leslie himself had remarkable intuitive powers, and a brother and a sister had even more. The whole family was interested and made quite a study of it.

They too, like Norman's family, read a good deal, and later became interested in folk music — and later still, launched the Cudjoe Minstrels[1], which was the first song and dance group I ever heard. In fact I think they were the original pioneers who ultimately became the stock entertainers for concerts, and for entertaining VIPs who were passing through, or when the Royal family paid their routine visits. Norman was very interested in them. The group was largely made up of family and close friends, and at a critical moment would not have died out if they had been flexible and able to absorb new, young talent.

The present Olive Lewin group[2] has carried on the tradition, to achieve recognition far away from Jamaican shores, and yet is filling the same function in a wider, deeper sense.

I think Leslie's chief interest for Norman lay in neither of these interests, but because in his own way he had remarkable gifts of wisdom and intuitive insights. They would have talked law and its problems endlessly – they would have tried to fathom the mysteries of human personality – they shared a love of music, and Leslie would have learnt much from Norman's love of the fine arts and from his wider reading. And yet I don't think either dominated the other – there was never any question of that – they were happy together, and they relaxed each other. Both were good swimmers – Norman would have excelled there – boats, horse racing, boxing – all these things they relaxed with and made a part of the woven fabric of their lives. Leslie was by profession a piano tuner, and he worked hard for a living, but an outstanding quality I think was his independence – a sort of personal pride that kept him inviolate throughout his long life.

Later in life he took up sculpting and painting, and finally became one of our finest stone carvers.

And here hangs the big question mark over his friendship with N. He finally left Jamaica altogether and took all his work with him, and went to live in Canada – one of the early migrants away from the Independent Jamaica.

When Norman went into politics the friendship was often strained, but still very much intact, and N. still turned to him very powerfully in moments of crisis, for understanding and spiritual help. But finally something seemed to become too much for Leslie, and although they never broke their relationship, something began to become apparent – Leslie was very much a product of his class and his background. There were no black faces in the Cudjoes, and although Leslie, who was a typical "light brown' Jamaican, had black friends, something began to appear in his conversation that hadn't been apparent before – and with the greater part of his family, he turned his back on Jamaica and left.

Two other people I remember being close to him were W.A. Campbell, Postmaster General, the man who wrote the book, *Did the Jews Kill Jesus?* and Rob Braithwaite, a barrister, who died young in a car accident. Norman used to say of Rob that he was the most 'civilized' man he knew. W.A. Campbell was an avid reader and an extremely interesting conversationalist. He loved the sea and the boats and they used to spend their Sundays in and out of the harbour with a boat. It had an outboard motor and a sail and oars, and when they did particularly reckless things, and friends and families protested, we were left to console ourselves with the thought that at least they were ready for all emergencies. The amazing thing was that Braithwaite, who couldn't swim, had nearly been drowned as a child − but nevertheless he had the courage or the foolhardiness to go with them.

On a different plane altogether, the women he was friendly with I remember as Margery Stewart, an Irish member of the Jamaica Welfare staff; Edith Clarke, social anthropologist; and perhaps closest, and a very relaxed, happy relationship, Iris King, member for W. Kingston.

Much later in life he was friendly with Dr Harriet Berger, a lecturer at Drexell College, with whom for several years he corresponded − he was very fond of her, and they had much in common.

Two very important young people in his life were Pam O'Gorman, now Head of the School of Music, and his own granddaughter, Rachel. Pam and Norman talked music a great deal, but there was more to their friendship than that − in spite of the years between them, Norman was tremendously attracted to a certain gallant courage, a quick, sharp mind and a wonderful warmth and sense of humour.

Rachel and Norman were something else again − he saw the acute problems she had lived through as a result of leaving her mother − but he also saw a potentially big person, who could get crushed, or even led away by her own charm and impulsiveness.

It was a very valid relationship, and is a source of great inspiration, and always will be to her for the rest of her life.

He also was friendly with his two sons − not in the later years as a father/son pattern, but as two very different people with whom he could discuss people and events and decisions. Michael, with his gift for under-standing people in the mass − and Douglas, who has a gift of understanding people as individuals. Those relationships grew in strength and depth with the years, and were a tremendous comfort to him.

And last there was his doctor who was also his brother-in-law, his sister Vera's husband, Ludlow Moody.

Moody, as he was called even by his wife, was a remarkable person both as a doctor and as a man and friend. As a doctor, he had that gift of imparting strength to someone fighting for life, or enduring great pain. People had tremendous faith in him. He was a quiet, reserved man with a mischievous sense of humour, and a tendency to tell stories with a sly ending that left the laughter to break out long after he had left the room. Norman envied him this gift, and would beat his head and say: 'Why can't I remember jokes – Moody's head must be a storehouse of them.'

He was also a crack rifle shot and along with Dr Ben Machado, had a world ranking. He and Norman, and sometimes Leslie Clerk, would go bird shooting together. As far as Norman was concerned, it was more the day in the open, for they would leave in the dark – long before the sun was up. He often talked of the logwood trees with the bees hanging over them, and the smell of the swamp – he could become quite nostalgic over it in later years. But his shooting wasn't very successful. In a moment of impulse he had bought a French shotgun which had its own unique method of loading, and which everyone felt didn't suit Norman's build, because he didn't bring home lots of birds like the others. Perhaps he didn't want to – perhaps it was more the joy of being in the open that made him happy and perhaps, and this is a very big question mark, perhaps he was loyal to that gun because it was French and it made a connecting link with his service in the war. Who knows – who knows the strange realities of a man's mind – what things come up out of the past and make a link with the present.

Anyway, he didn't only share shooting with Moody. They often worked together in Norman's law cases, when he would call Moody as an expert where medical opinions were needed.

They were both at the height of their powers during the famous murder case always referred to as *The* Alexander case. And here Moody's knowledge of guns, which was quite phenomenal, played a vital role. What sort of a mark a particular revolver would leave on a bullet, and they would take clay from my studio and roll the bullet in it, and spend hours comparing the kinks that were left in the clay.

I was commissioned to do a head of Alexander, which was cast into plaster of paris and actually taken into court to demonstrate various hypotheses. And these two men worked on the ballistics of that case with such concentration that they were asked to send the notes of that case to a law journal abroad, because it was known that they had broken new ground, and made a vital contribution.

But as a doctor Norman gave him a hard time, but then he gave his health a hard time too. He would never take advice, and as he had a way of reading medical journals, often stolen from his sister who kept herself very up to date, he would go storming into Moody's office and demand all sorts of new treatments, which Moody would fend off in his laconic, humorous way. But he managed to keep Norman fairly fit, in spite of the threat of an ulcer which hung over him all his life, and which was almost inevitable with the pace that he drove himself.

They both loved fast driving too, and the feel of a powerful engine. It was a great relationship and survived even when Vera and Moody were divorced. I don't think he took sides — he had too much experience as a divorce lawyer to do that. He must have known that marriages often break up because of an inner tension, not because anyone was to blame.

Of the lawyers Norman worked with, the only man I feel came close to being a friend was the solicitor, Aston Simpson — as a pair they were fantastically suited to each other in a barrister/solicitor relationship, and Aston lived down near the sea and loved boats and shooting. Norman always said he felt so safe with Aston in court behind him. He was also friendly with John Carberry, later Chief Justice. He felt that Carberry was honest to a fault, and he liked him and his wife, who used to give him wonderful presents of sweets and pickles she had made herself, and he would chuckle and say: 'Mind, you corrupt me — don't tell the judge, you know.'

He used to play the mouth organ, all the old Jamaican mentos. We used to say that if he would stop making speeches in the hills of St Andrew and just walk along the mountain paths playing, he would, like the Pied Piper, pull the world after him.

But I think his most intense happiness came once a year, when he played after Xmas dinner and we threw back the chairs and danced like a lot of crazy people, and then he couldn't bear being still himself, and he would throw down the mouth organ and shout to someone to put on the gramophone and he would *dance* — with the staff, with anyone and everyone — reaching top heights with his daughter-in-law, Carmen, and later with Rachel, both of whom were the only people who could match him for speed and a sort of demonic energy.

When Douglas was a baby and was restless, he would play beside his cradle, a sort of endlessly spinning tune something like, 'The Campbells Are Coming', and when it had to go on too long, I would hold a saucer under the 'organ' and catch the saliva falling from it — for Douglas quickly discovered this was a way of holding our attention, and if Norman stopped playing he would immediately start crying again, and the whole thing would have to be re-enacted once more.

Norman had extraordinary and erratic eating habits. It could be all summed up in an incident with Michael, who arrived home from travels and said: 'Mother, I don't understand a present I have brought for Dad — someone in London tells me that the one thing in the whole world he wants as a present is a fatless frying pan — so here it is. But tell me — the last time I was home, Dad was insisting that all his food had to be fried in olive oil.'

He was like that — if you called him a food faddist he would be furious. But he swung from fruit diets to vegetarianism, to T-bone steaks. Sometimes he was a non-drinker, and sometimes it was a remarkable number of, in the early

154

days, rum and gingers, and in the later days, gin and tonics. And the truth is, there was probably some intuitive wisdom in it all, because he did live to be seventy-six with remarkable health and fantastic energy. Somewhere along the way he checked excesses and rested his body — and I know that at seventy he could wear out men in their prime with late hours and a load of work. Partly I think because he had an outstanding ability to keep relaxed whilst in action — when he was campaigning, for instance, he always looked fit and confident and could sleep in a car at top speed, or doze whilst the other speakers built up the meeting.

Also his gift of patience — it wasn't the patience of an iron control — it was a 'waiting' patience born of a knowledge of human behaviour, and a certainty about his own objectives.

But where food was concerned he had always a sort of mischievous, prank-loving inquisitiveness about the effects of something new — a bit hard on the cook, however, who kept young and flexible to meet an unknown request. But a Bombay mango would top all fruit — that he could become poetic about!

Diary Three

13 March 1977

The two elections[1] have passed with a certain amount of violence and the usual scares and panics and quite nightmarish rumours. But the people have spoken very decisively and now there is a mammoth task confronting every well-thinking person. This deadly period of international strain and depression — the very frightening drought which I still believe will resolve itself. I hope so anyway.

There's a lot of illness around. Michael, Doug, Bev have all had unusually bad attacks of flu and poor little Natasha[2] got the vomiting virus which scared us all.

We have one of the worst, if not the worst, spates of rumour mongering this country has ever known. The stories embrace Michael with every kind of illness, and even that he had been shot.

Then the twice repeated, with some months apart, rumour that he had broken every bone in my body and knocked Bev's teeth out.

It's hardly worth recording, but I feel a little tough about it, it's so ugly — it's so obviously deliberately inspired — but we repeat it, we love it, and under cover of sworn secrecy we spread it — non-stop.

But the giant jobs that face the government, and the hope that somehow there will be enough dedicated men and women to give their lives to pulling us through. It's difficult to write of anything else — difficult to think of anything else.

But I'm facing a show at the end of the week and I know that I am not ready for it. But it's a charming idea — Jamaica Mutual — back to Jamaica Mutual after all these years.

I look back at the show that Koren[3] and I gave, and how we failed to turn up at the opening, but sat on the pier down by the Victoria Market and dappled our feet in the water. Koren would have attended but I led him astray and ran out on it!

But one has learnt a lot since then — the mask goes on and one smiles, and yet over all the years I have never changed — I still feel as if I have lost my outside skin!! Michael has had a few days off, part by the sea, with a little boat Trudeau gave him[4] – he and Joseph must have had a marvellous time – and today he phoned on his way up to the mountains for a last week.

Doug too – who is desperately tired – is taking a week down in Ocho Rios with Rachel and Paul[5]. Doug has become quite a politician. He felt the loss of that seat on a Court's decision badly – it hung over him for five years. It's odd, he doesn't like competitive things. I think I agree with him – it always makes a hole in my tummy and I feel weak.

One never changes in life – the things that stimulated or wrecked you as a child stay the same – one builds all sorts of defences to the bad ones, but it's just the same, and the challenges that call to one are as much music as ever.

Last year was a tough year for me health-wise – fibreglass nearly finished me off, and yet when I look at the amount of work I got through, it is a miracle. A strong sense of lengthening shadows and time running out seemed to enable me to drive every ounce of effort out of myself.

It's interesting that after all these years time is at last catching up with the *Gleaner*. All over the years they have pursued the progressive movement with a cynicism that appals me.

In any event, radio is a better medium in a modern world. But what is amusing is that they have themselves frightened away their own supporters by painting the picture dark and dangerous, the business people who advertised with them, who bought their papers, have gone, and now it's too late.

But when I remember how they treated Norman, for years and years, and for *no reason* – pretending he was a communist – it was a cruel farce. It's useless remembering who did it – one only remembers why they did it.

So now they go for Michael, but somehow time has been moving on.

I'm working hard again. I finished 'The Message' and Gonzales[6] did a fine cast and Carter did a lovely 'finish'. So I'm flying into 'The Wave' with all its problems, and doing a bit of drawing too.

Rachel has done some new poems – a big stride forward.

Norman has recovered from his two accidents[7] and is back at his law again.

I must stop now and go to bed – I'll try and keep a better record now so much is happening – I'll try to begin tomorrow.

15 March 1977

Yesterday I went up to Nomdmi to get it ready for Danny and Sarah.[1] In spite of the drought there were a few flowers, and Vincent had it fairly tidy. I had to lay him off, unfortunately, as I simply can't carry the cost of keeping the two houses. I explained to him and I feel he understood. If I can go up for a week in April that will be wonderful, and I will just draw and draw.

I saw Michael for an hour, but he had just had an upsetting bit of news, so Joseph[2] and I read and discussed his poetry. He has a sensitive mind – and quite a feel for words – only sometimes he can't resist the urge to let a bit of intellectualism impinge, which breaks the flow. I think he saw the point – it's easy talking with him as he doesn't take offence. Natasha was there too.

Last night I had a storm over the new work 'The Wave' – tore bits off it, and thumped it in anger, and as a result it's slightly off plumb and I'll have to get my darling Mr Richards to prize it back up and support. Damn – because I love it and it'll be alright.

Rachel phoned from Ocho Rios, so happy to have Doug with them. He spent the first two days and nights doing nothing but sleep. He was completely exhausted – he hasn't had a holiday for years. I think this should really help – that heavy flu and the return attack played the devil with him, so it will be interesting to see how he handles 'Health'[3] when he comes back.

I'm finding myself drawn closer and closer to Prokofiev – I think I'm nearer to him than any other of his contemporaries. There's a humour – a total lack of self pity – perhaps he works the latter off in that nihilistic mood in some of his piano works.

I have been able to stand the strain of Mahler, and I read an interesting article on him today which refers to his passionate sorrow, grief – almost neurotic – and comments: but he is not Hamlet, if anything, he had the outwardness of a Job. But I always remind myself that, in the way that all great artists have a certain prophetic instinct and certainly a psychic foresight, he was writing music not so long before the great Hitler massacres and brutalizing of the Jews. He *must* have sensed it coming and so one is constantly reminded of the wailing wall and the great archetypal image of grief laid at the feet of the Almighty.

17 March 1977

Yesterday Jamaica Mutual bought the head of the Old Woman[1] – they have been *so* nice over this whole retrospective show – they couldn't have been more appreciative of the whole effort. Just as they were forty years ago.

It's been a help to me personally and David has been marvellously imaginative and intelligent – the work he puts into a show is quite fantastic.

I hope and believe that David, Vera and Jean Smith[2] will make a fine trio if we are to organize the fine arts on a sounder basis.

We are going through such difficult times – and the drought – when nature takes a hand, that's something else again.

20 March 1977

Today is Sunday — all of last week I was so depressed — several reasons — nearly all political. But also having to give this exhibition — I don't think that it's a valid activity for me.

Showing things to other people is what I need to get away from — all the hidden worry that it engenders, when somewhere inside myself the need to test each step into a world and on a road that is very short.

21 March 1977

Had to reconstruct support for 'Wave' — time to get back to organized work.

The casting of 'The Message' seemed to paralyse all work in the studio, and its continued presence leaves me feeling cramped and dominated by it.

Gandhi has just lost her seat — I think it must be an impossible job to govern India — I wouldn't like the job — the press of the world is so unreliable over facts. I wish I could understand what she did that so outraged people. I know she was totally undemocratic, but was her opposition truly honest and will they do a better job?

Sterilization — it's such an ugly word in human terms — people can't swallow that.

29 March 1977

Yesterday was quite a day — went to the photographic show at the Mutual Life — very good nudes. Jamaican photography is of a high standard; Glave had some lovely work with not good titles, and Robinson[1] is mostly always good. Wanted to see the guild show in the same building and up to 10 a.m. the door was locked, which is what happens when artists become administrators.

The JBC TV and radio men came in at 3 p.m. to 'take' 'Tell No One' and Rachel reading her poem about the 'carving'. It's a remarkable poem and she read it with such poised feeling that all six of us were spellbound. Wycliffe[2] came himself, which was terribly good of him to give the time, and he handled Ra very well. She has this great talent, but is so nervous and insecure — her posture and her breathing reveal this and he got her to lift her torso and let her voice come full and round. She had clung to Bev who is a 'pro' on TV[3], quite marvellous, and Bev held the mike for her, giving her confidence. It went well and they brought my darling Ken Dawson[4] for the shots — one of the best cameramen in Jamaica. I really love him — he worked with Boxer on several 'artist' films, mine included.

I was so proud of Rachel and Bev sitting there battling it out together. And then Dorothy Hill came in with Stephen's[5] idea of my doing a New York show — but where to get the peace — because that would require at least ten unsold works. Anyway, let's see.

Meanwhile M.G. phoned that his son Dan had reluctantly taken a substitute flight back home — his flight was having problems. Dan is an interesting case of a young man born in Jamaica, and coming back at twenty-five, and simply falling in love with his mother country, at the same time perhaps understanding his Jamaican father for the first time. M.G. is so happy, so happy over it.

Then we all three went with Michael to the last night of the Cuba Ballet. Michael had given Bev and Ra new dresses for the occasion so we were very gala, and they came back to me for drinks after, and we all shook off the terrible strain of the weekend when the PNP had its Retreat and fought out some big internal policy and personality problems.

Michael is an interesting leader — he grows, but my God, the problems are great, and the press as always making them greater, and spreading discord and negativism.

The fire at Nomdmi was quite shattering, a raging fire coming up from the great valley behind Minni. Some little man, a half-crazy person who smokes ganja, went down and cut a bunch of bananas, lit a fire, and when the people on the hill called to him, he cursed back a lot of bad words and walked off — and in a moment the fire spread. It almost surrounded my three little buildings — circled the ortaniques —

Two fire brigades, police and the people of the area fought it from 10 a.m. to 9 p.m. We all went up around 6.30 p.m. when we heard of it. Michael was in Cabinet, but Doug went — Bev and I and the two Smiths.

The people said afterwards: 'The old man would never let that little house burn — see not one of him fruit trees touch.' That was Norman, watching from the skies.

31 March 1977

Went yesterday with Laura Facey[1] and Cecil Ward[2] to her little house between Bernard Lodge and the sea — I'm not sure where it is because the track wound so erratically.

There was a silent creek with water birds — it had been there for a long time — and a little immaculate and purposeful petchary overlooking us all — waiting for a dive.

And her little hut — set in an area of empty loneliness the like of which I have never seen. The girl has strong nerves — lots of skulls and bones — a mobile of bones that clanked in the wind — and a finally and totally melancholy Koto played by a Japanese on a tape.

A tremendous spot — somewhere that was 'before'. The ghosts of the Arawaks were there peeping through the fine little fine-leafed trees. Dead trees standing and lying from the world began — and the ground under one's feet — like silk — untrod.

The strangest part of Jamaica I have ever been in.

5 April 1977

That was a wonderful weekend, so much what I needed — the children! I have spent so much of my life trying to be at peace inside, and just for a little while I captured it.

The sound of children is a riot through the house and garden (with Ra in Ocho Rios). Two are armed bad boys — the police and the army. Two are good boys, cowboys — the cowboys are not armed. The parents are playing dominoes inside, two mothers and two fathers.

This morning there was poetry — four new poems and talk of a line here, a word there. Poems that went down to the nitty gritty of truth and feeling and experience.

6 April 1977

Am I too old for it — I simply loathe this 'woman's lib' business. There's something spiteful, almost revengeful over it. I remember as a child at school the suffragette movement was coming in, and how my sister Lena — *so* pretty, so feminine — used to sell tags to help the movement. It was an incredibly courageous thing to do because Penzance was a very conservative place. Coming home from school, I didn't take the normal short cut way through the fields. I went through High Street and there she was in the middle of the cross streets — flushed, frightened, but totally believing in what she was doing. She must have been about sixteen. I was proud of her, but I knew I couldn't have done it — and in those days one would have been dumb and deaf not to see the need for women having the vote.

But now women have all the doors open, and the energy they spend organizing and destroying so much in their own personal relations, with their fathers, their husbands, their lovers, their sons, their nephews, their grandsons. The doors are there — walk through them with brains and hard work and imagination — men are a little promiscuous — OK, so what — deal with it another way.

Women sometimes haven't the courage to face their own weaknesses or they might be promiscuous too — only men and women are not the same.

9 April 1977

What nonsense one writes — never mind — people say it always rains on Good Friday and yesterday in the middle of a set, hard drought in the late afternoon a little thunder and rain! Not all that — but just now pure heaven.

I meant to take the day off, but the thought of that inert mass of clay drove me out of bed.

That damned 'Wave' — the back view — I really fought it, or it fought me.

Can't play anything but Prokofiev just now. He had the *energy*, the just sheer energy: the second, the third movement — anyway the seventh sonata — for sheer power and construction mounting, mounting — that acceptance of and triumph in the whole of contemporary life, and Richter sitting like a demonic angel at the heart of it all. How it builds up — chunks of sound in juxtaposition, and yet the thread that leads it all forward. Odd musician — because he just collapses into his sudden lyricism and dreams away — and recovers!! And the cello sonata with Rostropovich and Richter — the cello allowed to be totally dominating until the very end when Richter comes racing in.

11 April 1977

I think, I think, I think I've found the 'Wave'. I searched and wandered and in doing so found at the end of the Michelangelo paintings some things I had never seen before — the conversion of St Paul and the crucifixion of St Peter. Both in the Vatican. That strange backward-looking glance of Peter — and the figure of Paul being so strongly and so wonderfully held by a soldier.

There was no wave there — but I can't think how after all these years I missed them — and the Peter has a strange, unearthly dawn-lit sky — and the light coming down from God on to Paul has a lightness, a floating ephemeral beauty and mystery — and yet God is, as always, with Michelangelo — very solid, very real, and such a welcoming, gentle face.

Greta and Henry gave me this superb present last year.

I wandered on and found *The God Beneath the Sea* with Charles Keeping's amazing illustrations — this was nearer home — I wish I had drawn those horses!

The Chinese are too tranquil with their mountains and mists, but so lovely — then I couldn't find, nor really look for, the famous Japanese wave.

So I walked at the dam where the water was quiet with a metallic shimmer from the sun setting behind a cloud. The watchman was listening to cricket on a transistor — and at that moment the Jamaicans were in a strong position.

Came home, had a cup of jasmine tea, and after supper wandered into the studio, not meaning to open up the clay — but I did, and sat and looked and looked. Where was the key?

I pulled out a book on animals in art — leafed it through, and there it was: Delacroix's 'Lion in a Wind' — a masterly study — there's the lion, there's the wind, there's some trace of scent on the wind that he has lifted his head to detect, and there is a remarkable, sensuous enjoyment of wind and scent, and with eyes closed he stretches his head up — in his young awareness of life. Turn the picture upside down and the blown mane is like spray.

I worked for nearly two hours stretching up from the ground, not climbing on to the stool, because in the very act of stretching in my own arched back and upreaching arms I seemed to come near to the emotive power that was necessary to lift that inert mass of clay. I wasn't tired at 10 p.m., I was exhilarated — the veil had lifted and, with any luck at all, the toughest problem had been solved.

Mr Delacroix and Mr Prokofiev I salute you — from my lowly position, I follow dumbly a trail — if I could know such joy — magnify me by a thousand — what joy you must have known.

Going with Doug to Nomdmi today — bought some pizzas. Tonight Rachel's poem comes over JBC at seven-thirty — I pray for her — she has real creativity and enormous perceptivity. Incidentally, the horse in St Paul has taken fright and is bolting like mad — horses are *so* superstitious, but how did Michelangelo know that!!

14 April 1977

I don't know what date the Guyanese Festival was, but I remember that Louise and I were asked to be their special guests, and I lost my head and couldn't go. I just couldn't go — not as a special guest — I was afraid. Ultimately I pulled myself together and realized that no Fine Arts show had gone. I tended to blame everyone for this, but the truth is I should have been part of it all, and then we would have got into action with our show.

So I did actually find myself down there. They did a brilliant job — a small country with limited funds, never having tackled such a thing before. I will never forget their great tent with its wonderful wicker lampshades and decoration. There all the dance and drama and music and everything took place. But I simply crumpled up when I got there — frightened, ill at ease. I know I offended them — especially Seymour and Pilgrim[1] — they couldn't understand and I felt mortified. It has taken me till now to realize that one of the strange things that happened after Norman's death, was that I fell apart — all my confidence went — I was lost. I didn't attribute it to that — that was all a trauma — but I found myself clutching at people, at places, madly pursuing things that were totally unreal and meeting reality as if it was some frightening ghost.

The same thing happened over Dennis Scott's[2] book of poetry for which I was to write the foreword. It shouldn't have been a difficult task, for the poetry has much quality, but I put it off until the last moment and then completely botched it. I don't think he has ever forgiven me, and yet I know that if he knew the circumstances he would have understood. (He has forgiven me. I talked to him later.) It was even so bad that that nice American poet who was promoting Dennis, gave me a copy of MacLeish's poetry, and I swore to God that I had never received it.

All these *years* and the clouds are just clearing, and I am recognizing that I was living in a no-man's land and merely functioning on reflexes.

Calmness is coming back at last — a precious calmness.

The fibreglass poisoning forced me to study and do correct breathing, and the exercises that promote it, and then young David Smith[3] sent me a book on Yoga. I haven't the brain nor the physical capacity to understand, let alone practice Yoga — but some of it rubs off — and I am developing a simple and very limited method of control.

If when the pressures come, one captures a kind of breath control, one can steady one's emotions — just that — nothing more, and a serenity descends on one.

'And such a tide
As moving seems to sleep
Too full
For tide or foam.'

15 April 1977

After that things became very difficult politically and all the calm slipped!

Watching Michael deal with the tensions and problems — I can only watch and believe.

2 May 1977 (on Friday, 29 April 1977)

What a remarkable morning!

Went down with Jean Smith and Pansy Hart and a Mr Harris to meet Bertram[1] at X marks the spot — where the truck was parked in 1938, when Norman brought Bustamante out of gaol[2] to the people. We drove down Hagley Park Road, turned left at Marcus Garvey Drive and went as far as Pier 2 — is that right — I'm not sure — where there is a clearing and something laid out that will no doubt, some day, be a little park.

Then we got out the car and walked back to the corner of Pechon Street and Port Royal Street. It was all changed and built up since 1938 – with odd, insecure-looking, freeport shops – quite incredible. One of Moses Matalon's[3] dreams or nightmares – I am not sure which. I got terribly confused. The pier building seemed familiar, nothing else did. Where was I with forty years of a past memory haunting me. A vast crowd – tension – waiting – perched on the side of the truck.

I challenged Mr Harris that this couldn't be the right spot – I felt that it should have been nearer into Kingston – nearer to Parade. He smiled whimsically: 'But Mrs Manley, I was there – I worked in the Pier office – I was part of the crowd. It was just here on the corner of the two streets.'

At that moment Bertram arrived with an aide and a strange little young lady who had attached herself, and then Jerry Craig[4] turned up.

Workers Week had printed about 100,000 copies of a pamphlet with 'Negro Aroused'[5] on the cover – and we were gathered at 'the spot' to plan for next year – a replica of N.A. three times the size of the wood carving – to be placed on a brick foundation, right where the truck so long ago had been parked.

The carving would be about 5 ft on a 7 ½ ft base. Something in me really stirred – the past came pouring over me and I realized too that I had always wanted 'Negro Aroused' to be monumental, and here was my chance.

It was a wonderfully imaginative bit of thinking on Bertram's part – to use the old carving which had grown over the years into a sort of symbol – *Workers Week* 1978, Negro Aroused.

Jerry had done a brilliant sketch of the whole concept, and as we talked a little crowd gathered – fascinated.

I shook hands and was introduced as 'Mrs Joshua' (what WOULD Bev say!). They wanted to know just how it all happened, and one man said: 'Cho don't introduce me – I know the lady for years and I was in the crowd and see where she sit down.' So I said: 'That's not possible, you wouldn't have been born!' and he said: 'Oh yes – well I'm fifty – so I was there.' And we talked of Aggie Bernard and of how we served food side by side, and how we'd collected money – Aggie is blind now, but very cheerful – I'm going to see her. I must go as soon as I get my car back.

So I told them how we were watching Pechon Street to see the great arrival, and then we heard the roar of the crowd – they were coming up Port Royal Street. I should have thought of that – coming from the prison it would be Tower Street and down into Port Royal.

So we measured it all up and Jerry and I walked down P. Royal to see how high it should be, to be seen from a fair distance.

It was a great morning – I'll never forget it, and it was so strange to be reliving it — all that passion and pain, and Norman hovering over everything. So strange that this young Bertram should be recognizing 'Negro Aroused'. I remembered the flash of vision I had when it first came to me, and how never for one moment had I doubted myself. With this strange new half-abstracted, half-distorted form that had come to me, and now after all these years — recognized — and the chance to do it in its right proportions.

Norman, what do you think darling — are you glad — you and the faith you gave me — and I so proud of you and the strength and courage and wisdom that you showed at that great moment — so long ago.

No one saw us to our car — the crowd surged away after Bustamante, and alone we drove home together — happy in spite of a strange ending!

Not bitter nor reproachful — a first taste of what it was all going to be like.

12 May 1977

Finished 'The Wave' except for a few minor details which I'll complete today. Gonzales came in to discuss casting. I think very, very highly of Gonzales — he has a good brain, and picks his way clearly through all the morass of theories about art.

Neville Dawes[1] uses this phrase, writing of Guillen: 'His directness, his clarity, his refusal to invent private images in sheer self indulgence.'

I expect great things of Gonzales and I believe that he is a *real* teacher, as different from someone who projects himself and sees in the work of his pupils an extension of his own work. He talked about his ideas of teaching and I was *very* impressed.

13 June 1977

Michael is at the Commonwealth Conference[1] — letting fire at Amin. Rachel is in Barbados having great trouble with her health, and things in Jamaica are terribly in the balance, and underneath on the boil.

A crying need for administrative efforts and so many young people in charge for the first time.

I have a cough which turned into a shocking attack of asthma, and I remember Suite's analysis — 40% emotional. Well either the dust from the cement factory or emotional stress — or both!

But as I sit here writing at 11.30 a.m., I have a real sense of foreboding — of a bridge that has to be crossed — that anything I plan or do is subject to something that will happen either inside me, or affecting not only me, but all of us.

There it is —

There is enough threat in the world situation to cause one to feel that at 11.30 a.m. every morning until it happens — so perhaps I should not pay it any mind. But this morning I felt it in a peculiarly personal way. We will see.

I wonder if I should write to Bev or Michael and tell them — how the leaders in China get out amongst the people and *work*. Administration now is everything.

14 June 1977

The premonition is still there, but I've sort of got it under check. Phoned Norman this a.m. to wish him luck with his exams. Doug was excellent on TV last night — he has his own style. Had a long talk with Roy and he's cleaning the swimming pool.

David has brought in his gauze self-portrait — it's a lovely thing, I do wish I could afford it. We had a talk about art and the subconscious — it's so strange, with the vast age gap we think along similar lines.

I'm working at my lion[1] — growling as the dawn comes up — the mutter of thunder in the hills.

Mary[2] really should write now that the boys have grown up. She has a potential style there that's not ordinary, and a perception about people.

10 July 1977

Ah! Had a good night's sleep again. Pete, Richards, Sue and I meet this morning to plan an armature for monumental reproduction of 'Negro Aroused'.

It's a big challenge, particularly for Pete[1] who is going to 'put it up'. I will get a note book and keep a day-to-day record — also of materials. We will go down to the site today as it's Sunday and quiet.

An important thing is to establish a relaxed attitude to Pete and think very clearly about instructions.

'Negro Aroused' was carved in wood — which confined it to the sense of mass in a block. Now I think we are free to let loose some sweeping curves and to dramatize the figure for monumental purposes, and for being seen at a distance. It's funny that after all these years I get a chance to do it *large* — in those days I was so preoccupied with the world of wood and carving. I never thought it should be violent — more throbbing up —

11 July 1977

Negro Aroused

Yesterday was Sunday, but we went down to the spot — the stone base is 8ft 6ins by 4ft 6ins by 2ft 8ins. This means that we have to enlarge the idea of the sculpture to 70 ins. in order to use the full space on the top of the base — otherwise, the figure being placed so high, the lower section of it will be hidden behind the base — things like the hands, etc. won't really show from below. But if they are to come out to the edge of the base, this gives the figure a volume which must be compensated for by a greater height.

We came back and began the armature after much discussion — we knocked off at about 3 p.m., Sue having worked out most of the proportions in figures on paper — and Peter and Mr Richards doing most of the cutting and hammering.

Peter was back at 7.45 this a.m. and we went right on until 2 p.m. creating the armature. He left then after a hard day's work, and Richards and I took a long, quiet look, and added a fair amount of strengthening. Mike came in later and suggested adding a little more support.

Pansy Hart came in this evening — a fine and interesting person — she felt 'Negro' would look very impressive at 70 ins. but we both agreed that the reaction of the public would be dicey. We also discussed the fact that Bogle had turned nearly white and needed treatment — investigating polyurethane paint or graphite. I'd like to try 'The Message' in open air, and see what would happen.

Lots of rain today — don't think I'll go up to Nomdmi — perhaps it's wiser to stay near Peter and see that he is confident and happy.

14 July 1977

So glad I stayed down as Ra came and Paul couldn't meet her — and she needed comfort and help as her health is in a precarious condition.

But on the work front Peter discovered the joys of 'wet clay throwing' and in three hours he had the frame of that enormous figure up — it looked very imposing.

But we've run out of clay — so that means a day off and I can get personal things done and also find the means of keeping the clay damp. We have to keep it going in sharp planes.

24 July 1977

Had meant to keep a blow-by-blow account of Peter working on 'Negro Aroused' — but events have crowded in so thick and fast.

He is such an intelligent and sensitive young man, and he works like a tiger.

He's like his father – he can't stand frustration – so when the clay runs out or is too wet to use and we have to hold up, it looks like the end of the world to him, and then things straighten out again and he's happy and tearing along.

I don't know how I'll be able to take it over from him and finish it.

A strange metamorphosis is coming over me – my strength is ebbing very fast.

26 July 1977

Peter accomplished the roughing out yesterday. It was a gamble sending for him – a bit of pure intuition because I didn't know him very well – and he has, after all, only done a year at art school. But he is an interesting person – I imagine very moody underneath, but he has a quick brain and an excellent combination of hand and eye.

We had great amusement when I discovered he could throw dead straight, and with the violence of a person shying a ball – wham!! exactly where the bit of clay could go or should go. I really enjoyed watching him – he has put up that huge figure, 6 ft high, in under three weeks, and this when we were often held up waiting for clay. Cecil Baugh took him off one day and they actually dug the clay out of a bank – where, according to Cecil, it was coming out absolutely pure – capable of being used without straining, only needing a little kneading. He took Peter and two other students with him, and I think they had a great time. Cecil has just won the Manley Award and he is tremendously happy. There's a whole new cycle of work in him again.

We have had a wonderful rain – which has cleared the pollution – and almost immediately this awful breathing problem of mine has eased, and I feel able to pick up the work on 'Negro Aroused' and move on to the finishing of it.

Tony Spaulding[1] seems to have written a speech, which someone read at the opening of the Fine Arts Festival, which has got the art world into a furore. Archie Lindo has a copy of it. and he is bringing it here today. I refuse to be angry until I actually read what was said – but apparently Scottie got up and protested – with the backing of all the artists present. Anyway, everyone felt that their freedom was threatened.

27 July 1977

They are preparing a film and a sort of record of Norman[1] – Harry Dayes is doing the legal side and a Mrs Theobalds the more personal angle. She asked me to give her some sort of key to what I felt was the motive and mainspring of some sides of his actions. An absolutely crazy thing to ask, but because I have learnt from experience that a thing like that, if refused, can lead to a misconception, in some fear and a sense of bafflement, I write this:

He seemed to have a very powerful inner life — a world where his values, his integrity, were of tremendous importance to him — and which he fought to preserve, sometimes in the teeth of incredible pressures.

And this world was not stationary, the values changed and grew and always in the direction of a greater understanding and detachment.

He always said that when catastrophe overtook him, it always seemed as if he were being guided into new worlds of consciousness — actually even new worlds of responsibility.

I think he had a strong sense of destiny — hidden, unexpressed. He also had a tremendous sense of compassion for suffering.

But you asked me what really made him go the road he travelled — I really don't know, except that possibly, *possibly*, he had to use himself to the full — he had to move on.

Law palled in the end because he knew it too well.

He was a shy man and public life placed a great personal strain on him — it was a price he had to pay — but the need to serve, to accept responsibility, far outweighed everything else.

He deeply loved Jamaica, he could never have lived anywhere else; he loved being with his own people. He loved the earthiness, even what one would call the 'badness', and he had a big streak of the earthiness, even the badness himself.

I don't think he died regretting anything — he had come to terms with it all.

5 August 1977

Michael has just phoned that Busta has just died. We will go to see Lady B. tomorrow.

How the past comes sweeping back over me — in a sense it's a sort of shock — although we have known for such a long time that this would happen any minute.

Half of one's life — the tension, the struggle — what can I summon from the depths of memory, of all that might have been, of all that was — the road that started with such innocence of the future. The suffering that there was then amongst the people — and now, after all these years, it seems to be worse.

Busta himself, who changed as he passed through the period of agitator into the realms of power. Something basic in him never changed — but he grew stronger and quieter. His death suddenly confronts me with Norman's death. I feel shaken and unable to clear my thoughts — unable to peer into the past.

I remember Busta young — I remember his periodic visits, mostly from abroad.

I remember that he and Norman seemed fond of each other — in the way people who have grown up together and then separated often are.

Remembering old days and yet talking of the present more in the terms of their personal problems — not so much in general terms — not related to world events, but how Norman had won a case or why Busta wanted to come home to Jamaica and what he planned to do, if he did return, with his money and his life. In a way we used to enjoy his visits and there was then never any of the quality about Norman that Busta later so resented. He seemed proud of N.'s success, something that he expected of him.

What he felt inside himself of his own way of life it was difficult to tell. He told tales of his life in Panama and Cuba, and I believe he spoke Spanish quite fluently, though we had no way of judging this.

We were very friendly with his two half-sisters, Daisy Cotterell and Ida Clarke — but far more friendly with his full sister, Louise Purcell, who was married to the overseer of Gibralta Vale . . . was it there or another property quite close to Annotto Bay?[1]

Their son Donald, who was at school at Wolmer's, used to live with us during term time, and on one of our trips to England, Louise came with us and used to help me with Doug and Michael, so we were fairly close. Busta's mother used to live with Louise in Annotto Bay. I remember her as a fine featured, erect, not very tall woman, about the colour of Norman.

Louise was more Busta's colour with freckles — her husband Bertie was from Canada — related, I think, to John Carberry. I think John knew about the case that was brought against Busta for charging 20% on loans — he used to speak very bitterly about it.

Then Busta disappeared from our lives until he came back into the news with his letters to the press protesting conditions and wages. I never knew what caused this sudden change of heart, and I am not prepared to be cynical about it. Something perhaps that happened to him abroad — maybe in the States, some injustice that he met, or watched someone else meet. I don't know — I don't believe that he started out with some grandiose scheme to be president. Perhaps as money-lender, perhaps feeling the pinch, being frustrated through lack of a good education, perhaps even being sorry for the poor about whom he had very few illusions — perhaps he was just staggered at wage rates in Jamaica as compared with the States — I don't know. But as a figure in the public eye, life and luck were remarkably kind to him —

Whether he came at the moment, or the moment created him, isn't very important — though I have heard men argue for hours over this. Anyway, Jamaica was on the boil and he seemed to lift the lid. When he was imprisoned, he immediately sent for Norman, and I remember Norman returning from the gaol — and the way he spoke — you could see still that natural, genuine affection and concern. I remember his saying that Busta had described how he felt when the iron door clanged shut and he realized that he was locked in.

173

Busta, like Norman, had this thing about being *free* − a sort of wild animal quality − the sort of animal that beat itself to death in captivity − they both had it.

Just then friends came in.

JBC had done a shocking broadcast, ungenerous, inopportune − NOT the sort of thing one does at a great man's death.

Of course the faults will be recorded, but this was crude and graceless. API[2] and JBC between them, I suppose − or rather, the young ruthless group that stem from the University.

How they let Michael down, and he had done one just before − generous, factual and an example of how to behave at such a moment. I'm afraid one can't leave the running of the world to youth − they are too gauche, too bloody-minded.

I'm implacable over Busta's betrayals, over his cheapness, but he had his qualities − he made his contribution for whatever inexplicable reason − he was a giant in comparison to the silly little girl who read his obituary. Only Dennis gave it a touch of grandeur, that saved it from utter meanness.

We went to see Lady B., Michael, Bev and I − it was a remarkable hour. Now both men are gone, would the bitterness, the cleft, die down? Sitting there in her house − making a little genuinely warm and desultory conversation − we seemed to go back to before the great upheaval. Some iron hand that had held us all in its grip seemed to ease, and coming home down Hope Road an extraordinary thing happened − Norman's voice came over RJR explaining exactly why that tremendous division had to be realized and faced.

So I go back to 1939.

When Busta came out of gaol and Norman got him out, he fought the Governor[3] over it. I know the inside story and I knew both men − the Governor was adamant he wouldn't have listened to anyone else but Norman. Norman had the influence, the status, and importantly, the perception of what would happen − he knew the mood of the people, and above all else, he had the advocacy, the ability to lift the whole subject above personalities, above fear, above the need for face-saving. In any event, lifted as it was in their discussions, it became a matter of writing history one of two ways − the old way of using force and power in the face of suffering and need, or seeing through the madness of the moment into the deep roots of the need for change.

I didn't know Denham very well − either he had the imagination, or he listened to a voice of reason, I don't know. What I do know is there was no one else who could have taken the whole decision on to a plane of discussion where a new road, a whole new road, could open up.

There was no one in the circle of the Governor's advisors — and Norman pledged his own word and his own freedom that the release was the only way as an alternative to endless bloodshed and broken faith.

I think within the confines of being a British Governor, and all that implied, Denham may have been an honest man — but I also know he must have had an eye also fixed very firmly on his future and his career. After the release these two men (N.W. and Busta) toured Jamaica together — and I never heard a breath of friction for months between them.

So what was it that ultimately caused the great divide?

Bustamante was beginning to react, like a sponge absorbing water, to a feeling of power — fed him by the reaction of the people to his charismatic powers. He knew that whatever he did, whatever he said, it was like a divine will for the crowds that flocked out to greet him. He wasn't an orator — he uttered a series of ejaculations as they came to him, often hauling the speaker of the moment from the mike, saying what he had to say, and flinging himself back into his chair, and so the power grew — and the realization of his phenomenal success.

But Norman was touring with him — working alongside of him — and Norman had a brain and will of his own — he also, in his own sphere, and perhaps at a more thoughtful level, had a following of his own.

There were differences of opinion and of method — differences between the followers of both of them. Total belief in Bustamante on one side, and on the other a concept of a party based on a council of voices with Norman as their leader. So in any event, I think there would have been a division.

But deeper than this — it's just possible, and I hesitate to put this on the record, except that it is human. Over the years Busta, I think, was proud — at least he expressed pride in Norman's phenomenal success as a lawyer. I think it was sincere, but under it may have been hidden a lack of satisfaction with his own life and achievements. He had lacked higher education — not, I think, because he couldn't have got it if he had tried, but because he was a good deal at the mercy of his own restless, roaming temperament.

Now here was something that he felt he had earned himself; whatever the motive, whatever the pressures, he was the mouthpiece of the oppressed masses — and no one else could share it, guide it, or divide it. Somewhere along the line he had found a cause — found a source of self-expression — and it was his, and would take whatever shape or form his mood and his will demanded.

Close to him was Norman, equally dedicated, but in a different way. I think Busta couldn't and wouldn't share it — N. could have taken a back seat and possibly even been a confidante and counsellor in times of trouble. 'You, Norman, have your world and your success — leave it to me and leave me alone.' That is possibly how he felt.

But driving down on that Sunday from Irish Town — Busta now having died, and the security man saying, 'Can I turn the radio on — Mr Manley is speaking now.' I said, 'Yes', thinking to hear Michael's voice.

But by some strange twist of fate, it was Norman's beloved voice, strong and clear, like a ringing bell.

If it had been left to Bustamante we would have had a one man rule on a Latin American pattern. He had the charisma to lead the people, and ultimately Jamaica, that way.

We had to form a party on democratic lines, led by a council of ministers and an elected leader. There was no other way.

I was stunned — his voice was so powerful, so alive, so persuasive. I walked into an empty house, glad to be alone, fighting to keep back a terrible sense of loss, a sense of the unrecapturable past. One moment — out of the heavens the voice had come on that little radio, and there I was back in the house again, alone, and with nothing but the dogs and the garden to comfort me.

So there it was — those two who had grown up together with a friendly and a family bond, precipitated by fate into an arena where perhaps only death could end the struggle of two different sets of values.

I know that Busta'a death came like the sudden release of a rope in a tug of war for me.

He did Norman and Jamaica many things which I never forgave — he never saw a new image that was waiting to be born. One couldn't hold him responsible for that, he had never seen it in those terms — but all his life he did look out for the cause of the poor and the needy, and in his own vain, arrogant way he was kind.

I want to go on record for one more event in which he was totally wrong, but not tonight — tonight I am tired.

9 August 1977

I think I must try to get the exact words of that radio of Norman's voice — it's important — my own scrappy account of it is not good enough.

Louise always said that it was total nonsense that she and her brother had grown up in a thatched hut — she said they lived in an ordinary wood house with several rooms — but I used to tease Norman that even his home seemed to get smaller and smaller, and he would laugh and say, 'Yes, but it had a shingled roof, and the acreage is known,' and then he would add, 'It isn't I who make it smaller — It's the Comrades!' So perhaps Busta's followers did the same thing. I don't think Busta would at all fancy his home being denigrated in this way — he was a vain and proud man. It's all a symptom of the times, in the effort to identify with the people.

But the people like Frank Hill simply clobbered me when I said to him, 'Frank dear, why don't you stick to the *facts* — Busta was so loved by the people it isn't necessary to tell falsehoods and even commemorate them — as at Blenheim[1].'

28 August 1977

Opened mould — absolutely perfect job — 'Hero' Johnson, Oliver Chung, Peter Smith — under direction of Christopher Gonzales —

Re-assembled and awaiting casting into fibreglass, we hope by Sam Harrison — will phone Kay.

Have just said goodbye to the boys, and particularly to Peter for the fantastic job he did on the clay — he put it up single-handed, with just basic directions, and the texture was his work. Perhaps the head and the hands alone were mine. He's a great worker and a very promising person in every way. Tremendously honest, and although he's almost too sensitive, it never borders on being touchy or difficult. I hope he'll have a great life — I see many storms ahead, but I think he'll fight through.

We all had our last lunch on the patio. Mike and Mary came in so we were eight in all. We were quiet and humorous but there was a lot of emotion running under the surface. We knew we'd had a great experience together, and we were a little sad that it was over.

Gonzales is brilliant — a first-class professional — and he directed even though he was working on an enormous panel of welding steel rods for Linstead Hospital.

He's such an interesting person — he has chosen as his subject the involvement of herbal medicine and science. It's fairly, no it's very abstract, but if he can pull it off, it will be an amazing achievement — it's a 10ft by 8ft panel, and welding is no fun.

I think over my life and some of the best things have been left for the end. This two months with Peter on 'Negro Aroused', and this last week casting.

Thank you life.

31 August 1977

Saw Don Mills[1] recasting of 'Negro Aroused' into bronze, and discussed possibility of its being placed at the United Nations, two copies, one in fibreglass for here.

1 September 1977

Have today written to the Fowlers at UNESCO in Paris, to investigate the possibility of either a fellowship for someone to go and study bronze casting − possibly Germany − or the even better idea of getting someone to come here and do general professional casting in all media, but finally a bronze caster. I threw out the suggestion that he might possibly use students etc. to get up a hand-mounted foundry for doing small things until such time when either Government or a business enterprise would set up a professional foundry, capable of handling industrial casting as well. I think I'll dedicate my last strength to this project. I can't bear to see people like Kay, whose work is utterly crying out for bronze, battering her spirit and her energies on fibreglass and its off-shoot unsatisfactory and unattractive materials.

14 September 1977

What a week! N.'s anniversary and wreath laying − at 5 p.m. the Women's Conference, at 7 p.m. mass rally at Heroes Circle.

St William Grant's funeral[1] − it made me very sad.

Bev's father's funeral.

And on Sunday the final day of a four day PNP Annual Conference. The bitterest conference since the expulsion of the Four H's − only this was more bitter, more massive and more dangerous, and we have only seen the beginning of it − not the end. The extreme left wing have been wreckers, not wanting anything to succeed − just dragging down the whole effort.

I hardly know how to write about it − the youth utterly uncurbed, running wild over this beloved country.

When I am calmer I will write what I think of Michael's effort on Sunday − Doug has just been in and he thinks what's been going on is just as bloody as I do.

But secretly tremendously proud of Michael's staggering, unflagging effort towards the truth − that waiting, agonizing audience − some in a misplaced triumph at their misplaced viciousness, and some waiting, aching to be led out of the morass.

15 September 1977

Have been up re-reading my diary, the typed copy − it's so disappointing and scrappy − sometimes almost a year goes by and nothing.

Vic and I talked of my writing a book − he's just finishing his, and borrowing my diary.

I can't write a book, but re-reading this, I realize that there are things I could factually record. I can't do any high-flown literary effort, but I was eyewitness to so many things — and if I am careful to put down exactly what I remember, and not go off on to flights of fancy, it might add a microscopic view point to interesting things that happened.

So let's try.

16 September 1977

Had a supper last night for Mike and Mary who are leaving — Michael and Bev, John and Carole, Dick and Shirley,[1] Kay, Val[2] — it went wonderfully I think. I presented Mike with a large box of cigar cuttings from those darlings at Gore's factory. There's no pipe tobacco at the moment, and he has been suffering — to my surprise he was very touched.

The night-blooming Cereus bloomed, and all the women went home with a flower.

Perhaps it healed some wounds, because the left wing had pretty well slaughtered Mike and made his very great contribution well nigh impossible[3] — farm prices, land policy, Banana Board. Oh they were rude to him alright, and simply cut him off at the root whenever they could.

Michael and Bev are oh so tired — but if I know him, he is at his best when and where the fighting is toughest — so long as he is at peace with himself inside, and they have solidarity between them.

Speaking of the conference, Doug said, 'Well, I am waiting to get to the country to hear what my delegates are saying; one has to wait and hear — but at least we have a message to carry.'

But to make the evening nigh perfect, Roy phoned to say that he had got into CAST,[4] with a fabulous story about Doug making a mistake with the cheque for his fees, and how when he got back the bank was closed, whilst he sweated in agony, feeling he'd lost his chance at CAST. But what I love about Roy is his humorous understanding of his father's eccentricities!! The person in the world who would make me want to live longer in order to see him come through — that's Roy — I love him and I believe in him.

Zethilda[5] cooked a fabulous dinner —

I think I will collapse the day that Zethilda, Batiste, the garden and the dogs fall out of my life — it's a magic circle!

Discussion —

The difference between the left wingedness of the Four H's and our present set. The Four H's wanted to go too fast. This set want to wreck, to pull down, anarchism, to destroy in order to start again. There may be some periods of history when this is valid — I challenge that this is the moment here and now.

17 September 1977

Michael wrote Mike a wonderful letter of evaluation of the work he had achieved − naming each item − and he also had a long talk with Mary, thanking her on behalf of Mike, and saying how much he would miss them.

Mike has been pretty mauled by D.K. and Co. He came with such high hopes and they blocked him at every turn − he's a bit of a tiger, and he fought back, and slowly had his effect. He is such a loyal person and believes in Michael completely in spite of so much strain − he knows Michael is the only person who can change this terribly unjust society, at whatever the cost.

So M. and M. will leave with great sadness − but I am confident now that they will come back − and both of them will work and serve.

Six months in Nigeria and then the Yale job − and it's so easy for them to get here from Yale − it's a quick flight. The son, Danny, is coming to work at the AMC[1]. God help him, he will have to have guts and intelligence, and it's a new world to him, but he was determined. It's a sort of call of the blood − the fact that he's Jamaican seems to be a deep chord in his life − but I have watched so many youngsters trying to adapt after years abroad. Anyway, let's have a little faith.

Trying an old idea, which I boggled at in 1941−5, went back at it again around the sixties, and now finally coming to roost − I've given away my carving tools!! So it's a point of no return, after 'Journey'[2]; I put the last ounce of everything I had into 'Journey', so no more wood. And then I did about six or eight works in concrete, including 'Manchild' and 'The Message', both large, life size − I also did the 'Rainbow Serpent' and 'Rio Bueno' in fibreglass. The Serpent made me seriously ill with enphesymia, can't spell it, and I'm left with the damage from that for the rest of my life. The slightest strain or a cold, and my breathing brings on this maddening cough − makes sleep difficult sometimes − I'll never be the same again.

Then Peter worked on 'Negro Aroused' for me − the enlargement − he was wonderful, with all the energy of youth, and great intelligence. Gonzales with Oliver and Hero, two students, have done this colossal mould which is waiting to dry, and the decision awaits as to its final fate. It took twelve men to carry 'The Message' out!!! and we can't cast Negro in concrete, no way you could move it!! So, we'll see − but I think it will end up in bronze, which means shipping it away, possibly two copies.

But now I am free to work small and fast, and experiment with a new approach which I have been putting off for over thirty years. I did a drawing in 1941, and Cicely teased me gently over it, and in a flash I turned against the whole conception.

The unity of man and nature − men and women part rock, part earth, even water. I've started the first one. It's now something well inside my physical strength. I've always loved clay. But I will work with solely concrete in mind — it's Jamaican clay and Jamaican concrete which keeps it well within bounds from a cost or hazard point of view, and I can be free to do as I like.

I forgot to mention 'The Wave' which we have cast into plaster of paris, which involves ultimate bronzing, a big expense and a big hazard.

Actually I've done twelve fairly major works since 1976. You see the speed of clay, it suits my temperament, and I think one can do many experiments with concrete. Cast in colour — texture from the use of sand or gravel or grog in the mix — oh I see a fascinating road ahead — bless you life.

23 September 1977

Haven't had a chance to write — the press — the *Gleaner* in the last month have been unspeakably foul. John Hearne[1] — of all people — John always had a mannerly way with him, a restraint — a good mind — well read — fun to talk with — has written an article — it's libel really — calling Michael and the Ministers contemptible liars and cowards — a shocker really. Then, seeking publicity on the very day of the article, attends Party Conference — Doug says he was sitting near him and he was perfectly safe — he left the arena whilst Michael was speaking, and some people outside who were hostile to the Conference got into an altercation with him, and bounced him about a bit — not enough for him to go to UWH for treatment, but he played his little part to the end.

Well, if you must be a hero, you must pay the price — I've lived through too much to give it a thought. The JLP would have done far worse to Maxwell!![2]

But the whole four-day conference has at least produced a confrontation which has ended in the relief of D.K.'s resignation, and then the Ministry resigned with him. It was a sorry little group he had gathered around him to do that gigantic task. People didn't even know who they were.

It has been a shattering year.

It's so strange, Karl Marx made his titanic contribution when we were youngsters — and then, bearing his thinking in our minds, we worked, we wrestled with the Jamaican context.

The ideal state became a dream — but we had lived through that dream — and now these kids seem a little quaint with their bibles and their theories. Looking back, we did it all thirty years ago, there being no ideal society, no dream world — but the truths that he wrote are real, and they are the yeast in the dough of political and social evils. God bless Marx, but God help his followers.

If only Mike Smith had been less abrasive, less dogmatic, he could have had *such* influence – not on the left wing, they are too young to understand, but on the moderates. Anyway that is past history now.

The women are the force in the Caribbean now – in Jamaica anyway. They have borne the loads.

Coming home today, I said to myself, 'Michael must start laughing again.' One has to know to laugh in the Caribbean, or one loses all. And as I walked through the door he was there on the phone at his most cheerful and amusing self. Michael always flirts when he's happy, and plays cricket strokes with imaginary balls. If he'll only go back to his gramophone again!

It was a good day – because Doug came in full of beans from Cuba – he had two and a half hours with Castro in his gayest mood – showing them around his cattle farms.[3] Doug was in a MOOD – it did me good, and he's so witty and dry and down to earth – a great companion.

I was watching TV when the Black Rhodesian leader arrived home and was trying to walk from the plane to his car – half the time we couldn't see him, we could only hear his voice – press, radio and photographers poking their microphones and cameras right into his face, scores of them. He kept his poise and gave his answers, and finally in an amused voice said, 'Gentlemen this is embarrassing,' and the screen flicked off.

How much longer is it going to take for the world to permit this licence – this abominable and dangerous approach to a job – more vulgarity? How much longer are journalists going to be allowed to call the leaders of a country the dirtiest words – without rebuke or restraint?

But I can't bear to put John into that category of violent, unbridled use of language; it's not like John – and I am very sorry.

23 October 1977

So Castro came, conquered and departed.

Quite a unique week – and what is interesting is that it is Michael who had the nerve and intelligence to bring him – and people of course don't realize or don't remember – so he doesn't get the credit for it, but it has changed the picture in a hundred ways and left the opposition – and by that I mean the forces of evil, at one level of intensity, and of conservatism on the other – with one weapon less with which to fight. The great bogey man, the monster, the devil, the evil man – and he comes with remarkable wisdom, with warmth, with charm, with common sense. I have watched it, fascinated.

The two things that stand out in my mind – his meeting with the churchmen and his understanding of the absolute havoc the young left group of anarchists can create. I get the feeling, talking to Michael, that he is a man with a first class mind, a great deal of a poet, and always this quality of love, love for and understanding of people. I think he poured out everything he had of mind and heart to help us, and particularly to help Michael. He warned Michael of something we had begun to suspect — that Seaga is now totally tied to the CIA, and that is a dangerous combination.

8 November 1977

The publication of the *Penthouse* article[1] and its denial by the CIA brings finally into the open the fear that has been haunting me for a year or more. That horrible story of the blackout of the pilot flying Michael across the country in that little plane[2], and the near crash — saved only by the second pilot's amazing speed and coolness.

It's interesting too, that after an experience like that, the pilot transferred to another company. He must have doubted what could have happened to him and whether he had been tampered with. Anyway, perhaps with Carter in charge that danger may iron itself out — I hope so — but I think our security have much to learn from the Cubans who do the same job for Castro. Anyway, let's have a little faith — but I feel better that the publicity should come from abroad rather than from ourselves.

The crime wave here has shifted its focus, obviously. The minute you get banks and large sums of money involved, it smacks of professional criminals, probably organizing from abroad.

I have been reading *Trinity* by Uris, and Levenson's *Maud Gonne*, both of course on Ireland, and it makes me wonder if there isn't a restlessness, a divisiveness, about Jamaica that could lead us into a permanent instability, out of which much creativeness could come, but which would make it difficult for us to achieve on the economic or social plane. Of course we are in the grip of trade union demands which are blind to the fate of the thousands of unemployed — and the world depression and turbulence is giving us more than our fair share of battering.

This is a difficult spot in world history, like living in the midst of a minor but endless earthquake. The fundamentals deep down are still intact, but the surface rumbles and rocks. Youth on the march demanding — demanding and disrupting their own worlds.

I think a little while ago I was getting very irritated with American 'Women's Lib', but Golda Meir's autobiography sobered me up — the Eastern woman, the African woman, the *Muslim* woman. But here in Jamaica, it's not that women are freer, it's as if women are more real. Dr Fraser, head of the Norman Manley Law School, was emphatic to me the other day that women make much better jurors, and in some cases better judges, particularly in criminal cases. Their lives demand that they understand people, and the relation of people to events.

14 November 1977

Michael is back from his three weeks abroad — the American leg of the trip seems to have gone very well, particularly business and press.

Norway he fell in love with — both the landscape and political thinking of the people. He feels he's made a good contact there — particularly for the future.

Sweden was impressive but he didn't feel as at home there — but Yugoslavia is all that he thought. Belgrade is apparently a very beautiful city, and the accepted successor to Tito, a terrific personality.

Next month, he meets Jimmy Carter. I'll be curious to see what he thinks. Carter's abandonment of the ILO[1] has shaken even Jamaica. What wolves the reactionary forces in America are. Can Carter cope? On our front we have the poisoning of D.K. Duncan[2] — let's say it's the CIA, but who is the local agent, and above all who is the small and intimate hand who was able to consistently keep it up until the man was hospitalized, when it all came to light? I feel we are living in a hostile and bloody world — a sick world really, and as Rachel put it to me tonight, if some remedy isn't found for the youth, the way they are set at the moment they will pull society down and destroy the West.

15 November 1977

Thinking over the situation with D.K. I find that in my mind he is the symbol of what took place after the election — irresponsible talk — double talk — which was swiftly spreading panic amongst the middle and professional classes. During the election he had been guilty of it — one thing on the platform and another in the rum shop. When the election was over he became either the hidden leader of, or the prisoner of the Y.O., the fringe Munro-ites,[1] and ultimately total confusion reigned. He had no idea how to handle the general public — people were either Comrades or were nothing. Maxine's[2] handling of the public was reputedly beyond belief, and did more to paralyze D.K.'s effectiveness as Minister than any other single factor. That whole group saw themselves as the real power — and in a power-drunk way, thought they knew so much more than any leader.

Actually, the nitty gritty of it lay in the failure to become the establishment in any real way — they held office, but they still were the enemies of office —

they seemed unable to make any change in their own minds.

And arrogance – mercy what arrogance – stupid to be quite so arrogant, and oh so dangerous – and in the wild panic that spread, with people leaving in their thousands and using every means in their power to get their money away. Michael rode it all out. It's not been easy for anyone – for any of us.

And here is my little creed – simple, pragmatic. The people suffer – the people need – everything – can we build a society that can change that? Can we work and govern as a nation and never take our eyes off that objective?

I am not an anarchist – it takes time and dedication. I know I write from an old generation.

Talking with Rachel yesterday, we both looked squarely at the fact that Jamaica is now caught in, or part of, a world upheaval where crime, violence, revenge dominate the entire scene. Even little Barbados has it. But except for moments alone at night, I am not afraid – and I am not afraid of being alone at night – it's not that – but when one is alone there is time to think.

One has to keep one's faith. I send my faith to Michael to play with the cards close to his chest, keep his own counsel, and be strong and quiet.

20 November 1977

Last night I worked for an hour or so in the studio and came back to search for Matisse, Renoir etc., sculptors. I fell upon Giacometti – not quite what I was looking for, I really wanted ...

Doing this little series of study figures for concrete – to learn about *fondu* and just following any nonsense that came into my head – I had done one little study that seemed important, I call it 'The Sleeping Hills' – but the two after it lacked any quality that I was searching for – I slipped back again.

So tonight I got so far and *stopped* at the precise moment that I had reached before I strayed away again. And I sat and brooded and brooded with Giacometti before me – something that Marini seemed to have to a lesser degree – and then went to bed.

This morning the phrase comes to me to work so that the work reveals something to me – not the other way around. This question of stopping in time, but far deeper than that – here is involved *process,* so that surface is not a subsequently applied thing which kills the beginnings, drowns them, swamps them – but in this way you learn to understand and express something that is taking place before thought.

I did this in a drawing once – 'Before Thought'[1].

I suppose in other terms it is just the subconscious finding its way through, or even the identification with something in the collective unconscious.

26 November 1977

I am deeply, deeply grieved over Duncan's unwarranted, unexpected dragging of Bustamante back into the arena[1] — what on earth can be achieved by it? Past history, past hurts, past mistakes or glories. Raking into the past intent on tearing everything down — dividing — when we need to build, build, build. Leave people their loves — we all need to love, to be proud, to look back not in anger, but seeing it all in perspective with the wounds healed. He was coming into the House to make his first speech as a back bencher — it could have been a triumph of inspiration, of leadership.

So the inevitable happens and Perkins[2] gets into the fray to rip everything apart — so we are back where we were — hating, dividing, at war. I'd like to get into D.K.'s mind for a while and discover what goes on in there — a total confusion I'm afraid — a mind pinned on certain theories, and a conviction perhaps that to pull down is essential before we build — but this is clearly based on theory, because so little is there to be pulled down.

For a long time I have been so worried 'in my small corner' about the Women's Lib movement, judging it I suppose on the sounds that come out of America, which are quite hideous — the savage expressions of hostility about the war and humiliation of the battle of the bed, and the repudiation of the bras!! Whatever the developed nations may feel about lesbianism etc., etc., surely this is not relevant to the needs and the position of women in a developing nation.

Is it possible that America has grown too fast? She is such a young country and yet she seems so like a falling culture — of some old and weary European country. She has telescoped everything —

I hope and believe that Bev will do her *own* thinking — based on our problems. She is so realistic, basically, in spite of her love affair with Karl Marx, which I must say moves through in her own way. To be a little prophetic, she made *her* mark there, for our women do need guidance, they carry such a helluva load and have done for so long, and there is a latent tendency to be hostile over it.

You see marriage in the Christian sense doesn't add up anymore, and with the fluid sex relationships that exist, children will now be brought up in a different way. Don't think of it as broken homes, that evokes an image that is *fait accompli* — rather think of the relationship that produced the child as something temporary, but something that must quietly evolve with the child still as the hub of the wheel, holding something together in a loose bond without bitterness. Above all without bitterness — children adapt to almost anything if the people handling them are happy.

Well we can all carry almost any load if inside we are at peace with ourselves.

I think Rachel is handling her own situation remarkably well,[3] and trying not to be possessive over it — with the result that the tensions are easing and the children are really lovely — both of them — and yet so different, as different as Doug and Michael are. Those two have made good lives for themselves — it gives me an area of happiness, for which I thank life.

Paul too is behaving very well and the children love him, and this fact, which Rachel sees clearly and respects, makes her move in as an unselfish a way as she possibly can — this is what I feel is our modern pattern at its best, with all its flaws.

27 November 1977

Went to Boxer's show this a.m. with Hope's on the ground floor. Two remarkable shows — David with his strange death urge, and Hope feeling her way into a brave new world. They both filled me with confidence and I came home on air — especially as David Johns was there, and planning a concert with Nerine Barrett.[1] They're playing Copland — I must brush up on Copland — so far I've never got past the two great Russians who seem to mark — what is it — there's plenty of Ravel there and plenty of Mahler, but oh the vitality of the unashamed emotion. Prokofiev with his Sonatas 7 and 9 and his *cello* concerto, and Shostakovich with Quartet No. 13.

So let's have a look at Copland.

Schoenberg bores me to tears. I've listened a lot — one day I'll go deep into Bartok, but not now. Sometimes I think one should be blind to get the best out of Bartok with his so sensitive (hearing?) and his night noises!

It was a lovely morning with lovely people there. I came home so happy.

7 December 1977

Certain things happened yesterday — I was shaken — and now a strange new light has dawned. Yesterday evening, looking through my big window — just the corner of the tree lit up — pure gold — with sky behind it silver blue. Behind the house the sun was setting and just by chance it must have caught a corner of the tree. I stared at it — it could have been just that — but it was more — something inside of me stirred — I know I said aloud, 'But that's Norman's corner.'

This morning I awoke at about five-thirty and in my mind's eye I review my present work and somehow I know I have to choose a different path. Only the old woman[1] is right — no, that isn't correct. The weary old woman[2] comes first, and then the sleeping figure[3], and then rising, waking woman[4] and then the little figure working[5], and then the two little archetypal figures[6] sitting very still — and suddenly a raging lion[7] — very small — and then I went over to the couch and sat and thought, and the breakthrough came.

The woman with her baby carrying the bundle of clothes. The dispossessed — I have the courage now to go into the present scene of violence and unemployment and poverty. Have I the skill — have I the passion — I am old now. But the light on the tree — that's it — that will show me the way — and I have gone on record.

15 January 1978

No, I never did this — instead I am working on 'The Ancestor'[1]. The truth is that I can't really work on something of which I have no direct experience.

The man in 'The Ancestor' — and his relation with the tall figure of the past. His past — his ancestor. We all see ourselves as either having to smash the contact with the past, or as taking great strength from it.

I can feel passionately about the dispossessed, but I can't actually give birth to it — give it life.

On New Year's Eve, Ra, Jarmila[2], Dan, Sarah[3], Norman, Roy, Rose[4], Johnnie and Melanie[5] — played dominoes and cards, and I told fortunes, and we saw the New Year in with Mr B., thundering out his 5th Symphony — tut, tut, tut, *tum*. It was quite unique and we all kissed each other. It was simple and real and unforced.

I had Norman staying with me getting ready to go to England to do more study, and to work and earn the money and try to be free of family and name — to break, in brief, with his Ancestors.

20 January 1978

I hadn't really wanted that book of Lawrence — I left it lying on the table for a long time, and then I ran into some reference to him and without conscious thought I picked it up to look up and check the facts, and of course I got caught and fell —

One thing leads to another, so I went to the bookshelf to see how many of his books were left after all the years. *Women in Love* was gone, but *The Lost Girl* was there.

I couldn't put it down, and as I read the last phrase, I found that the tears were running down my face. I cried and cried and for two or three days, somewhere in the back of my head, I realized that I was walking around in a kind of trance. So much had flooded back — my lost youth — all the passion and the glory of what had been.

But far deeper and more than that.

This genius of perception, of awareness. This man who could make a whole
landscape take on the palpitating life of his own body, his own spirit, nothing
is missed, nothing left out, the very stones cry out in praise:

Oh Lawrence.
Why did I have to meet you again?
One had lived the best one could,
but so often one has compromised
with the naked truth. How else to
survive?

But this, this is different — this *is* the naked truth. So the book was left
behind and I found again:

'Reach me a gentian, give me a torch
Let me guide myself with the blue-forked torch of this flower
Down the darker and darker stairs, where blue is darkened on blueness
. . .
And Persephone herself is but a voice.'
'This sea will never die, neither will it ever grow old nor cease to be blue, nor in the
dawn
cease to lift up its hills
and let the slim black ship of Dionysus come sailing in.'

And somewhere I half remember, though it is not quoted here — 'It is not
easy to fall out of the hands of the living God: They are so large, and they
cradle so much of a man.' Does it go like that — it's just a faint memory.
'Frieda you have killed me.'
So I won't go to France after all. I'll stay here with the simplicities and try
to keep faith with life — a little more faith.

30 January 1978

I am glad I recorded that, though it is a bit emotional! Because lots of things
happened after that — because I felt that Munroe was unsympathetic to Frieda,
I pulled out a book I had been meaning to read for a long time: *The Richthoften
Sisters* by Martin Green — and then I got a shock. It has left me depressed for
days. It gives the whole picture of intellectual Germany before the First World
War.
The story of Otto Gross and the two Weber brothers, Heidelburg and
Munich. Patriarchal and matriarchal societies. A fascinating book, a brilliant
book, and if nowhere along the line you are involved, a very worthwhile book

to read. But Otto Gross — that's a story all to itself — anarchic, destructive, almost totally mad — a pupil of Freud.

But I have read of Frieda — sensed the truly great influence in Lawrence's life and his art she contributed — but never for the wildest, brief moment did I realize the sort of background she sprang from. She lived with Gross — and absorbed or even contributed to much of the madness — totally wild, totally free, totally even creative in her own way — but not this other thing — and then she captures Lawrence. They seem to have lived a very tortured life and out of it his art sprang. He burnt himself out — very quickly, very brightly — very, very brightly —

Munroe closes his book with the quote, 'Frieda you have killed me.' Martin Green uses the phrase: 'Lawrence was Frieda's secretary,' with all that implies.

I just can't bear it — he meant so much to Norman and to me — we learnt so much from him — we were young and I think we understood ourselves so much more. The poem 'Look we have come through', we felt we could have written it, and neither of us sensed any overpowering force in Frieda. A life force, yes — but not this destructiveness, so that when Mabel Luhan published her book, we repudiated it. Now I wonder — perhaps if she had written that book in a more detached way an aspect of truth might have emerged.

Anyway, I feel shattered — I really do — I always knew that something quite fantastic was going on in Germany — one had read references to it so often. But I can't *make* my mind attach or associate Lawrence with it in anyway.

But I do remember my sister Lena, who was married to a Radford, whose family was closely associated with the Weekleys and who knew Frieda's first husband very well and was near to him over the separation, saying to me one day, 'Do you know you don't understand that situation with Lawrence at all — one day you will, and you will be disappointed and surprised. Everything he wrote came back to a sense of guilt which impelled him to denigrate Weekley and attempt to destroy him.' She felt that Chatterley was Weekley and she despised Lawrence for making Chatterley physically disabled. I hate the fact that anyone could write that he had imbibed so much from Gross via Frieda — and no one can tell me that his genius for description, for evoking sheer landscape, quite apart from whatever he had of the prophet in him, or any statements he made about society, flowed from any gift of Frieda's at all.

He was an artist in his own right. I don't know — I am upset, and perhaps they have exaggerated her faults — for at least she had the gift of laughter and enjoying life, which must have helped him. I think I will quietly re-read him and assess it for myself.

He obviously used people he knew to build his novels — he upset his friends often by doing it — and perhaps most of what he knew about the man-woman relationship he learnt with Frieda.

And was Frieda really the product of Gross? Even so, Lawrence was a very strong person spiritually – he wasn't Frieda's secretary, never on your life.

So, I've re-read Frieda's letters, and that photo of her in her seventies, and I feel a little happier – she was strong and she loved life – perhaps she helped him more with the actual writing in the early days than I realized – but still he was a great artist – a thinker or a 'feeler', and she – she was just herself.

The account of her death sent to Barbara Baur by Joe Glasco – no one could have written of her like that if she had been the demon Green makes out, and her own reaction to Munroe's book: 'There is Harry Munroe's Lawrence. But there is a Lawrence I knew that is not there.'

7 February 1978

So then Leavis got in on the act defending Lawrence, and between them all – these critics who earn fame and a livelihood writing about other men's work. (*sic*).

Well I have nearly finished *Aaron's Rod*, a fascinating book, with the other side of Lawrence – his genius for dialogue. Candidly I would rather never have read a word about Lawrence – but just known him through his work.

David is sending me his Last Poems from England – at least I hope so. So I will re-trace some steps for a little while and then R.I.P.

Megan[1], passing through Jamaica, came to dinner last night with David B. and later Lloyd[2] and Colin[3] came to pick her up. Megan has a mind – we had an amusing little skirmish on the use of the word 'happy'. David and Megan don't like the word – maybe not – but as a condition?

17 March 1978

All hell is popping on the political front. David[1] has been transplanted (supplanted?) by Bell[2] at Finance – it's all a little sad and hurtful for David and Michael. Michael had a hard time over it – he and David are life friends, and we all love David, but it needs a man like Bell to try.

The truth is, as an advocate for Jamaica's cause, you couldn't have a better man than David, but the Ministry runs itself – oh, the old story of who is a good administrator. That's a tough ministry. I remember it of old. they're used to taking orders from an English Governor, or doing as they like under confused and insecure ministers. But that sort of set-up in this changing scene doesn't work. Mercy, it's a difficult world.

And the PNPYO – I have no words that can describe how I feel about them. The chance they have thrown away – and pretty little Mr Trevor Munroe,[3] thinking he will change Jamaica – perhaps he will – but the change won't suit him either.

191

Still, on the credit side so much is happening that is good – whilst the press pour out their bile, the great opportunity to build confidence and energy and faith is in danger of being lost – but I will never lose my faith – I believe we will not only survive, we will pull through ahead.

I'm a bit tired myself – need a week by the sea – as soon as I finish 'The Ancestor', I'll go – possibly to Dragon Bay.

2 April 1978

Reading Gilchrist's *Life of Blake* – printed in 1863? I am struck by its beauty in style and its honesty in searching for and revealing the character of the man. I cannot help comparing it with the modern trend in biographies which seem to search to reveal the most private, and even the most trivial details of a man's life. Inasmuch that quite often you can't see the wood for the trees.

There is Samuel Palmer's wonderful letter written years after he had known Blake, who had died long before.

All the sordid details that surround some of the books about Lawrence and particularly the recent book on . . . (*sic*) where sex seems to be almost the sole preoccupation and so much is interpreted in the light of abnormality – the fine line between what is and is not normal is not of great importance when attempting to follow human relationships.

This is a little beside the point, I suppose, in the light of what I am trying to come to grips with in the Gilchrist book.

There is a grace, a wisdom, even a touch of humour! It would be hard to find that in a contemporary biography.

29 April 1978

Took four days off and went down to Port Antonio to just lie down and think, and pinpoint the final, ultimate seat of this upsetting and depressing fear. Have had a lot of emphysema which doesn't exactly help, and I've suddenly dropped over 20lbs weight – which is good in a way, but makes me look very haggard. I lay and counted the good things and the bad things. On the credit side, Rachel has brought her book[1] with considerable courage and determination, and that little book has remarkable, I use the word 'quality' after a good deal of thought. She never does a cheap thing, and when she is obscure, she makes you wrestle with the thought, and above all her verses sing.

Also on the credit side, it seems as if Norman Jnr has taken his step into manhood – by going abroad, working in a job and planning hopefully to go on with his law study, also Gray's Inn. If it comes through, he may make himself qualified to practise in England.

We will see — but it is a good move; people are so loyal to his grandfather's memory that they don't even realize how tactless they are. Hard on a young man, and he must do what he wants and stand on his own feet. So I'm relieved over that. Then Drum fell off the roof,[2] and after an awful scare, survived. He and Luke[3] were here — they and Natasha are a warm, lovely note in my life.

But this depression — it surfaced at last and I realized that I can stand like a rock now that I *know* what it is. Everything that is happening to Michael — not what happens from the *Gleaner* — the press of the world is the problem of the world, and my life with Norman has taught me that at the heart and core of the *Gleaner* is something that moves with the stealth of evil — an evil born of an intention to be the sole seat of power. Once you see and know that, you learn to live with it.

But the ugly, ugly struggle that goes on inside the party, whilst Jamaica's future hangs in the balance. This poses Michael with a problem and demands of him a strength and a caution that are not ordinary. We will see — but in the meantime all I can do is to be steady — even cheerfulness can be almost insensitive — but steady and quiet — and keep near to Bev who grows under adversity.

I am reading Bronowski's *Man Without a Mask* and in an eerie way it helps. That period of industrialism, the French Revolution, the American war, and the people starving, and little children working fifteen hours a day from when they were four years old. Is God strange to have allowed the human race to evolve on such terms? And our little lads up for murder at fourteen and sixteen. One day I must give myself the time to write my picture of what is happening to Jamaica today — desperation stalking the land — hunger, hopelessness, brutality — and the answer the guns?

Oh, keep me calm and steady.

7 May 1978

What helps a lot — though difficult to achieve in these days of stress — is to clutch on to some sort of sense of history.

We are going through a period of change — change that has been forced on us by the conditions at the bottom — change long, long overdue. So that we are *all* finding ourselves challenged at the most demanding levels. We speak bitterly, even contemptuously, of the professional class who run away — of the businessmen who move their money out, of the 'spoilt' women who don't want their children to grow up under equal educational facilities, and even those who run because of the new colour prejudice and the fear of being attacked, raped, everything. These things happen in every revolutionary period, and although so far this has not been a very bloody revolution, it could become that at the drop of a hat. The incidences of violence come nearer and nearer home − and when it happens to us, will we be bitter, will we still see it as part of a process? So it's no sense being angry at the lack of patriotism − those who run don't like the look of the new Jamaica, and even if it were bearable, the interim passage prolongs itself into a long future.

Sometimes in a weak moment I wish Michael could have been spared this moment in history − Douglas too − and then the list spreads out to so many people that I love who are caught in the storm − but they would be being saved from one of the greatest periods − the greatest perhaps since the riots that were linked with the post-slavery agony and struggle.

So stay steady, and steady in the face of any eventuality − one has to hold on to history. I spend the long weekend completely alone, and the thought often crosses my mind − no longer − it won't happen to me − instead I sometimes think when will my turn come, and if it does, how will I handle myself − not only outwardly, but inwardly − what sort of scars will it leave?

Anyway −

24 June 1978

Dan and Sarah got married today. I do wish them a lasting relationship. They are a gallant pair, and remarkably intelligent. It seems such a long time since I wrote here, and yet it isn't − but so much has happened. I've had a very hard time healthwise − and it really shook me, as my doctor had gone away. I still don't feel 100% but life seems to be a little more real. It came home to me very forcibly that one can feel so weak that to slip over the edge is now for me just a matter of time, and then what?

Reading Blake, Lawrence and even Jung − all three at least kept an open mind, though both Blake and Lawrence had a deep conviction that death is only part of a vast experience, just as birth is − I don't know. I think my strongest, but hidden, conviction is that somehow, somewhere my relationship with Norman is unfinished.

Working on the 'Creation' drawing just towards the end, I suddenly realized that the creative spirit was Norman − and I was so excited and *glad*. I don't really understand the drawing myself − it is possible that it has to do with the sheer energy required to create, or it could be the fear of birth engendered on the political scene right now. All the pressures and restraints have been lifted off, chiefly I think by Michael himself − and so everyone who would be going about their work cheerfully, now suddenly feels the inadequacies of their lives − the itch and rub of their work or their daily round, and so feel free to protest, to demand more, and so we get this rash of strikes. But deep in the core of our society is something far more serious, far more saddening − is the unemployment. This is the thing at the moment that just crushes me — isn't it at the heart of the violence and crime?

Michael made a tremendous statement in his Budget speech. It has, I think, cleared the air. But a 'follow-up' is an imperative, and at the heart of the PNP there is no strong person such as Arnett was. I wonder — what step can be started there?

We have been through a year that sometimes I wonder how we survived. Every kind of problem and often catastrophe. All the old problems of inertia, inefficiency, rumour, scandal, violence, cruelty and often just plain callousness. There is no doubt that mediocrity will always defeat and destroy vision, positiveness, enthusiasm, a desire to help and to change.

The old defeat too of civilization from the barbaric hordes — so that even here where music once was a standard, it is now swamped by the commercial pandering to what is the easiest appeal to sell.

I remember Norman reading Toynbee — where he says there aren't any barbarous hordes left to destroy what man has built. Now we contain the barbarous strain within our own culture — our youth, our underprivileged, now dictate the standards and 'Rock' is king — manners, dress, uncouthness, even dirtiness, personal dirtiness, are in the saddle and anything else belongs to a past that must be obliterated.

I don't really mean all this ... the truth is I haven't the patience to sift out exactly what I do mean.

25 June 1978

Had a talk with Michael. I think the fact that he had been driven into an inhibited posture was really wearing me down. I don't know how he could have reacted in any other way to the storm of *personal* abuse as different from tough, valid criticism, pouring out of sick people like Hearne and Perkins.[1] There has been a vulgarity that has never been equalled. It was quite a shock to me that a man like Hearne who, up to a few months ago, came weekly, drank my vodka and talked literature with me, could write anything as vile as when he made the bold assertion that Jamaica was being governed by a dog as Prime Minister.

There was once a Hearne who lived in Jamaican history — but surely something has gone astray. Strangely enough it helped me to at last decide never to open a *Gleaner* again — and now I'm happy with the *Daily News*, which criticizes, but which leaves the mud where it belongs, in the pig-sty.

Michael's Budget speech brought him back sane, fighting, almost fatherly at times, and then he let fly on the achievements in spite of all the agony and ills of our present times — totally uninhibited when he is himself speaking. You can feel the rapport with the *people*.

He's got guts, my God — just like his father, and Eric Bell just made me so proud — may his health hold and may he be for the years ahead, tough, cool, intelligent and honest. Doug was marvellous too — he never leaves anything to chance. When I asked him what he thought, his answer was, 'Well, I'll tell you when I get back from South Manchester.²' He really grows, does Dougie — and he looks happier and physically much fitter.

I am slowly fighting back to health — not easy though. Scottie has bought the big 'Creation' drawing which will steady the bank — but I do wish I could get a full-time person to run the house for me and leave me free to work.

10 July 1978

This last week was a bit stunning. 'Negro Aroused' had been stored at B.L. Williams waiting to be packed — someone set fire to Woolworth next door and the fire spread and both places were completely burnt out.¹

When they told me, I sort of couldn't register, and then last night it came home to me with a bang — what had happened. Well, it was a labour of love and I was giving it to the government to mark the famous spot. It's been a tough year one way and another.

Things are so confusing I'm revoking a decision — coffee has soared to $5.20 per pound, and when I think of all my coffee planting at Nomdmi, I think I'll go back up and take charge!

Also I've just got to get a holiday this year — out of the heat and worries. Actually I would have liked to go and lie down in a posh hotel and watch the sea — but with George and Odilia² coming and Rachel likely to be here, I think I'd better provide a base where I am totally comfortable and can entertain.

Mike leaves tomorrow, and Ra and the kids come up from Barbados. I'm so glad they're coming.

Ra's writing is growing stronger and becoming more a part of her life.

So let me get ready for the summer.

15 July 1978

It's a terribly hot Saturday afternoon — the house is very silent as the dogs make the only sound, panting with a fast rhythm that makes one think of a fast-moving machine. There's no one here but me.

This morning Lorna Goodison¹ came to see me. She works on the National Gallery Board. I was very struck by her at the last meeting and asked her to come in for a morning here. My health has kept me from attending a lot of art shows, and so I feel terribly out of touch with the youngest set. I am going to

196

make an effort, and Lorna has promised to help me make the contacts. There's a Wainwright Robinson who has done a social commentary picture called 'The Runner' which we are going to see, and she has promised to bring a small group up for drinks one evening. There's a strange, bitter resentfulness against the older artists who take no interest in anyone but themselves — coming under the category would be Marriott[2], Abrahams[3], Barry[4], Huie, and possibly even Hyde![5]

This is true — but there is no doubt that there is a group of youngsters who are in a devil of a hurry — want to get fantastic prices — $2,000 for a fourth-year student's work — demanding to be represented in the National Collection, putting on one-man shows before they are remotely ready. In other words, worshipping the bitch goddess. Youngsters who want to use their art to be successful, recognized — instead of working and learning the craft of their profession — struggling to find themselves not in society, but in their work. Perhaps all this is an exaggeration, so I am going to try to find out for myself.

Margaret Chen[6], who did my *fondu* massive woman with the breasts, came to see me. She is studying in Canada and she brought with her a girl who has just graduated from the art school, who impressed me very much. She made a good point that Michael made years ago — that the students will miss much when they leave North Street and go to the new building in the Training Centre.

Garish colouring — blue tube lights — terrible heat — instead of the old high ceilings and mature gentleness of the old building. Well, Jerry Craig got his way — a brash new building, but they lost a lot in the move.

I was very impressed with her and with Margaret. The latter brought some photos of very interesting abstract wood carvings. I asked her if she is going entirely abstract and she said no, she wanted to do both. I was very glad because she has done some brilliant nudes and portraits — whatever she does has that sense of design and style, and I think she's a real worker. I have great hopes for her. I gave her my last wonderful piece of mahogany. She seemed happy and I only hope it won't crack with the Canadian air-conditioning.

Scottie asked Marriott to cast my 'Ancestor' for me, which he has promised to send to England to get two bronzes, one for him and one for me. Marriott agreed to do it, and it gave me a wonderful chance after all these years to get near to him. He has been through a harrowing time, with his wife in a nursing home with a permanent breakdown. It has drained him and worn him out. He was hardly strong enough to tackle the job — but it was a joy to watch him cast. He is a perfectionist who leaves nothing to chance. He did a superb job and I am forever grateful to him. Bless him, bless him. He has lived a courageous life and tackled some vast jobs — but if it hadn't been for Scottie's support and friendship, he might have died a bitter man. Scottie has been quite great over the arts — he has backed Abrahams over all the years, who comes through to a triumphant period in these last two years. His biblical pictures are magnificent and are very sure in feeling and design. David has a massive collection both personally and at the gallery.

I have just bought his, David's, last picture, 'I Saw My Land'. A priceless agreement! I paid his telephone bill and gave him my *fondu* 'Woman on a Hillside'[7], also a little sketchbook I had of studies for the life of Moses which I never did. I know I got the best of it — but he wanted it that way.

There's a Rastafarian Bishop living on our road now with magnificent, great, tall iron gates installed — with the golden Lion of Judah crowned on both gates. But that is the least — he has a rooster that crows day and night — and there is something doomed about that little cry. It must be a very small rooster because it has a tiny, desolate crow, as if it knows that one day it will be sacrificed — not to feed someone, but in some strange, ancient rite.

All day, particularly when I am quiet and working — and it seems to be the last thing before I go to sleep and the first thing as I wake!! It always makes me think of an Aztec ritual sacrifice?! So I put on the gramophone and drown it —
God help me!

20 July 1978

So that's over — it was a colossal strain — a sort of disruption of a kind of peaceful work. Anyway, it went fairly well. The Vice Premier of China, Keng Piao, and his wife, plus Ambassador and his wife, etc., etc.,[1] Bev was an angel and lent me her Jamaica House staff who provided tea and soft drinks. I was very impressed with him — for a Chinese he is quite tall. He also is very strikingly good looking and carries himself with an air of quiet authority and charm, plus a warm, outgoing manner. There's no doubt the top Chinese leadership is very impressive — we were struck by it all the time we were in China. You get on the one hand the old revolutionary type — you get the same type in Israel, and certainly in Cuba — and then above and beyond that are those who have settled into the harness of making that revolution work. They have a sort of confidence, often an apparent idealism, and always a dedication to the job in hand. I enjoyed meeting him, but then I believe in China, and although they have clearly swung right — away from persecuting Mr Beethoven — I believe that they *possibly* have a better chance of remaining rooted in the people's power. I do hope so —

What I find completely bewildering is the bitterness I find all around me, and the willingness to condemn the whole Chinese effort because of her foreign policy. One shows enormous sympathy with Israel — then why not with China? The Russians are going to ruthlessly exploit Africa – and a big question mark hangs over Cuba. All my life I have searched in vain for altruism in foreign policy – perhaps as the result of growing up under British Imperialism. China has Russia like a snarling beast on her boundary – with an eye to uniting her to the 'wall'. Has everyone forgotten the plight of China after the Japanese devastation? So she turns to the States, so what? She dare not fail her own people – well I for one stand by her – and if it's a choice of Stalin or Mao, is there any question? Both countries will fall back into original, traditional patterns. Russia is doing it already and much blood has been shed, but vast changes have taken place and so it will be, only I hope to a lesser extent, with China.

8 August 1978

George Campbell is back in Jamaica. He was very thin and nervy when he came, but he's looking much better and he has had a remarkable welcome back. I think Jamaica has just caught up with his poetry. Many of his poems are known in the schools – and certainly politically. Actually, Norman did more than anyone to publicize them – he quoted them so often, and in his last speech he made one famous: 'Oh when I lift my hands and pray.'

I hope I'll see something of him, and in circumstances when we can relax and talk. Rachel is in Europe and I'll be very interested to see them meet, for he has influenced her poetry a great deal and always for the good. He brings back so much of the past – the gay holidays – he was part of our lives from 1936 onwards. We all loved him, each in our own way.

Douglas, Michael and George – and Norman watched him with a twinkle in his eyes and wondered about the freedom of his poetry, and in a doubting way would ask him: 'George, do you ever *work* on your poetry?'

And he would flush up in the defensive: 'Oh, Mr Manley, of course I do.' And Norman would fix him with a penetrating eye and would say: 'Humph ...' and there would be peals of laughter from all of us – George too.

27 August 1978

Yesterday John Hearne wrote his libellous article[1] – about Michael and ruling by torture. Somehow through this there is going to be a great need for calm – for an ability just to go on with one's life. Unfortunately Rachel has gone down with the gastroenteritis that we all have had. It's a pity, for she returned from her little trip abroad looking so well.

She's staying at Melanie's and I spent the evening with her and Melanie's two children, who are charming. We played cards and Ra watched, but the article came up — Ra is so perceptive, and she picked up the current that underneath I was upset. I didn't bother her about it, so there it was.

It's 6 a.m. — at 7.30 I'm going down to Norman's grave with his orchid, which is blooming — George and Odilia are coming too.

I always get a little strength when I go there. I don't go very often. So let me get dressed for the dawn is here.

2 September 1978

Saw Rachel off yesterday, she was feeling much better — but still far from well. But it was a cheerful send off — with hundreds of people milling around at the airport, as all sorts of rumours and news about strikes in the control tower grew and rumbled. Anyway, Melanie and I saw her off — cheerfully. The house was very quiet without her when I got back — she's such fun and full of life, and so much better living away from worry over her father and the endless tensions.

Today I must see George and try to have a quiet talk about his future. The job at the Institute is there for him, but I wonder if at sixty he can pull up all his roots and leave that warm family of four daughters and Odilia, and suddenly come here. If Odilia were coming too, but she has an interesting and very necessary job herself. I don't believe he could bear to leave it all, even though I think he does want to come back.

I must get back to a work routine myself — it's the only way to keep steady under what are becoming rather dangerous pressures. I believe we will survive — but what we need now is a good party organization — a good annual conference, and not to slip in the by-elections.

Blake[1] has gone and it makes me sad — and Coore[2] — but life is like that right now — some people can't face this changing scene. I am not sure what is the mixture of toughness and flexibility that is needed. To face the youth of 1978 — the bitter, frustrated youth — forces change, change in oneself. It's easy to write — it's easy to think about — but when the fourteen-year-olds are had up for murder — something inside one asks to die instead. And those who 'have' and can't face giving it all up — no, not all — but just some of it.

The violence. I can understand the run away from that — it's a pretty shattering experience. Oh, I can understand a lot of things, but the reality is here, and it has to be faced.

5 December 1978

Muschette[1] came to see me today to let me know that 'The Wave' had at last been shipped to the States for bronzing. He had a hard time getting the materials for packing — but in the end he did a marvellous job and wouldn't charge me. I think he felt very deeply over 'Negro Aroused' being destroyed. He only brought the bill for the shipping — we sent it by sea.

I love 'The Wave' — and I do hope that it will bronze safely and give an honest and illuminating representation of the work. I have had a hard time — since I went into clay — with all the problems of casting, with no professional help. Marriott did a wonderful job with 'The Ancestor', which is still waiting to be shipped, and Gonzales did a marvellous cast with 'The Message'. But 'The Wave' gave trouble because the wrong plaster was used. So I keep my fingers crossed.

The Drumblair Dance went off very well. I even danced a little, a thing I haven't done since I was ill with the fibreglass.[2] It's the first dance I have even remotely enjoyed since Norman died — I saw Michael and Bev dancing and obviously very happy. I didn't get home till four and they were the last people on the floor, singing 'Auld Lang Syne'. It made me so happy to see them so happy — they've had such a hard year, we all have had —

I wonder what next year will bring — this ghastly and strange happening in Jonestown, Guyana,[2] with over 900 people committing suicide. I think it has shocked the world. I keep remembering Mittelholzer's[3] book, *My Bones and My Flute*, and I wonder if that Guyanese jungle was a contributing factor in this appalling happening. I went into the fringe of it once and it left a grim memory that I've never forgotten — the sort of thing Joseph Conrad would understand.

But we are undoubtedly living in an amazing period. This cultism — everywhere the church seems to have failed so completely, and men grope for something to satisfy this craving for religion. At first I was very interested in, and in a way sympathetic to, Rastafarians, but not now — out of it grows nothing positive — and there are factors in it now that are terribly unattractive. Of course it's difficult to sift the real and the good from the phoney and the downright dishonest.

The truth is the world has become a very dangerous place.

24 March 1979

There, I have just seen Mike off at the airport. It was a brief visit and he worked hard on a project for Michael, then he had two days with a mysterious virus which came suddenly and left almost as quickly.

The house is silent with no one here but the two dogs, Johan and Nansi — so I take out this book and, with a new pen, I look back over the last stormy two months. Every sort of problem pressing in on the local scene and the world tip-tilting at the most horrific danger spots — with war in so many areas one can't keep up with it. Well, it's very explosive — but one mustn't be frightened, just be 'cool' as the youngsters say.

I was very ill two months ago with my enemy emphysema. Mercy, that was something; I was in hospital for eleven days. For Xmas I went down to Barbados where Rachel was living under great strain. As soon as I got back I was ill and as I came out of hospital I heard that she was gravely ill. She came up to Jamaica for tests and then was sent on to England for further tests. As soon as she came back she had a lump removed from just below a breast – we are still awaiting the report, but hopefully. She has behaved well – but she has been through a very difficult strain. If she could get her health settled and go on with her Masters Degree[1], it would be wonderful, for she is growing into a remarkable person and poet.

The political situation calls for unending stamina, intelligence, patience and faith. I think years ago I stated what I feel about the stand the *Gleaner* takes in our public affairs. They dogged Norman and now they are back at Michael at a time when this country has to have some sort of faith to hold on to to produce, to endure world conditions of the rising cost of living. At a time when Jamaica needs, and its leaders, to have some sort of meeting ground of confidence. I don't read the *Gleaner* anymore except for its badly reported world news and the racing and boxing.

But John Hearne – what has happened to him? When he was young he seemed to believe in a brave new world, but he has made such a tawdry mess of the fine talents he had.

Do I sound bitter? Not really – I'm not bitter, I have nothing to be bitter about. I have been blessed with a family and friends who had extraordinary powers of understanding, of loyalty, of love – I have loved many people and rarely, if ever, not learnt and received more than I gave. So why be bitter? And anyway, it's so bad for one's health.

I had a long talk with Louise Bennett, who is someone I truly love and respect. I learn so much from her. She has an uncanny insight into how people feel and think. I tend to create people in the way I would like to think they are. Louise seems with complete realism to see them as they are, and with such understanding – always accepting people – never trying to change them – because they are the world we live in – and there isn't any other world.

George Campbell came back to Jamaica after thirty years – it's been a bit of a shock to him and he's a brittle person. Terribly insecure, but still our finest poet – he stayed with me for a bit and it was wonderful to see him react with such sensitivity to the coo of the peadove – the mountains – a garden – after living on the fortieth floor in a New York flat. He so needs affection and recognition, always hard to come by. He's living up at Olympia – at A.D. Scott's – he's the sort of person one misses. I have always loved George, and the poetry is pouring out.

Tomorrow night I have dinner with Michael and Bev.

I heard accounts of last night's great meeting.

We have been living in the political doldrums for months — and Michael called this meeting to explain the 'crawling peg', his visit to Moscow, to cut across the distortions and viciousness of the press. A vast crowd estimated at 25,000. I hear you could hear a pin drop as he spoke. He felt that the crowd was desperately trying to understand and to keep faith.

Mike saw him the next day and said he was weary — but that something was restored in him.

Tonight I go to 'Masquerade'[4] with Easton Lee — it should be fun — I need a little, and these young people are so charming to me — I do appreciate it.

Roy is growing into a wonderful person. I'm taking him and George to Morant Bay to see old Bogle — who I hear has gone snow white[5] — and just for the drive and a little outing.

20 November 1979[1]

Sold my Benz October 31.

It's a sort of milestone — life will be different now, but I face it with great buoyancy — meeting taxi-men, having to organize one's day, making lists before setting forth to save the mileage and to save a second trip when you forget anything. So life begins at eighty!!!

My work has been a bit in the doldrums as I wrestle with finishing the Adam painting[2] — you know I don't know how to paint! I'm so clumsy — using the fine end of the brush instead of one's fingers or a cutting tool.

21 June 1979

Extract from a letter from Mike Smith:

I've been dipping into Jung's *Dreams, Memories and Reflections* not reading consecutively — so much is pure gold — and so much is inevitably dross. We need to distinguish Jung the man, the fighter, from Jung the message, the text, the creed. The man himself would reject any creed — but in his situation he had to try to provide one. I believe his courage and his experience, his sensitivity and his turbulent spiritual life are far in advance of his best efforts to integrate them — or anyone else's that I know, and also perhaps his unyielding honesty and determination to meet whatever came his way head on — but I'll continue reading with attentive ears — no fear.

Just for the record, I took to their first pocomania[1] meeting (pukko) Sherlock, Edith Clarke[2], Madelaine Kerr[3], Zora Hurston[4], M.G. Smith, George Campbell, Katherine Dunham[5], Leslie Clerk[6] *and* N.W. Manley.

7 July 1979
On the night of the third, API brought the start of a film on Norman's life. It opened with his funeral. There were just a few friends and family present — but it was a terrible shock to see my own face, over and over again, to see Rachel and Michael and Doug, and the mourning crowds. When it was over, I wanted *desperately* to be alone — but they stayed on for a little while and were kind and sweet to me. I have been haunted ever since — and when one searches for a pattern for the future, the only thing that brings me peace is a mood of tenderness. It's the only solution to the memories that hurt — being gentle with and about people and being a little gentle with oneself.

I'm going up to Nomdmi with John and Mike for a few hours — to see the extent of the damage that the bulldozer has wrought near Minni.

Some drawings I did in 1940, which were never completed, have been stirring in me again. Why shouldn't I go back and give birth to them. I find my work is breaking through into wild, free movements and shapes. All the things I avoided when I was young — except for the period around 1940–45? when I became terribly near to an almost cosmic consciousness — with the 'Dying God' series etc. But I found two battered 'browned' paper drawings and both of them were notes for future work, thirty years ago. Clay into bronze was what was indicated, but I was so frustrated by the practical problems that such a course created for me, that I used wood like 'Moon' and 'The Horse of the Morning'.

Rachel has been unwell and snowed under by financial problems. She so needs something stable in her life. I see all the struggle in her poetry — I see how near to the nerves her creative life springs. It worries me deeply and I strive to help her, but she has a strong sense of her own destiny, and interference achieves very little — one must just keep near and help in the practical details and with love and understanding.

Doug will be in Barbados now — and they have a wonderful relationship — it will give her strength and make him happy.

17 July 1979
The Fringe of Leaves by Patrick White — what quality did she[1] possess that brought her surviving through unbelievable horrors — not only intact, but with her conscience still the strongest element in her life. It's as great a novel as *The Idiot* and far wider in its intent and experience. There is a grandeur about her humility.

21 August 1979
Now why have I opened this old diary to write when I have nothing at all to say. The year moves from one bump to another — politically, personally, physically.

It's quite hard to keep some sort of hand on the steering wheel, but there is always the joy in the little things — the birds coming down for some grain, the black birds bathing in such a 'drastic' way that all the water is emptied out of the bath. Johan is such a gay, such a joyful dog, and little Nansi is so earnest with her big eyes showing the whites. 'The Ancestor' is back in bronze — it's made me so happy. Rex has one and Scottie one — and 'The Wave' should be on its way back now. The little mother is finished. I wish I had the foreign currency to bronze it — but that's an idle dream. 'The Trees Were Joyful' is being bronzed I hope, I hope.

As I write I feel a little calmer.

Doug is coming safely through that big operation[1] — he looks so much better.

There! The scene is over!! Michael wrote to Ra and accidentally signed the letter M.N. Manley, oh dear — oh dear!!! Anyway we're all friends again — thank God.

18 September 1979

Today is September 18th 1979 and it has rained and rained for days and weeks — though it seems like months and years. And yet we are so lucky — USA with billions of damage, Dominica wiped out, Santo Domingo with 3,000 dead — Cuba has taken a beating. We have had appalling floods at the end of the island in one spot a month ago — 50 ins in ten hours. But here it just weeps — 'old woman rain'.

But these weeks I have been facing the fact that I am living way beyond my means and the moment has come when I may have to leave 'Regardless'.

It's the first time I have tried to bring the subject up — but now I have mentioned it to Doug and he is coming in this morning to discuss it with me.

You see I can't always expect to work as hard to supplement my pension, and I sometimes think one shouldn't leave a thing like a move till the last second — isn't it wiser to do it whilst one is still strong enough to do it with a fresh sense of adventure! I sort of check the losses and the gains, and strangely enough the first thing that comes into my mind would be the loss of the dogs!!

I've always had a dog, ever since a child — when my Irish terrier, Mike, used to come to meet me from school. He was a remarkable little dog; we would leave for school together down the lanes and across a large field, over a stile, and when we got to the stile I would say, 'Home, Mike, home,' and he would pause and hesitate and turn back home. Then when school was over someone would say: 'Fetch Edna, go on fetch her,' and I would meet him cheerfully trotting down the lane to meet me and great joy and leaping about and barking when we met and went home together.

Then there was the dog that I bought for one pound with long, shaggy hair – and three weeks after I got her she produced eleven squeaking puppies. I was an art student and in digs at the time – working in an office in the day, and at art school at night – and I came to find my landlady simply furious and demanding that I get rid of the dog and pups *immediately!*

So if I move into a flat and rent 'Regardless', there'll be no more dogs. No handsome Doberman Johan the Gay, or mini Boxer Sentimental Miss Nansi.

Let's think about it – where can I cut down and save – the drink bill is a problem, and they never read the meter, but they send me colossal light bills. There's something inefficient going on there alright. Anyway I have taken that step instanto. I have written the Jamaica Public Service Co. an investigating letter – the last time they read the meter was in February this year – and they can't read the meter behind my back, so to speak, because the man would be afraid of the dogs. Nansi's bed is directly under the meter!!

Then the next thing is I would have to have a studio somewhere – because I do believe that with the grace of God I will be able to go on working small things to almost the end.

I know that the present large relief of the dancers[1] is my last very large thing. You see I have to climb up and down, up and down on to the table to work, and then to stand back and look at the work from a distance. It's good for me in a way – it's good for my concentration – but it will become increasingly arduous. So let's be realistic and think in terms of small experimental things. My chief problem is casting, but somehow we've just *got* to get someone to specialize and become a professional caster.

2 October 1979

Yesterday I saw the bank manager – he was so kind – but the picture is pretty grim. I've raised another loan to try and hold on until February, when I hope to give my show, and that all depends on my health. Anyway I have made a final decision to face realities and to work small and to try to draw more, so that I have stuff to sell. I am scrapping my big relief[1], the joyous one; it is too big and the casting etcetera create too big, too formidable a problem.

I am desperately unhappy today – this mix-up with Cuba and the States over Russian troops in Cuba[2]. I don't know how or why we have got ourselves all mixed up in it – as if we haven't got troubles enough of our own.

The *Gleaner* and the JLP are off on a flying gallop over it, but as George says, it will be interesting to see what Kennedy has to say after Carter's statement. It's the first time I've felt that Carter has played to the election. Michael thinks that Kennedy would have moved the US soldiers out of Cuba long before all this would have happened.

This last vicious attack of flu has left me almost deaf!! I have to find a new and more profitable and less risky line of work.

I think I am emotionally and practically prepared in my own mind for the inevitable change in my life to meet the rising debts and inability to face the cost of living. Never mind, I will adjust when the time comes — the important thing is to make whatever step I take a wise one.

What I have to remember at all costs is to keep a deep sense of joy inside because I have been blessed with such a marvellous life. I would like very much to do a series of studies of goats — both drawing and small models — and face the bogey of casting!

30 October 1979

There! So much has happened — I've sold 'The Mother' to be bronzed one day, and possibly too the picture of Adam which isn't finished yet.

I am very pleased with this 'Old Goat', — Old Ram, Dylan Thomas would say — but I don't want to make mistakes in the casting. It is just made for *fondu,* but there are problems so I've wrapped it up till next week, when Scottie is bringing Marriott to advise me over the moulding.

I think I have sold the Benz, it's a big step to take — but I believe it will free me financially if I can make an economic arrangement.

20 November 1979

I got lost in this book and put the sale of the car in a section dated March 24!!

I am worried about George's future[1]. Some coin has to drop in his mind so that he can come out in the open and face the fact that it's not a good job as it stands — no money and no publications. If it would move into something wider and more significant.

21 November 1979

Yesterday I took a taxi down to Mrs Keane[1], and all the way down the driver was tearing Michael to rags — there was a pause and I said, 'And yet you know I think he is trying so hard — he works terribly hard.'

'That's all dam rot he don't do a thing, how can he be tired only going to Cuba all the time.'

'But he is trying tremendously but this is a world slump — it's not us alone.'

'How you know he is tired — he's *not* tired.'

'But I am his mother, I must know.'

He went on ranting as if he hadn't heard. Then we came to the stop and I opened the car door. Suddenly he turned and with a look of grief on his face: 'I didn't know you were his mother or I wouldn't have said all that.'

'Never mind, I understand – but believe me he is doing his best.'

'Will you believe me, I'm sorry, I really am sorry. I shouldn't have talked so.'

My hand was resting on the back of the front seat. He took it in both of his. I thought he was going to cry.

'Please believe me I am sorry. A mother is a mother.'

'Never mind, dear. Don't worry over it, just have a little faith – try to understand.'

'Goodbye Mrs Manley, I'm glad I had a chance to drive you.'

'Goodbye dear – drive carefully and God bless.'

I felt happy in a sad-happy sort of way.

And this morning I have woken with such a sense of foreboding – I can't work – can't even face the studio. So I've walked in the garden a bit and I'm sitting on the patio although it isn't 10 a.m. yet.

What on earth is it – I hope it's only my imagination, but I feel terrible, and yet I'm so well physically.

George has just phoned that Doubleday want his new poetry and he has lost it!

25 February 1980

H.P. Jacobs[1] published a story in the *Gleaner* that I persuaded Norman to go into politics, persuaded by Fairclough to do so. This is not true. Norman wrestled that one out in his own very unique way. He knew that the country needed something – people were suffering poverty, unemployment – low wages were crushing a vast section of the country. He had learnt just how bad this was in his work in Jamaica Welfare. He wanted powerfully to help – what he was unsure of was what would make the surest contribution, what was the right road, how to achieve results.

Fairclough was afired by the Haitian history – that politics and power were the only way. The difference between Fairclough and Norman was that Fairclough repudiated adult suffrage – he didn't trust the people in the sense that he felt that you could do things to help them, but that they couldn't be part of the process.

Norman felt you must lift from the bottom up – that you must go to the people, not hand down gifts. He wouldn't serve any organization that didn't include adult suffrage, and it was part of his greatness that he doubted his own powers, but once committed, he totally accepted the responsibility.

Fairclough saw a need for political birth – but what he saw was a far more limited horizon – Fairclough said politics alone can do it, in the hands of a Jamaican élite.

Norman's problem was that he saw a far vaster effort, and this made his struggle to see the way infinitely greater and harder.

I knew nothing of politics – but seeing it in the terms Norman saw it in, I learnt from him.

The contribution that Fairclough made to my life was that he helped me to meet and understand a new group of young people – like the Reader's and Writer's Club etc., and he helped me to face doing group work and what I called, we all called, backyard meetings. I learnt from him how people will give the answer that you want, or even expect to get, and so you are totally misled.

I learnt that you have to be trusted before you can expect to get frankness and the truth.

I also learnt to understand all the difficulties of overcoming a sort of still strangeness that comes from difference of colour and class.

Meanwhile Norman was learning how to talk the language of the streets – from public platforms – without talking down to people. How to meet the fact that rural audiences are tired if meetings are late, because they get up so early to work.

It was hard – but he learnt, and in those early days we were so *happy* – we felt a team.

8 April 1980

1980 has opened full of foreboding – prices rising, violence everywhere. Very reluctantly I have agreed to give a show – the last decade of the seventies[1]. I feel very queasy about going before the public in the mood they are in. Only one or two or possibly three things seem to come through to real finality. Anyway it's in a week's time, so not to worry!

Went to Nomdmi for a weekend – the first harmonious period I have had there for a long time, particularly regarding health. And the hard, dry weather which brings out a quality in Nomdmi that particularly releases me.

You get the pungent smell of the pines – you can walk and sit anywhere. The drought is so hard on the people with water shortages. I am aware of that all the time – but the triumph of the sun is there pulling at all one's sense of the eternalness of the world – out of time and space.

So when this show is over its opening, I am going to pray for enough good health to spend what might be my last chance to go to Nomdmi, and find the inner peace and strength, and let it talk to me once more – and for the last time – as it has done in the past. It's difficult to know if it is because one can be alone and quiet there − if it is the challenge of the landscape − with the towering blue mountain range that one looks across at. Or is there some special quality as I used to claim in the past.

I know that all my life I have been conscious of suppressing something inside myself. An awareness of family and of the public opinion of a country that I deeply love. Now, even if I destroy everything, I want to be alone with myself and my thoughts and my work. The times are so appalling, both in Jamaica and internationally, that one is driven inside oneself, and that is a journey into a little-known sphere − one hasn't time to know oneself.

This morning I opened the newspapers and headline news is − USA breaks off relations with Iran − for the first time on any large scale − there has been (sic) in South Africa. Sadat, Begin and Carter are to have a difficult meeting with Palestine looming over their heads. Massive rioting by blacks in Bristol, and so on and so on − what comes to me very strongly is that it *can't* get any better. Unemployment in Britain mounts as it does everywhere else in the world. Here it has reached a point where it is quite shattering and hence the endless brutality and violence.

I can't explain why, but on Good Friday when I left the hills I once again took out Blake − the little Tate Gallery book − and I spent the weekend looking and brooding and thinking.

After the show − a new road − a very, very personal road, more disciplined in my personal life, and with a tremendous effort to conquer the sense of loneliness.

One isn't really lonely − that's just a state of mind − one must be unafraid of the next step one has to take.

I find Garcia Marquez almost biblical in style and thought: 'And so she understood, not through love, nor through hate, but through the measureless understanding of solitude.'

11 April 1980

So the exhibition is mounted, all except 'Mountain Women', coming from USA and the lights are sliding into place. David is really remarkably gifted, and he has surely put his back into this show as he does for ALL his shows. He has that combination of the creative and critical that is very unusual − also he is so many-sided − music, fine arts, writing and TV.

I'm facing the opening with what calm I have left after a gruelling year − politically, family − and on top of all, world pressures. I will be glad when it's over and I hope it helps me financially − if I could just get on to a material balance, I think my spirits could soar.

I worry over Rachel and Norman − life is not easy for that generation −

and Michael and Doug are really facing the battle.

Daily News coming for an interview — hope I'll keep control of the situation.

13 April 1980

Thinking back over 'The Faun'[1] which I haven't seen for years. The work puzzled me when I was doing it — but now, looking back, it comes to me like this — the Faun — the whole concept of the Faun died out hundreds of years ago — an elemental creature — but deep in all of us the Faun exists — something elemental, passionate, fear-ridden and utterly untameable.

It's hard to find the words — this creature of the woods and mountains — sometimes brutal — sometimes laughter-filled — utterly shy.

And the Faun in the modern world crammed down under all that is so-called civilized — but is really the dominance of technology. For after all the Faun could live safely in the great civilization of Greece.

So the Faun today is grief-stricken — terrorized.

11 May 1980

What an appalling start 1980 has got off with. It's unbelievable — everywhere in the world tension, bitterness, explosions of every sort.

In some dim way, after the hazards of the seventies, I believe that in our pathetically human way we were looking for a beam of light or hope that it would not continue going from bad to worse. But that is just what is happening. And in our own small world here, there is something quite cruel taking place — cruel because it seems to have no sense of direction. As each event piles up — each act of violence and brutality — no one seems to know where we are going. I certainly don't.

It's so tough to keep faith, so difficult to believe that everything we fought for has ended like this. Not ended, that's a wrong concept — but that it should have to pass through such a difficult road. Anyway, it's happening, and alongside of it all much good is coming in ways that are swamped by the noise and confusion. Time, time, time is what we need — these things take time and it is obvious that the 'people' explosion that we are living through here is the same explosion that is everywhere else.

The people are on the march — they don't march with a clear purpose — they only know that something has to 'give' somewhere, that their world shall improve.

And can you blame them — gunmen don't provide leadership or give a direction — but they let the world know that they have had enough of want

211

and oppression. I'll never forget what the Black Power movement achieved for the Black race in the States. Decent people were shocked and afraid of the direction things were taking — but the Black Power movement did more for the decent people than anything they had been able to achieve for themselves.

So here we go — I can't work myself just now — I've smashed up some powerful beginnings — I begin to see an element of complaisance in my work and I don't like it — but what does one do with a hurricane?

19 May 1980

I have to chip out 'The Dancers' in *ciment fondu* today — it's strange how one can suffer from this inner *panic*.

Later —
It was still dark when I turned on the studio light and started the long job.

Also I hate this Fellowship and OM[1] business — I hope I'll get through tonight. But if one goes on refusing, it looks as if one is being aloof, and perish that thought.

Never mind — feeling better now. Do the nightingales feel panic as they persuade the young ones to leave the comparative safety of the nest for the first time? This is about to take place in the garden — soon, soon.

I worked until breakfast time — cut away the outer layer with the wood and burlap reinforcement. I was weak and tired — but feeling more confident.

After breakfast I started to get down to the *fondu* — heavy going, but confident and careful — and then my caster turned smiling and interested — he said he knew how to chip out — so I gave him tools and side by side we had it all out in time for lunch. A good cast — not perfect but lively and a nice colour.

So that's my future insured, at last I've found a caster!! After sixty years of struggle.

This is a bas relief and easy to cast — so I showed him a clay sketch that I am going to enlarge and it's in the round, and he's confident he can cast it — but I'll go carefully before I land him with important work — oh glory be!

5 June 1980

Been browsing through many books on sculpture — Moore, Lipchitz — and reading even as much as looking, back into Herbert Read, looking at Bourdelle and Maillol. Bits of Janson's History of Art — but on the sculpture.

A book on Modern Italian. Boccioni, Marino Marini — read a whole life of Marini and looked hard at him and Martini and Manzu, and finally worked my way round back to my source, Mestrovic. I hadn't realized how deeply he inspired and influenced me. His great 'Cariatid', his wood reliefs, the taut line of his neck with the head drawn sideways.

I come up finally amongst the 'moderns' with Marino Marini and Lipchitz. At least equal in power with Moore – but with Lipchitz the outstanding quality is that he presses on and on right to his death – whereas I think both Moore and Marini got bogged down a bit, one with lying women, and the other with lying horses!

And then I picked up my old friend Mestrovic – with his heroic creatures and his deeply spiritual side. But never mediocre, never a cliché, rooted in humanity, rooted in craftsmanship – and, too, always pressing on.

But what a grand sense of history – what a humility in the face of the Titans of the past.

I do respect and revere his whole attitude to sculpture and too in its relation to architecture.

24 July 1980

How in the name of God are we all living through this reign of terror; it is impossible to describe.

Not fear for oneself, though that is all part of it, but the burning down of two old people's community homes – where over a hundred people die – and the deliberate shooting down of children at play – little children five and three years old.[1]

I haven't written about it – because I can't – that the beloved Jamaica should come to this; but perhaps it is something the whole world will pass through – the pent-up wild anger of the poor – centuries of neglect.

And now a madness – without mercy, without compassion – just a blind rage to kill, kill – and at the moment they are killing each other. How to write of it – how to keep faith and understanding.

One has lived too long!

I've done a sketch of an archetypal woman trying to protect some children[2]. I would like to put it into a permanent form – but my spirit quails before the challenge. One has to believe – one has to be positive. I try to peer into the future – I spend half my conscious life trying to pull away the thin film that separates us from the future – not again for oneself – for my future is very short – but what way is the world going?

Let me go back to work – but each day one realizes one is living on a diet of some new killing, new arson, new brutality. It is claimed that the men who commit these crimes are kept going on cocaine – but whatever the prize money, whatever the cause, whatever the internal mental disease – it is our people who pull the gun — light the fire — and it is *our* people who protect and hide the criminals. I hadn't thought — even though I expected and knew that the explosion was bound to come — not the Eventide Home — but most of all not the little children at play.

Anyway we're casting in the studio — three jobs since my show and two others already cast. Errol Lewis[3] and Basil Watson — they seem to have what it takes — they seem to be careful and disciplined. This afternoon we will chip out the first of the three in *ciment fondu* — when it's a success it's a great material, I love it — but when the casting hasn't been well done, it can be pretty awful.

So I'll check out now.

But before I leave — why is it that these crimes are committed almost entirely by men? Are men — under pressure — more brutal, nearer to the animal than women? Women in the Irish movement commit murder. Then there's Patty Hearst. Is it that men assume responsibility even in their crimes — because it seems to me a woman murderer is a rare thing.

Rex was saying the other day that a man who couldn't kill with a knife, could conceivably kill with a gun. There's something almost detached about killing with a gun. You can stand back from the mess. I remember during the World Wars — bayonet killing placed a far greater strain on a soldier than any other form of attack. There's a lack of contact, shooting with a gun — and in any event for a century now guns have been glorified. To kill five men with a knife has an element of danger in it that is formidable and even impossible — but in one minute six bullets can destroy six people and hold a whole crowd up to ransom.

So all the movies and novels and pictures and TVs have come true at last with one man with his one revolver.

God, oh God.

6 August 1980

Whilst preparing for hurricane Allen yesterday — what a storm — in the back of my mind the form that the new work would take started shaping in my head, and I realized what the new work is pursuing — something more stark, more primitive — the emotion expressed in the form and not any humanly naturalistic expression. Dawn and the head with the flaming hair[1] are first steps — but I think that the new head may press it through further.

I stared and stared at primitive work, comparing it with the late Greek sculpture — so I feel that with hard work and hard emotions there may be a year of work ahead down this road. You see that is the way to release the subconscious untrammelled by thought, and more and more I know I haven't released my subconscious to any great extent. These two last heads[2] – perhaps.

No, that is nonsense – I haven't released it in clay and concrete. The *fondu* is enthralling – it is old-new – it can be so primal in its massiveness.

Johan hurt my finger accidentally, so I won't go to work. I have the sketch in pencil and anyway when I finished the winged horse power plaque[3] I knew I was tired after the show – a week's rest, much though I resent it – I'll go and tidy my cupboards.

Thank God only one life lost – though the poor will suffer *terribly* – and we just can't afford a hurricane, with the endless damage. We – in our concrete houses – whilst the little shacks go down – Michael feels terribly, terribly. At the last moment it veered off Kingston, but places like Port Maria have had a terrible time.

30 August 1980

Lamming[1] said I should write an autobiography – I have often thought of it, but I don't feel up to the task – the scene is too big for me. There are too many imponderables and my view is bound to be very biased. Looking back I remember how much I suffered from deep fears, a sort of inner panic that was a relic from childhood – but to this day I still suffer from it.

One of the things that future generations may not understand is that with all our faults, our weaknesses, we nevertheless were breaking new soil – doing things that had never been done by Jamaicans before. There had never been a Jamaican Prime Minister, never been the wife or the child of one. There had never been a minister of government in any aspect of life. People were voting for the first time – how did we find guidance? Certainly not from the past.

So we walked enthusiastically into a tremendous and fearsome responsibility. A slip, a mistake could be blown up into astronomical proportions – pressmen have to live, and they don't live on certitudes, they live on the frailty of humanity – the frailty of life.

The attempt to be totally honest is beset with some strange shocks. To be honest with oneself – that is a rare privilege – but somehow one has to hold on to it – however secret, however privately that is protected. You see people don't always want the truth – in fact the truth is a very personal thing – your truth and my truth. Nothing in our personal lives had prepared us – we stood, part of and yet facing a public in the full glare of a blazing, a searching light. Action was demanded – how to find a common denominator for a programme. I don't mean only in policy decisions, I mean in the day-to-day contacts of questions answered – or subjects deferred.

'I can't look into your heart – you can't look into my heart – we can only trust one another.' A man told me that in an election campaign. But how often does one meet a response like that? The business of party politics in Jamaica has been not so much the selling of a programme as the destruction of your opponent by any means.

We went into our first election on a programme — and we were chopped into little bits!!! No regrets, no bitterness — but with a certain amount of humour we learnt a sharp lesson.

Here I sit quietly writing whilst the 1980 election is raging around us. New forces, new factors, and a dangerous period ahead for everyone.

How would you like to wake one morning after an election and discover that you are the wife of a Prime Minister? You have to sit and quietly think through every value that you have held most strongly — all the things most dear to you.

It is something life had dropped on you — a tremendous job — like putting an unbroken horse to draw a chariot. You're there — there's no running away and the footlights are on. Strangely enough I doubt if many people think into that aspect of the future — until the door is actually open. In a country like England the Conservative Party would come from a world used, to a certain extent, to what now confronts them. The Labour Party — with a few rare exceptions — with their totally different backgrounds — would more understand what I mean. Professional people and 'workers' facing and leading a class-conscious country like England — where every slightest sign of inexperience or lack of formality would be sniggered at behind elegant fingers.

So after that long, quiet moment of appraisement, of assessment — you are left with a slightly apprehensive decision to be yourself — come what may — but of course it isn't quite as easy as that. Clothing matters, a schooled patience has to grow — and always you are haunted by that inner panic that steals your calm, when you most need it.

And to learn public speaking — however slight and unrehearsed. I made my first public speech in Clayton Powell's[2] Abyssinia Baptist Church in Harlem. Norman was ill and I spoke for him — well — I survived — because people are kind!

10 September 1980

Now why did I go down with a fever like that — I went to bed tired but alright, and then I woke at 2 a.m. shivering and aching from head to foot, not even aspirin worked. Michael came in at about 8.45 a.m. and I was completely confused — thought it was Thursday and noon, and couldn't find either Batiste or Ellen[1] — and Ellen, who had gone to the country for the weekend, arrived and said: 'But it is Monday — I'm back on time.' I was quite wandery.

It was horrid. I slept nearly all day and most of yesterday still with a fever, and today, Wednesday, I feel it all had something to do with the effort to rough out this new head of a Rastafari singing.[2]

George saw the beginning and being honest, said very little. Then Wayne Brown turned up after seven years.

Frederick Karl's book on Conrad is the most important thing that has happened to me for many years. The quality of thought − perceptiveness − even of invention . . .!! Norman would love it.

God I feel weak − but I must make that head S I N G −

25 September 1980

Casting going fairly smoothly −

My hands hurt sometimes when I work − so I'm using hammers two different sizes − to hit and mould the clay.

Bev's baby has come prematurely[1]. I do HOPE all goes well − she is fine. Michael is very caught in the underground of worry for both their safety.

Anyway the Venezuelan oil deal has come through[2] − he worked so hard for it − bless him.

Doug is having a bumpy patch with his future still uncertain[3]. It's a strain but he's holding on.

20 October 1980

I can't let this quite brutal election campaign pass without a comment. Roy McGann[1] and his bodyguard have been killed and the whole country has had a shock −

Never in all my years' experience − forty years of politics − has there been anything like this. One can't go into details about it − it would take a book and also one would be writing all day −

There are certain basic facts about it that one either accepts or not. United States interference − I took a long time before I began to see the pattern − and there it is. America attempts to rule the world, and not only that, but to force other smaller and weaker countries to accept her way of life and to force it, not at the hands of an open surrender, but to be battered in the back by illicit arms handed out to the men of the ghetto − who, because life is terribly, terribly hard, will take money to ease their frustration and their hopelessness. That is 1980 for you.

Yesterday I was near Dudley Thompson's[2] political office − so as the friend I was with wanted to see Dudley on election affairs, I went along too.

Whilst we were there, a woman came in screaming − totally distraught −

her two daughters had been shot before her eyes — and killed. The daughters attended I think it is St Andrew High School — two lovely girls.

It was simply awful — what could one say or do — her whole life had been destroyed — and she was so worn out that when I held her against my shoulder she quietened and actually dozed asleep — only to break out in a wild crying as someone entered the room. The whole family were PNP, there's no need to say anything else.

So polling day is ten days off — will we survive without a total explosion — I hope and believe we will.

Michael and Bev are fantastically courageous people and this struggle will be won by those that can endure to the end.

21 October 1980

It is quite unbelievable to be living in this world of murder and gunmen and bitterness and brutality.

All our confidence circles around tales of horror and violence — tonight I said to Douglas, what will we talk about when and if this is ever over.

One tries to read and to release one's thoughts from the one overbearing preoccupation — the will to win — and hovering over it all is not the desire for power, but a deep-seated conviction that if we don't win, with all our faults, something very dangerous and very different will come to this land we love. Something undemocratic — that's it in a single word.

Bev with her baby boy looked so starry eyed in the midst of all the worries.

Oh let us try to be positive and unafraid — sometimes I get so terribly, terribly down and then I realize it doesn't help anyone.

Anyway I am starting my woman and the frightened children. God help me — because it will be a tremendous effort — but it will keep me calm.

31 October 1980

Early morning — I woke and lay quietly whilst the knowledge pressed through my brain that we have lost.[1] At first I was only dumbly conscious of all that has happened in the last four years that has led up to this.

The first reaction is to flee from it ALL — and then I let out Johan and made a cup of Chinese tea and I lay and thought and thought.

A touch of gold is in the room as the sun comes up.

Another day — last night I was a little bitter, but today that has gone — we have to blame ourselves as well. It's no moment for a post mortem — it's enough to meet a new day. We fought a heroic election. And now what of the future? Where from here? Many will go away but many will stay and life goes on. I think I will stay.

Just at that moment Rex phoned from Ottawa – he and Ramphal and Trudeau got the news together.

I felt better for talking to him – it's what is called facing the unknown.

Rex felt what I have felt very strongly for a very long time – that Michael has been very isolated.

It's so strange –

I feel he must be left to make some very difficult decisions – without pressure from his family or friends.

Defeat is the surest way to find exactly what you want of life.

1 November 1980

Spent an hour with Michael and Bev last night – after the initial shock they are resilient people – and both of them have tremendous inner resources.

There are so many things they can do with their lives. Michael already is on the way to a fellowship to do a book on Third World Economics[1]. He needs a rest – not too long! or he would merely fret and chafe.

I find myself strangely relieved that it is all over! 1938–1980 – quite long enough, but I am going to draw people around me. I am not going to isolate myself.

Ra comes on Monday for a week. Oh I am so glad – she's bringing Luke with her and that will be fun for Natasha.

So we move into a new and perhaps more fascinating phase.

Douglas worked terribly hard in South Manchester. I guess he is as shocked as everyone else. He phoned me to tell me of the imminence of the arrest of Michael[2] – but since then I haven't seen nor heard from him.

I hope he gets this University job – he needs to get out of this tight circle for a while.

Mike[3] leaves tomorrow – he did a tremendous job for us, and he is pretty well worn out, but Yale will relax him and he will be at peace with himself that he got the chance to serve his homeland in a crisis. He cares so much for Jamaica – but he can't find a life here because he is another of these people who is ahead of his times – in this area of the world anyway.

12 November 1980

So yesterday Bev and I – with a little group of faithfuls saw Michael off to London, to Spain where the Socialist International is meeting. Michael is a vice president – I think Willy Brandt is president. It was terribly sad – the next day – I cracked up temporarily and went down to see Bev at about five-thirty – only to discover that the same thing had happened to her – we talked for a while and I think both of us felt better. This gun case is hanging over Duncan's head[1] and his two bodyguards. I think he is a tired man — or maybe, not well. Shades of Pernel Charles'[2] internment long ago hang over his head. I hope he doesn't get a sentence — the police are in a vicious mood and I would tremble for him.

Carole came in to see me, to tell me that they held up her office woman and split her cheek open from the forehead to her jaw, with the bone showing.

Ra and Luke were a godsend to me and made that week into a big thing of love and gentleness — whilst the nightmare we are facing was held off for a time.

I started working on the woman with the petrified children: 'And Would Not Be Comforted'. But it's too big a subject for me and I feel too deeply over it — gunmen in cold blood killing little children at play just for the hell of it.

I want somehow to write an account of this few months — but I want to be fair to 'the people'. Norman would say the people have spoken, or perhaps even the voice of the people is the voice of God. I don't quarrel with the people — but I feel bitterly over the guns coming in over the police and soldiers, this has never happened before — and I find myself saying I never want to step on American soil again. I have always been happy in the States — and then I began to read people like Schlesinger — the books on the Kennedys, and the play upon the pressures, the fears — just one phrase, 'the CIA' — and somewhere around the joint Britain had a hand in there too.

America with her inept and often phoney leaders — America with her foreign policies. America determined to rule the world — it's a nasty picture.

But let me cool off a little first — an election now seems to be total war — but why can't we fight it out locally. I hate communism — really hate it — but the voice of the people — with their griefs, their 'no-life', the ghetto — the voice of the people must be heard.

Let us watch and see if the JLP will listen to that voice in the way we tried to do.

I think we all have to go on — just as before, forgetting the tribalism — so that in some way we can heal an open wound.

17 November 1980

All of a sudden the strange premonition of danger that haunted me for months before the election has returned. It could of course be a terrible heartache for Michael. How will he return from his travels — how will he live with the future. What *is* it — that is looming over us? Or is it just the return of the shock of the election.

The weather has turned cool — and the November light is here — Xmas is just around the corner — what a Xmas.

I try to see it through as a blessed relief from a nightmare of strain and violence and fear – a freedom to live one's own life. But Michael can't see it that way – oh my God I wish that I had died before all this happened, and yet alive it may be possible to help. Poor Rachel stuck away in Barbados – Douglas got his hurt with the loss of his ministry, and slowly he is fighting back to get a hold of his future. Bev is meeting disaster for the first time with great courage – and on the fringe of it all, I suffer for all of them.

20 February 1981

Things are beginning to swamp me a little – the perpetual worry of the present situation. Doug has not yet got a job and he and Roy are cramped in that little bedroom – Roy came home from work last week and announced that the boss had fired the whole department because some employees had moved to bring the union in. So both he and Doug are out of jobs – it's a terrifically depressing situation for them both. I am so glad that I can help by having them here – but for Doug it is an appalling situation and he's beginning to show strain. It's nearly four months of idleness – by the mercy of God I have hit a little patch of good health. I don't know how they would fare if I were coughing all night as I do sometimes.

The atmosphere in the country is one of tension – people are being fired from jobs in a shattering way. Seaga talks of money coming – but in the perspective of the needs of the country it is a drop in a bucket, and the oftener he talks of it, the more the demands of the people grow.

Fortunately for him the army and the police are with him, because we are facing a possible explosion – if not an overall one, a continuing series of small ones.

Perhaps I am wrong, but I sense an atmosphere and an attitude of loss of faith in all the areas that had a clear concept of a good nationalism – now it is every man for himself, for whatever he can get for himself. I think the teachers are the most notable example. John, as head of Waterford School, felt it intensely – the staff would not make the sacrifices, or give the devotion that had inspired the people of his generation when self-government was coming to Jamaica. The truth is that it is a world trend and the whole picture is of depression, of a slackening of a sense of honour and the enthusiasm of doing something for its own sake.

At this moment of crisis and need there seems to be no way you can rally public opinion or behaviour to help to make Jamaica grow and succeed. I know that Michael felt it intensely – that there was nothing, no way you can call on people's patriotism to make the supreme effort that is called for.

The cultural movement is the most alive area – but the painters are handicapped by exorbitant prices on paints, and often a complete absence of what they need. But there *is* a fire amongst some artists and art lovers – even though the area is small.

A shining example of an exception is Easton Lee's effort[1] in the area of theatre in the church, particularly in the rural areas.

The dance still has its followers – who are totally loyal and interested in the very real growth of the dance movement.

The National Gallery is pioneering a whole new approach to exhibitions and the production of catalogues which are 'mini' art books and can one day be bound to keep a historical record of the work of our times. There are small galleries that come and go – that have their followings – and music at last gives signs of stirring.

22 February 1981

How can one grow when one hasn't stopped to understand impatience.

I think impatience is the refusal to allow that truth has an existence outside oneself – you move along carrying your truth with you – someone cuts across your trail – and you are wildly irritated.

You emanate something and it meets another source of truth.

25 February 1981

There! I've signed off 'And Would Not be Comforted', later 'Weeping for Her Children'. I wonder if it will prove so difficult after all to cast. The boys don't seem afraid of it.

It's been a strange experience, there's been no duality over it – only a shrinking away from the subject, a fear that it was negative, and then finally I felt it is the truth. I didn't mean to do it – I didn't want to do it, and those drawings that just came out of me – in one horrible burst – the cocaine in the men's eyes – MY GOD[1].

I'm tidying up the studio and putting away tools. I don't feel tired – it just came slowly – almost doggedly – and now I don't know where to go from there. Perhaps I will rest a little, or perhaps I will draw – thank God for nothing perhaps to do.

The last movement of that Mahler 9th symphony carried me through the last days of it – it seemed to mean something to me for the first time – I've always been afraid of Mahler.

7 March 1981

From today I must keep an accurate account of how I spend my days.

Three people out of work pressing on my heart – Doug, Roy and George

— so that I find that my mind is being pulled totally away from its own axis — and even reading confronts me with an extra-acute effort to concentrate.

Reading Greene's *The Power and the Glory*, I found that I had to read and re-read parts of it several times and look back to discover where I had lost the thread.

Now that 'Woman and Children' is finished and about to be cast, my mind would normally either cut off completely and I would find some new target, or it would already be feeling towards some new work.

Instead of which, I seem to be waterlogged in some vast sea of worry and have to put up a tremendous fight not to succumb to a haunting and haunted fear.

To combat it, I take on small, practical jobs of no extraordinary value — but useful and at least practically absorbing.

I think I am slowly trying to form a plan to get away for at least a week, and give my mind a moment of untramelled idleness — which is a life pattern and has always helped me to preserve an area of creativity which is essential to my life.

I have checked and collected or located all the material for the casting, so that is one job done, and the boys start work on Monday. I've done things like fixing the shower curtains — cleaned the studio for action.

It's getting cooler now — so I think I will go and water the garden as it's Saturday and Batiste is off — he is getting very shaky and I have to look after his health. Apparently he has no woman at home, so he is very battered, but I dread the day when he isn't there anymore — it's a lifetime relationship which I value very deeply.

So off I go for the moment.

After the garden, Roy was lonely and bored so I did what Doug had suggested. I tested his arithmetic only to discover that he had forgotten most of it — and in any event the use of a calculator had taken the place of most of his figure problems! So we plunged in and I found that he wanted me to help — with more enthusiasm than he had shown over his reading — then Norman came in and I gave them supper and washed up — and tried to read — but I feel sleepy and it's only 10 p.m. so I'm going to bed.

Doug went out to Con Allison's[1] funeral, which showed every sign of ending up a 'wake'!! organized by Basil Keane[2] — who read the lesson in the true style of 'The Harder They Come'!

14 March 1981

Last night I asked in Dorrette and Gem[1] and Basil and Silver — to cheer Doug a little. Roy and Norman were here too, and Dorrette's adopted daughter. It was great fun — and we all laughed a lot and remembered the old Drumblair Dance meetings, which were often hilarious. We even danced a little. It did Doug good. He was more relaxed than he has been since the election. It is a ghastly experience being without work, both Roy and himself, and the days hang heavy on their hands. Anyway, Doug has taken the step and has decided to go back to planting on Fern Hill[2].

It will be hard on his car — the up and down — but perhaps he can get a lift up occasionally in Michael's car. Anyway to be motivated again — and of course if he could get water on his St Catherine land, he would not really have to worry about the future — with his pension. This ekeing out of time is troublesome.

Monday, 16 April 1981

I will organize myself to start on a new phase of drawing. Perhaps a year — who knows. I would like to organize myself into illustrations of some tale, some legend, some bible story if I could just find one.

3 May 1981

Of course God can't be a monologue, God must be a dialogue. In spite of his tremendous genius, Blake saw God as a father figure, but what about the mother figure.

When I was at Nomdmi, and very inspired, I was feeling my way toward a Man Woman Godhead.

Lawrence says all this in 'The Man Who Died'.

But the balance of the Man Woman state is not the marital concept. This is a massive mistake — the great compromise.

11 May 1981

Today George received the advance notice of the publication of his book. A new edition of *First Poems*[1] with some later poems.[1]

It has been a long wait and a very painful one, because to keep some hope and faith alive in George has not been easy. He dreamt for thirty-five years of returning to Jamaica one day, and it has been such a tragic disappointment to him. He has been through a near breakdown — a bad one — and then just when it seemed that the end had come and there was no sense in even trying to hold on, at last this breakthrough. It came today just as we were finally doing the layout of this little book on the 'Rural Carvers of Jamaica'[2] that we have worked on together.

So we looked at each other and prayed for the future! For there is no money anywhere, and our whole family is having a tough time financially. Anyway we have to believe that just as we held on for two years waiting and hoping that the publication of his book would come through, so we have to hold on and believe that this little venture will materialize.

Then he has also about sixty new poems which sometime will have to find their way into publication.

Faith, faith is the thing.

The new poetry is full of a mystic love and faith — I believe in it, but I also believe that it isn't easy to understand.

After all this I want to sort out the best of Rachel's poems — she can't write just now as her job and her children are very demanding, but her time will come — we'll see!

31 May 1981

I keep wondering if one had to make a statement, perhaps a speech about Art in Jamaica 'then' and now, how on earth would one handle the subject. Going right back to the '30s when it was all British inspired, to now when some of our artists are fighting to be free from what some call an oppressive nationalism — even a sentimental nationalism. Free to play with theories — with all forms of abstractionism — 'isms' generally. Free to be citizens of the world.

That is one side of our present coin — but on the other, there is this deep, passionate, savagely expressed *racialism*. There has always been a racialism in the arts from 1935–8, but it came from one or two isolated artists — and often through the channel of portraiture. Much has been written by writers about the history of writing, and they can handle it with clear perception.

I can only write of the earnest days — times that are often referred to as the battle of the 'daffodils and the snow'. I know a lot about that — Roger and I had our famous 'head-on' over that! But since then much that is sophisticated has been written about the place of the Jamaican writer in his confrontation with life 'at home and abroad'.

So let's leave that in their hands.

But the fine arts, from the days of Dunkley, Marriott, Abrahams and myself, have travelled a long way and it has been a chequered journey.

11 June 1981

Things are so tough right now — so tough — think I have to get out for a while. There's Carifesta[1] — it might help. Trying to keep still inside — let things take their own course — whatever may happen. Feeling of being overwhelmed, feeling that any action, any speech will only precipitate more trouble — but I am tired — one has to trust life.

Yes, but what you have to do is to *understand* other people's problems, problems that are 'themselves'. One knows that one's own life is a struggle with 'oneself'. The image of a boat on a rough sea — the sea is there and one can do nothing about it — but the boat — yes — that is it — the problems are there — out of one's control.

But to handle the boat —

I feel a little better — but ...

Oh God — what a sea —

20 June 1981

It's getting even worse — no jobs, very expensive living — !! The thing, the only thing to do is to have F A I T H — somehow it will all work out.

I can't work — can't even draw — the uncertainty everywhere, and the people near to love are so unhappy — and I am so unhappy for *them*.

5 August 1981

Got back from Barbados — it was a remarkable two weeks — such friendliness and warmth — and so much to see from all round the Caribbean. It was a stimulus — there's no doubt about that. I came back to find things much the same — Roy has gone on as an apprentice in a video place, he isn't earning yet, but it's a real chance for him, and I hope it clicks.

Barbados appealed to me — I wonder if one could work there for a while — and Rachel needs help. She is struggling with a difficult but interesting job and those two not so easy children.

However — I am still in a period when I need calm — to be still inside — if only I could work.

Last night Douglas had the two wheels stolen off his car, and the car next door had the same fate!! The violence and robbery are everywhere.

12 August 1981

George tells me he was in Papine and two men were talking, and one said to the other, 'Do you see those young girls over by the gas station — you know three of them making picnee for me.' No comment!! Caribbean man is the thought that I have been brooding over for the longest time — I have done so many Jamaica women — my favourite theme — but N E V E R Jamaica man.

And yet in Barbados, where one becomes very Caribbean conscious, over and over I have tried to draw something — just something — that could be a root statement about our 'man'. There is a comparatively easy statement — a powerful negative one — as the muscled, physical, magnificent 'pretty boy'.

But the male who is wrestling with himself — as an artist, particularly as a writer — the Lammings, the Braithwaites[1], the Vic Reids — the Errol Hills[2].

21 August 1981

Mike brought me two books on Käthe Kollwitz[1] — he brought them in July to Carifesta in Barbados. I had never seen them before — I just had a little booklet on her that made me want to see more, and then to my amazement I saw her drawings of women and children. This was months after I had finished 'The Cry of the Children' and they are so alike. Only hers are much stronger than mine.

It has hurt me — because the one work I know I have done that has come straight out of my *heart* is this one. It is, I know, a naked statement of *me* — and all I went through in 1980 with the killing of the children here.

2 October 1981

Bev and I talked yesterday for the first time about what we have lived through since the beginning of 1980. I think we were beginning to be able to talk because something inside her was quietly steadying.

It's like living on a road with heavy traffic — the background of noise becomes part of one's consciousness — but only that — one does not pay it any mind.

7 October 1981

Yesterday the news of the assassination of Sadat. I can't judge him as a ruler or a person — I know that he did one very brave thing, when he went to Israel — I think that it amazed the world. But now everyone is judged by the one measuring rod of the pro-Russia or pro-America.

What I personally feel is that to kill blurs all the issues — and one of the issues is that in this year 1981 it is almost impossible to govern at all — the problems are so great. The voice from the ghetto insists on being heard, and how do you solve *that* problem.

The very morning (that's yesterday morning) I showed Doug an article in the *Guardian* with an account of the people Sadat had suddenly arrested. So he must have felt the pressure coming and he acted that way, a desperate man, selling out completely to America? I don't understand anything!!

Rachel is coming to stay here until she is well enough to go back to Barbados after her operation. I wish she could get work in Jamaica — she doesn't like being so far from the family. But Jamaica isn't an easy country to get work in — Jamaica isn't an easy country — period — not just now! So many people out of work — some losing their jobs as a result of a change of government — it's very difficult.

13 October 1981

Party conference was a startling affair. Thousands of people and such a spirit — all they wanted was Michael, it is absolutely weird. After the smashing defeat in the election and now this — and a massive *unity*, left wing, right wing, middle of the roaders, all there. Well one keeps calm, because it could lead to all sorts of things, and elections are far away. So I pray that people will keep their heads and not precipitate some crisis.

I am trying very hard to keep calm myself, the family is in a very uneven patch — particularly Rachel and Norman in two very different ways. Rachel wants to come home from Barbados; she is now very lonely there as George and her friends have left. It will be costly moving all her furniture — and she will then be out of work. But I think she is right — she can't cope with the children and that heavy job. Here at least we can help her with the children — I feel that I can.

Saturday night. We've had Heritage Week — and tonight was Norman's night. A shockingly bad broadcast — opening with a photo of him as a child, only it was a photo of his grandchild Joseph. The photos were so bad they were hardly visible, and the whole broadcast concentrated on Federation and Busta's defeat of it. There was no mention of his great achievements with adult suffrage, self-government and ultimately independence.

I feel very bitter over it — after all, on the smallest plane — well never mind.

I'm thinking about a lot of things tonight and perhaps I am allowing people, family, to get completely on top of me — so that my own life is becoming quite submerged.

Well tomorrow is another day — perhaps many things can be wiped out with a good sleep.

So I've finished the Dancers and done eight other pieces since the show closed. One head, 'Dark Flame', came out of some unknown corner of my 'other' self. And although the caster spoilt some of the effect I wanted by applying black oxide and making it a uniform colour when I wanted it to be smoky, we nevertheless scrubbed most of it off, leaving a natural patina everywhere except in the eyes, which are more or less black.

The other important little one is (*diagram*) which for me is a new attempt to let the form alone express the agony. The big work, 'The Word', is something that I worked on at top speed around twelve hours. It all grew up from the hair, and it is a *definite* expression about the Rastafarians, who have always fascinated me, and wrong or right I think are going to stay and spread. It's a new social pattern based on an easily appreciated expression of FAITH, also a repudiation of the Christian faith which has so badly failed the black man, plus the inevitable pull of Islam which was the faith in the world from which a large part of the slave trade was tapped. So where does the road lead from here? I started by wanting to do a drummer, and then I wobbled.

29 October 1981

Wouldn't it be wonderful if God was a drummer and in the beginning it just whispered out the first pulse beats − and man was born on a sound-wave, a pulse beat − and from his creation, from his inception, he grew in a foetus of music − it would account for so much!

3 November 1981

It's strange the things you remember − we were coming to Jamaica, coming home, it was 4 a.m. and I crept up on deck and lay there in the dark, watching the stars go out and the first sign of dawn flaming a deep crimson behind what seemed like black purple mountains, and the calmest sea I had ever experienced. Flame and purple mountains. Norman, who had been up late playing bridge, was asleep in the cabin with Douglas in his little crib.

The beat of the ship's engine − how we had grown to love it − like the heart of God: unfailing, regular, and infinitely sonorous. With the faintest possible chill, the old saying came to me: 'Red in the morning, shepherd's warning' but I stifled it quickly. I was too happy, too excited − we were here and life was beginning, and suddenly I felt someone behind me: 'Looks good, eh?' and there he was on the rails watching the magnificence of the dawn and smelling the land after weeks at sea.

I think the challenge of the future was all there in his face and something taut in his pose − leaning on the rail − like a runner about to take off − a handsome spirit of a man.

Later
This is an age where one dives into the bottomless well of truth. Henry Miller is writing and John Updike has brought out *Couples*.

Where sex is portrayed in the movies on the heroic scale of a vast cinema screen, the orgasm is that times larger than life — is a bony facial struggle under arc lamps that would pick out the skull under the flesh of the Mona Lisa.

I go too, we both went too, we always were cinema fans, from the beginnings of Charlie Chaplin — and we loved the pouring out with the vast crowds into living world of traffic and taxis and neon signs — and even when TV came in, we never really succumbed.

Our first set was given us by the JBC, but we returned it in a dramatic but ineffectual gesture during the JBC strike. When all the youngsters came out and lay down in the streets to block traffic in the rush hours as a protest against repressive policies. I remember Michael flat on his back with knees cocked up, reading the *Gleaner* in the middle of King Street, and the *Gleaner,* instead of thanking him for the free publicity, merely attacked him and the JBC as a bunch of middle-class young nuisances. I've never quite understood why a middle-class nuisance is any different from any other kind of nuisance, but I guess it's all in the eye of the journalist as beholder.

Anyway, the JBC is still repressive, and later on we bought our own TV just to keep in touch with that influential part of the world, and restore the balance of humour.

7 November 1981

People so often ask me for stories of Norman — what he was like at home as a father — what he was like with his friends — and I realize how different he was as a private person, and he was a very private person, from how he was as a public figure; and yet if you watched closely, the two were not so far apart.

The first time I got a glimpse into a new-to-me side of him was when we were walking from St John's Wood[1] station to my little room which was over a fish shop — he used to see me back safely, stay and have a cup of coffee and depart.

There is a little cemetery on the way and sometimes we would go in and sit on a bench and talk. One night, I must have been about nineteen — that makes it 1919 — he had been talking about the Left Book Club books and the Fabians and socialism, and his mind seemed to have swung back to Jamaica, and he said after a long pause, 'You know one day I might go into politics — one day when I have succeeded at my career, when I have made a home and a life professionally, so that I can do it with confidence. I think that is what Jamaica needs.'

I can't swear for the absolute word-for-word accuracy of that — the build up of it — but the phrase, 'I might go in for politics,' I can hear as if he said it today.

Telling this little story opens up my mind to what his interests and his activities were in those days — and that takes me back to 1914 and surprisingly the memories, the impressions of him all come crowding in.

One has to keep in mind that I was in my early teens for some of that period and he was in the army — but there were some rare letters.

When he arrived in England — in the summer — his two sisters, Vera and Muriel, had planned a holiday for him — to show him England. He had just recovered from a near-death fight with typhoid in Jamaica and needed a holiday, and things to interest him. Vera and Muriel were people with wide interests — Vera was a musician and music was one of Norman's passionate loves. So they had plays and concerts and much book reading and discussion.

Norman was closely attached to Muriel — she proved to be a friend of a lifetime. Vera he respected, but fought eternally with — he considered her too conventional, too conservative, and too conscious of what other people 'thought'. They both outgrew this over the years, largely through the draw of music on both of them. I remember once staying with the three of them — and a ridiculous fight over a salt cellar into which Norman had stuck his knife to help himself, and Vera threw up her hands in horror! Long after I talked to Norman about this trivial incident, for they didn't speak to each other for days!

He said: 'Listen Edna — Vera is never satisfied till she totally dominates the people she loves. She's a fine person but this damnable will of hers destroys love, destroys relationships, and I am not allowing her to get even a toe-hold in my preserves or my life — I will meet her halfway, so long as she leaves me alone.'

In the years to come they worked it out — but she did not approve of his politics, and particularly what she felt were his left-wing tendencies.

I tell this little story because I learnt a lot about him in that brief encounter. Because of course he went on shovelling salt into his plate, scattering a good deal on the table. Then another side of him appeared — he was superstitious about spilt salt, not much else! and he solemnly took three pinches of salt off the table in the fingers of his right hand and threw it over his left shoulder, and then calmly ate his dinner.

He had one or two other so-called superstitions — one was embedded in the saying: 'chicken merry hawk near'. If he saw anyone wildly, irrationally carefree and excitedly happy — even when it applied to himself — he always felt that something would happen to end it dramatically — like bad news or illness.

But on a more serious level, if he felt or saw anyone over-confident he would say: 'Let not he who putteth on his armour boast himself as he who taketh it off.'

It showed that deep streak of caution which he developed to protect himself from his own very impulsive, reckless, freedom-loving nature.

I know that I seem to wander from my tale — but as I remember things I have to put them down as they have a way of sliding down into the world of no memory that hangs over all of us. Freud would have a lot to say about memory — and the individual — and what and why he does not remember.

They brought Norman down to meet my mother and her family — and then we all drifted apart as the war fell like a thunderbolt on us — with so many losses in our family and circle.

Norman's brother, Roy, who we knew very well, and who was a constant visitor, and who adored my mother, was so different from Norman. He too was handsome, but where Norman was a shy, intensely reserved person, Roy was outgoing — a terrific flirt and lover of women, up to any prank — and quite unconscious of the impression he was creating. He picked up friends everywhere — was a lively conversationalist, interested in everything and very original.

He was trying his hand at play-writing when the war struck him down. He was darker than Norman, but apparently totally unselfconscious about racialism, except that once when a picture of him came out in the rifle shooting team for the high class public school, Felstead, where he attended, he said: 'See the photo of the team and me in it — they've done their best to scrub me white.' And thus for the first time, the very first time, racialism walked into my life — I must have been about thirteen or fourteen.

The relationship of Norman and Roy was very strong and meant a great deal to both of them — as children they had fought bitterly in the way of brothers, but alone in an alien and strange world they were driven together in an intensely loyal friendship. Norman saw all the originality of Roy's mind and valued it — always with the comment that it was a quality he lacked. This was a sort of humility that he carried with him all his days — but when he came up against pretentiousness, shallowness, intellectual dishonesty, he could be savagely, ruthlessly condemnatory. What a critic — but he demanded of himself a total truth.

Roy's death left him with only Muriel. All his life he was a man with few friends — and usually he was attracted to people the absolute opposite of himself.

In Jamaica he had a family — the Clerks — whose home meant a place of safety to him after his mother died and the rest had moved to England. They were a very unusual family for those days — all the girls had careers — mostly teaching or in the civil service — and one of the boys, Leslie Clerk, was Norman's lifetime friend.

They were a very musical family: piano and violin. They had an uncle, Astley Clerk, who ran a store where pianos and other musical instruments were sold — he even wrote music, I think accompaniments for poems. So

Leslie grew up in that sort of world, and because he had perfect pitch he almost automatically made a living tuning and caring for pianos. He has tuned pianos for all the visiting musicians and in those days they came regularly – Rubinstein, Brailowski, Moiseiwitch, Arrau, and the Memilien accompanists for Heifetz, the cellist Casals, Ginette Neveu, all sorts of people – and as he had a gift with people, he was very appreciated for himself as well as his work. I write of him because he was a very, very close friend, and someone whose advice Norman took.

The family had very strong ESP interest and talent. The oldest girl, Grace, a strong, intelligent teacher of music, certainly had strange experiences, and so did Leslie. But Leslie had one unique gift that I personally have never met in anyone else. He could be handed an article belonging to someone he didn't know – a personal article like a ring or something that the person used a great deal. He would hold it in his hand quite still for a long time, and then he would begin to talk about the owner. Sometimes it would be recognizable character sketches, sometimes some activity involved – or a trend in the future. I have seen him almost change personality as he made a closer and closer telepathic, if you will, contact. He would look older or tired or even mischievous. He always had someone to write what he said – and in order not to have mind-reading, he always made sure that the article he was expressing was unknown to anyone present.

I played a practical joke on him once – I gave him something of mine which I told him had come from some unknown (to me) person. He took it home with him and a little later the phone rang and it was Leslie laughing and he said: 'You're too clever! The first thing I got was the room full of wood chips – you must have done a lot of work today.' He was good at it, he really was, and people from overseas tested him in all sorts of ways.

Now Norman was the most rational person, and this sort of thing was not up his street at all. Vera was very interested and was herself a very telepathic person – if there is such a thing. Muriel was a scientist and not interested.

Norman believed in a real way in Leslie's integrity – they were very close – but in his attitude to table rappings etc., he refused to allow himself to get mixed up. I think he was a true son of the twentieth century – Freud, Jung, Whitehead, Spengler, Einstein, Shaw, and then on a totally different plane, D.H. Lawrence, that's where he learnt human relationships and much about men and women. Spengler and Collingwood were the thing then, with H.G. Wells skating around on the periphery.

27 January 1982

For so many years I have 'wrestled' with the story of 'Jacob and the Angel'[1], from before Norman died, sometime before when I showed him my first sketch – and he smiled and said in disagreement, 'But they both look too much the same,' or something like that. 'They look too alike,' and I was piqued and put it away, but kept it.

Since then I have had periods when I went back to it again and drew.

Then finally the whole of the period from December 27th to now, it has been on my mind – and finally having decided on doing it life-size, which with wings would make it 8ft, and having made all the preparation for an enormous board to carry a clay relief, I received a 'back-tax' property bill. So I sat down and worked out what the whole production of Jacob could be without my work, and it couldn't be under $3,500.00. Well, that was that. So I scrapped the whole idea ...

Then just by chance I went into Sangsters to buy a book for someone, couldn't get it, and bought a 1979 book on Jung – by Van der Post, *Jung and the Story of our Time*, and going home in the taxi, the first sentence my eyes took in was: 'For the increase of human awareness as the dark night of exile in the Old Testament wherein Jacob the father of Joseph the Dreamer, wrestled alone and long with an Angel. Only then does one reach the chapter, the work.'

Then yesterday I was making a list of things to be noted and done, and suddenly I wrote: 'Sublimation, sublimation, sublimation.'

I went and looked for Salvador Dali's book and its closing chapter: 'Moses is flesh of sublimation ... integrate, integrate, integrate.' A book Nethersole had given me in 1945 when I was in the Nuttall from a riding accident.

I simply must make a breakthrough – I must, but how?

I must go somewhere by myself?

Sublimate – what? by myself?

The Oxford Dictionary says: 'Hallucination – a diseased perception of an object as present which is not.'

5 February 1982

I tried so hard to do a little thing – NOT to bother with Jacob – I can't afford even the board, let alone the casting, because it has to be 8ft.

But I couldn't get anywhere with the little thing like the ones I had been doing with pocomania shepherd etc.

Anyway I went on reading my Shelley book – which for some strange reason I find inspiring – he was quite a man – and then I went back to the Jung quotation, then I thought I was going to be ill.

And then the day before yesterday, feeling awful, I went to sit in the big old chair in the studio. After a long time I said DAMN let me try again – so I stuck up the big last sketch I'd done and studied it, and I did another drawing just as unsatisfactory. So after a long time I said: 'You're in clean clothes — you can't work in clay,' and the clay looked too hard, not properly prepared — it made me tired to look at it.

And I said damn, damn, damn, and I went and found a little board about 18ins and I started to work non-stop, and in an hour there it was — a little, scratchy, lived-in maquette — I'd got it, after twelve years, from before Norman died. So there! And then I thought of the size and I said NO — not 8ft, which was your idea. I can't cope financially or physically, and I asked and I looked and I brooded — Jung had clearly told me to do it — so let it be 5ft.

So I rang Scottie and he said, 'Edna, I will give you the board with the expanding metal on it.'

And I said, 'Scottie, I THINK you might go to heaven after this.'

23 March 1982

A week of coughing and asthma.

9 April 1982

Good Friday — a roaring wind, blazing sunshine, and not even the smallest indication of rain. Water we get for only two hours, morning and evening, often a bare trickle.

The great Mr Reagan has come and gone, with Government and some of the people genuflecting passionately to the Saviour of Jamaica. Oh dear ...!

Watching him on TV he's a remarkable communicator, with a marvellous memory. I doubt he's dishonest, it's possible that he believes what he says about Salvador etc., whilst the CIA rampage behind his benign shadow. BUT his gaffe about the past previous Communist government[1] — Michael caught him on that one, and elements in the *Gleaner* obviously resented it too.

But it's a dangerous world. And the comic opera of the Falklands could turn into anything, especially as the Russian power man is obviously dying — and who knows what influence will lead Russia after he goes.

This last illness has left me drained of all energy — I don't want to work on Jacob anymore — and the ideas for the small things, which I was full of, have vanished, and I'm desperately in debt. I hope something will come soon. The house is full of the family and the desperate worry over Norman, and sometimes I feel desperate to be alone and silent, or able to play my gramophone, without the endless TV and pop music.

I may try to get away for a few days — but *where?*

10 April 1982

Today is a crisis day — I have lain down all day — no energy, no hope, no wish to live any longer — I don't know why I feel so ill — and for about an hour I had a faint, racing little pulse — it was really awful. I can't work, I can't think — I am shaken and utterly worn out. It seems one can't be happy anymore. The world is in crisis, there's no doubt about that, and there is little to be happy about — I feel half dead. What can I do to take control of myself again — to want to live —

Oh God, I'm weary of it all — I'm just weary —

But somehow I have to have a plan — I have to reduce the situation to some *order*. I HAVE to fight back or I will die — I feel so weak, so shattered by all the alcoholism around me — people not really in control of themselves. But I have to try —

I have to make some decisions and stand by them — and try to begin work and *living* again. Please God help me —

Today, now, now, now.

11 May 1982

Just heard that Doug has got the Fulbright[1] — oh what joy and what a relief — that opens a whole new world for him — thank God. And George has got a job part-time — on the new paper *The Rising Sun* to do a cultural page — he too is very happy over it and has started well.

So it leaves Roy now — if only we can place him in something more worthwhile — he so deserves it.

We started the new small bronze of 'Negro Aroused'[2] — they've paid half in advance or God knows how I would face the bank.

I am making a great effort and beginning to get on top of my breathing problem and fighting back the weakness. I actually trimmed some plants in the garden today — and it didn't affect my breathing, and I wasn't too weak, so I think I'll soon be back at work again. Doug's good news has helped me so much —

I don't think I can get another book like this — I don't see any on the shelves and this is the end of this one.

We are all sitting on the edge of this Falkland fracas — the world is in a *perilous*, dangerous mood.

13 May 1982

This book is nearly finished and looking back in it I am surprised that of all that had happened so little has been recorded. Why? Is it that when the BIG pressures are on, one hasn't the time or the peace in which to record them? Or is it that one's energies are going another way.

I am glad to say that my main big worry after Doug's position has been Norman. He has moved his base to Mandeville and gone in with another firm.

George too has bitten on to this job with the *Rising Sun*, and is showing great imagination and application. It has made a big change in him — and he has all the talent it takes. Thank God, because he has been like a ship without a rudder without a job, and in that lonely, empty block of flats.

Roy is the person now who needs the help — solve that and there'll be a load off my mind — and he's such a steady, decent person.

'Jacob and the Angel' is slowly, oh so slowly, moving forward. I am in debt up to my eyes — I daren't buy anything — and prices go up and up. It's a desperate situation and I find that it drains me — I feel so *unsafe*.

This is my last page — so let me not record negative nor unhappy thoughts.

Poor Batiste is trying to turn out for a day's work — after months of illness. I hope he can even do a day a week to keep him cheerful and not feeling too old and useless, poor darling —

Ernest, who works for him, is so like him — slow and a perfectionist. It's wonderful to watch his hands when he's planting or covering a clay model, which is tricky work.

Have just read a life of Ingrid Bergman — what a remarkable woman — she has had terminal cancer for so many years, and yet she has come out and done a film of Golda Meir, which must have been a tremendous challenge.

I must go to bed and to sleep — didn't like Anais Nin's biography at all at first — but the section when she is seeing Otto Rank has great perception.

The terrible weakness is beginning to go, and I am beginning to move more normally again — thank GOD!!!

15 May 1982

There is something about this fight over the Falklands that is packed with a sort of obsessive fear for me. At first it seemed like a comic opera and then it began to become ugly and serious.

But once the weather became a factor, the icy, icy weather, with mountainous seas and a raging non-stop wind, it began to evoke all sorts of memories. Cornwall in the winter, with great towering waves crashing down on the pier — and endless cold.

And the English lads — used to a London fog or a Scotch mist — having to hold firm and be full of courage, and never once having visualised a sea in Antarctica and zero weather. The fear it must arouse — oh I can't bear it, and so far from home. I know Scott's expedition to the Pole had the same horrifying effect on me. I once crossed the Atlantic in the winter and ran into a fantastic storm and we ended up off the coast of Ireland. I remembered the way the sea rose up like a wall in one's face one minute and the next there was nothing but sky.

Why *don't* they make peace and let the lads go back home. All for that bit of rock stone. Democracy? What hell! Like the war to end wars and the last World War. Maybe Thatcher is afraid to make peace — because they'll say she's a woman and daren't face what will happen. Well, better to be a woman.

30 June 1982

I have tried everywhere and I cannot find a new manuscript book like this one to continue my diary in this year of deprivation, 1982. No light and power, no water, and now today no bread!

What a deliverance!¹

It's hideous at the moment with the financial strain. George out of a job and unable to collect his pension or his royalties from his book, and he's showing such courage. Roy not working for money, just running his life away and trying so hard to hold his own — and it's another colossal strain.

But my health has improved a lot and I can work hard. 'Jacob and the Angel' is nearly finished. I have set myself a terrible problem with its size — so hard to get down from the wall to cast — it's such a great weight — but once we can get it down and I can do any repair job, I hope and believe that the boys can cast it — Errol and Basil.

It's the last thing of its kind I am going to do. From now on I have to think of the need to have enough money to keep the ship steady.

There! Mike has phoned in a rage at George's publisher.

And now Rachel has phoned, and Doug — and it's midnight so I guess I will go to sleep.

Diary Four

14 July 1982

There! I have tried for weeks to get a new diary and couldn't find one, and then Douglas, who was doing research at Party Headquarters, found this one dumped.

So I try to pick up a thread – in this extraordinary, unpredictable, frightening time in the history of the world, and I call it that because never, ever before can the world have been so completely informed about what *is* going on as it is in this year 1982. Of course there are whole areas that are totally out of touch, but when one reads that over a billion and a third people are tuned in for the World Cup Football and living from day to day hanging on the results – it is the most significant assessment of how WORLD conscious we are.

Someone said to me the other day, 'What on earth do you see in football?' – well I didn't tell her about my passion for sport, a legitimate passion for a sculptor. I simply said, 'What do I see in it? All the things the billion other people see in it – at least I'm not lonely!!'

But perhaps all that is frivolous – but the Falklands – Israel and Beirut – Iran and Iraq – El Salvador, Guatemala and the whole of Africa like a kettle on the boil.

You see, one shouldn't know about these things – one should just deal with conditions in Jamaica – no water for days on end – wiping down with Limacol – looking askance at someone drinking the last drop of water instead of drinking a Coke!

No light and power from 7 p.m. to 1 p.m. – no light, and if you haven't a gas stove, no power –

For ten days no bread – crackers.

All the business places depending on electricity, air-conditioning – even the hairdressers are afraid to wet the client's hair in case there is no current to dry it!!!!

I'm so grateful that we aren't the government because conditions are pretty grim and it's a world complaint – no work, people really suffering –

So one goes on — and yet we talk and laugh and in our own way enjoy living. But I can't pretend that I don't wake in the mornings with that weird, indefinable sense of foreboding — wondering what new catastrophe will erupt today.

Today there has been a news item that they are moving in the House that Belafonte should be declared *persona non grata* for his speech the night of the Manley Award.[1] Mercy what a storm —

I am expressing no opinions — I am truly glad Jimmy Cliff won the Award and *how* he rose to the occasion — his voice rang out with that wonderful song, 'Many Rivers to Cross'. Sitting so near to him as he sang, I came to feel what tremendous spiritual and physical passion comes through with singers like himself and Marley. The place was packed and, in spite of a few who differ, I think the Award was well received — Rex did a remarkable citation.

17 July 1982

It has now become a ritual — You wake at 5.30 a.m. to the sound of the water coming on bubbling in the pipe. You leap out of bed and, with the help of Roy and Ellen, we fill all our containers — working in the half light before dawn.

Then you turn on the bath heater and you wait — holding your breath for fifteen minutes to let it warm up a bit. Then I go — Roy goes — Ellen goes — and finally Doug goes — and all of this has to take place before 6.45 a.m!! Every now and then Doug takes a week-end in Mandeville and sleeps late in the mornings and takes his bath when he feels like it!!

And then another part of the ritual is — you're sitting peacefully watching the news on TV, and just as the blurb is over and the nitty gritty of the news is coming you are plunged into darkness and that lasts till 11 p.m., by which time you wake from an appalling and useless doze — unable to go to bed and sleep because you are not sleepy anymore — and you are cross and bored and frustrated.

And then there is the garden: slowly the 'special' hibiscus die — and you try to keep a few pot plants alive and water in the bird baths —

If it comes to rain, I don't think we are getting any before August, and then maybe there will be too much — a storm?

I can't do any casting without water — it's sort of elemental, what's happening to us all.

The government screams at us all to produce, but raw materials, spare parts, any of the basic things that are needed can't be had and people, from the quite big industrialists to the little man, can't get what they need to enable them to produce.

Then, quite new — well not so new — I suppose five years or so — are the higglers[1]. It has to be seen to be believed. The woman without a bread-earning man has got to feed her children, has got to clothe them and send them to school – that's on one side of the fence – and on the other, the public of Jamaica needs to buy certain items – shoes, shirts, what have you. She doesn't cross the door of the merchant's sanctuary, she goes to the Plaza and she bends down and picks up what she needs and buys it right there from the higglers. This government carried the promise to the merchants that the higglers must go, but the higglers don't go, they grow and grow – move them into tidy stalls and by next morning a new group have taken over the streets.

When Roy wants shoes he doesn't follow the uncertain course of asking prices in the big stores – he asks the lady right there beside the shoes and he comes home satisfied that he's got the best buy, and he hasn't been embarrassed in the act. But when the higglers are shopping abroad, first Miami, then Cayman, then Haiti and now Panama, and they enter a plane to return home – that is a RIOT!! How can a little air hostess control a Jamaican market woman – that's not the way it goes. She has enormous parcels – probably seven hats on, one on top of the other, and she jams the passage between seats and refuses to move. Doug, returning from Puerto Rico, told a story – it was something!!! And when they sail through Customs, the officers are afraid to stop them ...!

Then the language differences – in Haiti handsome young lads of eighteen learn a little pidgin English and earn a nice little living translating, conducting and guiding, all of course for a nice rake-off fee for both buyer and seller!!

So we survive – with a certain humour, a certain resignation – but somewhere underneath there might be something a little explosive – who knows WHAT the future holds –

I have been thinking of saving my little money and planning a fortnight in New York. Doug would be there by then, and to see and hear all things new and strange – I got quite excited over it – but since then I have been thinking, weighing the relative values, thinking of what could improve my life here and be of more lasting value. What can New York add to my life here – when the excitement dies down and one is back in the flow of one's life.

Actually, I am bursting with ways I want to work. I don't need a stimulant. I think to add to my leisure time is more important, and to add to it right here, than to spend all that money on entertainment abroad.

Take music – to spend a sum of money on records, to explore this Latin American music and literature – but the gramophone covers that. I don't find North American painting and sculpture inspiring – it's born of technology and all that goes with it – give me the man, not the machine.

Bookshops, yes – concerts, plays, fine arts, for a brief moment – and then home again.

I have grown to understand the serious people who have taken to video. Video has taught me something, and that is that the films that were made twenty years ago have something, a true artistry, perhaps, and they are very worth watching.

I have no transport — going out is a problem, therefore. One has to leave one's house empty — that's a hazard — the violence and house-breaking is right back — so why not find something at home — a little greater care of the garden, the house — having one's friends in — let people understand you don't go to openings and first nights anymore. You live quietly — and try to create an oasis of peace.

21 July 1982

So tomorrow we will lift the clay model of 'Jacob and the Angel' down from the wall to cast it. It is now 4ft 2 ins and very heavy — and if they shake it, it will crack all over!! So let's hope there's enough left on which to do a repair job!!

I have loved doing it — to me it's the inner struggle — elemental, earthy man at war with the light that would lead him.

Also man unwilling to accept the agony of leadership.

Man and his Angel.

It has had problems of texture — all sorts of problems — anyway, there it is, and I hope it will still be there after the move. I hope so. And then I'll cast it in *fondu*, I hope a soft, light shade, and perhaps I can use a little colour on it.

Rachel has been unwell again — also she's having a terrible time making 'two ends meet', and it's so hard getting permission to send out of the country any sort of money that can help.

Doug's affairs are moving at last and he hopes to get away by September — he's much more cheerful.

I can't help looking back at the start of 'Jacob'; I just couldn't stand, I was so weak. I had had this weird bug that was going around — and asthma too — with my heart doing all sorts of funny things. I actually thought I was going to die. Each time I get ill I do feel a little weaker.

The furore keeps up over Belafonte. I don't think he will ever understand Jamaica, so I guess he'll be a bit of a liability.

Ottey[1] and Cameron[2] have just won the 100 and 400 metres on TV. It was a triumph!

22 July 1982

So, 'Jacob' came down safely! At first we each and collectively blew up, and then I took George out. He was in a state bordering on hysteria, he was so afraid of it being dropped.

Presently — within six minutes — Scottie called me back in and there it was safely on its back, not damaged in any way *at all*!

Scottie coped in his own inimitable way and so we move on to the next stage. He begged me not to do it in *fondu* and I think he is right — so we will cast in plaster and hope and believe that one day it will go into BRONZE — it's a natural for bronze.

28 July 1982

We had such a wonderful shower — it won't fill the dams, but the plants and the grass look so different this morning. The only thing is, it's clear which will and which won't recover.

The casting is going on steadily — so hold thumbs.

There is a world background of storm and fear and uncertainty.

It's no good saying who is right and who is wrong out of the USA and Russia grinding away in their ugly power struggle. Call all things ideology — call all things a way of life — choose which you will. How much idealism lies behind Salvador or Afghanistan — how I despise them both.[1].

Iran and Iraq — that old horror.

Khomeni — with his tortures and deaths and horrors, all in the name of a faith. Think of Israel — tormented and driven into conduct that makes your blood go cold — as Beirut becomes a hideous, fear-ridden, stampeding shambles —

Oh, I know I am blowing up — but what does one believe in?

Let's say Thatcher *had* to stand up to Argentina — and it was a great and a right victory. But should it have ever happened?

And here in Jamaica — the violence is growing again.

And one comparatively small point, but a point that is strangely significant — we have a Festival and a competitive Festival song, and at this moment, when we are straining to *lift* ourselves, we give out $10,000 in prizes, and the coarsest, the most empty, the most degrading song has won. And little Joyce[2] comes down from Mavis Bank furiously angry — people don't want that song — 'It's a dirty song and little children shouldn't sing it,' and her story is that the region is angry and protesting — you see Kingston people don't represent Jamaica, they represent Kingston, and the country people are quite, quite different.

Anyway, I feel better for blowing up — I really do — but as the editorial in the newspaper points out, this hot time of the year is the silly season and we all have to be on guard.

5 August 1982

Talking to Doug over Arnett's autobiography[1] — only about a hundred pages — we got on to the subject of the Four H probe. I told Doug of the visit to the church of Wills Isaacs and Glasspole, and their theory of what was happening. I then went into my diary where I thought I had written an account of it — but could only find a single sentence that I would leave to Michael the job of telling that story, as he had been in and out of the whole thing.

It looked as if I had removed something from the diary — perhaps feeling that I had been harsh in my judgement of the whole story. And out of it all I think I had better leave any statement about it to him.

Right now, I want to slide quietly out of the whole thing — such small contribution that I have made belongs to a different time.

Michael and Beverley are working out something that may be of value in that it has a basis on the need to survive — and survive we must.

The thought of a one-party state gives me the cold shivers.

24 August 1982

Paul Bell[1] has just died — it's awful — I can't believe it — He was so young, so valuable — he has meant so much to our whole family, especially to Michael — and to me. He was quite unconsciously helping me to lose this terrible fear of dying. Everywhere you turn people are so grieved — there's such a sense of loss.

The weather has set like iron. I haven't had a bath for days and with the heat over ninety degrees the current goes off and there are no electric fans.

It's a pretty grim time.

But one has to keep cheerful and positive — the world is in such a ghastly mess.

Anyway, they are moving the guerillas out of Beirut, so maybe that will quieten down at last.

Wrong or right — Begin has played the devil with Jewish tolerance.

11 September 1982

Yesterday I sat in the studio and thought about all sorts of things.

First that Roy was going that afternoon — going to Cuba with Joseph[1], to have some tests done to discover his best capabilities and to get some training. The idea came from Bev and Michael. Bev first said it in the car coming back from Norman's graveside service. Michael moved like lightning over it, and the invitation to come arrived. It is a golden chance for Roy to get his feet on the road to finding a man's place in the earning world.

But as I looked at the little couch in the corner, I realized how close we had grown to each other — each with our particular brand of loneliness.

Then I looked at the plaster cast of 'Negro Aroused' and all of the past came back — the deep surging excitement I had felt in 1936 when I realized that something of importance was being born. The massive formalism — the only bit of wood I had of that width necessary was too small really for the concept, but I tore into it and somehow it arrived — proud, defiant. I felt an irresistible urge not to give the face an emphasis — it's often been criticized for that — but the straining form was what came to me.

Now forty years later I go over the road again — legitimately, I think. They want to show it abroad, and it's wood and David values it — so the commission came to do a small one in bronze.

That interesting Wallace Campbell[2] is financing two bronzes — little ones.

As I worked, I had planned it just a shade smaller — I didn't want to do it SMALL, and of course it grew and grew and now it's about five inches taller!! It gave me trouble at first, because I never work from what I see but from what I feel.

At first I made the head angry and threatening — it still is, if, as Michael says, you climb up and look down at it: 'Oh, Mother, how many times have I met that man in the Union, in politics. *Demanding* — oh my God I know that man — you better not try to fool him — he'll fold his arms and watch your every step at the bargaining table — no — treat him, treat him honest — or look out for yourself — but why haven't you made that the dominating theme?'

I said, 'Yes, but there is something more timeless for the Negro to arouse, not in anger, not in fear, not in weakness or bitterness — but just to be there — aroused — resolute.'

George's poem screams[3] — George's poem reflects in passionate language the eruptive feeling of the moment, in poetry that only George can write.

Sculpture is different — sculpture is the symbol, the archetype, the image in frozen form of the world of feeling, emotion.

A man can't form his life on defiance, so what one carves is the core of all the conflicting passions — the residue.

I think I like my plaster cast — I don't think it's as good a work of art as the carving, but in some mysterious way it is nearer to me, and the experiment I did with the surface has, I think, worked out.

And now for some quiet — a period of germination — a brooding, a silence — eddying down to the core of one's being.

18 September 1982

Party Conference with an innovation of night sessions.

Bishop DeSouza[1] on first on Thursday night. A fine voice — powerful delivery, a sense of humour and a remarkable gift of communication. I will always remember the surprise and pleasure of his speech. Strong, honest and with an intense awareness of the sea of troubles we all struggle in. I was greatly drawn to him, and the crowd followed him with wonderful response.

BUT the American last night was something again: Mayor Richard Hatcher-Gayle, Illinois, four times elected — also president of the black mayors' organization. He's a vice president of the American Democratic Party.

He made a tremendous speech — speaking with the utmost boldness in criticism of all that Reagan did and stood for. He attacked Reagan, but he did it with infinitely greater skill than Belafonte had done. Still, that he attacked him at all gave ultimate support to the people who strongly agreed that Belafonte had every right to do the same thing. When 'B' did it for the first time, people were very shocked — those who had never heard it done before. But Hatcher's more authoritative manner silenced the criticism of Belafonte once and for all.

But there was so much more to his speech than that. He made constructive, valuable suggestions that could have far-reaching effects. He had something of Martin Luther King about him — extremely serious, but warm, intelligent and infinitely understanding of the vast world problem we face in the building of nuclear weapons etc., and a quite heart-breaking picture of the danger of the black man's position in our world — the poverty, the ghetto conditions, etc., etc., and all that it could and did lead to.

It was a *magic* evening — we all felt it — and when he finished the applause came over again and again and again in great waves — dying down and roaring up again, and then, with divine inspiration, someone at the back of the hall started 'We Shall Overcome' and it mounted to a great roar, Martin Luther King's great song, and then, 'The Trumpet'[2] and the National Anthem, led by that absolute darling, Jimmy Tucker,[3] whose voice has lost not one bit of power and musicality. The night before he had sung 'I Saw My Land in the Morning'[4] and I shed tears!

Doug, George, Joe Bush[5] and I went together to all the sessions, and after Hatcher spoke I've never see Doug so uninhibitedly with excitement *thrilled* — and we all shot up on to the platform to shake hands and be joyful!!

But today I sit at home and wait and wait for the election of officers.[6] So *much* hangs on it — our whole new image could emerge or we could be hurled back into the old confusion and mess.

Let's wait and see!!

19 September 1982

Last night we went down to hear Gil Noble[1] — a radio, TV journalist — apparently pretty top notch.

It was an amazing night — he put on his film on drugs. I've never in my life seen anything so horrifying. A world I didn't know existed. Bodies covered in destroyed conditions. Nowhere, from head to foot, an area of healthy flesh capable of taking a hypodermic needle. Rotting sores, great swollen lumps left as hands or feet, and still the needle searching for a place where the drugs could be injected.

And Noble talked with them – would they, if their life could be lived over, would they do it again?

And the astounding statement that, to destroy the Black Panther Movement, drugs were given away in the schools in the ghettos. The schools were notoriously the easiest and cheapest place to get any amount of drugs and each one taught one, and so the community was silenced, and the great effort to bring a more just world. Those who were, or who would have been, leaders were destroyed. And the news media? With all its chance for good – deliberately debunking, distorting, twisting the reality of the moment to preserve the status quo of the all powerful, few, rich.

Even the twisting of the militant folk songs, pure in aim and powerful in impact, degraded into something coarse and foul. Well I think the same thing is happening here, whilst the Seagas make a fortune selling records – $10,000 for 'I Wan a Woman fe Jam.'

22 October 1982

It's interesting how important it is sometimes to have a bad and sleepless night – you catch up on all your thinking. Anyway – I have had a wonderful picture of the sort of work I want to do for the next year. It's not good to put these things into words – you blow your creativeness that way – but roughly I know it's the Jamaica woman – the woman who bears the loads – nuff said.

Had Rachel for a wonderful and peaceful week. She really rested. Her job, her children, her poetry – this is enough – and the acting she did in Walcott's play, and which she did well, I am sure was too much for her.

Michael has cancelled his lectures, and for three weeks has a real rest – the States and England – staying with friends. Michael has had a hard time on too many fronts. I don't know how he has come through – but he's coming through I feel sure. He has seen a lot of Doug, who seems profoundly happy and lifted from three years of utter battering. I'm glad he's back at his academic work – he did politics very, very well – he's such a grass roots person in one way, but he has a good mind and sound, and I do pray that the next year or two will give him all he deserves.

It's difficult to know the future right now. I have had patches of furious depression over East-West-North-South – Israel, PLO, the whole works, and these two idiotic, vast and powerful countries snarling at each other like delinquent children, each with a weapon that could blow up the human race.

I watch it on TV and the newspapers, and my spirit goes down and down.

I had a bad night — it's still dark outside and slowly the feeling has grown on me that the human race is not that bad — somehow it will save itself — much will be destroyed, but much will survive. One has to just get rid of the feeling that survival doesn't bring peace and solutions — survival is just the capacity to go on — through all the storms and maddening mistakes. It will always be like this — and as I think of survival, I think of my Jamaican woman. I called my woman and children in the end, 'Ghetto Mother' — the agony of the ghetto mother.

I wish the morning would come, it has been a long night!! But it has brought me a kind of convincing peace.

Strange how Seaga is trying to make what we called in the old days 'pocomania' into an established church. He is an astute politician, but he's walking a very strange road for a social anthropologist. He's a queer man — maybe he will succeed — I watch and am glad that Michael is out for a bit.

23 October 1982

It was wonderful sitting in the little old house and listening to Miss B., who is ninety-two, telling me how it used to be. How there was a toll gate at Matilda's Corner, a real gate across the road. And the people coming down from the hills had to pay threepence before they could go on down to Kingston to sell their products.

She lives at 96 Hope Road, and if they wanted to go into town they had to walk to Half Way Tree, and there they would catch a mule-drawn bus. The mules did very well into Kingston and back — but they couldn't take the steep hill up to Matilda's Corner.

We sat there in the spotlessly clean and rather artistic little house, with good Jamaican pictures on the walls, for she loved artistic things, like putting dry branches with bronzed leaves in large jars standing on the floor.

She lived and worked with us for years, running the house, doing the shopping, and above all, being a second mother to Douglas and Michael. She was 4ft 8ins, a tiny person, with a gift for wearing a pretty dress. And when Rachel came along, once more she had a young person in the house. How we loved her and still do.

Norman trusted her in every way — she is so discreet, so able to weigh her values and give the right advice when asked, for she rarely offered advice. Her mother lived to a hundred, a wonderfully dignified and wise little lady, and her sister, Miriam Campbell, the mother of George Campbell, was one of the best nurses I have ever known. She was only a 'practical' nurse — but as she walked quietly into the room with that mischievous smile, you relaxed and felt confident that all would be well. Everyone loved to see her handle Norman.

She used to 'get around him', as the saying goes, and once when he had a high temperature she persuaded him to have a 'Bush Bath' and my God it worked! We were all jubilant, particularly Mrs C., and Norman was sheepishly relieved. Norman was a terror, there's no getting away from that. He used to tell us about old man Shearer[1] who became blind ultimately, and how the women of the house fluttered around him taking turns to cut his toenails and read to him.

Then there was our mutual grandmother who was a horsewoman *par excellence*, who rode a black horse called Emperor — who used to *bow* deeply up and down when reigned in. She could ride any horse (like me!!), only she was beautiful and had a magic side-saddle seat — whilst I rode like a street 'gamin', no seat, no grace, but GOOD and sensitive hands.

27 October 1982

Theatre in Jamaica — I have a titanic love and respect for Louise the incomparable. I always loved Ranny[1] from the days when he campaigned with me and visited the most threatening and difficult PNP groups, and what an actor, what a sense of timing — and in later days, Barbara Gloudon.[2]

Greta and Henry were theatre to a vast public. Pantomime was always with it — always dead cool and right on the contemporary scene. But the person I look most to as Jamaican theatre is Trevor Rhone[3] — difficult to say why — an oddly attractive, very shy man — have never exchanged a sensible word with him, my fault of course, but I believe in him — I believe he's tuned in on Jamaica. I believe he could be marvellously popular, with pop plays, but I also believe he has a strange compassion. He understands why people laugh at the wrong moments and come to theatre with all the wrong motives, and he doesn't let himself get upset. He believes that when they go home, something else sticks. He's right up my street and on a different level entirely, so is Charles Hyatt.[4] But Trevor is something again.

Later —

Up to now I had preferred McCalla as Gloria, but tonight Grace McGhie[5] put on a *superb* performance and Trevor was so charming, he wouldn't let us pay for our seats. I was very touched — a remarkable person — he isn't on anyone's market.

2 January 1983

5 a.m. What an awful night — I couldn't sleep, and I felt *cold*. I'm just over an appalling type of flu, much more like Dengue Fever — agonizing aches and cold, cold. I've got over it in a way, but it has left me not quite myself.

Ra and her friend Israel[1] and the two children are here from Barbados staying with Carole. They leave this morning to go back to Barbados. An aura of sadness hangs over the whole exercise – New Year's Day was spoilt by too much alcohol, and George was in one of his utterly unreasonable moods.

I had a little group here on New Year's Eve and somehow it was friendly and a little comforting.

Norman's girl has arrived from USA. I gave them sandwiches and fruit juice, whilst he looked frantically for a bedroom in one of the small hotels, so tomorrow we have to persuade her to return home until he can make some sort of provision for her.

Rachel wants to throw up her job in Barbados and come home, but it's an impossible situation without a job and without a home.

I am looking for Roy to turn up from Cuba at any moment; we have twice been to the airport to meet him.

So 1983 starts with a bang.

On the credit side, George has got sponsorship for his book of poems,[2] and my last sculpture has apparently been a great success.[3] As soon as I can get the home running smoothly again, I want to go back and do another figure in the round of about the same dimensions.

But in the meantime, I will press on with the drawings for George's book.

12 January 1983

Things seem to come toppling down on one. There's this libel case with the *Gleaner* – and the lawyers afraid to take the case!! People afraid to give personal evidence – what are they all afraid of – Jamaica is a place that has changed beyond all knowing.

Actually, it sounds a bit pompous to write, but if you look around the world today, HOW the values have changed. The age of idealism is dead. People won't lay down their lives for a concept anymore – the things we fought for – sometimes paying a high price.

All this neo-colonialism – it leaves me a little stunned. The flooding, the swamping the country with America; anything for what 'really matters' – money, economic growth, etc. Of course they're right in a way, one has to survive. There are problems staring us in the face and somehow they have to be solved – unemployment, poverty – oh God, and it all moves so slowly.

And now the cricketers and apartheid. Long, long ago I remember going to cricket in England at Lords, and some of the players entered from one door and some from another.

Gentlemen and players – cricket has travelled a long way since that, and the paying salaries to tennis stars has risen to an earning capacity of one million US dollars in a year. So the cricketer is still almost starved when it comes to money.

But nothing, nothing, *nothing* excuses this move by the West Indies team to take vast sums of money to play in an apartheid South Africa. It's awful — I don't care *what* excuse is offered, and it would seem that Rowe[1] had grouses — so he didn't just sell out — he attempts to justify it.

Sport is terribly important in this modern world. Public entertainment is worth almost anything, with shorter work hours, etc., etc., and any ...

13 January 1983

I got as far as that 'black balling' of cricketers, Michael's quite ghastly case against Hearne, and things started happening on the domestic scene and I had to stop. We're having a hard drive on proof-reading George's new book of poems. It's about eighty-four poems — 'Earth Testament'.

Aaron Matalon,[1] bless his heart, is sponsoring the publication, so we haven't got to do a skin-flint publication. The poems are lovely, something entirely new for George, and, in all humility I say, something new in our Jamaican, Caribbean and West Indian Poetry. Also, and here I am diffident because I am out of touch with world poetry — I feel that it is something new in poetry, free of place or time.

Michael came in, deeply moved over Patterson's[2] opening speech in his case. He felt it had a passion, a care of facts, an ability to confront the court with the full horror of what Hearne wrote. At the time I never read what he was writing, I was too deeply disturbed and shattered, really, over everything that was happening. So that the article has fallen like a bombshell for the first time. Hearne totally baffles me — he has a fine wife — I like her so much, and John from boyhood times I knew and was very fond of. I hope that the truth will emerge, for knowing Michael for a lifetime, with all his faults, cruelty, torture, murder are not part of him.

I must stop now and have a *hot* bath — it's so cold.

I have been ill on and off for weeks. I am trying to build back my strength for one more year of work.

22 January 1983

It's a difficult moment, chiefly financially, and also the household is costing me far too much. I am over-staffed, and in a way they are overpaid. I am trying to settle Roy into the small studio, and this means a certain expense for furniture — but it's a step I must take because I must get back the big studio free of anyone sleeping there – and free of TV, music, etc., etc. It's a bit of a nightmare at the moment.

George has settled into the one spare bedroom, and if he could either get his pension or a decent job he would contribute to the household, which he is anxious to do.

Getting his poetry into book form has required a great use of time as he is easily discouraged, and then I took on the drawings before we got the sponsor, when we wanted to give the book an extra public appeal of two contributors.

As it turned out it wasn't necessary, but having started I don't want to let him or his great poetry down too badly.

There's no doubt he is a remarkable poet, and these poems are, I feel, breaking new ground. We have finished the second proof-reading, so it is really beginning to get off the ground, and it should be a fine contribution. I doubt it will have the immediate appeal of *First Poems*, which was a historical event, free of a strong racialism or even nationalism – it has, nevertheless, that deep humanism that characterizes all his writing.

Anyway I have one drawing left to do and then I am hoping to pour my energies back to my own work.

The local scene is unpleasant. I am so angry over this nasty libel case.

I think I'll stop now and try to find something useful to do!!!

I think I need to be alone – I need to brood, to think. I've been ill so often recently it is good to just feel a little *well* – but I don't want to share it with anyone.

I find I spend a lot of time reading and thinking about world affairs – and I must say it's not very inspiring and there is almost a sameness in the pattern everywhere you turn until an unbelievable thing happens like a hurricane in Copenhagen – with roofs off!

Kingston is having an awful drought – my poor little garden is completely burnt up and the hills beyond are so dry and so few clouds.

Rachel is DOWN again – I worry so much over her. The right man would help so much. Douglas sounds well and cheerful – I hope this is so. And Norman has recovered from Xmas – he has so many nice qualities, if only he could mature.

23 January 1983

Each morning I get up now, I feel a strange uncertainty about how to direct my energies. It's so queer because I don't doubt the energy, I feel that it is there – but which way to go. It's a work preoccupation underneath, but because I still have that final drawing to do for George's book, the fact that Xmas knocked my work and myself sideways – I got ill, I ran into fantastic financial difficulties, and it was imperative that somehow or other I must survive through all the storms that were piling up on the family around me.

But as I sit quietly in the studio writing this now that things have quieted down a bit, it comes to me that I should just stay quiet for a little while and trust life — that it will flow again.

I am reading '*The Autumn of the Patriarch*' — it is a remarkable work. To quote '*Alice in Wonderland*': 'No pictures or conversations'!! It must be an incredibly difficult style to handle, and must demand a unique type of concentration. It certainly demands a total attention from the reader. Miss a line, a paragraph, and the whole build-up of events can pass you by — events that are going to culminate in something extraordinarily significant, sometimes catastrophic, but which takes place in a few words lightly thrown in — and the action changes, setting off on a quite new aspect of the patriarch's character, which is about to become obsessive.

An interesting case of this is when he decides he wants his fortune, future, told by an old, old woman who lives in a distantly remote spot — a journey that he has to take of quite challenging difficulties, not to say dangers, and he has to go almost alone so that as few people as possible will know. You are carried along with deeply felt and described events and places, but the strangling of the old woman after the future reading takes just a few lines — and the fact that she has to die so that no one will know what she has told him — the nonchalance of that brief act — tells you more about the patriarch than a whole book could do, handled differently.

I know, I know — something is coming to me about the work road — let me stop writing and let it just flow.

12 February 1983

So I had a moment of happiness — it's strange — a great harmony, a great happiness. And then blow after blow fell with Michael's case, and here we are stuck with the likelihood of an appeal to the Privy Council in England.[1]

He has extraordinary courage and resourcefulness, but my God what a life, what a reward for his long years of service — he has loved the people — laboured for the people — he really cares and they know it. I think he has a great love from them, but the vicious handful of men — just a few families — who want to own this country — they will stop at nothing.

And now America arrives on the scene.

It's so sad to get caught in this cross-fire between these two powerful countries — their hatred — their refusal to trust each other. Then there's Cuba and the price we have paid for that friendship. But one mustn't be bitter — it serves no purpose.

One has to live — to love life — to love people to the end.

17 February 1983

So the Royal visit is over. I said to Michael, Jamaica hasn't changed one iota in the forty years since 1938 — of course that was a silly distortion of the truth. The trade union movement is what has changed Jamaica. Every domestic help will demand double pay for working on a holiday. Everyone says 'help' instead of 'servant'.

Black and white work in stores and banks — preponderantly black. Oh, everything has changed except our love of pageantry and stadium shows. The few people of Beverley's generation who will stay angrily at home, and the few like Michael who totally disapprove of monarchies, but go out of courtesy or because he knows his people will go and they will want passionately to see him there as *their* representative.

Seaga has produced the Queen and Reagan so he looks triumphant — the only enormous crowd was at the stadium, but Montego Bay was a smashing success. Anyway, let's get peacefully on with our lives. I'm glad I went to the dinner, and Glasspole was glad I was there. Michael and I went together and he looked very handsome!!

The violence is growing on us in a frightening way — the press put it on the back pages now, but it grows and grows, and people are suffering terribly. The most pathetic thing is the young, fresh-faced teenagers with their 'pieces of paper' in their hands which they toiled to earn, but no job, nothing for them — it breaks my heart.

19 February 1983

It's too early for coffee and I think I would like to try to recall what the early political pioneers seemed to me to be like.

The first ones that spring to mind are always Fairclough, Nethersole, Arnett, Glasspole, Wills Isaacs — and looking back after all these years, they seem as vivid, as real, to use a funny word, as valid. Then there are of course the men of the left wing — Ken and Frank Hill and Richard Hart.

The two early women in politics, Edith James[1] and Iris King[2] — and, not so strictly a politician, Amy Bailey.

These are the people I knew closely; people like Ivan Lloyd[3] and Father Coombs[4] I was never near to. I think that being from rural Jamaica I never had the opportunity ever to sit and talk with them.

Another very vivid and much loved memory is *Public Opinion*. I remember the struggles that went on over it — to keep it alive, to face the realities of the newspaper world in a country like Jamaica. The ceaseless effort to give publicity to the struggling talent in every field. I remember too the almost bitter struggle to make the PNP understand that if you ran a completely political paper you would be forever limiting yourself to preaching to the converted. *Public Opinion* had to spring out of all the new ideas that were coming alive politically − but it had to have a freedom to criticize or support. If a man were a good poet, his political beliefs were of secondary importance. If he were an out and out opponent that would be different.

Fairclough believed that the paper could serve the literary and artistic as well as the new political thinkers. But if it ran on a strict party line it would not attract the readers who did not see eye to eye with it. This often angered the over-enthusiastic politicians who needed every inch of space to propagandize the new ideas. He was right, as it has often been proved in the years that have followed, where party organs have flourished and faded under the stimulus of elections.*Public Opinion* lasted nearly forty years, with an unfailing reputation as a free paper of staunch liberal, even radical, ideas. But it was always the paper that gave to the struggling writers a chance to cut their literary teeth, and it carried the flag for all the new efforts of fine art, theatre, dance.

Fairclough was a dedicated man − he loved his country − he was loyal to his people, but he had absolutely no illusions about either. He knew and understood the total conservatism of the small country man and woman. He knew that theories and ideologies would cut no ice with them.

From 1938-83 a British queen would rouse a storm of loyalty and excitement: as she did last week in exactly the same way that Queen Victoria would have been felt to be the repository of all wisdom, all power.

Say the words 'Queen's visit' and only Haile Selassie could pull a bigger crowd; an American President certainly couldn't.

That's why he (Fairclough) feared and fought the idea of universal suffrage, and was a passionate believer in self-government. The first would give 'quashie'⁵ rights and powers he could not handle, but the second would give the intellectual, the thinking, forward-looking, intelligent man of education an area in which he could change the public image. The educated black and brown man could replace the aristocracy of the ruling white, or near white, small and powerful class.

Fairclough was a man of considerable dignity and poise.

Conversation with him was not the small talk of the average citizen. But in conversation he was stubborn and inflexible if you touched on subjects that were a matter of opinion.

He quarrelled with a series of editors of PO − people said he had a father complex whenever the paper was concerned, whatever that ambiguous phrase might mean! He was conscious that it was the one area where he could get *his* ideas expressed in a world that was getting increasingly strident, as left and right struggled for political power. The group surrounding him in 1937 would have been the Hills, Hart, H.P. Jacobs, and the most powerful as a matter of prestige and public image would have been Nethersole.

23 February 1983

I had just reached there when we went down to Michael's with a parcel for Rachel — he was leaving for Barbados. Michael with Bev and the children were having dinner.

After the greetings, Beverley said something like: 'Did Michael tell you about what I found, doing research in Washington?'

She is doing her doctorate — Jamaican History.

I said — 'Yes — the letter that the American Embassy had sent to Hoover.'[1]

She said: 'Did he tell you all — about you too?'

I said, 'No, he didn't mention me.'

'Oh', she said, 'That you were a committed communist.'

I was quite stunned for the moment.

I will always remember the feeling that I had. This is how history is written. Not the truth about people — but just the records of man's prejudices and distortions. Well, I am not, and never have been, a communist. I believe that there are things in society that have to be changed. But I believe passionately that the *way* this is done is an important factor in the end result.

The starving-out of peasants in Russia because they couldn't or wouldn't change.

The silencing of the voice of criticism and the freedom of the arts.

I could go on for a long time but I won't.

No, I am not, and could never be, a communist. I would never choose that road. I think that with all its bungling and confusion and slowness, the change has to come under democratic ways.

I don't think I answered Beverley. I don't think I said anything — and I left it for a day before I write this.

Whoever was in the Embassy wasn't apparently in a position to know anything about me — but he wrote what he chose to write. He had his own motives.

It was all a long time ago — but what about history? Does it lie in the hands of responsible people, who want the truth and nothing but the truth?

Research is a good thing — it keeps the past alive — but it too must place the truth above an interesting story. I believe that Beverley thinks just that — and will strive for the truth.

23 March 1983

The news seems to be so bad all the time — violence and cruelty — a terrible revenge against society — against life. That's on the level of the gunmen, the hold-ups — and on the national and international level, the struggle for power goes on. Latin America, Iran and Iraq, the fight around Israel. And behind it all the States and Russia — piling up armaments, and the horror of nuclear weapons.

I get awake sometimes too early — it's too late to go back to sleep and it's too early by far for dressing and getting up, and I lie and think about it all and I wonder how does one find and keep peace inside.

When one gets so near to the end, one longs for the end to come — to have it over with— and that seems so cowardly. Let me write to Gehrke,[1] she must be having an awful time in Guatemala with the political struggle that is going on there. We are both the same age and both of us have gone on working — just as we did as students. Today I will write her.

I have this girl who wants to bring out this book of my work.[2] I don't know what will come of it — but there's a sort of catharsis in getting out the old photographs, seeing where one failed and what has stood the test of time.

I will get out the catalogues too, and send Gehrke what she hasn't seen. She brought out a lovely book of Guatemalan costumes, and her line drawings, especially of trees, are wonderful.

I am feeling calmer now, time has passed and it will soon be six o'clock. The sky is getting touches of fire as the dawn draws near. If I can help where it is needed; if I can let love take charge of all the rough moments. One is so lucky to have little children near one — Natasha and her friends, and little David and Drum.

18 April 1983

'Praise' is finished and being cast — there's nothing I can say until it's out of the plaster.

My two young men weren't available. Basil Watson is now in Guyana with his wife, who has a government contract to fulfill. Errol Lewis is now living in Montego Bay — and living off his sculpture. He phoned me and said he would come up and cast for me — but he hasn't turned up and I didn't want to hold up too long. Fitzroy Harrack,[1] who is a fine sculptor, is doing it for me. I HOPE it comes out alright, but we have no experience of each other, and I hope and believe that he will come through alright. He's coming in to chip out this evening. I keep my fingers crossed.

I find that I am selling fairly regularly now; after all these years I begin to feel that I can now depend more on a sale.

But of course there are always the works that don't sell, and sculpture is such an expensive thing — you have to carry a heavy load of expenses. For instance, I haven't sold 'Ghetto Mother' and it cost the earth to produce, certainly over $2,000.

Well, I will try to keep accounts from now on and see if I make anything to do more than help me to pay my expenses.

'Praise' has come out very well indeed!

I hope it will be bronzed, it needs it, but I am happy over it.

I hear that 'Ghetto Mother' is attracting attention at the new opening show at the new Gallery.[2]

30 July 1983

There, I finished Diminuenda[1] — how do you spell that? — but whereas I finished 'Praise' so happy, so happy, not so Diminuenda — it started with such joy, but I never got completely lost in it. The house was full of pressures, full of needless explosions — one could never get on to that fine line of awareness, so the feet hold like roots and it nowhere floats.

One always has to take the blame, take the failure — but there are pressures in Regardless just now that are out of my control — but what to do about it — I have tried so hard — but ...

18 October 1983

Today is a day of total exhaustion — never felt like this before, but there is a sort of stillness with it — an unknown way. Where, how, when — it hangs over me like a gigantic question mark. Does any road lead from here?

24 October 1983

George went into hospital yesterday. It's been an awful day; after he left Roy and I felt terrible.

But he will come through — I know he will come through — his poetry, that book *'Earth Testament'*, it was worth all the suffering. If he hadn't brought that out of himself he would have died with a broken heart — if he can just live long enough to know and recognize what he has achieved after all these years with it bottled up inside him. The love that pours out of it — love of man and woman and God. Love of the Universe — the sun, the moon, the stars — what poetry — George, get well again, dear, and know and understand everything.[1]

25 October 1983

George phoned, totally bewildered that the doctors had apparently forgotten him as he was left alone. I couldn't say: George you are forgotten, we are all forgotten, whilst the horror that has taken place in Grenada[1] sweeps everyone and everything off the map — out of our consciousness. I believe how I felt on the 18th was this coming — I don't know what to write or what to think, but

I put my small opinion on record — I may be wrong, but I think it's the most brilliant coup the CIA has ever pulled off.

13 November 1983

It's after breakfast Sunday a.m. Roy has gone to post letters for me, Joyce is tidying the house, Michael has phoned and asked Roy and me to dinner. He's going abroad for two weeks, we miss him, but it's valuable work and in any event he can't just do opposition moves — he's bound to become a focal point for unrest, and no one wants to be responsible for an outburst of violence or unrest — anymore than there is already.

The firing of Joseph[1] has deeply upset him in every way — as a father, as a politician and as a citizen. Joseph shows a fierce anger — at first I thought it was a mask — but I think the main thing is that he seems unafraid. I don't think he is pretending at all. Every commentator has been on the air over it on the programmes like 'Public Eye'.[2]

The popular polls had Michael way ahead until Grenada came along — then like Thatcher and Falklands, Reagan and the 'jumbo jet',[3] Seaga now has the invasion of Grenada. It's all very odd because everyone forgot that there is a Commonwealth, and America invaded the Commonwealth, and the British government said and did nothing.

It's funny how those little letters CIA hang over my head like a bell tolling. From long ago that all started, poor Bishop. Anyway this has never been a political diary, or record of public events. Many things occupy my mind now, for one a great worry over George — that's been the bond of a lifetime, and his book is so lovely. I know he will find his way through all the confusion.

There's tremendous pressure everywhere — all sorts of people are cracking up — loss of memory, confusion, senility.

I myself realize that I have allowed my life to get caught in all the intense cross currents and it isn't good — it leads to reckless talk, a drink too many, saying things that you don't mean either to shock or make people laugh — quite stupid things.

Then I also realize that I have become strangely afraid of being alone. It isn't quite as simple as that, it's more that when I am alone I become aware that there is very little time left.

Last year I dropped into a habit of just sitting, watching the birds feed on the bird table, and the clouds as they drift over the mountains. All very charming and harmless, but when it began to go from minutes to hours, I realized something very bad was happening. I wasn't *doing* anything, and when people came in I would listen for a little while and then drift off into myself again.

Rachel on one of her visits spotted it, and then George complained that I wasn't living my normal, full life. So slowly I am learning to laugh again – to tell funny stories and actually tackle things like clearing cupboards and drawers – working a little in the garden – in other words using myself.

Several of our friends, three in all, have succumbed to what, for want of a different word, let's call senility. How does one stave that off? I imagine one just has to guard oneself – take infinite care of how one talks, be aware of people's reactions to what you say – like that, you are measuring yourself against reality.

There! Roy came back from the post with a carefully guarded *Newsweek* to which, as he had paid for it, he was entitled to the first look! Cover – blood running from a soldier wounded in the great bomb blast.

No one has been in this morning and, as usual, I have that strange, lost, deserted feeling!! So until the 12.30 concert comes over on TV instead of moping I'll go on scribbling.

There! as I wrote that the phone went and Corina is coming.

It really is fantastic the way telepathy can work, for I needed someone BADLY.

14 November 1983

Yesterday was a struggle all day after Corina left, with a quite ghastly sense of exhaustion – all day it dogged me – exhaustion and a profound depression – a need to die – to just have it all over with, and then that haunting sense of fear. What is death? A cessation of all movement? But is it also a cessation of consciousness. Oh it was a BAD day – and then Michael, who is going abroad, asked Roy and me down to supper, the two children, Bev, Michael, Roy and myself.

He is being criticized for being abroad so much, but what else can he do? I suppose he is bound to be a focal point for restlessness, not that he is doing anything about it. Because it would be wrong to stir up trouble, when nothing in the world can be achieved by it. Also it keeps his mind keenly alive. It's a challenge – I imagine it does distance him from Jamaica and the village pump preoccupation with life and its difficulties here.

So, I had a bad night – got awake at 3 a.m. and that was that. I have been taking sleeping tablets, just a light dose, and I had run out. At 4 a.m., I took two aspirin and a drink but it didn't work. What *was* haunting me?

Around 6 a.m. I think I dozed and at 7 a.m. I got up and got some coffee. After breakfast I went and sat in the studio and literally went to pieces. I finally got up and pulled out a book, *Ecce Homo*, and in it Norman had written, 'The best is yet to be, 1962.'

I pulled myself together and got out some clay and started a little ten-inch standing figure. Then Pam phoned and was coming down for a talk as I had asked her to.

We had a long talk. It was very good. I have such love and admiration for her. She had just returned from Venezuela from some music commission she is a part of and her account of the passionate dislike of the N. Americans — their fury over the invasion of Grenada and their whole intense anger over their interference in South America.

She too is aware of a problem looming in her own life since Ronnie Thwaites[1] was held up by two motor bicycles in broad daylight on that Content Road. She stays up at Content by herself a great deal, and of course Martin[2] was chopped up at Flamstead.

It is all such a tragedy — as we lock up and stay indoors as night comes down.

Verona[3] came in this evening — she too lives alone and we talked of many things, but as the sun went down she went home. She's such an experienced and lovable person. She really knows her Jamaica.

I think I'll try and go to bed now as I am tired — but my spirits have lifted and the awful exhaustion is not as bad — that little bit of clay in the studio is a help!

19 November 1983

It's past 5 p.m. and the sun has gone down — there's just that golden glow over the hills and tree tops. The dogs are playing on what ought to be a lawn — but no rain — Johan and Cindy, a Doberman and an Alsatian. He is enormous and a nice dog — full of strength and grace, but an awful snob, a very prejudiced person! — but if he likes you he's very loyal and over-affectionate. Cindy is small and fox-like — she has a streak of real wildness — but without being a 'correct in form' Alsatian, there is something touchingly beautiful about her. Sensitive, nervous — she doesn't like visitors and goes and hides when they come! Last night in the moonlight, at about 10 p.m., they were absolutely wild — circling round and round the garden and then a great collision and a near fight — only Johan is so much bigger, he knocks her over and she goes at him showing her teeth.

Horowitz is filling the world with Scarlatti — Scarlatti of all people — quite exquisite — a delicate world of speed and dexterity and flowing form — truly, truly, wondrous and beautiful.

It's been one of those look over your shoulder days. Roy is terribly depressed and lonely — so lonely that at last I see that he must live with young people. He must live with *people* — I love him very much — he and Norman are so different, but both very sensitive. On Monday, Doug comes to stay. I have had a hell of a job sorting his things, George's and Rachel's, and coming on old and forgotten papers, photos and things.

And I can hear Zethildah moving around the house. What a mixture of toughness and an incredible sweetness. She is like my own sister with this long,

long relationship. She cooked Norman's last meal and knew with unerring judgement that his end was very near. She has a great flair for clothes – always simple but with a touch of style and she has kept her figure – oh certainly one in a million, if that phrase means anything.

The music has stopped and a great full moon is coming over the hills, and then BANG – a blackout – lights gone – TV gone – music gone. Well that's the way it goes.

I always remember being at Nomdmi on a magnificent evening – the world shrouded in a golden net of light and air – the sort of evening one remembers forever – and a car arrived and I could see a figure hurrying from the gate. Norman had sent a message that he was coming but would be late, but warning me that there was a storm warning out – it must have been '56? He did come just as the storm broke and we had that wild night when the little house – it was only two rooms then – rocked like a ship in a storm making strange, grunting sounds. We had the three children with us and a nurse – Rachel, Juanita and Milton,[1] and of course they slept through the whole thing only to wake next morning to see the debacle – hundreds of pine trees down – the whole place a shambles – you couldn't walk to the gate – you had to have a path axed out. It was a wonderful experience – terrifying but REAL – Nature let loose, as if directed and directing against mankind.

Jamaica can give you the whole gamut of emotion and thought – it's a marvellous country to be part of!!!

I seem to have used a mighty lot of superlatives – and a rose-coloured world. It's interesting because all day I've fought.

26 November 1983

Last night it came over the news that Seaga has asked the GG to 'dissolve' parliament as he wanted to call an election. I'm putting that badly because I am a bit tired. It's 6 p.m. and I am all alone in the house. Doug and Roy have gone off to Mandeville.

Last night Yvonne[1] came and picked me up and we went and watched NDTC rehearsing for about two and a half hours. It was *fascinating* – I loved it – and, as Yvonne said, I couldn't sit all evening and fret. When we got back at about ten-thirty, Roy said Michael had phoned twice from New York. So I immediately phoned him – he had very good control of himself and was watching Larry Holmes beat that poor youngster in one round. It was, as Bev said, his way of giving himself time to think. Bev sounded excited but unafraid.

This morning I saw Doug and Roy off and Norman, who had dropped in with a client, said he'd appreciate some dinner tonight. Then I dressed and went to the Soroptimist 21 – I was glad I went. I was their first president years ago.

When I got back at 3.30 p.m., the dogs were glad to see me. Joyce had put dinner in the oven for Norman. He hasn't turned up yet but I expect he soon will.

I haven't had time to talk with anyone – or really to think. I phoned M.G. and he said right off – boycott – I said I think you're wrong.[2] They are having what will be a monster meeting at Half Way Tree, and Seaga will announce the date. Rex said it'll be the 16th, which is a bare three weeks. It's to be the old enumeration – which was pretty corrupt.

I feel we are at a great crossroad. I am not clear at all about it, but that's the image that presents itself to me.

There is a raucous sound system up at Four Roads, pelting out a reggae to end all reggaes – really something. It reminds me of what used to happen when Norman was in his last illness – and I asked them to quieten it a bit and he said, 'Oh no, I like to hear it. It doesn't sound like a sound system – it sounds like real people.'

I am writing to calm myself – I think I am afraid and I don't like being alone. Anyway, Yvonne has a birthday and Rex and Barbara Gloudon are going so it should be lovely!! And we will be together when Seaga makes his announcement of the date, which will be a comfort. If Norman turns up I am going to ask him to sleep here – I must go and dress to go out.

29 November 1983

2 a.m. Still waiting for Doug to come home and to hear if we are going to fight the election or not. At that moment I heard the sound of Michael's car next door – and I phoned. 'We are ready for an election – and the minute the new voters lists are ready – we are ready for an election. We welcome an election – but we cannot take part in a sham.'

There, now I'll wait and give Doug some supper if he comes straight home – he should be here any minute now.

30 November 1983

2.30 p.m. This morning I went and had my hair washed – came in and had lunch. I saw Michael for a minute – he's getting a cold and we can't find Beaubrun[1] anywhere. I think he's in a panic at the power he will feel Seaga will now have.

Nomination morning passed off peacefully. The JLP nominated sixty candidates unopposed by the PNP. Some independents and rather weird little new parties nominated a handful of candidates. Trevor Munroe boycotted. This means they will have to create a Leader of the Opposition because in the Constitution there has to be an Opposition Leader. There are all sorts of occasions that require it. So we will see – many things – sixty pairs of hands stretching forward for Xmas work, for contracts for every known need. Sixty MPs are a lot of MPs to satisfy. It's funny that I think of that first!! That's a memory!! From the days when Norman was an MP.

There!! At last Beaubrun turned up, so that's one big worry off my mind.

I've just sold the 'Little Drummer'² and Susan and Neville Alexander³ are coming in to pick it up for a client.

I'm glad I have nothing on tonight. I'm a bit tired and tomorrow I just have to go to Hope Brooks'⁴ show. I'm fond of her and I think she shows great courage following that 'textured' road! Pam O'Gorman is opening and to me she is a very, very special person. There! I feel better now – I get these periods of panic and nowadays I really have to fight them.

Michael is so RIGHT in this matter – but it will take time and strength and patience for the road to become clear. I think of the Referendum and Federation and all we went through. But if we had federated, America couldn't have intervened in this ghastly Grenadian business.

So I'll stop now.

Actually when I think what I have lived through this last two weeks I deeply regret the fact that I haven't been able to get it down on paper. It's as if it took all my strength just surviving!

What a horrible pen – one of these wretched little cheap ball points that they give away in the stores.

A cup of rosemary tea – that's what will fix me!

3 December 1983

I find I can't write about this debacle. 'The sanctity of agreement' on which all civilized societies rest – this is Michael's theme – a theme which he feels is his last contribution to the road we Jamaicans have to travel. He is putting everything he has into it – I hope that his health will stand up to the strain.

The whole country is seething one way or another – over not fighting the election in spite of Seaga's break of faith. Busta and Norman in spite of their faults never broke faith over agreements. Shearer and Michael all through the union struggle, and politically, never broke faith with each other. But this – son of a gun – will do anything to retain a place of power at whatever the spiritual cost to Jamaica.

There! I can't write of it objectively so let me go to bed.

I was up till three o'clock this a.m. dancing at the Drumblair Dance and what a dance and what a band!

I was as high as a kite – can't dance any other way nowadays. I'm old and I feel I must be inspired by an alcoholic freedom. It was marvellous – my feet aren't even tired this evening.

Then Michael came in and we had our first serious talk since the last crisis of nomination day — at last I understood exactly what his mission is in this new step of growth.

Had to sit next to Glasspole at the dinner — never mind, I love Glasspole's wife. I think she's a darling and true as gold all through.

6 December 1983

I don't know what to write. Michael is touring, holding meetings and explaining the refusal to nominate. The press is terribly and viciously against him — oh God — places like the University were vibrantly with him and understanding. I gather parts of the PSOJ[1] agree.

Last night I went to the Alvin Ailey Show[2] at the Arena. One member of the party had had too many drinks and it made me very nervy — so coming down the stairs I had a terrific fall. It was horrible so today I am lazing around — a bit apprehensive of everything and most of all of myself.

Several things have happened recently that are sort of alien to me — things that happen to me — thoughts that tend to dominate the consciousness of my day.

I wish I could write of the present political situation — I know Michael is right, but I can't see the future in any logical way — it almost seems to be in the hands of fate, of chance — oh God.

Norman Jnr has just come in — he's off to the States tomorrow.

10 December 1983

Tonight I know that there is nothing worth going on living for. Whatever course the family is set on they will wisely or unwisely go on their way.

In different circumstances, I could have lived on longer but to what gain?

No, I think I'll clean my house — put everything in order and then pray for an end.

24 December 1983

3 p.m. and the rain is falling lightly outside — but fairly steadily — rather spoiling Xmas Eve for those that have no car and no easy transport.

Doug and Roy are out and I can hear Joyce and Zethilda fixing up the ham and picking the sorrel buds to make the drink. I've spent money I haven't got trying to make my contribution to Xmas for those around me —

But nothing can make it feel like Christmas — everywhere I go everyone says the same thing — but it doesn't feel like Christmas. It's horrid — people just eating and drinking too much — particularly the latter!!

266

I am trying very hard to remain calm — inside as well as out — but a strange sense of doom seems to hang over.

Now that is absurd and something I shouldn't have written.

Music seems to upset me. Schumann's cello concerto, Mozart's harp and flute and this strange man I have never heard before playing the pipes of pan, 'The Lonely Shepherd'. It all made me feel *more* disturbed — so I've taken out this record and I am trying to find some peace. But in the silence I can hear my own heart and it seems so frail — that's all one has to hold on to — the one evidence of life.

30 December 1983

The Americans — yes just that.

We quite correctly boycott the elections. But the Americans — the star spangled banner and what have you? It will take a few years and we will right the pattern.

I love them occasionally as individuals, the BASTARDS — the world hates them, but like Grenada prays for their presence.

I am old and going out — if I can just make it quickly — as I can't call to the youth of Jamaica to give Jamaica a chance, to give it support, leadership, imagination. To HELL with America and Russia too — why can't WE give our own leadership?

It's so late — Rachel has gone with her father to play bridge and Drum and I can't sleep so we sit and wait and wait — whilst Michael gets tight on the telephone because we want Ra to come home and give us a chance to *sleep*.

George came to dinner and has gone home in one of his tantrums. It's so sad — I think he too is slipping.

26 January 1984

After that terrible scene last night I couldn't sleep and today I am trembling all over. I *have* to get calm and be in charge of myself. I have no one to turn to when there is a crisis.

I wish, I really wish, I could go. I feel my time is up — there's nothing going really well at the moment. It's an out of joint period in history.

13 February 1984

Today is the first I have got out of the house for over two weeks. This time I was ill and I was left with a weakness that could have been the end. And of course for the first time I asked the question — is it wise to get better? Isn't it wiser, safer to get out of the world *now* whilst one still has the strength to end it?

Day after day — at night really I knew I had the right number of tablets to end it — end a marvellous life — with nothing new, just bad health, deterioration ahead.

This brought the great confrontation uppermost in my mind. I don't know why I decided not yet — but I did. But it's an experience that has changed my approach to living.

In the background of my mind I'm wrestling with some work. I think of sea — I think of a wave and I remember that 'The Listener' is also Orpheus — so I draw and draw rough sketches to be destroyed. Meanwhile I am coming to grips with the knowledge that I believe I have found the strength and the way to say farewell.

Then Rachel's poem arrives and she writes of Eurydice — and there it is at a bound — NOT farewell — but 'and she looked back'. In Rilke's great poem Orpheus is summoning her back from death — the Gods grant Orpheus the chance to challenge them and play his heavenly music, which defies even death. But she must follow the music as it seems to precede her — but only the music must prevail — she must not look back to see its source. But she looked back.

How does one put that into contemporary and acceptable form — an old Greek legend — born in the land of reggae — born in the land of a place where life and death are perhaps not accepted as tragedy but with a robust, almost emotionally excited and excitable (sic).

16 February 1984

You see I got the story wrong. He looked back to see if she was following.

10 March 1984

I asked Mike — does unconsciousness go on forever after you die, and he sent me this wonderful account of how he sees and feels it.

'You asked what I believe about death and the aftermath. At death metabolism ceases, the organism ceases to function — becomes cold and inert and begins to decompose. Few, if any, dispute that, but there are many diverse opinions and beliefs about the fate of the soul. As you know, I believe it persists as an awareness of its surroundings and loved ones for an individually variable period before withdrawing finally into its own world of impersonal, universal awareness of all living things, all natural phenomena and processes. I do not believe in immortality, nor that individual souls retain their individuality or even the memory or idea of it for very long. But I also believe that for some indefinite period after its separation from the brain and the body, what we think of as the spirit or the soul retains its individual attachments and sensitivity until with time and experience here and elsewhere these ties lose their intensity and the spirit its individual centre so that it can dissolve into the universal being or process of life. Love always,
Mike MGS

3 April 1984

I understand that Yvonne is in grave danger tonight.[1] Since the tests, except for her liver, she seems stronger, calmer. Doug and I went to see her on Sunday for just a few minutes. But tonight her mother phoned in floods of tears — she has made a sudden change for the worse. God — why don't you let me go and give her a little longer to live? She has made such a great contribution to all of us with her dancing — Yvonne in 'Dialogue for Three' — Yvonne dancing with Rex in church.

I love her so much — we all do — and her many kindnesses to me I can never count.

Take me God and let her stay — *please*.

Rachel phoned — but I didn't tell her. She is sending me the Winter Sports Skating Cassette — I wanted it so badly, but I never said it in front of her. She is so good to me — darling, darling Ra.

20 August 1984

Since April life has passed so swiftly and I have recorded nothing. Only today I seem to have the energy to open the book and yet so much has happened and I have been through such deep waters spiritually and physically.

You see recovery from any kind of ill health depends so much on the life span ahead.

One can fight and recover, but at eighty-four one is only recovering to go through the same thing again quite quickly. It's not worth it. However, when I did 'Praise' I found a new spontaneity, a sureness — I love 'Praise' — and then 'The Listener'[1] seemed to start with the same sureness — and at a critical moment George had to move into his new little cottage — very cramped but near to interesting people and at least a restaurant a few yards away.

It was a nerve-wracking experience for all of us — particularly him — and I lost touch with the sureness I had started 'The Listener' with, which I never recaptured, and then I became ill with the cold.

I managed to hide those long nights of fear whilst I wrestled and battled to breathe — and death would have been so welcome. I had it all planned and I know what held me back — the hope of helping Norman and Roy to a greater sureness.

I started the goat[2] at the end of July — it is a commission. I could only work sometimes for half an hour and I would collapse into a chair and fall fast asleep.

Now it is August and it's barely roughed out.

Uninspired and uninspiring — and today I remember the sureness of 'Praise' and I realize this isn't sure enough. So, I think I'll scrap it though there's nothing to put in its place.

The boys seem so calm and happy, particularly Norman for whom it is so necessary. This I have helped them to achieve, but Roy is still not motivated. It will come.

Let me draw back into myself and wait.

Meanwhile so much is happening here and in the world. I follow it all — it interests me passionately and Douglas and Michael so involved — and Rachel battling with fate.

Oh let me follow my instinct and read Eliot's *Four Quartets*. 'In my end is my beginning,' and, 'I said to my soul, be still ...'

22 August 1984

The strangest things are happening. That's a massive understatement. But in one week two Ministers have resigned, or rather, Irvine[1] and Abrahams[2] have. Whether one links the two together no one knows, but it is believed that they were bitterly opposed to each other. Anyway, from the outside where we are, it's all very sudden. Irvine, I guess, is a very good man with a reputation for integrity.

2 September 1984

It seems that I don't write in my diary anymore.

Events follow one another so swiftly and with such a dangerous slant for all of us. Also I think it would take so much energy to write of it clearly and honestly. Douglas and I follow the foreign news and it seems to get worse and worse. The coal miners' strike in England with the threat of the closing of so many mines, and somehow, even from here, one wonders if Scargill couldn't have handled it differently. I always have passionate sympathy for miners — it's such a grim life. We'll have to find a new source of energy — coal and oil can't last much longer.

Today I was thinking of my youth clubs and what a happy time that was. The Shortwood Club on the Drumblair land turned out some remarkable people and August Town, and Hope Tavern and even for a while, Hope Flat.

21 September 1984

Yesterday was David's birthday. I bought him a most expensive present!! But I didn't attend his party. Partly I was working late on 'Goatee the goat' and I was tired — the party was at the poolside at Pegasus and that meant dressing up and getting a taxi. So decided to save the present for one of his visits and I would have something to amuse him. He is a dear little boy, bright and courageous — I am very fond of him. Since Michael and Bev broke up I wonder about those two children. Natasha is a very strong-minded child — intelligent and, in a way, detached. We used to be very close, but since Bev is not there I think she is more jealous of her father — she's very close to him. I think she will grow into a very intelligent person — intelligent in an interesting way. She has a very interesting pair of eyes that seem to notice everything, but she doesn't give away what she sees. I am very fond of her too and I watch her with great interest.

The political stage is quite incredible at the moment — it's almost impossible to believe it is happening.

We are in the middle of Party Conference — I hope to go on Sunday. It's odd, I have been so sworn to secrecy over Michael's health and the coming operation that I have instinctively not even written of it here. He has a lump on his thyroid which has to be removed. He loses that gland, but that isn't the worry. Until the lab test is done we none of us feel too happy. He has been very tired recently, which is not surprising when one thinks of the life he has been living recently. Lecturing and even taking classes all over the States[1] — in the Universities — with political appointments as well — the long flight to England and back several times and his job on the Socialist International as one of the vice presidents.

He's going into hospital on Monday. The operation will be on Tuesday and then the business of persuading him to rest. I know that's going to be a serious problem. Anyway I feel the outcome won't be too serious — I believe — I pray.

23 September 1984

So today is Party Conference — open to the public — I wonder, maybe it will be my last — I hope so! I'll go and hear Michael. Tomorrow he goes into hospital — so let's pray.

I spoke to Mike today — no, not today, last night. He leaves for Barbados today and will be there tonight. I asked him to reassure Rachel over Michael's health — I think and hope he will help for she must be terribly worried — I also want him to meet Israel and let them talk a bit.

Mike was very funny last night — apparently Yale goes on strike today — and Mike says, 'It's like a strike in heaven.' With all the strain of everything I let out a hoot of laughter. Mike can be so witty!! *When he's ready.*

I wish to God I weren't having these dreams — so vivid, so disturbing — it's hard to go back to sleep. Oh Lord, I just remember Zethilda didn't come to work yesterday, which means she won't be out today and there's a huge washing-up waiting for me in the kitchen which I should have done last night.

But I was tired after coming home from the Law School Graduation ceremony.

Jean C. told me to wear a long dress, with both Norman and Roy protesting!! And I was the only one. I told Jean, people have been murdered for less.

Anyway, I'd better stop and get on with the job.

There, the washing-up is done but it's too early to get breakfast. May today go through in positive strength and as much calm as possible!

I think I'll phone Ra and Israel to let them know Mike will be passing through.

26 September 1984

Conference was absolutely wonderful – almost the spirit of the 70s and Michael – well it was a complete break from his old style – it was the whole, more integrated Michael speaking – it was a great speech – and the whole spirit of the conference much more mature, more serious, and yet it had a great dynamism – a vast crowd in and out of the arena.

Sometimes I was very moved.

Doug got such a 'hand' as he was announced as a candidate – it made Michael and me very happy.

There is a growing feeling against D.K. Duncan – he attacks Michael in the most vicious way – I've never liked nor trusted him.

Michael came through the operation very well but he goes home tomorrow to a house that has no one to look after him – it's really so sad – anyway if the children are there it will help. They are remarkable children.

The future is very strange – how long will we be without an election – we *don't* want it soon – every day that passes we seem to move forward in our thinking. But whilst we are really preparing ourselves in thought and behaviour the time will come and we'll get another chance to serve – you'll see!! I don't feel sad over it, but then I believed in the boycott of the election from every point of view – so I have no regrets.

Meanwhile Reagan is running a fantastic campaign in the States. Mondale hasn't a chance. Reagan is an actor in a part – a part he loves and it probably makes it less of a strain. It suits Seaga fine for Reagan to win but I have a deep conviction Reagan isn't going to last much longer. In spite of that brilliant smile, there's an underlying frailty hidden by the most superbly fitting clothes.

There! It has just come over the night news that Hong Kong is going back to China – here we go!!!

But the attack on Ferraro makes me terribly sad – how could they do her that – but Mondale should have vetted his choice very carefully whereas I think he acted on instinct. Whatever the motive, she is a brilliant choice and adds something that he hasn't got. But it has let her in for what must be much agony. Still she will battle through to a brave defeat unless Reagan drops dead *before* the count, of a heart attack. He's doing some remarkable bobbing and weaving in his foreign policy, which the Americans either like or ignore, but vote him back they will.

29 October 1984

I haven't the inclination to write very much these days – but the 'Goat' is nearly finished and it has restored my joy in life and a certain degree of self confidence.

Seaga has shut down the KSAC – so we now have no councillor. I know it has been done before but have we a Byrd or Rodriguez to handle it?[1]

People seem to be spending a lot of money but complain of the COL and high taxes.

I don't know, but I don't feel that there is the bitterness against the government that the PNP claim is there. Even Douglas seems to get caught in the belief that Jamaica wants an election – I don't see it that way but I may be wrong. Talking to Rosie[2] the other day, I don't think she thinks so either.

Michael had a hard time over that thyroid operation. He was pitchforked into action with no bed rest or hospital care. Sent home in thirty-six hours to a home that wasn't really ready for him and back to work. He wouldn't listen to me, they none of them do – they feel that my age would be too big a factor in my advice!!

There, I've summed that up in a good little sentence and I will leave it there.

Jessie is seriously ill – I am very worried about her. Harry died – not in her arms – but for her I think. Harry was Jessie's life – it goes back to the days of Roger's[3] confinement. Jessie is one of the remarkable women I have known. I hope she recovers.

I think I could write a whole book on Grenada – God, the media of the world indeed *inform* the world exactly what they want to.

7 April 1985

Things are so tough I think I had better start keeping a record. Tomorrow George goes into hospital for his cataract – the operation is for the 8th – the financial strain is going to be fantastic.

Anyway I guess that somehow he will manage to get through. He is drinking very heavily which isn't very wise, but nothing will change him over that – that's George – and at a moment like this, Doug's car has gone on the blink –

Then above all else I am so worried over Michael I can hardly function. This last attack of diverticulitis beats any attack he has ever had – with all the haemorrhaging that has gone with it. Doug and I saw him today – he was looking better and much more cheerful. But I discovered that he had had a violent attack of ague with a temperature of 103 degrees, and this only three days before his operation.[1]

Let's say no more.

Ra is coming up on Wednesday and I am so glad that she will be with us — it's awful for her stuck away at a distance and not knowing just what is happening. The phone is fantastically uncertain — oh the sound of an inefficient phone when it matters so much to be able to communicate drives one to despair.

Somehow I have got to get hold of a car to get George in tomorrow — I think he's frightened to death, poor soul.

I must try to get some sleep to face tomorrow.

Midnight

I just haven't been able to sleep — so finally I called the hospital but the nurse says he's alright — he's resting.

So I'll try to keep calm and have some sleep. Strangely, both dogs have decided to sleep in the room tonight — as if they were aware of strange things happening. Only Johan is not well. I think he is in pain — so it probably comforted him to curl up on my mat!

27 April 1985

Oh I wish I could have a little silence for a while without the endless snarl of the television going. I wish I could peacefully play the music that I love and miss so badly.

There, I came over to the studio and sat quietly by myself. I was trying to remember the Lord's Prayer. Whenever I am emotionally upset I usually say it quietly to myself. And then sometimes I forget it and I struggle with everything I have got to remember how it goes. Tonight this has happened, so I went over and brought a bible back with me and I searched and couldn't find it — I still haven't found it — but I've written down what I have remembered — but I think it probably isn't right. It's a sort of trauma. I suddenly realize that I don't hear the TV anymore — I think Norman, who is reading quietly in bed, must have got Roy to turn it down a bit.

It's still going, but very quietly — 'Tomorrow'[1] is really beginning to come, but I need to find some sensitive bit of music to help me find its face. I need to get away by myself quietly to find this strange little work. I will go to bed later thinking the right thoughts.

I am worried about Michael. He is a great person and has stood this battering with such insight. And Douglas, who has stood this long uncertainty and emptiness — I am very proud of both of them.

And Rachel, the way she grew overnight in order to help him — she has been too wonderful. And Joseph who has stood late hours and great strain — he has really shown amazing steadiness and courage. But really, I think Rachel held him through the worst crisis — Michael says he will never forget it.

28 April 1985

So Michael came home this morning — he phoned this evening and phoned Ra and Drum — it was a wonderfully kind thing to do. I do hope things will stay fairly steady for him.

Norman is up in the air — I am very weary — really weary. I wish I could get away to Barbados and be with Ra for a bit and hope that the problems here will resolve themselves.

'Tomorrow' is going along in a strangely peaceful way — I only hope that it will cast safely. I do love it and it seems as if I am drawing nearer to the solution of the 'Wave'.[1] I have a large sketch on the wall — but it won't be as effective in sculpture — that still needs a little more wrestling. My eyes are giving me a hard time.

16 May 1985

It is strange that with all the madness that is going on I don't write anything about the politics of Jamaica. The truth is that Jamaica has got on to a chronic wail about the problems of our time. We wail about the cost of living that goes up and up. The well-off people can still afford to live — so they grumble but they buy. Most of the middle class still cling on to living beyond their means — they don't really give up any of their comforts — but they do more than wail, they protest loudly. But it is the children of the poor in the rural areas who leave for school in the mornings with a cup of tea with no milk and a little sugar to make it palatable.

Now sugar has gone up!

There's a whole age group who are going to grow up second-class citizens because they are so underfed — they won't have the health and the stamina to be anything else. People talk of a coming explosion — but I don't see it. The whole atmosphere is too soggy to have the energy — also they know that the army is standing by with a strange man in charge of everything. Someone not like a Busta, nor a Manley, nor a Shearer, nor a Michael.

We'll see.

Ra is ill in Barbados — low blood pressure, anaemia etc. She's had a rough time in her personal life and was a wonderful help with her father's illness.

I hope to get away by the 24th[1] but Michael has run a temperature again and we don't feel he's out of the woods yet. It's going to be a long time and he needs to get out of the country and its problems for a break. I hope this will materialize.

It's very interesting: Seaga has made this shattering announcement that the number of councillors is going to be cut down, and obviously is shifting so that local government has much less power or effectiveness. Ordinarily there would be a howl of protest — particularly from the small man and woman — and talk of constitutional rights. But people are so desperate trying to keep alive, trying to feed their children, to cope with the transport, to get them to school with books, that this absolutely fundamental proposal just passes them by.

Mike phoned me from Yale, quite shocked at the whole thing; and I told him people aren't thinking about it at all — all they are worried about is the cost of living — the endless blackouts — water locked off — letters that arrive a week late.

The insane Public Service Company bills. My pension just about covers light, water, telephone and transport. For the rest I work hard. So I must get up and get my cup of herb tea — it's $35 for a bottle of coffee, grown and produced in Jamaica.

I still feed my wild birds, though their feed has gone up. Every morning at six o'clock a baldpate calls three or four times and flies away. I never see him — I wish I could — whilst the nightingales and white wings fight for territorial rights in the garden. Even the birds are at war.

Only the yellow canaries, conscious of their beauty, fly in and out unafraid and confident — beauty must be very reassuring.

But the lizards still fight to dominate the old bench — that's been going on for years. It makes me think of Alsace-Lorraine years ago.

27 May 1985

My father was the son — one of three sons and one daughter — of James Swithenbank. The family were well off — they owned a wool factory in Leeds. I remember the family photos of my grandparents — my grandmother had that premature white hair which Douglas, my son, and I inherited from her. My grandfather was a keen businessman and his eldest son Oliver inherited this quality.

I remember my Uncle Oliver was extremely handsome, with charming manners which impressed even me. He was extremely kind and helpful to my mother when my father died, and I certainly owed my first year of art study to him.

My Uncle Seth was in the church and was Chairman of the Northern division of the Wesley Church. The third brother was also in the Church, and the story about him is that he was very frail, with chest problems and a passionate love of music — he naturally played the organ and even composed some hymns.

How do I remember my mother? I remember one or two storms we had when I wouldn't obey and she stood up to me very strongly. I remember her as a small-boned, strong woman, with a sort of gentle sweetness in her voice and manner. I remember her most clearly and vividly the night my father died. We had all been called in to see him and say goodbye. He lay there, very white and still. Someone tried to stop me and my mother said, 'Don't stop her.' I kissed him on the side of his face and then I started to weep, because his face was cold and still and in a childish way I knew that he was gone.

She used to talk to us about Jamaica. She missed Jamaica terribly — Roxborough, an old two-storey house, split-level really, had a great, sweeping view across the plains and back up to far away mountains. The mist used to stand in the valley below the house in the early mornings, and as day dawned the chorus of birds rose through it. Mother used to call it the Roxborough Choir. She always told us that Jamaican girls had the sweetest singing voices in the world. The Church choirs were a great event in Church life.

Strange things I remember about my mother — how she grew up in a house that had a staff of several men and women who did all the house and field work. My mother didn't even tidy her own room, and yet, caught in England without a husband, with very limited means, she took charge of the whole stage of her life. She learnt to launder, to iron on Mondays and Tuesdays, don't forget for a family of ten — she became a magnificent cook, and I will remember most vividly of all how, when my oldest sister at eighteen married in the midst of the First World War, she tackled the sewing of all but the bride's and bridesmaids' dresses. Looking back it was incredible.

My father's family were quite wealthy, so that I know that she got help from them, but they never knew, for she wouldn't let them know, the endless struggle to live that she endured.

As she grew up, the older ones learnt to help, and we adopted a girl from Dominica who just appeared at the door one day and asked for a job — a black girl, bonny and strong, but hopelessly homesick. My mother paid her a salary, small I have no doubt, but she looked after her and helped her in everything. I think there must have been a deep bond between them — both from the Caribbean. She didn't stay very long, somehow she managed to get back home. We all missed her, especially my mother.

Mother had a great gift with people — the postman, the butcher, the women working in the shops all adored her — very like her great grand-daughter Rachel, who too has this gift with the everyday person whom she comes across in the routine of life. She also made very different friends, like the brilliant headmistress of our school, West Cornwall College. Another great and lifelong friend, was the woman who became assistant Matron at a big London hospital, but who came from Cornwall where she worked ultimately as Sister in either Falmouth or Penzance. These were rare women and they seemed to find some chord of interest and sympathy in Mother.

3 June 1985

As I let my mind drift along about the past, I remember another extraordinary achievement of my mother's. She had a way of knowing where influence and influential people lived and worked. From I can remember she always felt that a holiday should be a regular and possibly annual affair, if not oftener.

Well, a woman alone with nine children depending on her, with very little money, would have to be a genius to contrive a holiday that would be worth remembering. Suddenly from nowhere some army people arrived with two bell-shaped tents!! We were all summoned as the summer holidays started and the exciting news was broken to us – we were going to pitch our tents on Hayle Towans in Cornwall, and live by the sea for two weeks. The soldiers would pitch the tents and leave us – we were responsible for the removal of ourselves and the essential things we needed. The tents were put suitably within easy reach of tap water, and the spot was well chosen in that it was sandy and clear, with a few isolated trees that had grown within a short distance of the sea. We were *wild* with joy.

One tent all the females would sleep in – the other was the food and kitchen tent and the three brothers slept there. We girls quickly realized that this was leaving the food at the mercy of the boys and we loudly protested, so some sort of compromise was agreed upon.

We lived in the sea, we wore the minimum of clothes, and to this day it is one of the happiest memories of my life. That my mother alone had achieved this, we didn't stop to think – we had to grow to maturity to realize what an amazing woman she was. What sort of influence did she wield, what sort of imagination was she capable of?

We went each year, and I think must have stopped obviously as war drew near, for the coasts of Cornwall were closely guarded – the nearness of Ireland, of Europe, the danger of landings on the miles of empty coast line, and undoubtedly the ancient memory of the Armada!! So that ended our beloved summer migration.

I remember her as a passionately independent person. From when we were children she announced that when we all grew up and she was old that never, never, never under any circumstances would she ever come and make her home with any of us.

She will have spent her life living in crowded houses, packed with her own children, and visited so often by our friends. She had to leave Cornwall when we all gravitated away — in those days Neasden was lovely open country, so she wrenched herself away from Cornwall and put herself in a spot that we could all make our home as we moved out into jobs.

I can't remember clearly how her final break with us all came. I know that during the war she lived with my sister Nora, who was in school in London at the Mary Datchelor. I know it was a charming little two-storey house, and that it was heavily bombed in the Second World War, and they used to sleep under the stairs. What a war!

But her final home was alone in Orpington. I went to see her once, when I had gone to England with Norman, and I remember hearing her talking as I walked up the path. I thought she had a guest, but she was feeding the wild birds and calling them by name: 'Twinky, don't be greedy, don't do that!' I spent two nights with her — such a happy, happy visit — she was a great cook, and here again were her friendships with the postman and all the people in the shops who were serving.

27 June 1985

I don't know what to do this year, this month, this week, this *day*.

No water — this is the fourth day!

The light is back for the moment — but gas is short so transport is curtailed.

Even if I wanted to I can't draw. My eyes are obviously on the out and my vision is double sometimes and almost always — for the first time — unclear, so I can't read, and I have had to wait for days to get them tested.

At that moment the Water Commission men came in to look at our water situation. This is Thursday and we haven't had one drop of water since 7 a.m. on Monday. Today I had to send out a taxi to bring water because we hadn't a drop to cook lunch.

One can't write about this general strike[1] — it's too big and too complicated. One thing I know, it's a justified strike — the teachers alone have a shocking case and tied to it are the nurses and junior doctors. Whether the Government has the money or not, the strikers have a very strong case. It has spread in an amazing way — it has the general support of the country and I think Seaga entirely missed this fact when he made his speech on his return from Washington, when he calmly said that he expected everyone to return to work the next day and that after this had happened, he would meet the Union Leaders. Naturally, the next day the workers said the unions can't send us back to work. We, the workers, voted on the strike and we have to meet and agree what steps we take.

I wish I could read — it's so hard as one waits — not only for the strike ending – satisfactorily – but one also waits for the Almighty to turn on the rain.

29 June 1985

I don't think I have ever in my life been in such a mood – my eyes are giving me no end of trouble – they have no lenses that are right in Jamaica. This means importing and that means I will be unable to work for probably two months – so I can't read either and when it comes to writing, which I can do for brief periods, there's nothing I want to say – we are in a hopelessly negative situation. Nothing seems to go right.

As I sit writing at 2 p.m. the temperature is ninety-two degrees in the shade and there's a horrible tearing wind.

Michael is coming back a week early from his busman's holiday and he's coming in to a situation that no one seems to comprehend.

The drought is unbelievable – and it's five days now and we haven't had a drop of water through the pipes. One of the men who drives me lives on the St Catherine border and he is overflowing with water, so he has been bringing water for us. But of course, it's costly.

Anyway, at last we had a visit from a tank and we were able to fill every possible sort of container and we could at least flush the toilets.

But the days seem incredibly long.

I hear someone has been poisoning rats at Nomdmi and the grand old tank which is still half full is now full of dead rats, so it has to be emptied and cleaned out. Doug has probably got to go up next week so I'll go with him – I'm longing to get up.

But I hear the drought is awful up there and Michael's flowers are dying by the hundreds.

Tomorrow I want to go down to the show at the National Gallery where six painters, two Americans and four Jamaicans, are doing an interesting experiment – 'Six Options'.[1] They have, I think, been given a piece of wall on which they express themselves – choosing a subject that is both relevant personally, but also an alternative to something that's of current importance. I think that is more or less the idea though I don't think I've given a good picture of it!!!

Anyway, I think it's going to be very interesting. I only hope we don't have a blackout in this heat.

Whilst I burble along Jamaica is passing through a crisis, the like of which is near only to 1938. Only this is in a strange way more thoughtful – organizations like the Civil Service Association and the churches etc., are uttering words of support and warning.[2] Certainly the Civil Service do it on a risk of later victimization. It's all growing quite chaotic — some are back at work — the soldiers are driving the tanks.

7 August 1985

It's difficult these days with my eyes playing up to read so much — so here's to remembering.

The family — nine of us — what did we all do? Lena — easily the prettiest and the most stylish. She married at eighteen with the First World War smashing up everything. She married a county surveyor, young, vigorous and the son of an old Cornish family who lived in a lovely old house overlooking the Tamar valley. They were very in love — certainly he was madly in love with her. He had a fine warm voice — baritone, so I have early recollections of his singing, either accompanying her or one of the family, 'Coming Through the Rye', 'Thora', 'Where the Mountains of Mourne', 'The Little Gray Home in the West'.

He joined the army and in nine months he was dead. Later in life I discovered that they didn't make love completely because he was afraid that he might die and leave her alone to bring up a child. It smashed her up for years.

She came and stayed with me at my Young Woman's Hostel in London and I used to wake at night and hear her sobbing with her head under the blanket so as not to waken me. But she was a very bright person. Took up war work at the branch of the war office PIO where I worked, and soon rose to be a supervisor. After the war she had a secretary's job with a Dr Fairburn of Harley Street. He was a very well known gynaecologist with an enormous and wealthy practice. She was deeply loved and appreciated by her boss and his family. She worked there for some years and ultimately married again — an economist at Nottingham University, Arthur Radford. I stayed with her once for a brief holiday and watched with intense interest the charm and tact she showed in her handling of people. She ran a lovely home.

When she was a schoolgirl she joined a movement of 'Votes for Women' and actually sold tags at a rally they had in the Square in Penzance. I wasn't against votes for women but I went another way home from school!! I was very shy about the whole business. Lena wasn't at all aggressive but she felt strongly about many things and was totally unafraid.

11 August 1985

Gladys, who was the next in line, was as different from Lena as was possible. Gladys was a straight-forward, plain, outspoken Yorkshire woman with a broad, plain face; straight, thin, brown hair, no eyebrows and a habit of thinking aloud. But she too made a success of her life. She owned and ran what in those days was an innovation, a Froebel and Montessori school for young children in an area that was expensive upper middle class. The school was a great success. She herself had been well trained and gifted. When we were children it was to Gladys that my mother turned. 'Gladys, please *cope* with the children for me,' and Gladys would organize a walk to the sea, or a story-telling little group, and when Harvey and I 'caught fight' she could distract us with the minimum of authority to be reasonable. She too ran a good home, tasteful, but not with the glamour Lena could conjure up.

She married a remarkable man – very Yorkshire too. He had a brilliant degree – first class Cambridge honours – but he could never get what he deserved, a first-class job, because he had been a declared pacifist in World War Number One. He used to say, 'You can't fight to end war – you just don't resolve the problem by fighting,' so he had to be content with second-class jobs all his life. He wasn't bitter, but he didn't like to talk about it and somehow Gladys respected him so much for it that no one opened up the subject.

I ultimately drifted away from Gladys, which I have always regretted – she had her faults like all of us.

I would arrive in England utterly exhausted from a political battering at home, and needing a few days of quiet to just face the challenge of English upper-class snobbery or more happily the English Labour Party. No time to be by yourself – a problem of clothes, little money and a husband who had the weakness of not understanding the strain of switching from the lively, much loved Jamaican scene, to the well-dressed, well-composed wife of a leader in the Caribbean – a political wife. To the English I was, I suppose, an oddity – in spite of my Jamaican roots, I didn't look the part. I did the best I could, and was happier with the Labour Party than going to Ascot with lunch at Lord Salisbury's table – or the Derby and meeting the Queen or Princess Margaret.

Well, to continue, my contact with England and my great love was for Nora – so I would phone her and travel out to see her. We would talk and I would sit quietly by her fire or in her London garden, and when I had steadied myself I would phone Gladys, or 'Swiddle' as we called her.

So this happened – I phoned and she complained that I had been in England so long and had never contacted her. I think it happened once too often and it soured our relationship – which was such a pity because I should have understood.

She was such fun – full of a sort of Yorkshire dry humour – she could be so humorous about her quite brilliant husband who nevertheless loved Yorkshire, football and cricket. I don't know how much Gladys understood about games – but she did love to drive to the scene of the action with him and come home exhausted to their comfortable flat and many glasses of wine to celebrate or console themselves.

They followed London theatre closely and could always take us to or advise us what was worth seeing. When she died she left quite a sum of money to us — those who were left — born of her Yorkshire carefulness.

11 August 1985

Dear Swiddle — I should have *needed* you more — and we would have been happy. A wonderful memory was when I went over for my big operation etc., etc. and health revival.[1] It was in Swiddle's house that I recuperated and they were both so kind to me and made it a memory I have always treasured.

Then there was Leslie, my beloved brother — the friend of my stormy youth. Leslie to whom I could always go when the storms with my mother and older sisters raged. He would comfort me and understand what I couldn't understand myself. He was a quiet, gentle, withdrawn person, more English than Jamaican — a great reader — and one day two things happened when he was sixteen. One — he came out with a vivid smile to me, his younger sister, and said — 'There, I've got a hundred books' — and so he had — all the good writers of his and his past. (*sic*)

The other thing he did with that deep seriousness that was his most memorable quality, a sort of fundamental spiritual seriousness — he lied and put his age up to seventeen and joined World War One as an ambulance carrier, RAMC. My poor mother was so shocked — we all were — and yet in the image of 1914 we were all so deeply proud of him, and within nine months he was dead. I still have the letter announcing his death — the message from his comrades who worked with him. It had profound effect on me. He was my port in a storm. I was shattered and it has left me permanently with a sort of shock fear of death.

Followed as it was with Lena's husband's death — Gladys' fiancé's death, and Roy, Norman's beloved brother — four tragic deaths in one family.

The war to end all wars.

31 August 1985

Yesterday there was something lovely in my life — all day. Oh how I love Vic's book[1] — the 'eye witness' account — the perception, the imaginativeness. But this morning I read of how he used to feel in the months before he died. How one day he would feel marvellous and the next day awful, lousy — not anything.

I sat and cried in the studio because it was an exact description of how I feel and I became aware this a.m. that my end is very near.

I cried and cried — I used to say, 'To die would be a great adventure.' Was I afraid to die? I have died many deaths in my eighty-five years — the wise man dies but once. I sit very quiet sometimes and I feel it rise like a mist around — just a touch and one is over the edge — then I remember people I love and would not leave — to be with them one last time.

Am I afraid? I am drawing those strange, full of fear, drawings of the ocean, my mother — all life comes from the sea. I will try again — the sea without fear. Owen[2] has given me some special paper, paper that is not full of the weakness of temporary art material.

I found a drawing I had done, and I am walking across rushing water on flat river stones and Norman is crouched on the bank on the 'other side' holding out a hand to help me.

My whole youth was surrounded by, enveloped in my relationship with the sea — not the sunny, loved, Caribbean sea, but the mighty power of the sea off Land's End. I remember our long walk to school could be shortened by half a mile if one took the narrow path over the harbour — a path about five feet wide with a sheer drop on one side and the solid rock going up the other. In my dreams I had always got just halfway across and suddenly a gigantic wave appeared, crashing down on my head and me unable to go forward or back.

This is haunting me these days — so my drawings are full of prenatal fear.

Perhaps I could take Owen's paper and draw again — full of power to cope with the sea, with the wave — with death — for cope I must. If one could just get it over — like pulling a tooth. But what is the other side? I sit and I fall into a sort of coma — and Norman says, 'I did it, you can do it' — but I wouldn't see Rachel again — and Doug and Michael and Roy *and* Norman — he doesn't want to join the family circle, he prefers to go it alone — and *Drum*, and Sarah — is brave — I could name them all, my family — and John and Carole for years and years.

It's time to go and have lunch with George — his sight is giving him a hard time — there's only one abominable but lovable George. I think I feel more normal now and I will stop — but dear God I really am afraid — no? not really!!!

Corina came in sort of intuitively — she knew or felt that I was DOWN.

We talked — she has a lively strong mind and looks into what happens and why it happens — I talked a bit too much I'm afraid. One shouldn't do that to one's friends.

Death is a rather obscure, obscien — obscene — which is right? None are, death isn't right anyhow. To die is to break the whole struggle of your life — one comes up against it — bam — no answer — no argument — just no nothing and a rotting body and all the things that have mattered don't matter any more.

Next to Leslie comes Nora — who was for years my favourite sister. When she and I were little I used to think that she was self-righteous – a prig, in fact. But she wasn't – she wasn't – she actually was a deep thinker. She had a great love of literature which went very deep. She got a very good degree at Reading University and ultimately ended up as head of that department at the Mary Datchelor[3]. They had a fantastic reputation and won awards at all sorts of Festivals – but the peak of her career was when she put on Bernard Shaw's 'Joan of Arc' and got a write-up in the London Sunday Observer from St John Irving.

She retired early and when I was in England, seeing her was my great moment.

She was handsome and dressed very well. She hadn't Lena's elegance, but she chose her clothes to suit her type. Her clothes were always right whether in winter or summer. She had a remarkable gift in judging and appraising literature. I remember her saying of Marlowe one day, 'If only he had lived – he was such a poet – a better poet than Shakespeare – but he hadn't Shakespeare's genius as a dramatist – as a student of human beings and human occasions.'

She too fed her birds and every year a slightly deformed nightingale would turn up – he knew Nora so well – he had a permanently deformed wing.

She shared her house with a woman friend, Margaret Grey, who was Headmistress of one of the big London Schools – I can't remember the school. She kept a lovely house – not as expensive!!! as Lena's, but in lovely taste.

She was fond of me in a way – she understood my maverick ways and she was interested in my art. I think I was responsible for introducing her to music and she fell in a great way for Mozart and Bach. When she died, I had nothing to attract me back to England. I felt her death terribly.

19 September 1985

The ocean my mother – I think I need to keep some sort of record of this series of drawings all hung around this name and theme, to try to give some sort of idea of the order in which they have come. Already at this early date I come upon drawings that I have no recollection doing – which means I am working fast and pushing aside drawings that don't satisfy me – 'which said' often turn out to be the best – the reason being perhaps that over-occupied with a particular theme, I don't realize that one's subconscious is at work releasing something deeper than the set plan which I'm pursuing.

I started by doing a single head – a disturbing, even frightening head. I started with nothing in my mind at all except the need to release all the inhibitions that plague me all the time. It certainly was not meant to be an ocean drawing – God forbid – but it sets me off with a great deal of confidence to *find* my ocean – drawing, on the whole, much larger and bolder than I generally do. I think I was trying to recapture the spirit and freedom of the Nomdmi drawings.

The small head in charcoal with great eyes and the mouth open – and the face so twisted that it is almost like looking through water at an object, and as the water moves, the object seems to twist and partially move. It gave me quite a shock – but this is an ocean study. And then I did two or three big drawings with a woman's figure or just a head and hand.

Before this new effort, which started with that strange head (not ocean), I had been wrestling with the idea of an ocean sculpture and all the drawings are locked into the almost obsession about a woman's figure lying in the water. I didn't really achieve anything organic at all – nothing cosmic.

But the head had opened a door that there was deep fear in my 'being' of the raging Cornwall seas. As a child I had been a little obsessed with the danger – 'moods and calm' – almost playful moods of a summer sea. Now as I write I remember in the studio this morning, how the thought came of a Caribbean sea – and this I think came after I had released and faced the fear.

Then I wander on and the next theme comes – what oh what is the *Face* of the sea – and instinctively I went searching for the inspiration. I got it, and three or four line drawings, because with a pen there's no chance to correct a line as you can in charcoal – I found I was trying to let the pen steer itself with some interesting results. But it is an extraordinary head – ancient and still frightening in another way. But once again it isn't definitive.

And I thought a little about Neptune, the Greek god associated with the sea, and I did two male heads, almost by accident, and didn't think of them as Neptune at all. But there is a possibility there – I feel that anything or anyone connected with ocean should have just the shadow of memory of a fish, and this drawing – the pen and ink one – has it.

I must stop now, now that fear has been drawn out – one has to get the size and majesty of the ocean – so I've been driven from Debussy and (?) back to Beethoven – Op 110 – oh the height and depth of all beauty – sonata 31.

24 January 1986

Xmas has come and gone and New Year also. Rachel and her sons were here and it was lovely having them. Xmas is truly a time for children.

I am revolted – yes that is the word – for the commercialization of Xmas. Have you done your shopping nine days to Xmas? – eight days to Xmas? – start shopping or you will be late, and then you make anxious lists for presents with the sinking feeling that you are buying all the wrong things and your mind becomes a slough of doubt and worry and the money – the money will *never* stretch. Xmas without money, what a worry and a nightmare.

But when the day actually comes, the deep, deep family love prevails and one is truly happy – not quite in the natural and untroubled days of one's own youth, which also was short of money, but the magic was more convincing – more all pervading.

Anyway with the world in the precarious situation it has brought on itself – we had our moments. Jamaica has not often been in a more difficult position before. I am fully interested, fully absorbed, but I find I have no desire to write of it, to attempt to analyse it. It seems to take always imagination and perception to live through each day at a time and pray God for a good night's sleep.

I lost my wonderful Doberman, the biggest and most noble looking I have ever seen. I really loved him and vowed I'd never have another puppy to battle with and train.

But Cindy the Alsatian is shattered. I have never seen a dog show such grief before and being a very nervous dog it became worse – so I fell and got a halfbred German Shepherd. Roy called him Butch, which is a difficult name to remember and often gets mixed and becomes the female of the species. She and Johan had a wonderful relationship, and with him big and strong and calm she depended on him and became a very good watchdog. Now she is lost and confused and at four months he is no comfort to her. Anyway they will soon shake down.

I've had a wonderful patch of creativity and selling drawings and prints like mad.

But now I need a break – I need a week of loneliness and silence to spring forward again. I have to wait and listen for that inner voice. I was coming on fine with my Ocean drawings and then Christmas came and put a stop to it. Never mind, it will come and it was so wonderful having the family together – Sarah, Natasha, Joseph and Della[1], David, Doug, Norman, Roy and Michael with Ra and Drum and Luke.

31 March 1986

Spent a strange Easter – mostly in hospital – about a week.

My thoughts were preoccupied with dying – how does it come on one? I was quite empty of anything creative and one moment came, I was sitting crouched over – the way that is easiest to breathe – and the thought of the risen Christ came to me. True or not true, he lived a tremendous life and died a terrible death. How would he look if he found himself regaining consciousness. How much of suffering would be left on his face and how much of a new dawning. Would he consciously free himself of his grave clothes?

It was almost dark – night was coming down and I couldn't really see to draw – but my mind carried my hand through the motions, and when I stopped and looked there was a crude little drawing of a rising figure gesturing away the wrapping clothes[1] – I haven't shown it to anyone – every now and then I have looked at it.

I am weak now from the illness so I couldn't do anything about it and it dawns on me that it can't be carried out as a conscious effort. It would come again in a finished form – as the first one did – just coming, no struggle.

Or am I wrong about that – when I get well again won't I, as almost always, go into a wrestle with many solutions. I don't know – let me feel well first.

22 April 1986

There! Butch caused me a nasty fall *and* an unknown man snatched my handbag with the week's housekeeping in it and one's glasses etc., etc. and a fairly new cheque book – so this meant closing one's account and issuing a new bank number. After I'd spent years remembering 74217, it's now frantic 0010612. Is that *right*?

But Butch is a problem, wild, wilful, and in a way dangerous. At first everyone spoilt him and now I'm paying the price. He's not too popular with me but I'll work on him because he's very confused.

The episode with the handbag was horrid and my shoulder hurts.

Had to do an interview with the BBC[2] just after and it wasn't good. I guess my ancient fear of cameras didn't help. The last part was good, about 'Negro Aroused', but the first part was old and wandering.

Anyway, I earned $200, not much, and I took for a cause the reanimating of the clinic in Four Roads[3] – which in the good times bore my name. Now it doesn't get any favours – only on my birthday I beg for help to paint it and clean it and find some of the necessaries.

The response was wonderful – Portia Simpson[4] carried an enthusiastic team that begged the paint, and painted and cleaned up the whole clinic – which has several rooms and much old, soiled and faded wall space.

I wish that long ago I had given the time and space in my life to learn to handle interviews. The press and cameras frighten me – let me be honest. After it's over I remember all the things that should have been said, and the interviewer, Nigel Finch, was such a darling, quick, clever, and for his age, very experienced – he helped me – but I am trying to find him to get him to let me edit it. There! I got David and we'll see if it's worth worrying over – maybe not.

Now to find Portia.

6 May 1986

Well, the Budget is out and we have endless sections of it with Eddie speaking — TV is very laden with it.

It is of course a fantastic budget with millions being spent on vote-getting and other good promises. I haven't been out much recently so I don't get the reaction. But if they think it's safe they'll jump a general election on us. American money and American pressures jump out at every corner — and how Jamaica loves America — how it mops up all the glamour propaganda — all the sell advertisements. Of course a lot of it is true, America does have a way of life that is attractive — they know how to enjoy themselves — their technology gives them something to 'sell', and how they sell it with their glamour ads.

When you look across the world at the arch enemy — what chance has Russia got — how many people want to go to Russia. Somehow, rightly or wrongly, you get a grim picture — of course all Russia's enemies paint a grim picture of her, but there's nothing coming out of Russia that is good salesmanship.

So in 1940 we eased Britain out of the picture, only to let America take over. Actually, the attraction of America has always been there — we're very close. But now we actually have a new political party that is dedicated to campaigning for Jamaica to become an American state!![1] Admit it's Jamaica's idea. America almost certainly would see it another way.

Anyway the Budget is out and the growls of a coming election — parochial or general — as the microphones tune up.

We're having lovely weather — with lots of rain — so far not *too* much with all it costs with road damage, etc., etc.

I have been very ill and I know I'm walking a tightrope so I must keep calm and try to be detached — when the whole thing is in full cry.

Being positive about big and little things will be the greatest and most necessary achievement.

I am cleaning the studio — putting away the clay and wood and hoping to give it new life by some form of drawing, pastel or paint. I'm also wondering if I can't bronze some of the work done in *fondu* or plaster. I must talk this over with David and Pat too.

14 October 1986

There, I am going to the Cultural Heritage Gala wind up and then tomorrow is the last Institute meeting, and then I am pulling out of all public occasions, small though they are.

I'll work and try to keep near me the people that I love.

I'm a bit scared of tonight, but having Louise Bennett with me makes a world of difference.

Going to try to make a new start and keep some record of the days.

24 October 1986

Had another attack of whatever it is that plagues me — unable to breathe — so maddening and in a way frightening. But I have got a 'new' doctor who is in 'residence' at the Chest Hospital. A Doctor Muriel Lowe. She is brilliant and obviously very sympathetic. As she enters the room, it's a sort of blessing, and she is intuitively aware that I know I'm living on borrowed time and even perhaps that I have a last work to produce. But for her, 'Birth'[1] would never have materialized — it's weak technically and the acrylic is a new experience for me. But if I can live to do my 'Lazarus',[2] I'll go happily. I really love my doctor — she is tough and humorous — but she has a *mind* and an understanding imagination.

Since she came on the scene I am not in a panic anymore and I hope I can go step for step — with Lazarus — who has passed through the doors of death and returned — and the Christ is facing what Lazarus endured. I want there to be a joy of reunion as Jesus summons Lazarus back. Twice he groaned aloud and then he wept. It tore him to pieces to do that miracle and the Marys watched — one in a supreme, painful confidence — the other, unconvinced, peers down at the empty grave as Lazarus soars at Christ's bidding. Together they unite — one to live on — the other to face a terrible death. Oh my God.

25 October 1986

Michael is back — so happy — so radiant — his work succeeded, all for the Socialist International.[1] The work succeeded and there was a glorious Indian summer over Europe and even over England. A golden Indian summer. He is so happy working on his big effort on cricket. I've read bits and it's marvellously good.

Doug has got his farm started at last — he finds the work very tiring, but he's happy and it's real. Rachel is laughing on the phone again and witty — she's finding a new life and the boys are in a happy period.

Roy shows quiet signs of growth and maturity and says he enjoys my classical music!!! Only Norman I grieve over and I'm going to find a way of getting his wave-length.

4 November 1986

Went to the eye man today. My eyes are really bad.

So I was right — the left eye is all clouded over and there's no remedy — an oncoming cataract. Lots of double vision – which is quite a challenge.

I draw big so that I'm not drawing from my wrist – I'm drawing from my shoulder.

Anyway as we drove home I felt a quiet peace move over me. It's a sharp beginning of the eye and I wasn't frightened – I looked at the garden – my beloved garden – and the mountains behind – I will learn – it's good to have taken the first step of passing out. And then I put on the earphones and played the Walkman, anything at random – the Brahms 1st Symphony – an immature work, but much of Brahms I adore.

13 December 1986

I stopped carving when Norman became Premier – there was so much else I had to do to help – so I didn't go to my studio in the grasspiece in Drumblair for a couple of years. One day I was riding home up the gully, walking the horses as the sun went down, and a young Rastafarian I knew walked and talked with me. All of a sudden he looked down at the sandals I was wearing and he could see that I had painted my toenails, and he said, 'You shouldn't do that you know, that is Babylon,' and we both laughed.

In those days I hadn't yet got to understand the Rastafarians. But when I did, I quickly understood the difference and I became fascinated with what I felt was a 'faith' that was going to grow and spread – I didn't identify it particularly with Haile Selassie, though I understood that – but to me it was the identification with a Black God. All the white imagery that consciously and unconsciously had found its creative expression in the white Christs all over Europe – all over the world – carried there with the Christian religion, couldn't *mean* the truth to the black people of the Caribbean or black America, and this was true not only in the case of the poor masses but also to the intelligent thinking youth of the middle classes.

Sometime after that someone came to the house and told me that the 'Rastas' were living in the studio. I sent a message down to them that they couldn't do that as I wanted to work there again. They cleared out overnight with no quarrel – but an amazing thing happened. I had been carving over a number of years a huge over-life-size figure of Sampson being led to the temple where Delilah had his eyes 'put out'.

The carving had been going on very slowly over a number of years and Norman's friend, Leslie Clerk, desperately wanted stone to carve and he begged me for the stone half-finished. I gave it to him, but I cut off the great head which was almost finished and very impressive. I had it mounted on a log of wood – and one day it disappeared – the Rastas had come and taken it away. So somewhere that stone is lying around — and the rest of the stone, carved by Leslie Clerk, is a lovely carving in the National Gallery.

I think that Sampson could be the first person to connect his strength and virility to his hair!

Last entry, undated

It is so long since I last wrote here and so much has happened it hardly seems worth while picking up the thread.

Notes

DIARY ONE

Nov. 1939 1. Arthur's Seat, a 600 acre cattle property in St Ann where the Manley family spent their summer holidays from 1933–41.

7.3.40 1. Sir Harry Luke, Chairman of the British Council. 2. Hugh Paget, possibly the local British Council representative.

8.3.40 1. Robert Kirkwood came to Jamaica in 1937 as Manager of the Frome Estate for the West Indies Sugar Co, part of the Tate and Lyle group. He was knighted for services rendered during his stay in Jamaica. He became Chairman of the Sugar Manufacturers' Association, and in the early 1950s formed the Farmers' Federation. He then launched the Farmers' Party to contest the 1954/55 elections. 2. The People's National Party. 3. Wills Isaacs, a founding member of the PNP and one of the leaders of the party's right wing. 4. Lady Molly Huggins, wife of Governor John Huggins. 5. Domingo, nationalist and political activist.

28.1.41 1. M.G. 'Mike' Smith, the Jamaican poet and anthropologist: a lifelong family friend. 'Realisis' was his shorthand for a concept drawn from *Adventures of Ideas* by A.N. Whitehead.

11.7.41 1. Edna Manley's two gods, part of the 'cosmic' series often referred to as the Dying God series, are described by her biographer, Dr David Boxer, as '... the embodiments of a system of opposites, couched in the most elemental terms – dark and light; night and day.'

8.1.44 1. 'The Horse of the Morning' became Edna Manley's most popular carving.

5.3.44 1. Vivian Dacres, the Manleys' driver for many years and a former Jamaican boxing champion, trained by Norman Manley. 2. Allan Isaacs, a founding member of the PNP, who changed his political ideology and affiliation several times.

10.3.44 1. *Public Opinion*, a weekly newspaper founded by O.T. Fairclough and H.P. Jacobs in 1937 to stimulate the national movement in Jamaica. 2. Edna Manley could be referring to either 'New Moon', owned by Gloria Cumper, or 'Moon', now in the National Gallery, dated 1943. 3. Claude Thompson, Jamaican short story writer.

12.3.44 1. N.N. Nethersole, 'Crab', Rhodes scholar, cricketer and founding member of the PNP. MP for Central St Andrew from 1948, he became Jamaica's Finance Minister in 1955 and held the post until his death. 2. Nethersole and Isaacs planned to resign when Governor Huggins increased the rates of personal and corporate taxes for the 1944-5 financial year.

14.3.44 1. The Kingston and St Andrew Corporation, a municipal body handling local government. 2. Gerald Mair, a senior partner in a firm of accountants, ran for the Jamaica Democratic Party (JDP) against Norman Manley in 1944. The JDP was formed by the upper classes to fight the 1944 elections but failed everywhere. Mair later joined Bustamante's Jamaica Labour Party. 3. Richard Hart was jailed for so-called subversive activity (see note, 20.3.44). 4. The concept of co-operatives was key to Norman Manley's thinking in the formation of Jamaica Welfare in 1937. This organization was created to encourage self-reliance and improve community welfare in rural Jamaica.

18.3.44 1. The issue was the taxation issue mentioned earlier, over which Nethersole resigned. 2. Vernon Arnett, a progressive and genuine socialist, was General Secretary of the PNP after O.T. Fairclough until he was elected to Parliament and took over as Minister of Finance after Nethersole's death. 3. Winston Grubb, a left-winger. 4. E.H.J. King, an English socialist who came to Jamaica College as a history teacher in the 1930s. 5. A strike at the *Daily Gleaner* newspaper by printers and clerical staff, organized by the Trade Union Congress.

20.3.44 1. 'Parliamentary delegates' refers to British MPs visiting Jamaica, which was still a Crown Colony. 2. 'The little group' refers to the Four H's – Ken and Frank Hill, Richard Hart and Arthur Henry – leaders of the PNP's left wing. They were jailed for 'subversive activities' along with Alexander Bustamante, 'Busta', Norman Manley's cousin and founder of the Jamaica Labour Party. 3. *Native Son*, a novel by the Black American writer, Richard Wright.

23.3.44 1. Governor Richards agreed to free Bustamante from internment to defeat the PNP and socialism. A deeply conservative man, but a shrewd populist, he was the preferred favourite ever after. 2. Wilmot was a British MP who had come to study Jamaica on the eve of the new constitution. 3. Florizel Glasspole, General Secretary of the TUC, then of the National Workers' Union (NWU) after the two split. A conservative member of the PNP, he was elected for East Kingston in 1944, was Minister of Education from 1955–9, and became Governor General in 1974.

26.3.44 1. Abe Issa, a wealthy merchant, was one of the JDP founders. 2. Lindsay was a black Jamaican who owned the Kingston Bus Company.

27.3.44 1. Marjorie Stewart, an English social worker. 2. Greta Fowler, see *n.* 16.6.73.

16.4.44 1. William Seivwright, master baker, deeply Christian patriot and lifelong PNP member.

Minister of Home Affairs and then Agriculture 1955–62. **2.** Major Nathan, British owner of 'Nathan's', one of Kingston's leading department stores. He was booed on his arrival at the election count when Nethersole won the KSAC seat.

Undated 1. Nomdmi, a rustic wooden house built by Edna and Norman Manley in the Blue Mountains.

13.6.44 1. Theodore Sealey, retired editor of the *Daily Gleaner*. **2.** Robert Verity, late head of the Institute of Jamaica's Junior Centre.

19.6.44 1. Esther Chapman, English author and editor.

28.12.44 1. Edward Fagan, a chiropractor, ran against Norman Manley in 1944 and defeated him, but was beaten by Manley in 1949 and afterwards joined the PNP.

7.3.48 1. The Doorly Hall one-man exhibition.

29.7.48 1. 'The Rising Sun' is the final carving in the cosmic series, a variant of 'Morning' on a more heroic scale.

20.11.48 1. Paul Robeson (1898-1976), the American singer. **2.** Overcrowding at the Robeson concert caused a stand to collapse, resulting in the death and injuries mentioned.

4.12.48 1. Edna Manley edited four editions of *Focus*, a literary anthology that was a vehicle for much Jamaican literature, exposing an authentic national voice.

7.12.48 1. Although many of M.G. Smith's poems featured in *Focus* they have never been published in a separate anthology, despite many efforts mentioned by Edna Manley in these diaries.

9.12.48 1. Louise Bennett, folklorist and Jamaica's foremost comedienne.

14.12.48 1. Rachel Manley, Ra, daughter of Michael and his first wife, Jacqueline, who were then living in London while Michael studied at the London School of Economics. **2.** Salvador Ley, a Guatemalan composer and friend of Edna and Norman Manley.

29.5.48 1. 'The Hills of Papine', a carving of an archetypal image of Mother Earth, cradling her child.

3.1.50 1. The general election was won by Bustamante on a vote of 19 seats to 12. Norman Manley won the East St Andrew seat.

7.3.51 1. The children are Rachel and her half-sister Anita Verity, who stayed with Edna Manley when Michael's first marriage broke down. **2.** The carving of the crucifix for All Saints Church in downtown Kingston. The drawings have disappeared. **3.** Norman Manley was detained on Ellis Island for two days on his way home from arguing the Vicks case in London – one of his greatest legal victories. The detention was never fully explained.

9.4.51 1. Jim Gore: the Gore Brothers owned a cigar factory and ran a terrazzo tiling business. **2.** Wright was chief groom and buggy driver at Drumblair.

11.4.51 1. Gallimore was a carpenter who did odd jobs at Drumblair.

12.4.51 1. Aimee Webster, a Jamaican writer.

14.4.51 1. Dr Muriel Manley, sister of Norman Manley, who ran the Children's Creche in Kingston for many years. **2.** Nurse: Evelyn Phillpotts, who came to look after Rachel.

16.5.51 1. Vera Moody, eldest sister of Norman Manley. A graduate of London's Royal College of Music and first Registrar of the Jamaican School of Music. She later moved permanently to England to join her daughter, Dr Pamela Moody. **2.** Grey: the Manleys' driver at the time.

16.6.51 1. A senseless and shocking killing in which Aston Folly (Woppie King) murdered Sydney Garel, aged 19, and wounded Garel's girlfriend, Bernadette Hugh.

13.3.52 1. 'The party split': the split in the PNP began when the right wing accused the Four H's (see note, 20.3.44) of teaching a Marxist document in a secret PNP class. A tribunal was set up to examine allegations of communist activity by the four.

2.6.52 1. The terracotta 'Mountains', a man and a woman in the form of two interlocking mountain ranges, was later cast in bronze. **2.** Lady Sylvia Foot, wife of the Governor, Sir Hugh Foot, who as Lord Caradon later became the UK representative to the United Nations. **3.** Edna carved the 'Unknown Political Prisoner' for an exhibition and competition won by the British sculptor, Reg Butler. **4.** Fagan joined the PNP in 1952.

6.7.52 1. The Farmers' Federation formed by Sir Robert Kirkwood in 1951. **2.** The 'Plan for Progress' was a PNP policy document. **3.** 'The Secret' – a small carving of a woman's head with raised hands. Owner not known.

20.7.52 1. 'Minni' was a little shingled one-room hut with a cement floor, under the pine trees at Nomdmi, which Edna Manley used as her studio.

27.7.52 1. Family and friends would be asked to pat the wood for good luck. Edna Manley described it as 'the laying on of hands'. **2.** Graham, the driver who succeeded Grey. **3.** At the Helsinki Olympics, the Jamaican 4 x 400 metres relay team of Wint, McKenley, Rhoden and Laing won the gold medal, setting a new world record.

7.8.52 **1.** The International Federation of Trade Unions was formed in 1951, when the World Federation of Trade Unions split over communism. The issue was whether the Jamaican TUC should stay with the WFTU or move to the ICFTU, as in fact happened. **2.** Sir Grantley Adams (1898–1971), founder and leader of the Barbados Labour Party, Premier of Barbados 1954–8, only Prime Minister of the short-lived West Indies Federation 1958–62. **3.** 'Anansi', a Jamaican mythological spider. Edna Manley did not, in the end, do this carving.

30.8.52 **1.** Carmen Manley, wife of Douglas, and their first son Norman.

1.12.52 **1.** See *n*. 28.1.41.

1.4.53 **1.** There is no record that they were exhibited, so she may have changed her mind about sending these carvings. **2.** The PNP's Adrian Gray won the seat in a by-election caused by the death of Sir Harold Allen, who had become the JLP Minister of Finance in 1949. **3.** A strike was called at Alcan's Kirkwood works after the company refused a wages claim by the National Workers' Union (NWU).

14.11.53 **1.** The 'HHO scandal' was caused by the misappropriation of the funds of the Hurricane Housing Organisation, set up after the 1952 hurricane. **2.** Simmonds – political reporter at the *Daily Gleaner*. **3.** Trotman – news editor at the *Daily Gleaner*. **4.** Abe Issa and Sir Alfred DaCosta were trying to protect Bustamante's Government. **5.** Michael DeCordova, then Managing Director of the *Daily Gleaner*.

2.4.55 **1.** Davidson was a marvellous singer, who would lead the crowds with hymns and party songs. **2.** Fagan, now a member of the PNP, lost the East Rural St Andrew seat. **3.** H.O.A. Dayes, a lawyer and founding member of the PNP. **4.** Magloire, President of Haiti before Duvalier. **5.** Princess Margaret. **6.** Thelma Manley, Michael's second wife.

Jan. 1957 **1.** The question of where to put the Federal capital became highly controversial. Trinidad won.

11.1.59 **1.** The Cadburys' carving was 'Girl with a Goat'.

24.1.59 **1.** Jock Campbell's carving 'And the Dawn Came' was a man and woman facing the dawn.

23.3.59 **1.** The death of N.N. Nethersole was both a great national loss and a personal tragedy for Norman Manley, who was devoted to him.

31.8.59 **1.** The 1959 election, sprung early but with adequate notice, was Norman Manley's greatest electoral victory.

24.2.60 **1.** George Campbell, the celebrated Jamaican poet. **2.** Derek Walcott, Trinidad and Tobago's leading poet and playwright. **3.** A reference to Bustamante being jailed during the 1938 strikes. **4.** St William Grant, see *n*.14. 9.77. **5.** Williams and Scarlett, political activists. **6.** Aggie Bernard and Edna Manley fed the 1938 strikers. Aggie had a luncheon business among the dockers at the waterfront. **7.** Frank Walcott, General Secretary of the Barbados Workers Union.

26.2.60 **1.** Eric Williams (1911–81), founder of the People's National Movement in 1955, father of Trinidad's independence in 1962 and Prime Minister of Trinidad and Tobago until his death; an authority on West Indian history.

5.3.60 **1.** The PNM was founded on similar lines to Jamaica's PNP.

24.6.60 **1.** Edna Manley refers to the start of the difficulties the PNP was to suffer over the question of socialism.

12.6.61 **1.** The Referendum gave the country the opportunity to decide whether or not to stay in the West Indies Federation. **2.** C.L.R. James, the great Trinidadian philosopher, writer and historian. **3.** Six of Campbell's poems were set to music by Salvador Ley; this performance was given by the American soprano, Vela Vincent.

24.7.61 **1.** Scarface, Adinah Spence and Marquis were three PNP martyrs, killed by political thugs in the early 1940s. **2.** Linwood was a staunch PNP 'comrade'.

Undated **1.** Dr Leslie, then a PNP candidate and MP for St Catherine. **2.** The Rastafarian Report was made by Dr Rex Nettleford and a delegation, including rastafarians, who were sent on a mission to Africa after mounting rastafarian trouble.

18.11.61 **1.** Drumblair, the family home, was sold for £30,000 to Maurice Facey, a developer, to pay Norman Manley's debts. **2.** 'The Land of Wood and Water' was the first of two children's stories written by Carmen, late wife of Douglas Manley, and illustrated by Edna Manley. **3.** 'The Bush that was not Consumed', a carving (bas relief) commissioned for Webster's Memorial Church. **4.** Batiste, long-time gardener at Drumblair, then Regardless – dearly loved by all. **5.** Drawings of rastafarians in preparation for 'Brother Man'.

3.9.62 **1.** Regardless was the little house built on a 'toe-hold' of Drumblair land to which the Manleys moved after selling Drumblair. **2.** The loss of the Referendum in 1961 signalled Jamaica's wish to become independent alone. Norman Manley called an election in April 1962 and was narrowly beaten. **3.** The 'Sheraton carving' is a large bas relief called 'It Cometh Up', now on loan to the National Gallery.

7.5.63 **1.** 'Owl', a terracotta, now in the National Gallery.

28.7.63 **1.** 'Tyger', a terracotta, given to Rachel. **2.** Nude: 'Faun', owned by Professor Rex Nettleford.

12.4.64 **1.** Charlie Lopez, a building contractor and political activist for the PNP. **2.** Miss B: Maud Boyd, officially the housekeeper at Drumblair and unofficially second mother to the Manley children and lifelong confidante of the whole family. Aunt of George Campbell. **3.** John Burrow, maths teacher and family friend. **4.** 'Scottie': A.D. Scott, architect, building contractor, painter and art patron. **5.** Roysterer: a roan grey gelding, locally bred and a triple three-year-old champion. After an injury he became Edna Manley's favourite riding horse.

19.11.64 **1.** A statue of Jamaica's national hero, Paul Bogle, was commissioned to mark the centenary of the Morant Bay Rebellion, which he led.

5.2.65 **1.** 'Atholl' and 'Newaralyia' were houses rented by Norman Manley before buying Drumblair.

July 1965 **1.** Tom Concannon, an architectural historian, assisted with the siting of Edna Manley's 'Bogle'. **2.** Edna Manley's mother, Ellie Swithenbank, *nee* Shearer, came from Hanover.

August 1968 **1.** 'Roxborough': the property in Manchester where Norman Manley was born, owned by his parents, Albert and Margaret Manley. **2.** Frank Hill, one of the Four H's, possibly referring to Richard Hart.

6.10.68 **1.** Barbara Manley, Michael's third wife. **2.** Thelma Manley, Michael's second wife and mother of Joseph. **3.** Sarah Manley, daughter of Michael and Barbara. **4.** The great banquet held at the Sheraton hotel by the PNP on Norman Manley's seventy-fifth birthday.

6.10.68 **1.** Ken McNeil and his wife, Valerie. He is an ENT specialist and plastic surgeon who became MP for East St Andrew when Norman Manley resigned. A close friend of Michael Manley. **2.** Moody: the late Ludlow Moody, a physician and friend, married to Norman Manley's sister, Vera. **3.** The late Professor John Gilmour and his wife, Mavis. She was a surgeon and served first in a PNP and then in a JLP government. **4.** Graham Binns, once head of Rediffusion Services in Jamaica, and his wife, Gillian, an actress. **5.** Dr Roy Levy, Norman and Edna Manley's family doctor. **6.** Dr Ken Stuart, medical specialist.

10.10.68 **1.** Roy Manley, Douglas and Carmen's second son. **2.** Dorit Hutson, close friend of Douglas Manley.

4.10.69 **1.** Chambers, Norman Manley's last driver.

28.11.69 **1.** Uhuru: Norman Manley's handsome Doberman.

1.12.69 **1.** Vivian Blake QC, PNP activist and family friend.

30.11.69 **1.** Rachel had been accepted as an air hostess by Pan Am airways.

10.12.69 **1.** Victor Stafford Read, Jamaican writer, who did eventually write Norman Manley's biography, *Horses of the Morning*. **2.** Philip Sherlock, former Vice-Chancellor of the University of the West Indies, also wrote a biography. **3.** Vivian Carrington, Longman's local representative at the time. **4.** John Maxwell, once editor of *Public Opinion*. He stood unsuccessfully as a candidate against Edward Seaga in West Kingston.

20.12.69 **1.** Leighton Holness, Tito Jemmott and Pat Anderson, three university graduates who helped Norman Manley with research for his unfinished autobiography.

1.1.70 **1.** Jessie Dayes, sister of the Jamaican author and painter, Roger Mais, and ex-wife of H.O.A. Dayes.

2. Beverley Anderson, who was to become Michael Manley's fourth wife in 1972.

20.6.70 **1.** A Russian ship put into Kingston harbour on the eve of the election, and the countryside was swept with rumours that this ship was filled with soldiers, who would take over if the PNP won.

3.7.70 **1.** Forbes Burnham, Prime Minister of Guyana. **2.** After Norman Manley's death, a foundation was formed in his memory. One of its functions was to provide an annual award for excellence in any field of endeavour chosen that year.

20.8.70 **1.** 'The Angel'.

July 1971 **1.** Basil McFarlane: Jamaican writer and poet.

DIARY TWO

31.8.71 **1.** Wayne Brown. Trinidadian poet and writer was working on a biography of Edna Manley, *Edna Manley – the Private Years 1900–1938*, which was published by André Deutsch in 1975. **2.** This one-man exhibition on sculpture at the Bolivar Gallery featured her 'mourning carvings', 'Adios', 'Angel', 'Woman', 'Phoenix', 'Mountain Women'. **3.** George Drummond, Rachel's first husband. **4.** Edna Manley lived in the fishing village of St Ives, Cornwall, England, from 1902–1906.

3.9.71 **1.** The PNP held a candlelight meeting at Bolivar's statue in Kingston to mark the anniversary of Norman Manley's death.

11.9.71   1. Rex Nettleford, a Professor at the University of the West Indies and Director of Extramural Studies: Rhodes Scholar and author, and founder and artistic director of the National Dance Theatre Company of Jamaica. He edited and annotated *Manley and the New Jamaica*, a selection of Norman Manley's speeches and writings published by Longman's in 1971.   2. David and Harriet Berger, friends of Edna and Norman Manley from Philadelphia.

7.2.72   1. The inaugural meeting for the 1972 election campaign.

10.2.72   1. The Remount Depot at Wembley, London, where Edna Manley worked in 1917, breaking in horses to be sent to British regiments in France.

Good Friday 1972   1. The PNP won the 1972 general election and Michael became Prime Minister.

7.6.72   1. Carole Edghill (*née* Brennan), lifelong friend of Rachel who lived with the Manleys during school terms.

July 1972   1. 'Faun', bas relief.

16.9.72   1. Norman Manley's memorial tomb was designed by the Jamaican architect Denny Repole.

17.12.72   1. *On the Coast*, Wayne Brown's first book of poems, published in 1972, was a Poetry Book Society recommendation and won the author the Commonwealth Prize for Poetry.

January 1973   1. 'The Sunshine Showdown', a world heavyweight title boxing match staged in Kingston featuring Frazier and Foreman. Foreman won by an early knock-out.

24.3.73   1. Henri Gaudier Brezska, major twentieth century sculptor.

16.6.73   1. Greta and Henry Fowler, theatre enthusiasts and co-founders of Jamaica's Little Theatre Movement (LTM).   2. Easton Lee, playwright, actor, dancer, PR Consultant, friend of Edna Manley.   3. Cecil Baugh, 'master' potter and friend of Edna Manley.   4. Edna Manley was commissioned to do a piece for the Little Theatre. It would be 'Rainbow Serpent'.

9.7.73   1. These two by-elections were caused by the vacating of the seats of Wills O. Isaacs and Florizel Glasspole.   2. Viv Blake was appointed to the Senate to be Minister of Trade and Industry.   3. David Boxer, artist, art scholar, head of the National Gallery of Jamaica, friend of Edna Manley.

17.9.73   1. This carving is of 'Journey' which is technically a bas relief but is so 'deep' that the semi-'relief', semi-'in the round' nature of the work was giving tremendous problems.

21.9.73   1. 'Nyumbani': Michael's mountain house next door to Nomdmi.   2. Douglas's case was an election petition by defeated JLP candidate Arthur Williams to unseat Douglas Manley. The case succeeded and Douglas had eventually to go to the Senate for the remainder of the term, though he won in 1976.   3. A.E. 'Tonti' Barrett, farmer and building and haulage contractor – close friend of Douglas.   4. Michael had recently visited Algiers.

25.9.73   1. Dwight Whylie, Jamaican broadcaster, and his wife Tangie, a nurse. They bought 'Ebony Hill' from Michael, becoming Edna Manley's neighbours.   2. Drumblair Dance Committee annually organized a Xmas dance, the proceeds providing treats for needy children.   3. Odel Flemming, pioneer worker at the Supervision Board, part of the Jamaica Welfare movement.   4. Carole Burrow, a social worker, wife of John Burrow (see note 12.4.64).

27.9.73   1. Roy Marshall, Vice Chancellor of the University of the West Indies, a Barbadian.   2. Harry Milner, Jamaican art critic.   3. Dossie Carberry, son of former Chief Justice of Jamaica, for years Clerk of Legislature, then Appeal Court Judge; poet and lifelong family friend of the Manleys. His wife Dorothea is a sister of John Burrow.

7.10.73   1. George Headley, one of the West Indies' greatest cricketers.

10.10.73   1. 'Journey', she refers to as the 'Translation' figure.   2. This was the request to do a one-man show at the Commonwealth Institute. The final result was the exhibition 'Ten Jamaican Sculptors' which included 30 works by Edna Manley.

November 1933   1. Michael's first book, *The Politics of Change*.

30.11.73   1. Corina Meeks, PR Consultant, then an assistant to Michael, also a close friend of the Manleys.   2. Joseph McPherson, then a Senator, was editor of the JLP paper *The Voice*.

22.4.74   1. The late Rev. Phillip Hart who was keenly interested in art.   2. Swopping guns for marijuana (ganja) was a notorious part of the trade.

Undated (after 22.4.74)   1. A complicated series of events prevented the headmastership of Kingston College being offered to John Burrow who was widely felt to deserve the position.   2. Mr Blake: a reference to a book on William Blake she was reading.

8.6.74   1. The relief for LTM: 'The Rainbow Serpent'.

3.7.74   1. Paul Ennevor, Rachel's second husband.

January 1975   1. This incident took place as a result of David Boxer telling Edna Manley he thought the original head of Adam 'effete', which upset her. Says Boxer: 'For my impertinence we got a much better head of Adam.'

8.2.75   1. The Government of China invited Edna Manley to visit. Douglas and Mike Smith accompanied her.   2. Edna Manley had visited Germany earlier that year.

22.4.75 1. Creation: first ideas for the 'Creation of Adam'.

23.4.75 1. Barrington Watson, Jamaican artist. 2. Susan Alexander, American-born painter and sculptor. 3. A second cast was made of 'Rainbow Serpent'. 4. A committee for purchases at the National Gallery was established in 1974.

24.4.75 1. 'Rainbow Serpent' is signed N.M.E. and the inscription is 'to Greta and Henry Fowler from Norman and Edna Manley'. Adam is clearly identified with Norman. 2. Mr Fung: Edna Manley's bank manager.

19.5.75 1. Shensi — a province of N.W. China where Edna Manley was shown, (long before the Chinese people were informed) the great find of pottery soldiers in the tomb of the Emperor Shih Huang Ti.

12.7.75 1. Albert Huie, renowned Jamaican artist. 2. Gertrude Swaby, won the Norman Manley Award for excellence in the field of nursing. 3. Horsemen: Edna Manley planned to do a drawing or painting perhaps leading to a sculpture of the Four Horsemen of the Apocalypse.

14.7.75 1. Norman Manley, Jnr., elder son of Douglas and Carmen, became a lawyer. 2. Roy Manley, son of Douglas and Carmen. 3. John Hearne, Jamaican writer and newspaper columnist. 4. Ian Blair, optician, music lover and close friend of Michael. 5. Marcella Martinez, veteran worker for Jamaican tourism. 6. This space indicates where Edna Manley crossed out three names she had written, so I have respected what I presume to be her wish.

9.8.75 1. The Commonwealth Institute show, Ten Jamaican Sculptors. 2. Osmond Watson, major Jamaican painter and sculptor, and one of those exhibiting in London. 3. May, an unstable cook who worked with Muriel. 4. Dr Rudolf Aub, a family doctor.

29.11.75 1. Dr Emile Khouri, Jamaican surgeon. 2. Reference to a substantial exodus from Jamaica of the middle classes and their money. 3. The problems occurred because there was no bronze foundry in Jamaica.

10.12.75 1. Rachel and Paul moved to Barbados in 1975, where he worked.

6.2.76 1. 'Sea God' was retitled 'Rio Bueno' and belongs to Pam O'Gorman. 2. Edna Manley was allergic to fibreglass, which gave her asthma.

30.4.76 1. Dan Berger, son of David and Harriet Berger (see note, 11.9.71).

14.7.76 1. Hugh Lawson Shearer, Prime Minister of Jamaica 1967–72. A distant cousin of the Manleys.

6.9.76 1. The 1976 election produced the PNP's greatest-ever victory, with 57% of the vote. 2. 'Tell No One' was retitled 'The Message'. 3. Noel Foster Davis, outstanding Jamaican musician and music teacher.

7.9.76 1. Pam O'Gorman, 'Pam', Australian music teacher, later head of the Jamaica School of Music; family friend and one of Norman Manley's beloved 'chosen few'.

8.9.76 1. Kay Sullivan, Jamaican sculptor. 2. These were the 'Creation' and 'Wind and Rain' drawings. 3. Sheila Graham.

Loose pages 1. The Cudjoe Minstrels were one of the earliest groups in Jamaica to specialize in the singing of Jamaican folk songs. 2. The Olive Lewin group, the 'Jamaican Folk Singers', are still active.

DIARY THREE

13.3.77 1. The February 1972 and December 1976 elections. 2. Natasha Manley, daughter of Michael and Beverly. 3. Koren der Harootian, an American artist and teacher, who came to Jamaica in 1930 and exhibited jointly with Edna Manley in 1931 at the Jamaica Mutual Life Assurance Co. 4. On a state visit to Canada in 1976, Michael received a gift from Pierre Trudeau of a little racing yacht for two people. 5. Rachel and Paul now lived in Ocho Rios. 6. Christopher Gonzalez, Jamaican sculptor. 7. Norman had two car accidents in which the car, not Norman, got hurt.

15.3.77 1. Danny Smith, son of Mike Smith, and Sarah, his future wife. 2. Joseph Manley, son of Michael and Thelma. 3. The Ministry of Health of which Douglas Manley was then Minister.

17.3.77 1. Head of old woman later titled 'Jamaica 1976'. 2. David Boxer and Vera Hyatt were Director and Deputy Director of the National Gallery, and Jean Smith was Director of Arts and Culture.

29.3.77 1. Clive Glave and Warren Robinson, photographers. 2. Wycliffe Bennett, then manager of the Jamaica Broadcasting Corporation. 3. Beverly Manley was a broadcaster before her marriage to Michael. 4. Ken Dawson: the JBC cameraman who shot the film 'Edna Manley, Sculptor' directed by David Boxer. **5.** Stephen Hill, Jamaican impresario, married to Dorothy. This show did not materialize.

31.3.77 1. Laura Facey, young Jamaican artist, graduate of Jamaica School of Art. **2.** Cecil Ward, a photographer. **3.** Koto: a Japanese plucked instrument.

14.4.77 1. Seymour, Pilgrim: officials of the Carifesta, a Caribbean cultural festival. This one was held in Guyana. **2.** Dennis Scott, Jamaican poet, playwright and actor. **3.** David Smith, son of M.G. Smith.

2.5.77 1. Arnold Bertram, then Minister of Youth and Culture in the PNP government. **2.** Bustamante's release from prison had been negotiated by Norman Manley. **3.** Moses Matalon, Jamaican developer. **4.** Jerry Craig, an artist and a Director of the School of Art. **5.** 'Negro Aroused', Edna Manley's famous carving of the1930s.

12.5.77 1. Neville Dawes, author, was then Executive Director of the Institute of Jamaica.

13.6.77 1. This London Commonwealth Conference produced the Gleneagles Agreement on sport and apartheid.

14.6.77 1. Edna Manley never finished this carving of a lion. **2.** Mary Smith, wife of M.G. Smith.

10.7.77 1. Peter Smith, son of M.G. Smith, a young sculptor, collaborated in the translation of 'Negro Aroused' from a carving to a monument.

26.7.77 1. Anthony Spaulding, then Minister of Housing in the PNP government.

27.7.77 1. A film being prepared by the Jamaican Information Service.

5.8.77 1. The property was actually 'Aquatto Vale'. **2.** The Agency for Public Information, a Jamaican government information agency. **3.** Sir Edward Denham, Governor during the 1938 unrest in Jamaica.

9.8.77 1. 'Blenheim' was the property in Hanover where Bustamante was born.

31.8.77 1. Don Mills, then Jamaica's representative to the United Nations, who became President for a term.

14.9.77 1. St William Grant, a Jamaican labour leader who broke with the BITU and became a PNP stalwart.

16.9.77 1. Richard and Shirley Fletcher. **2.** Valerie McNeil, wife of Dr Ken McNeil. **3.** M G Smith was an adviser to the government, researching questions of poverty. His objective, scientific approach was unpopular with the left-wing. **4.** CAST: College of Arts, Sciences & Technology in Jamaica. **5.** Zethilda Myrie, superb cook from Drumblair days, adored by Edna Manley.

17.9.77 1. AMC: Agricultural Marketing Co-operation (Jamaica). **2.** 'Journey' was Edna Manley's last carving. All subsequent sculptures were modelled in clay or plastelina and then cast into plaster for final casting in *ciment fondu*, fibreglass or bronze.

23.9.77 1. John Hearne, columnist with the *Daily Gleaner*, had by this time started a hostile campaign against Michael. **2.** John Maxwell (see note, 10.12.69). **3.** Douglas was accompanied by Tonti Barrett. When Fidel Castro discovered a fellow cattle farmer, he cancelled his other engagements and escorted them to see his farms, which had nothing to do with the original agenda of their meeting.

8.11.77 1. 'Murder as Usual' by Ernest Volkman and John Cummings appeared in *Penthouse* Magazine. **2.** At the end of the 1976 campaign Michael was in a helicopter which went out of control and nearly crashed on its way to Bog Walk in Jamaica.

14.11.77 1. President Carter denounced the International Labour Organization. **2.** D.K. Duncan, General Secretary of the PNP was poisoned by arsenic over a period of time, and had to lose one kidney in order to save his life.

15.11.77 1. The PNP Youth Organization caused untold trouble at this time. 'Munro-ites' would be the Marxist leftists. **2.** Maxine Henry, Duncan's personal assistant.

20.11.77 1. 'Before Thought', a drawing from 1942 of a tall spiritualized figure: in the National Gallery.

26.11.77 1. D.K. Duncan attacked Bustamante on National Heroes Day. **2.** Wilmot Perkins, columnist with the *Daily Gleaner*. **3.** Rachel's marriage to Paul was breaking down.

27.11.77 1. Edna Manley's memory erred in this entry. The other pianist was not Nerine Barrett but her contemporary Maxine Franklin. All three are leading Jamaican pianists resident abroad.

7.12.77 1. Old Woman: 'Jamaica 1976' **2.** Weary old woman: 'Old Woman Seated on a Rock'. **3.** Sleeping figure: 'Sleeping Hills'. **4.** Rising, waking woman: 'Morning'. **5.** Working figure: 'Washer Woman'. **6.** Two archetypal figures: 'The Mountains'. **7.** The Raging Lion was never cast.

15.1.78 1. 'The Ancestor', completed 1978. Two casts in bronze exist. **2.** Jarmila Taud, a friend of Rachel. **3.** Danny and Sarah Smith (see note, 15.3.77). **4.** Rose McFarlane, journalist, diplomat, friend and horoscope guide of Edna Manley. **5.** Johnnie and Melanie Martinez, family friends; she had been a friend of Rachel since childhood.

7.2.78 1. Megan Brown, wife of Wayne Brown (see note 31.8.71). 2. Lloyd Record, Jamaican stage director. 3. Colin Garland, Australian-born painter living in Jamaica, now regarded as one of Jamaica's leading painters.

17.3.78 1. David Coore, lawyer and friend of Michael since schooldays, who became Minister of Finance and Deputy Prime Minister in 1972 with the PNP Government.2.Eric Bell, also a lawyer, who replaced Coore as Finance Minister in a cabinet reshuffle after the failure of an IMF test, when Coore resigned. 3. Trevor Munroe, Secretary of the Workers' Party of Jamaica.

29.4.78 1. Rachel's second book of poems, *Poems 2*, published in Barbados. 2. 'Drum' (George Drummond jnr, Rachel's elder son), fell 20ft through a warehouse roof, breaking his back. 3. Luke, Rachel's son from her marriage to Paul.

25.7.78 1. There was intense and often very personal criticism of Michael by most *Daily Gleaner* columnists at the time, which reminded Edna Manley of similar hostilities endured by Norman Manley. 2. South Manchester, the constituency which Douglas represented in Parliament.

10.7.78 1. A sectional mould of 'Negro Aroused' had been created for shipment to New York for casting. It was destroyed in this fire. 2. George Campbell (see note, 12.6.61) and his wife Odilia.

15.7.78 1. Lorna Goodison, Jamaican poet. 2. Alvin Marriott, major Jamaican sculptor responsible for many Jamaican monuments. 3. Carl Abrahams, major Jamaican painter. 4. Barrington Watson, (see note 23.4.75). 5. Eugene Hyde, artist. 6. Margaret Chen – in 1978, a recent graduate of the Jamaica School of Art. Edna Manley had been an adjudicator examining the students when she acquired this sculpture. 7. 'Woman on a Hillside' was titled 'Mountains'.

20.7.78 1. Edna Manley entertained these Chinese dignitaries at her house.

27.8.78 1. Michael sued the *Daily Gleaner* for libel and eventually won, years later, when the newspaper apologized.

2.9.78 1. Vivian Blake resigned from politics and went to practise law in the Bahamas, where he later became Chief Justice. 2. David Coore moved to Washington, working for the World Bank.

5.12.78 1. Muschette – an employee of B.L. Williams. 2. Jonestown, Guyana, where there was a mass suicide of members of Jim Jones's cult, the People's Temple. 3. Edgar Mittelholzer, the Guyanese writer.

24.3.79 1. Rachel never completed this masters degree at Cave Hill. 2. 'Masquerade', a Jamaican play by Jim Nelson and Sylvia Wynter.
3. The original black patina of the statue of Bogle had bleached due to constant exposure to the sun.

20.11.79 1. Shortly after this entry is another similarly dated, but correctly placed, in which she refers to the fact that she had got lost in the diary (see p.0). 2. This 'Adam' painting was never finished.

21.6.79 1. 'Pocomania', literally translates as 'little madness' – a Jamaican religious cult. 2. Edith Clarke – anthropologist. 3. Madelaine Kerr – anthropologist. 4. Zora Hurston – folklorist. 5. Katherine Dunham – American dancer. 6. Leslie Clerk – piano tuner and Norman Manley's closest friend.

17.7.79 1. Ellen Roxburgh, the heroine of the novel.

21.8.79 1. Douglas had major surgery for an ulcerated stomach.

18.9.79 1. 'The Dancers' was originally planned as a large relief.

2.10.79 1. The big relief she refers to is 'The Dancers' of the previous entry. 2. On the eve of the Non-Aligned Summit in Havana, 1979, President Carter became indignant about Russian troops on Cuba.

20.11.79 1. George Campbell was then working at the Institute of Jamaica.

21.11.79 1. Frances Keane, Jamaican dress designer.

25.2.80 1. H.P. Jacobs, an Englishman and history teacher who co-founded '*Public Opinion*' with O.T. Fairclough.

8.4.80 1. 'Edna Manley: The Seventies' opened 14 April 1980 at the National Gallery and was a survey of Edna Manley's work for the decade.

13.4.80 1. 'The Faun' – one of Edna Manley's last carvings.

19.5.80 1. 'Fellowship and OM business' – Edna Manley refers to the Doctorate from UWI and the Order of Merit, second biggest honour in Jamaica, both of which she reluctantly agreed to accept.

24.7.80 1. The brutalities described were thought by many to have been part of a deliberate destabilization campaign against the Government. 2. This was an early sketch for 'Ghetto Mother'. 3. Errol Lewis, Basil Watson: young Jamaican sculptors recently graduated from Jamaica School of Art.

6.8.80 1. 'Dawn' was cast in a red ochre coloured *ciment fondu*, (Boxer collection). 2. 'Black Sun', cast in a black coloured *ciment fondu*, is the other head referred to. 3. 'Winged Horse Power' was a commission from Air Jamaica.

30.8.80 1. George Lamming, celebrated Barbadian writer. **2.** Rev. Adam Clayton Powell, controversial black Congressman for Harlem, a Baptist preacher and Pastor of the famous Abyssinia Baptist Church.

10.9.80 1. Ellen, the cook at 'Regardless' after Zethilda retired. **2.** 'The Voice', the singing rastafarian owned by A.D. Scott.

25.9.80 1. The birth of David Manley, Michael's fifth child. **2.** An arrangement for Venezuelan oil to be bought at discount with the difference going to an investment fund for countries like Jamaica. **3.** Douglas was asked to step down from full Minister to Minister of State as part of a huge contraction of the Cabinet, part of an effort to make the Government more cost effective.

20.10.80 1. Roy McGann, Parliamentary Secretary in the Ministry of National Security, was shot at a Gordon Town meeting in a campaign in which over 700 people were to die violently. **2.** Dudley Thompson, veteran Jamaican politician, then Minister of National Security for the PNP Government.

31.10.80 1. The PNP lost massively at the polls, ending their eight-year Government.

1.11.80 1. Michael was offered a fellowship from a Canadian International Trust, but turned it down when some members of Canadian Parliament criticized the offer. He later wrote the book, titled *Up the Down Escalator*. **2.** Arrest was believed to have been imminent, but never took place. **3.** Mike Smith was then the Professor of Anthropology at Yale University.

12.11.80 1. D.K. Duncan was caught with an unlicensed gun in a police roadblock during the election campaign, but was later acquitted. **2.** Pernel Charles, a JLP activist, was interned in 1976 during the state of emergency.

20.2.81 1. Easton Lee would stage plays and concerts in rural chuches throughout Jamaica at Easter.

25.2.81 1. The early drawings for 'Ghetto Mother' show a figure of a gunman towering above the mother with the cowering children. Edna Manley did not eventually use this figure in the sculpture.

7.3.81 1. Con Allison, a civil servant in Douglas's former Ministry. **2.** Basil Keane, a dentist: eccentric and charismatic friend of Douglas who acted the role of preacher in the Jamaican film 'The Harder They Come' starring Jimmy Cliff.

14.3.81 1. Dorette Tomlinson, and her sister Gem Abrahams, close friends of Douglas and the family. **2.** Fern Hill, a piece of land opposite 'Nomdmi' that Vera Moody bought and willed to Douglas.

11.5.81 1. George Campbell's *First Poems*, a new edition with additional poems published by Garland Publishing Inc., 1981. **2.** *Rural Carvers of Jamaica*: this book on rural carvings with many photographs remains incomplete and unpublished.

11.6.81 1. Carifesta – the Caribbean cultural festival, held in Barbados: she attended and was honoured there.

12.8.81 1. Edward Braithwaite, poet. **2.** Errol Hill, playwright.

21.8.81 1. Käthe Kollwitz, German expressionist graphic artist and sculptor.

7.11.81 1. St John's Wood, London, where Edna Manley lived in 1919.

27.1.82 1. 'Jacob and the Angel' was first considered c. 1968. Her renewed interest in the subject produced many drawings, leading to the 1982 bas relief, from which two casts were made. (Now in the A.D. Scott Collection and Pan-Jamaica Collection.)

9.4.82 1. President Reagan, in a speech, referred to the PNP government as communist.

11.5.82 1. Douglas Manley received a Fulbright Fellowship to do research at Columbia University. **2.** Edna Manley was commissioned by Wallace Campbell and David Boxer to produce a smaller version of 'Negro Aroused', with two casts, to provide a bronze to travel with the Smithsonian Show. However the result was larger than the original carving, and with three casts, the third of which was bought by the Wadsworth Atheneum, a major American museum.

30.6.82 1. 'Deliverance' was the slogan used by the JLP during the 1982 campaign, hence the tongue-in-cheek comment.

DIARY FOUR

14.7.82 1. Harry Belafonte made a controversial speech as guest speaker at the Norman Manley Award to Jimmy Cliff.

17.7.82 1. Higglers – unofficial street vendors.

21.7.82 1. Marlene Ottey, Jamaica's great 100/200 metres woman sprinter. **2.** Bertland Cameron, the world's No. 1 400 metre runner in 1983-4.

28.7.82 1. Edna Manley means that she despises both superpowers, not Salvador and

Afghanistan! **2.** Joyce, granddaughter of the housekeeper Blanche at Nomdmi.

5.8.82 1. Vernon Arnett wrote a fragment of an autobiography before his death.

24.8.82 1. Dr Paul Bell, Edna and Michael Manley's doctor after Dr Khourie left.

11.9.82 1. Joseph was then studying at the University of Havana, from where he later graduated. **2.** Wallace Campbell, a Jamaican businessman, who during the 1980s assembled perhaps the largest private collection of Jamaican and Caribbean art in existence. **3.** George Campbell's poem 'Negro Aroused' was written after the creation of Edna Manley's carving.

18.9.82 1. Bishop DeSouza, head of the Anglican Church in Jamaica. **2.** 'The Trumpet has sounded' – party anthem of the PNP. **3.** Jimmy Tucker, popular Jamaican singer. **4.** 'I Saw my land', a poem by M.G. Smith, was put to music three times. This version was that of Mapletoff Poulle. Lloyd Hall and Noelle Foster Davis also wrote music for the poem. **5.** Joseph Bush, grandnephew of Maud Boyd, and nephew of George Campbell. **6.** It was important for the PNP that the 'moderates' do well in the election of officers, as did happen.

19.9.82 1. Gil Noble: black American TV journalist and producer.

23.10.82 1. Old man Shearer was the mutual grandfather of Edna and Norman Manley.

27.10.82 1. Ranny Williams, late Jamaican comedian who often acted with Louise Bennett. **2.** Barbara Gloudan, Jamaican journalist, broadcaster and art critic. **3.** Trevor Rhone, celebrated Jamaican playwright. **4.** Charles Hyatt, veteran Jamaican actor. **5.** Barbara McCalla and Grace McGhie, Jamaican actresses who alternated playing 'Gloria' in the Trevor Rhone play 'Two Can Play'.

2.1.83 1. Israel Cinman, who later became Rachel's third husband. **2.** George Campbell's second book of poems *Earth Testament* was illustrated by Edna Manley. **3.** Reference to her 'last sculpture' refers to 'Future'.

12.1.83 1. Lawrence Rowe, one of Jamaica's star batsmen.

13.1.83 1. Aaron Matalon, Jamaican entrepreneur and developer. **2.** P.J. Patterson, lawyer and Vice President of PNP. Represented Michael in this libel case against the Gleaner Co.

12.2.83 1. Due to an oversight over a jury member, the case went to the Court of Appeal for a new jury, but they were split, so the appeal went to the Privy Council in England.

19.2.83 1. Edith Dalton James. **2.** Iris King, Councillor, then Mayor in the KSAC; then MP for West Central Kingston in 1962. **3.** Ivan Lloyd, from St Ann, was the first person to win a seat for the PNP in 1942 by-election. **4.** Father Coombs, an early unionist from Montego Bay who served under the 1955 PNP government until he was fired. **5.** 'Quashie': derives from the name of the slave rebellion leader, and now means rural or peasant.

23.2.83 1. This letter was sent by the then American mission in Jamaica in the 1940s to J. Edgar Hoover, the head of the FBI.

23.3.83 1. 'Gerhke' is the nickname of Carmen Lynd-Pettersen, Edna Manley's friend since art school. She married and settled in Guatemala. **2.** June Girvan is still compiling this book in Ottawa.

18.4.83 1. Fitzroy Harrack, a Grenadian born sculptor, Head of the Sculpture Department at the School of Art. **2.** In late 1982 the National Gallery was moved to its new location in downtown Kingston, where the opening exhibition was 'Jamaican Art 1922–82'.

30.7.83 1. 'Diminuenda' is possibly an alternate name for the sculpture of Orpheus, 'The Listener'.

24.10.83 1. George Campbell underwent successful surgery.

25.10.83 1. The murder of Maurice Bishop, the Prime Minister of Grenada, and other Cabinet Ministers led to the US invasion of the island.

13.11.83 1. Joseph, who was employed as a computer planner by the Jamaica Bauxite Institute, was fired by the Minister of Mining, a brother-in-law of Prime Minister Seaga, when he learned of the appointment. **2.** 'Public Eye', a popular current affairs call-in radio programme hosted by Ronnie Thwaites in Jamaica. **3.** Reference to the shooting down of a Korean Airline jet by the Russians.

14.11.83 1. Ronnie Thwaites lives on and operates a farm near to Pam O'Gorman. **2.** Martin, a Jamaican businessman who bought 'Flamstead', a house near to Nomdmi, where a madman wounded him. **3.** Verona Ashman, Secretary to the National Dance Theatre Co. of Jamaica.

19.11.83 1. Juanita and Milton Aiken, grandniece and grandnephew of Miss Boyd, who grew up with Rachel.

26.11.83 1. Yvonne DaCosta, late dancer and ballet mistress of NDTC. **2.** This election was boycotted by the PNP because Seaga and Michael had pledged in 1980 that whoever won the election would implement electoral reform, before calling another ; Seaga did not wait for these reforms and called the election with the old, out of date, lists of voters.

30.11.83 1. Dr Mathew Beaubrun, Michael's doctor and friend who became Edna Manley's doctor after Dr Bell's death, and until her death. **2.** 'The Little Drummer': a bas relief. **3.** Neville Alexander, husband of Susan Alexander (see note, 23.4.75). **4.** Hope Brooks, painter and current Director, Edna Manley School of Visual Arts.

6.12.83 **1.** PSOJ: the Private Sector Organization of Jamaica. **2.** Alvin Ailey Show: famous black New York dance group.

3.4.84 **1.** Yvonne DaCosta (see note 1, 26.11.83) died of this illness.

20.8.84 **1.** 'Listener' grew out of the 'Orpheus' drawings of the late 70s, but the floating figure is listening to, rather than playing the harp. **2.** This commission for sculpture of a goat was from the American Ambassador and Mrs Hewitt.

22.8.84 **1.** Dr Ronald Irvine, Chairman of the JLP resigned in opposition to Seaga's calling the '83 election. **2.** Anthony Abrahams, then Minister of Tourism.

21.9.84 **1.** Michael earned his living lecturing on the US college circuit.

29.10.84 **1.** This act was reminiscent of Bustamante in the 1950s, when he closed down the KSAC and appointed the two men, Byrd and Rodriguez, to run it. To everyone's surprise they did a good job. **2.** Rosie McDonald, a police sergeant who worked as part of Michael's security and became a friend and confidante of the family, keeping the household going after the breakdown of Michael and Beverley's marriage. **3.** Roger Mais was imprisoned for six months during the Second World War for writing an article 'Now We Know' in which he attacked Britain after Churchill's famous statement, 'I have not been elected His Majesty's First Minister to preside over the liquidation of the British Empire.'

7.4.85 **1.** The first of two operations for diverticulitis is performed on Michael.

27.4.85 **1.** 'Tomorrow': a recreation of 'Tomorrow' of 1939, which was conceived as a modelled work and created first in clay, but proved impossible to cast so was carved in wood.

28.4.85 **1.** There are numerous drawings which show Edna Manley wrestling with the concept of a female form representing the Ocean; this is 'My Mother the Ocean', sometimes called 'the Wave'.

16.5.85 **1.** This trip to Barbados was to be her last.

27.6.85 **1.** A two-day general strike was called by unions in protest over wages and economic policy.

29.6.85 **1.** 'Six Options: Gallery Spaces Transformed', organised by Rosalie Smith McRea at the National Gallery. Four Jamaican artists — Colin Garland, David Boxer, Laura Facey, Dawn Scott; and two Americans — Sam Gilliam and Joyce Scott. Jamaica's first major installation show. **2.** Even as the strike was failing the Civil Service Association and the Churches continued to speak out over the issues.

11.8.85 **1.** Edna Manley refers to her major surgery, an appendectomy with complications.

31.8.85 **1.** 'The Horses of the Morning' a biography of Norman Manley by Vic Reid, was published by Caribbean Authors Publishing Co. Ltd. in 1985. **2.** Owen Minott, one of Jamaica's leading photographers. **3.** Mary Datchelor: a girl's school in London.

24.1.86 **1.** Della Magnus, Joseph's wife.

31.3.86 **1.** 'Rising Figure', perhaps the earliest sketch of the 'Raising of Lazarus' series.

22.4.86 **1.** Edna Manley was robbed as she left the hairdressing salon. **2.** Edna Manley was interviewed by Nigel Finch for the BBC documentary on the Jamaican intuitive artist Kapo, the leader of St Michael's Tabernacle, a revivalist church. The interview was not used in the final tape. **3.** Reference to the Edna Manley Clinic in Four Roads, named in her honour. **4.** Portia Simpson, MP for the area and a PNP Vice President.

6.5.86 **1.** A small group proposed Jamaica becoming a state of the USA but the polls have always shown the majority of Jamaicans opposed to this idea.

24.10.86 **1.** 'Birth', a large painting, the culmination of 'My Mother the Ocean' series. The concept of the reclining 'wave' figure shifts to the vertical rising female holding aloft three horses. **2.** Lazarus was to be her final obsession, resulting in several sketches and large drawings in preparation for a painting she never had time to create.

25.10.86 **1.** Michael's work on the Economic Committee of Socialist International was a success.

Index

Index of Works by Edna Manley

Figures in italics refer to illustrations. Dates in brackets refer to notes where the title of a work has not been given in the diaries, but has been referred to in some other way.